Gendering Ethnicity
in African Women's Lives

WOMEN IN AFRICA AND THE DIASPORA

Series Editors

STANLIE JAMES
AILI MARI TRIPP

Gendering Ethnicity in African Women's Lives

Edited by

Jan Bender Shetler

THE UNIVERSITY OF WISCONSIN PRESS

Publication of this volume has been made possible, in part,
through the generous support of retired Goshen College history professor
James Hertzler and his wife, **Diane**.

The University of Wisconsin Press
1930 Monroe Street, 3rd Floor
Madison, Wisconsin 53711-2059
uwpress.wisc.edu

3 Henrietta Street, Covent Garden
London WC2E 8LU, United Kingdom
eurospanbookstore.com

Copyright © 2015
The Board of Regents of the University of Wisconsin System
All rights reserved. Except in the case of brief quotations embedded in critical articles and reviews,
no part of this publication may be reproduced, stored in a retrieval system, transmitted in any
format or by any means—digital, electronic, mechanical, photocopying, recording, or otherwise—
or conveyed via the Internet or a website without written permission of the University of Wisconsin
Press. Rights inquiries should be directed to rights@uwpress.wisc.edu.

Printed in the United States of America

Library of Congress Cataloging-in-Publication Data

Gendering ethnicity in African women's lives /
edited by Jan Bender Shetler.
pages   cm — (Women in Africa and the diaspora)
Includes bibliographical references and index.
ISBN 978-0-299-30394-5 (pbk.: alk. paper)
ISBN 978-0-299-30393-8 (e-book)
1. Women—Africa, Sub-Saharan—History.
2. Women—Africa, Sub-Saharan—Social conditions.
3. Ethnicity—Africa, Sub-Saharan.
I. Shetler, Jan Bender, editor.   II. Series: Women in Africa and the diaspora.
HQ1787.G457   2015
305.40967—dc23
2014030779

Contents

Acknowledgments

Thanks to the editors and readers at the University of Wisconsin Press for their helpful insights and suggestions and for their conviction that we could make a significant contribution to scholarship. We owe special thanks to Aili Tripp for seeing the importance of this topic at the first African Studies Association panel in 2010 and to Stanlie James, the series coeditor, as well as Gwen Walker and the great staff at the press. Thanks to Lauren Stoltzfus, a recent Goshen College graduate, who did much of the first round of editing, helping us to see how an undergraduate might experience our writing and showing amazing ability at a young age. Thanks to Goshen College for the grant money to do much of the editing and preparation work. Thanks to Dorothy Hodgson for providing guidance and support throughout the process, as well as insightful comments on drafts.

Chapter 4, "New African Marriage and Panethnic Politics in Segregationist South Africa" by Meghan Healy-Clancy, has been adapted from Meghan Healy-Clancy, "The Politics of New African Marriage in Segregationist South Africa," *African Studies Review* 57, no. 1 (April 2014), copyright © 2014 by African Studies Association. Reprinted with the permission of Cambridge University Press.

Chapter 8, "Sorting and Suffering: Social Classification in Postgenocide Rwanda" by Jennie E. Burnet, has been adapted from Jennie E. Burnet, *Genocide Lives in Us: Women, Memory, and Silence in Rwanda*, copyright © 2012 by the University of Wisconsin Press. Reprinted with the permission of the University of Wisconsin Press.

Chapter 11, "Muslim Women Legislators in Postcolonial Kenya: Between Gender, Ethnicity, and Religion " by Ousseina D. Alidou, has been adapted from Ousseina D. Alidou, *Muslim Women in Postcolonial Kenya: Leadership, Representation, and Social Change*, copyright © 2013 by the University of Wisconsin Press. Reprinted with the permission of the University of Wisconsin Press.

*Gendering Ethnicity
in African Women's Lives*

Introduction

Women's Alternative Practices
of Ethnicity in Africa

JAN BENDER SHETLER

Does ethnicity in Africa have a gender? Is ethnicity a gender-neutral identity, or do different men and women conceive of and act out their ethnicity in different ways? Although the analysis of male-centered ethnic discourse has defined the literature, in this collection we explore the gendering of ethnicity in disparate cases. Tanzanian women tell stories of their grandmothers coming from distant communities, South African women write a ladies' newspaper column as "New Africans," Zimbabwean churchwomen choose their sons' marriage partners within the ethnic subgroup, Nigerian women assert the preeminence of matrilineal ties, and Kenyan Muslim women parliamentarians carefully choose their ethnically cosmopolitan dress. All of these women made choices about the forms of ethnicity that they embraced, if any at all, sometimes providing alternatives to male-centered definitions. If gender matters to a central concept like ethnicity in African studies, then it is surely time for women's role in the process of ethnic formation to be given analytical priority.

Both gender and ethnicity are two of the most used but least defined elements of the much larger and potentially problematic analytical category of identity in African history. Recent scholarship has shown that gender, like ethnicity, cannot be assumed as a "category of analysis"; instead, it should be seen as a concept to be investigated.[1] Neither ethnicity nor gender is assumed as a "natural" object; instead, both are processes by which people make claims based on their identification as members of an imagined community. They construct these claims in everyday practice as a lived experience—whether in

3

the stories they tell, the marriage and family relationships in which they engage, the work they do, the collective action they undertake, the associations in which they find membership, or the status positions they assume. In this collection, we use the concept of "gendering ethnicity" as a verb rather than a noun. The state or other powerful institutions and individuals can classify someone by gender or ethnicity, but those same categories can also be subverted, resisted, or redefined as men and women work out claims of identity in everyday life. How any one person chooses to assert a particular identity depends on the specific historical context and the concerns of that individual. This work of identification is thus historically situated and contingent, reformulated in each new context, rather than being assumed as a given reality to be appropriated.[2]

Although Africanist scholarship has treated both gender and ethnicity in depth, the study of women's various relationships to ethnic identities and ethnically constituted communities has been limited and largely superficial. More often, when considering ethnic identity, scholars have assumed the dominant male-generated discourse in the colonial period as normative and stable. In his foundational study of the colonial construction of "tribalism," Leroy Vail cites the Tswana proverb that "women have no tribe" as an indication of a woman's loss of ethnicity as she married and moved into her husband's community. Historian John Lonsdale, too, discusses women's ethnicity in terms of their marginalized role as outsiders in the patriclan.[3] Yet this leaves women as passive victims of an absence rather than asking what other kinds of identities they embraced beyond "tribe."[4] It also does not acknowledge all of the variations outside of strictly patrilineal societies, for example, in places like Igbo society, where wives defined patriliny through women's associations, and matrilineal societies with patrilineal endogamy, where wives were also daughters (see Ndubueze L. Mbah, chapter 9).[5]

The African Studies Association panels (2010 and 2011) from which this collection grew explored the adage "women have no tribe" as a way to problematize the relationship between women and ethnicity.[6] The panelists discussed cases in which women did not necessarily reject ethnic categories altogether but seemed less invested in male-generated forms. In these cases, women's everyday practice reconfigured ethnic categories to fit their needs. Heidi Gengenbach (chapter 2) sees ethnicity as a "livelihood asset," a "form of social capital" that was salient to women's livelihood strategies, even if women deployed it very differently from men. The women whom I (chapter 1) asked specifically about this adage in the Mara Region, Tanzania, denied that "women have no tribe" and went on to talk in depth about the kinds of relationships they had with their father's or husband's kin groups. Jennie E. Burnet (chapter 8) translates the same adage in Rwanda as "wives have no classification [of their own]," meaning that a wife has to put her husband's patrilineage first.

The authors of this volume formed a group over a two-year period of pre-sentations, adding other members in the years since, that brings together a variety of perspectives, both regional (mostly East Africa and southern Africa, but also one from West Africa) and disciplinary (mostly history, but also anthro-pology, languages and literature, politics, and development studies), on past and current relationships of women to ethnicity in Africa. Time frames range from pre- to postcolonial. We worked collaboratively in defining our approach to the topic despite our varying contexts. The case studies in this volume, ranging widely in time and space, investigate the multiple ways that various African women have imagined their ethnicity and other communal identities.

This collection of essays builds on anthropologist Dorothy Hodgson's concept of the interconstruction of gender and ethnicity as historically dynamic categories that change over time in relation to one another. We move beyond thinking about adding gender plus ethnicity to considering the complex ways that they mutually constitute one another. Parallel work on gendering national-ism, specifically in relation to race rather than ethnicity, also provides a useful theoretical basis for exploring this question.[7] Hodgson's study shows how Maasai ethnicity was gendered male, particularly in relation to the politics of pastoralist development in the colonial and postcolonial eras.[8] Ethan R. Sanders's assertion (chapter 5) that ethnicity is "largely situational and strategic" is reflected in the diverse contexts of the chapters in this collection. The ways various people enact gender shape, and are shaped by, the larger societal struc-tures, including ethnicity, class, and generation. Women and men of different ages, statuses, roles, and levels of wealth perform their ethnic identity in differ-ent ways and reject it in other contexts. Heike I. Schmidt's work (chapter 10) shows that royal female chiefs were more invested in local power structures and therefore supported (male) concepts of ethnicity that included them in places of power. In other cases, young women, as well as young or disenfranchised men, performed subversive identities. Women also simultaneously held multiple identities, like Christian, nationalist, and feminist, while still asserting their rights in the ethnic or descent group communities of their father and husband (see Meghan Healy-Clancy, chapter 4; Wendy Urban-Mead, chapter 6).

Our study helps to explain the ability of numerous African women's political organizations today to overcome exclusivist ethnic affiliations and reach across that divide.[9] The performance of African ethnicities does, in fact, seem to be gendered, with some women having less investment in male conceptions that became dominant in the colonial era and that do not appeal to many women practically or emotionally. Ndubueze L. Mbah's exploration of gendered concepts of Ohafia-Igbo ethnicity (chapter 9) demonstrates how women main-tained diplomatic networks with non-Igbo matrilineal and bilateral ethnicities in the region. Throughout African history, far from being a natural biological trait, women's ability to play the role of peacemaker in a variety of circumstances was often a result of the gendered structural role that they played as boundary crossers and network creators. Women who married far from home maintained these networks to accomplish their everyday tasks as traders, farmers, artisans, and ritual specialists. That might explain why women are much more likely to have the resources to rise to the occasion at critical historical moments when the performance of a reconfigured ethnicity, or the rejection of ethnicity altogether, is paramount to the community's survival. Recent examples of this include Liberian or Congolese women uniting across ethnic or religious divides to bring men involved in the civil war to the peace table because of their long-standing role as social mothers.[10] Thus we explore this topic with some hope that it will have both pragmatic and scholarly benefits.

Our group wrote to the common organizing question: What difference does gender make to the practice of ethnicity? And more specifically: How did women's gendered practices contribute to the construction (or subversion) of ethnicity in relation to men's practice? Our critique of scholarship based solely on dominant forms of male ethnicity led us to explore how women reconceptualized and used, or rejected and reformulated, ethnicity in their day-to-day practice of identity. Our conclusion that African ethnicity is always gendered does not mean that there was ever a single form of male or female ethnicity, nor that the ways women chose to identify themselves were exclusively female. Rather, the diverse ways that various women interacted with ethnicity depended on the historical context, their gendered social roles and relationships, and the extent to which male-defined ethnicity served their interests. The parts in this book demonstrate how women variously formed interethnic networks, constructed new forms of identity, promoted ethnicity in gendered domains, and performed gendered ethnic power, each of which provided alternatives to male practices of ethnicity. Women claimed agency and power in determining the ways that they enacted or denied a variety of ethnic identities.

Theoretical Approaches to Gendering Ethnicity in Africa

Ethnicity is commonly understood as an identity based on shared history and culture: belief, language, origins, lifestyle, and so on. In this sense, religious groups with a shared culture and past experience are treated like ethnic groups.[11] This is the case in one of this volume's chapters (chapter 11), where Ousseina D. Alidou discusses Muslim women parliamentarians in Kenya who are members of both an ethnic and a religious group, but in some cases the two are nearly synonymous. While members of ethnic groups often see these cultural attributes as a static primordial tradition, they certainly change over time as the boundaries of membership shift. Gender, too, is commonly understood as an identity based on sexual difference that is also immutable. But what it means to be male and female also changes over time, is socially determined, and is embedded within a system of power relations. The social constructivist approach taken in this book does not understand identity as a primordial category that has existed unchanged throughout time,[12] nor as an entirely instrumentalist category used as a political resource to manipulate people.[13] While it is important to see the psychological and emotional power of identities understood as primordial and to recognize the very concrete ways that ethnicity and gender can be used in the interests of those who wield power, this book concentrates on the actions, practices, and performances of men and women as they worked within a socially constructed set of power relations rather than on the ethnic group itself.[14]

Ethnicity is defined as gendered and dynamic social practices that seek to distinguish a community in relation to its neighbors. Ethnicity as a performance or practice allows us to see this as a process that constructs the socially relevant yet fluid and shifting categories that both men and women deploy to make claims based on their belonging to an imagined community. Defining the ethnic unit in Africa historically is difficult because there are various levels or scales of social organization, sometimes nested within one another, that have been classified as an ethnic group with a shared history and culture. In the precolonial period, many African societies were heterarchical—small local groups without a centralized administration under a chief—consisting of various forms of authority and overlapping leadership roles. Ethnicity in this context was flexible, without rigid boundaries. Ethnic groups were often made up of a number of descent-based groups that may have been confined to one ethnic group or crossed over into others. Some clan groups achieved the status of an ethnic group when they established themselves in a permanent settlement and gained power in relation to others.[15] Among the case studies in this book, Mbah (chapter 9) describes Ohafia-Igbo in southeastern Nigeria as a smaller ethnic group nested within the larger panethnic group called Igbo, while my case (chapter 1) focuses on the Mara Region, Tanzania, which consists of many small ethnic communities without chiefs or larger panethnic identities. Those places in Africa under more hierarchical kingdoms or chiefdoms defined a central ethnic core of the kingdom but also incorporated other ethnic groups as tributary chiefdoms. In this volume, three papers deal with the emergence of hierarchical Nguni polities in South Africa (Jill E. Kelly, chapter 7) and in Zimbabwe and Tanzania (Wendy Urban-Mead, chapter 6; and Heike I. Schmidt, chapter 10), where royal clans kept their own, often endogamous, exclusionary subethnic boundaries as they incorporated people of other languages and cultures. Taken together, these chapters illustrate various ways that women related to and practiced or subverted the various constructions of Nguni ethnicity that developed over time and in different contexts.

Male forms of ethnicity became dominant in the colonial period, making invisible the female forms of identity that had long defined an alternative social practice. In the colonial period, authorities sought to regularize and systematize the administration of indirect rule by establishing "tribes," chiefs, and their geographical boundaries, which defined the basis for competition over colonial resources and power.[16] Thus a large part of the literature on ethnicity in Africa analyzes the creation or invention of "tribe" where it did not exist before colonial rule, making the term "tribe" problematic for analyzing pre-colonial ethnic units.[17] In this volume, Poppy Fry (chapter 3) describes the colonially constructed Fingo "tribe," which was elaborated by Xhosa people who began farming and gaining mission education. Gengenbach's case (chapter 2) in Mozambique concerns an ethnic group that was created through long-term commercial interaction with the Portuguese, while Kelly (chapter 7) addresses Zulu ethnicity in a region where the people did not identify as Zulu until the twentieth century. In some cases, smaller groups were amalgamated into pan-ethnic "tribes" under a colonial paramount chief. In Burnet's study of Rwanda (chapter 8), Tutsi and Hutu shared language, religion, culture, and origins but were redefined in colonial times as ethnic groups in opposition to one another. In other places, ethnic groups spanned national boundaries. Ethnicity was further elaborated in the context of urban migration and migratory labor, where men sought others from their home areas for support.[18]

The construction of colonial "tribes" depended on co-opting senior men to define the boundaries and tell the historical narratives. They created the "mythicohistories" that formed the basis for the emergence of the imagined moral communities, set up in opposition to others.[19] Lonsdale describes the construction of ethnicity as an internal debate to define moral meaning and civic virtue within the imagined community.[20] Women and young men were the objects of control in these narratives, and their part in the construction of a performed ethnicity was largely ignored. Scholars have followed this trend in using men's accounts to build their own ethnic histories and ethnographies. In this way, the study of ethnicity in Africa has largely followed a male discourse of both local actors and global scholars, marginalizing women's role in both external and internal debates.

In the late colonial and early postcolonial era, men and women began to find new ways to imagine themselves beyond the ethnic group. These new ethnic or non-ethnic identities took on the character of racial, national, or pan-ethnic entities. The case studies in South Africa (Meghan Healy-Clancy, chapter

4) and East Africa (Sanders, chapter 5) demonstrate the emergence of the racial category of African, as opposed to white, European, Indian, or colored. Even though racial categories were also a colonial imposition, the alliance of ethnic groups as African gained more political traction than did the colonial strategy of divide and rule. The case studies in this volume concern ethnic groups of all kinds and many levels of organization, the variety being helpful in theorizing ethnicity's intersection with gender.

Earlier scholarship portrayed women in Africa as victims of domination and overwork under patriarchal oppression created by men in both colonial and indigenous structures.[21] Other scholars have shown that gender relations were not so clearly binary and that women had agency in these structures, sometimes in cooperation with men, to create a cohesive community and to gain status.[22] In precolonial Africa, women maintained an extraordinary amount of autonomy within their own domain, particularly in matrilineal societies. But even in hierarchical societies, women served a variety of leadership roles, including chiefs and queens or kings. Women had authority in ritual activities, and their spiritual power was often understood to be superior to that of men because of their connection to fertility and reproduction. In many African societies, women controlled gendered spheres of influence such as subsistence agriculture. Women and men had gendered tasks and domains of power in most African societies, making their identities closely related to the gendered roles they played in everyday life. This authority, however, broke down with colonialism when Europeans failed to recognize women's political and spiritual roles and their economic importance in agriculture.[23] This has led some to question the use of patriarchy as a blanket term for African gender relations, since the current terms of inequality are largely a result of colonial policy.

Gender scholarship in Africa has also recognized that women are not a single category of analysis. In Africa, age matters as much as or more than gender, giving older women respected positions similar to men and younger women and men more subservient positions. In fact, some have argued that gender is not a relevant category in Africa at all, since a woman could become a husband (as the head of a homestead) and a man could become a wife (as the genitor of a female husband's children), while an older women could become a chief or king or take on an honorary male role.[24] Whether old or young, urban or rural, rich or poor, women from various descent groups may not claim a common identity or see themselves as a part of a single category of women. In this volume, we see various categories of women—for example, women as farmers (Shetler, chapter 1; Fry, chapter 3), mission-educated elite (Healy-Clancy, chapter 4; Urban-Mead, chapter 6), politicians (Alidou, chapter 11), party members (Sanders, chapter 5), kings or chiefs (Mbah, chapter 9; Schmidt, chapter 10), writers (Healy-Clancy, chapter 4), beer brewers (Gengenbach, chapter 2), land-lords (Sanders, chapter 5), church members (Urban-Mead, chapter 6; Kelly, chapter 7), mothers and wives (Urban-Mead, chapter 6; Burnet, chapter 8)—each of which has implications for the ways in which women assert or reject the claims of ethnicity.

In exploring this topic, we first had to overcome the lack of both historical sources and analytical concern about ways that the everyday performances of African women constructed alternatives to male ethnicity in the scholarly liter-ature, popular media, local discourse, and the archives. In the literature where women are understood as ethnic subjects, they fit into dominant male concep-tions of ethnicity. The scholarship often portrays women as victims of ethnic violence as a result of ethnicized masculinity rather than as agents in their own construction or deconstruction of ethnicity. Although literature does exist on how men use women symbolically to construct their ethnicity, this book is more specifically about women's claims to their own identities. In the strong tradition of gendered history in Africa, these contributions seek to understand women as agents, performing their own versions of identification with ethnic groups.

Understanding gendered ethnicity requires new methodologies, new sources, and new approaches to conventional sources. Each of the chapters pays close attention to the sources and methodologies necessary for making these alternatives visible. Fry (chapter 3) advocates reading sources in the ar-chives "against the grain," while I (chapter 1) analyze women's historical narra-tives as embedded in wide-reaching social networks that cross ethnic boundaries. Many of the cases are set at critical historical moments when, according to Fry, there was a breach of dominant norms that allowed women to assert alternative forms of identity. Kelly (chapter 7) claims the same for a moment of unrest in South Africa that opened up possibilities for reassessing ethnicity. Burnet's study (chapter 8) from Rwanda suggests that women are still working out al-ternative definitions in their performance of identities that no longer fit the assumed categories and leave women in limbo to construct their own livelihoods against enormous odds.

The women in these essays have often asserted an alternative to male eth-nicity because they have been excluded from communal identities that do not necessarily reflect their interests or desires. Women's practice of alternative identities in these cases is not often overtly opposed to men or male dominance or even to male forms of ethnicity. In fact, some chapters show how women supported practices of male ethnicity. Kelly (chapter 7) claims that a moment of unrest in South Africa enabled men and women to perform complementary gendered spheres of militant ethnicity but also prevented men and women from performing shared rituals and ceremonies. Alidou (chapter 11) shows how Muslim women parliamentarians bow to gendered ethnic expectations so that they can maintain their support in the constituency but also work tirelessly to bring women of all ethnicities together to achieve women's rights. Women's performances take a less obvious and more pragmatic approach, not necessarily opposing conventional gender roles but marking men's rights as contingent and men's ethnicity as partial.[25]

Scholars have long understood ethnicity as an identity that is constructed in relation to, or to distinguish oneself from, neighbors who are different rather than in isolation. As Frederick Barth claimed, ethnicity was defined by how people related to others across their cultural boundaries rather than internally with each other.[26] However, some scholars suggest that women's definitions of ethnicity may be formed in relation to male discourse rather than to someone who is culturally different, while others show that women perform their identity independently of men in ways related to women's own agenda.[27] In historian Phyllis Martin's work, Congolese women's call for unity across ethnic boundaries as mothers for peace was a direct response to violent forms of male ethnicity.[28] Likewise, three chapters in this volume demonstrate women's responses to ethnic identities of militant masculinity. Fry's argument (chapter 3) shows that Fingo defined a new ethnicity in the Cape Colony in opposition to militant Xhosaness, while Kelly (chapter 7) demonstrates that women's complementary and subverted forms of Zuluness in the transition-era conflict relied on identities of militant masculinity. Finally, Mbah's chapter (chapter 9) starts with the stereotypical representations of Ohafia-Igbo head-hunting, representations that ignore women's performances of a different kind of ethnicity. The concept of gendered ethnicity is not new, and scholars in many disciplines outside of Africa have used it to think about, for example, interethnic violence, immigrant identity, and democracy building.[29] But rarely has it been analyzed from the multiple perspectives of women's understandings.

Our definition of ethnicity as a social practice or performance of communal identity claims rejects its static form as a reified structure. Scholars have looked at music, dance, and theater as forms of popular culture that construct and reflect claims of nationalism in performance.[30] Similarly, women often perform their own forms of ethnic belonging in everyday discourse and practice, but they do so offstage, while men, at least in the colonial period, occupy center stage. However hidden and obscured within male-dominated discourse and documents, women's performances legitimized or provided alternatives to ethnic, national, racial, or other identities in pursuit of their own various interests. In other cases, such as Mbah's (chapter 9) and Schmidt's (chapter 10), the performance of female forms of ethnicity was quite public. In still other cases, ethnicity, or its rejection, was practiced not only for instrumental reasons but also more subjectively on the basis of altruism, love, beauty, nostalgia. Kelly (chapter 7) characterizes the practice of a female Zuluness as a coping strategy. Women might even assert identities that seemed to subvert their own material interests. But because these were all performances, they could be deployed in different ways depending on the circumstances.

Whatever the explanation for performances that defined various identity claims, these case studies show that women's practice of ethnicity is firmly rooted in local, and even household, contests of power. Schmidt's case study of female chiefs (chapter 10) explores the gendered performance of power "vis-à-vis their subject populations." These gendered forms of ethnicity, whether male or female, had significant consequences for everyone, but particularly for women. Women practiced gendered ethnicity in the realms of marriage and family, domestic livelihoods, political organization, ethnic conflict, and even genocide. Alidou's work (chapter 11) on Muslim women in Kenya's parliament demonstrates how they deploy different strategies to challenge their exclusion from political power. Once we see how ethnicity is gendered, it becomes clear that this scholarship is not just an esoteric exercise but one with life-or-death consequences for women in the context of genocide, civil war, or famine (see Gengenbach, chapter 2; Burnet, chapter 8). These case studies indicate that various African women in many contexts have had ambiguous and dynamic relationships with ethnicity, embracing and constructing it, as well as rejecting and redefining it. In some cases, they took the role of the keepers of "tradition," while in others, they took on that of the primary boundary crossers and champions of interethnic activism. In all of these ways, women performed ethnicity or other communal identities as alternative practices, asserting other interests and sensibilities within particular contexts of gendered power relations.

Women Practicing Precolonial Interethnic Crossings

While the authors of this volume accept the social constructivist scholarship on the creation of tradition, which asserts that colonialism encouraged the formation of a male ethnicity or "tribalism," we seek to bring to the center alternative female practices that are built on identities and strategies for livelihood with precolonial roots.[31] The colonial need for delineated administrative units and chiefs under indirect rule, young men's need for support away from home in cities or in migrant labor camps, older men's need to control youth and women who were taking advantage of colonial opportunities, and missionaries' need to translate the Bible into a single language understood by various dialects all conspired to construct isolated colonial "tribes" with clear boundaries. "Tribe" contrasted with much more flexible and overlapping precolonial forms of identity organized around kinship, economy, or polity. In the colonial model, ethnicity was specifically formulated by men—colonial officers, migrant youth, and rural elders. In Tanganyika, the colonial anthropologist Hans Cory called together chiefs and elders to document "traditional" governance patterns and laws that would be reinforced by indirect rule.[32] In places where no chiefs existed, colonial officials created them to fit the administrative pattern but used "traditional" forms dictated by the elders where possible. In analyses of the colonial construction of "tribalism," women are only mentioned in relation to their *lack* of ethnicity rather than in relation to the multiple ways that they provided alternatives and redefined ethnic categories.

The larger literature on gender that highlights women's agency in forming their own identities as boundary crossers and mediators in precolonial societies addresses this purported absence of ethnicity for women. For example, in 1976 historian George Brooks wrote about the women of the French Senegambia called *signares* as female entrepreneurs in the slave trade who served as cross-cultural brokers between the European traders and their African communities.[33] Walter Hawthorne's study of slavery among heterarchical Balanta society in Guinea-Bissau also depicts women as the main traders and intermediaries outside of communities fortified and secluded for protection from raiders.[34] For a later period in East Africa, Dorothy Hodgson and historians Cora Ann Presley and Margaret Jean Hay show that women were the main traders and links to neighboring peoples on whom their specialized lifestyles depended for grain and other caravan products like cloth, wire, beads, and tobacco.[35] In these examples, women were mobile, spoke multiple languages, used marriage to augment their trade position, and occupied autonomous spheres of activity respected by men. Although this rich literature on gender provides empirical cases for comparison, rarely is this material theorized or problematized in relation to ethnic identity. More commonly, the literature refers to women as "Kikuyu" or "Luo," for example, without questioning what that designation meant for women who crossed boundaries daily.

Ethnographers have explained women's role as the primary boundary crossers and alliance makers between ethnic groups by women's structural position outside of kinship systems. Jean Davison defined ethnicity as an enlargement of lineage and showed that the particular form of lineage ideology—whether matriliny or patriliny—determined women's access to resources like land and inheritance controlled by the lineage. Marriage patterns in either system were critical in determining whether a woman went to live in her husband's village, a patrilocal system, or stayed in her own, a matrilocal system. The majority of African women lived in patrilocal societies (even those practicing matriliny) and became boundary crossers between language, ethnic, clan, and lineage groups.[36] In my interviews (chapter 1), women described how their grandmothers taught them to relate to a new place while keeping their networks back home intact. Women in exogamous marriages were fully part of neither their father's nor their husband's ethnic groups but instead kept multiple identities in motion to preserve their options. Gengenbach's previous work characterized knowledge of these female cross-ethnic social networks as a "relational epistemology"—very different from men's knowledge, which was much more centered on the local clan and ethnic group.[37] Women's identities in patrilocal societies were cross-boundary, multiple, and relational beginning in the precolonial era and extending to the colonial era.

Although many scholars have challenged the creation-of-tradition assumption that ethnicity is solely a product of colonial relations, only recently have scholars noted women's role in the creation of precolonial forms of ethnicity. The period of African state building, conflict, and dispersal in southern Africa leading to the formation of Zulu and Ngoni polities provides documented cases of emerging male ethnicities in the precolonial period.[38] Schmidt (chapter 10) argues that Ngoni ethnicity was "masculine at its core, military in nature, and defined by exerting power over subjugate people," while women who married in could never become Ngoni. Other precolonial studies of pastoral people moving into contact with others demonstrate how ethnicities were built around male age or generation sets.[39] Mbah's work (chapter 9) shows how Ohafia-Igbo men built their ethnicity around a form of masculinity developed in military conquest and violence. The one study, in addition to Schmidt's previous work, that specifically sets out to explore how precolonial ethnicity is gendered male is that of Allen and Barbara Isaacman on Chikunda as military slaves of the Africanized Portuguese landholders or *prazeros* in Mozambique.[40]

However, instead of focusing on the exclusively male conceptions of ethnicity in Ghana, historian Sandra Greene demonstrates how women's choices in response to changing historical circumstances helped to create Anlo-Ewe ethnicity and its boundaries. Greene is concerned that previous studies of ethnicity do not consider how women and other marginalized peoples contributed to the formation of precolonial identities. She takes exception to the idea that women have no tribe by showing how women contributed to and identified with ethnicity.[41] Likewise, some chapters in this volume show how women were clearly invested in ethnicity. All of these cases demonstrate that there is evidence from earliest times in African history that women have been practicing their own ways of identifying with groups, often centered around boundary crossing and alliance making, as well as redefining ethnicity in response to particular circumstances.

Women Subverting and Supporting Colonial Ethnicities

In spite of these precolonial precedents, most of the scholarship on the creation of a gendered ethnicity is located in the colonial period, where women both supported men's emerging ethnic practices and provided subversive alternatives to it. Tabitha Kanogo's study of Kenyan womanhood surrounding the female circumcision crisis argues that during this time ethnicity became "feminized" as women's bodies began to represent Kikuyu nationhood leading up to the Mau Mau rebellion.[42] In this and other colonial cases, women became symbols of a male-defined ethnicity. The creation-of-tradition literature highlights women as ethnically conservative, wearing national dress or other bodily markers of ethnicity. In Tanzania, many women wear the *kanga* (Swahili wrap) in preference to Western dress, even if they are not originally from the coast where it originated. Women often bring out their old beaded ornaments or sing the traditional songs on special occasions. These forms of conservatism may be seen as imposed by men or as women redefining ethnicity for themselves in the way they arrange beads or do their hair.[43] Because men who left home to work as migrant laborers in the cities, mines, or plantations found themselves in a rapidly transforming political and economic landscape, they needed women to ground their own identification of ethnic belonging in the rural areas. The men themselves were the first to adopt Western dress, go to school, learn new languages, join the mission church, and take on cosmopolitan practices. Male migrants formed some of the first ethnic associations to bring back bodies for burial at home and to retrieve women who ran away to the city.[44]

Many scholars agree that colonial ethnicity created an extreme form of male dominance, often with negative consequences for women.[45] For example, in Hodgson's study, a masculinized Maasai ethnicity restricted women's mobility within the Maasai Reserve.[46] Conversely, colonial labor demands throughout Africa made men more mobile as migrant workers. Male dominance increased within the structures of gendered ethnic formation as men's power was enhanced with the consolidation of their control over cattle and cash crops within a monetized economy. Colonial policies also restricted women's mobility and autonomy. Colonial officers often collaborated with senior men, who were appointed to Native Authority courts, to confine women to rural areas in order to subsidize the low wages paid to men working on plantations and in mines.[47] The commoditization of cattle seems to run parallel to the commoditization of women as property to be exploited for agricultural labor (see Shetler, chapter 1).[48] Confining women to the boundaries of ethnicity kept them more firmly under the control of male elders in their descent groups and less free to start businesses or leave home. Yet women often subverted these restrictions on

their autonomy by running away to the city or to the mission stations.[49] Women
who ran away often found themselves in mixed ethnic communities and reconstructed their identities in non-ethnic ways, such as by embracing a more widely
encompassing racial identity to secure access to local structures of power (see
Sanders, chapter 5). Even those who stayed in the rural areas may have had
different definitions of the ethnicity they ostensibly shared with men. For example, Kenyan women may have supported female circumcision not in order
to defend Kikuyu nationhood but because they could not become adult women
and mothers without being circumcised—the basis on which their future security depended. Looking closely for women's alternative identifications helps us
to understand the impact of colonial policies on both men and women.

One of the most common ways that colonial women redefined their
identities was in the spiritual realm. Christianity in Africa became a "church
of women," and women became the main practitioners of folk Islam, which
drew on pre-Islamic African spiritual practices.[50] In precolonial societies,
women asserted their leadership as spirit mediums and prophets on the basis of
the recognized female nature of spirituality in reproduction and fertility.[51]
Schmidt's study (chapter 10) of female chiefs demonstrates how they used their
power as spirit mediums in this role. It is no accident, then, that women found
religious identification as a way to escape the confines of ethnicity and redefined
a gendered ethnicity in terms of moral values. A number of chapters in the collection demonstrate the power of women as spiritual leaders. For example,
Kelly (chapter 7) shows how Zulu women during the violent transition from
apartheid used religion as a protective strategy in forming their own definition
of what it meant to be Zulu. Urban-Mead (chapter 6) also demonstrates that
Protestant Ndebele women in Zimbabwe formed partnerships with women
from other subethnicities as evangelists and teachers. The literature on ethnicity in the colonial period has been so preoccupied with religion as a form of
resistance that little attention has been paid to religion as a place of belonging
for women in particular.

Women Practicing Alternative Identities
in an Era of Nationalism

A model for thinking about the interconstruction of gender and ethnicity has
been elaborated most clearly in the literature on nationalism and race in relation to gender, particularly during the independence period.[52] Historian Susan
Geiger argues not only that nationalism was a male construction but that certain
women, namely, "middle-aged Muslim women with little or no Western education" from "trans-tribal Swahili communities" in Dar es Salaam, played a crucial

role in performing their own brand of nationalism, which included the moral claims of gender and ethnic equality.[53] Elizabeth Schmidt's study of nationalist politics in Guinea during the independence era shows that women "joined the nationalist struggle as women" with their own interpretations of "ethnicity, class, and colonial oppression."[54] In this and other cases in our collection, women were attracted to nationalist and other interethnic political organizations that were responsive to women's issues and concerns. These organizations served as an arena of contested space where various members, such as a number of the women activists, bent the organization to their own purposes (see Sanders, chapter 5). Guinean women also "violated gender norms" even as they used preexisting cultural forms and social networks to promote the nationalist movement.[55] Both Schmidt and Geiger show how women transformed the methods of the nationalism movement by introducing popular songs, slogans, uniforms, and dances to raise support.

These cases of nationalism add weight to the assertion that women are more likely to step up to redefine and practice alternative claims of identification when crisis looms.[56] In Guinea, women took on the masculine role of "politicized street fighters," harking back to a much older West African tradition of women taking collective action against men in times of crisis. The prolific scholarship on the 1929 Igbo Women's War explores women's protests at colonial courts using the older methods of "sitting on a man" to express their grievances. In this tradition, if a man abused his wife, her neighbors might gather in his compound to bang on pots all night, refuse to cook in their own homes, or expose their genitals as a curse until the men brought the perpetrator to justice. Even though men might have had the same problems with colonial policies and economics, they did not turn out into the streets along with the women.[57]

A collection of essays edited by Nickie Charles and Helen Hintjens from cases around the world provides a larger context for theorizing the ambivalent and subversive relationship of women to nationalism and, by extension, ethnicity. Comparative cases show that nationalist organizations, like colonial "tribal" authorities, often used women as symbols of cultural identity in order to control their sexuality. Sexual violence thus became a weapon of genocide where nationalism was based on an exclusivist concept of blood rather than citizenship. In these cases, the dominant ideologies of nation or ethnicity had deadly consequences for women.[58] Yet here too women's alternate claims on nationalism or ethnicity subverted male-dominated forms so women could pursue their own interests. When women played the role of boundary crossers and unifiers across ethnic and national boundaries, they delegitimized ethnicities that provoked violence. The collection describes women who united around another identity, such as motherhood or religious membership; re-defined ethnicity in ways that protected women's interests; or rejected ethnicity for an interethnic, interracial, or international identity.

Women have also formed national-level political organizations based on alternative ways of identifying themselves. With the advent of capitalism in the colonial economy, the gendered spheres of public and private came to define men as wage earners and women as homemakers who cared for children. However, some women also used the private sphere as a site for the defense of family in the public realm. They transgressed those boundaries as they brought the private into the public sphere. In a comparative example, women in Argentina whose sons had disappeared or were imprisoned by the repressive regime defined motherhood as a political identity when they demanded to be reunited with their sons in the Plaza de Mayo in Buenos Aires every day until they saw action by the government.[59] Similarly, churchwomen in South Africa formed powerful associations around their role as mothers.[60] In the Igbo Women's War, noted above, women organized over a large geographic area in a protest movement using the strategy of "sitting on a man." Thus the private sphere became a site of resistance for women in the liberation struggle as they turned these definitions of gendered behavior on their heads.[61] In more recent cases, for example, Martin explains how Catholic women in Congo-Brazzaville united as mothers in a peace movement, while the Nobel Peace Prize was awarded in 2011 to Leymah Gbowee from Liberia for her work in uniting Muslim and Christian women for peace.[62] These women drew on past knowledge and gendered networks to form powerful groups that directly criticized men's destructively exclusive definitions of ethnicity. In all of these diverse ways, women have been involved from precolonial times to the present in constructing, deconstructing, and reconstructing ethnicities and other communal identities that have not always served their interests.

Conclusion

How, then, does our study speak to this broader literature about African ethnicity and gender? The broad question that unites our diverse research is: What difference does gender make to the practice of ethnicity? Our first conclusion at the highest level of abstraction is that we can no longer understand ethnicity apart from its gendered construction and practice. We found no case in which women's practice of ethnicity was identical to men's. Ethnicity always appeared and was performed in gendered ways, and gender cannot be ignored in an analysis of ethnicity. Men and women claimed different forms of ethnicity in different times and places. The historical context is critical to the variety of ways that this happens. But not all women or men approached ethnicity in the same way; there is no clear dichotomy between men's and women's performances of identity claims. While ethnic identification has often been used to control and restrict women, women have found numerous ways to assert alternative forms of ethnicity in order to make connections across those boundaries and redefine identity in their own terms. Gendered ethnicity matters in women's everyday concerns of home and family, as well as in political debate and under the extraordinary circumstances of civil war or genocide.

That this simple, though critical, fact of gendered ethnicity has been less than obvious in Africanist scholarship is cause for concern. Even male ethnic discourse cannot be understood without acknowledging it as a gendered practice. Analysis of male discourses of ethnicity as normative has endorsed the global perception of Africa as a place perpetually embroiled in ethnic conflict. Women's experience and identity, which offer alternatives to this narrative, have been marginalized and ignored in public discourse. Women have most often been seen as the victims of ethnic conflict rather than as participants in its construction or reconstruction along other lines. Yet women have often been the ones to organize cross-ethnic political organizations because women follow a long tradition of embodying alternative identities that can be mobilized when the community is in danger. In their myriad forms, those alternatives may provide new claims on the moral economy when ethnicity provokes violence. Becoming aware that ethnicity cannot be treated as a unitary form also brings into focus the severe consequences that may be borne by women and other marginalized people who do not benefit from the dominant conceptions of ethnicity.

Our analyses also suggest that the reason that ethnicity took particularly gendered forms in Africa is that women and men had fairly separate gendered roles in their work, kinship, authority structures, and social interaction. This meant that women's and men's life experiences took place in very different spheres with implications for identity. I (chapter 1) found that the key reason for gendered memory was that women moved to their husband's family homesteads in patrilocal marriages, while Mbah (chapter 9) demonstrates the consequences for ethnicity in matrilineal or patrilineal systems. Gengenbach's work (chapter 2) analyzes the gendered livelihood strategies that led to different forms of authority and ethnic strategies, while Fry (chapter 3) shows that Fingo ethnicity grew out of women's domain in agriculture. For Schmidt (chapter 10), women's role in spirit possession enhanced their authority as chiefs, while in Kelly's analysis (chapter 7), women's ritual role in funerals affected women's reaction to men's martial ethnicity in the Zulu civil wars.

The appeal to ethnic tradition was also a way to confine women's choices to particular gendered roles. In many societies around the world, women are expected to represent the ethnic group in their dress and connection to home and family. Women can also work with these expectations with their performances in the public domain, as Alidou (chapter 11) demonstrates with Kenya women parliamentarians who used dress both to gain the trust of their ethnic constituency and to reach across ethnic boundaries. Other chapters (Healy-Clancy, chapter 4; Urban-Mead, chapter 6; Alidou, chapter 11) show that ethnic expectations of women as "traditional" wives and mothers both confined women and provided the platform to promote other agendas. More research could be done on women's use of ethnically defined fashion, theater, or music. One might also explore whether the current era of globalization is breaking down gendered roles in African societies to the point where it would potentially give women and men the same stake in promoting antagonistic ethnicity.

Ethnicity defined by male discourse has often disempowered women. This is illustrated most starkly where women have been the victims of rape and sexual violence in the name of defending an ethnic nationalism. Both male elders and colonial authorities constructed colonial ethnicity in large part to control women's mobility and independence. Gengenbach (chapter 2) shows that gendered expectations of women in Mozambique resulted in keeping them out of certain economic enterprises, which in turn resulted in their impoverishment. Alidou's work (chapter 11) demonstrates how these gendered ethnic expectations also led to discrimination against women, particularly Muslim women, in politics. Most dramatically, the consequences of rigid ethnic categories were sometimes violently marked on women's bodies. I (chapter 1) show that in Tanzania the constriction of women's interethnic networks in the colonial era resulted in extreme forms of domestic violence when high bridewealth gave husbands impunity. Fry's work (chapter 3) on Fingo ethnicity in South Africa describes the wrath of men expressed in rape and violence when women broke out of gendered ethnic expectations. And most poignantly, Burnet's work (chapter 8) on women in Rwanda who experienced rape and sexual assault as a weapon of war during the genocide demonstrates the impoverishment and marginalization they suffered as a result of fixed ethnic categories. The collective work in this volume, however, demonstrates that, although women were constrained and even violated by the systems of power embodied in gendered forms of ethnicity, they were nevertheless instrumental in shaping new, alternative, or subversive ethnicities or turning to other forms of identity that made more sense in their lives.

Our more specific question for bringing this volume together was this: How did women's gendered practices contribute to the construction (or subversion) of ethnicity in relation to men's practice? We conclude that women's practice of ethnicity developed out of interaction with emerging male ethnic identities. Where women's interests were not coterminous with forms of ethnicity promoted by men that were sometimes particularly disempowering to women, they adopted forms that subverted those categories by creating interethnic networks or contributing to the construction of new forms of identity. Where some men and women had common interests in promoting a particular ethnicity, women were invested in this identity for their own purposes within gendered domains and performed ethnic power in gendered ways.

Part I of this book concerns the strategies that women used in forming interethnic alliances. Because rigid ethnic boundaries were often destructive to women's interests or because those boundaries were not conducive to women's need for widespread social networks in their everyday lives, women continued to reach out to form interethnic relationships and find other ways to make alliances. I (chapter 1) argue that women's interethnic relational experience and historical memory continued to offer alternatives to men's exclusive place-based ethnic identity. Gengenbach's comparative essay (chapter 2) contends that women in the Magude District of Mozambique cultivated multiple, fluid, and geographically expansive ethnic ties, while women in the Cheringoma District dismissed ethnicity as irrelevant and destructive in their economic struggle within the constraints of gendered roles.

In part II, we see women's response to destructive male ethnicity in constructing new forms of identity. These authors show that some women claimed identities that were interethnic, non-ethnic, or perhaps supraethnic when dominant ethnic forms did not serve their interests. Fry (chapter 3) explores the possibility that women were instrumental in constructing a new kind of Fingo ethnicity in opposition to a militant male Xhosa ethnicity in the colonial era. In some places, women have been instrumental in transcending ethnicity to build other national or Pan-African categories. Healy-Clancy (chapter 4) shows that women were central to constructing a New African identity for both men and women in South Africa. Sanders (chapter 5) argues that women chose to participate in the East African Association rather than ethnic organizations during the mid to late colonial era and by promoting their own interests significantly shaped a panethnic or racial identity.

Part III gives examples of women promoting gendered domains of ethnicity. Although in some places women accepted male-defined ethnic categories, they did so for their own reasons and within their own gendered domain, while other women sought ways to survive when the male categories did not fit them. Urban-Mead (chapter 6) contends that while royal-class Ndebele women supported male-constructed ethnicity in their promotion of endogamous marriages, they did so because of their own preferences in choosing a daughter-in-law and made enduring cross-ethnic relations in their church work. Kelly (chapter 7) argues that Zulu women during the civil wars in the transition from apartheid claimed their own form of Zulu ethnicity centered on spirituality and family while also both complementing and subverting the martial identity of men. Burnet (chapter 8) claims that the violence of rigid ethnic categorization took its toll on Rwandan women who were caught between the categories and who worked to forge lives for themselves.

Finally, in part IV, we see women performing ethnically gendered power. Women who had positions of authority in ethnically based polities performed their power in gendered ways. Mbah (chapter 9) argues that Ohafia-Igbo society in Nigeria was characterized by a contest between gendered forms of ethnicity and power carried out by the performances of men and women in ritual, lineage ideology, and authority structures. Schmidt (chapter 10) demonstrates that female chiefs in colonial Zimbabwe and Tanzania supported ethnic authority but performed their power in gendered ways. Finally, Alidou (chapter 11) contends that Muslim women politicians in Kenya today perform political power by maintaining a balance between conforming to expectations of gendered ethnicity and reaching across ethnic boundaries to form the cross-ethnic alliances necessary for championing women's rights.

However, it is obvious in each of these cases that women adopted these various gendered ethnic strategies because of their very particular circumstances and roles, not as a homogeneous category of women. Not all men or all women claimed the same gendered ethnicities. Urban women in interethnic contexts in Healy-Clancy's (chapter 4) and Sanders's studies (chapter 5) were more likely to adopt African identities rather than emphasize those of their home. Female chiefs in Schmidt's study (chapter 10) and high-caste women in Urban-Mead's case (chapter 6) supported ethnicity, albeit in a gendered way. Older women had a higher stake in ethnicity than did younger women (Burnet, chapter 8), and mothers had a higher stake than single women (Urban-Mead, chapter 6). Neither is it helpful to see the opposition of men and women in binary terms. In many of the cases presented here, men and women had similar interests in protecting their families, their communities, and their own class interests or in expressing their resistance to colonialism or racist societies. In some cases, men valued the role of women and promoted their inclusion in Pan-African associations (Sanders, chapter 5).

These case studies make it obvious that we can no longer think about ethnicity in Africa without seeing its claims on identity through gendered performances. But more importantly, we must include women's contributions to the construction or deconstruction of ethnicity. Rather than being complicit in promoting a unitary male version of ethnicity, Africanist scholars must not exclude other versions that may be less militant, rely on widespread networks rather than boundaries, or promote other forms of power. The knowledge production of generating ethnic categories within African communities, particularly beginning in the colonial period, was deeply gendered and often disempowering for women. Even so, women in many different historical circumstances, roles, and places throughout Africa exercised their agency and power in claiming their own forms of identity. Within these broad parameters, much work remains to be done in future research that will continue to uncover women's varied performances of ethnicity that contributed to their own well-being and that of their families and communities.

NOTES

I am indebted to the insightful comments of my colleagues on the introduction as it developed during our collaboration. Thanks especially to Ndubueze Mbah, Jill Kelly, Poppy Fry, Jennie Burnet, and Heike Schmidt, who provided critical insights on drafts of the introduction, and to Dorothy Hodgson and Ethan Sanders. I am also grateful to my writing group, with Marcia Good and Regina Shands-Stoltzfus, who read through numerous versions and talked it through with me. Without all of them the framework would not have appeared in its current form, and I am grateful.

1. Rogers Brubaker and Frederick Cooper, "Beyond 'Identity,'" *Theory and Society* 29 (2000): 1–47; Jeanne Boydston, "Gender as a Question of Historical Analysis," *Gender and History* 20, no. 3 (November 2008): 558–83. Allusion to Joan Wallach Scott, "Gender: A Useful Category of Historical Analysis," in *Gender and the Politics of History* (New York: Columbia University Press, 1999), 28–52.

2. Brubaker and Cooper, "Beyond 'Identity'"; Boydston, "Gender as a Question."

3. Leroy Vail, ed., *The Creation of Tribalism in Southern Africa* (Berkeley: University of California Press, 1991), 11; John Lonsdale, "African Pasts in Africa's Future," *Canadian Journal of African Studies/Revue canadienne des études africaines* 23, no. 1 (1989): 136; for a refutation of "women have no tribe," see Sandra E. Greene, *Gender, Ethnicity, and Social Change on the Upper Slave Coast: A History of the Anlo-Ewe* (Portsmouth, NH: Heinemann, 1996), 14.

4. Throughout this collection, "tribe" is used in quotation marks to indicate its contested and problematic status as an artifact of colonial history. When we want to refer to the African-generated communal identities we use the term "ethnicity."

5. Audrey Smedley, *Women Creating Patrilyny: Gender and Environment in West Africa* (Walnut Creek, CA: AltaMira Press, 2004).

6. These panels were titled: in 2010, "'Women Have No Tribe': Why Gendering Ethnicity Matters in African History"; and in 2012, "'Women Have No Tribe' Part II: Why Gendering Ethnicity Matters in the Ongoing Liberation Struggle."

7. Pamela Scully, *Race and Ethnicity in Women's and Gender History in Global Perspective* (Washington, DC: American Historical Association, 2006).

8.   Dorothy Hodgson, *Once Intrepid Warriors: Gender, Ethnicity, and the Cultural Politics of Maasai Development* (Bloomington: Indiana University Press, 2004), 13–14.

9.   Aili Mari Tripp et al., *African Women's Movements: Transforming Political Landscapes* (Cambridge: Cambridge University Press, 2009).

10.   *Pray the Devil Back to Hell*, video, Passion River Films, 2009; Phyllis M. Martin, *Catholic Women of Congo-Brazzaville: Mothers and Sisters in Troubled Times* (Bloomington: Indiana University Press, 2009).

11.   Barbara Harff and Ted Robert Gurr, *Ethnic Conflict in World Politics*, 2nd ed. (Boulder, CO: Westview, 2004), 3.

12.   Clifford Geertz, "The Integrative Revolution: Primordial Sentiments and Civil Politics in New States," in *The Interpretation of Cultures: Selected Essays by Clifford Geertz*, ed. Clifford Geertz (New York: Basic Books, 1973), 255–310.

13.   René Lemarchand, *Burundi: Ethnic Conflict and Genocide* (Cambridge: Cambridge University Press, 1996), 5.

14.   Bruno Latour, *Reassembling the Social: An Introduction to Actor-Network Theory* (Oxford: Oxford University Press, 2005), 27–42.

15.   Michael R. Mahoney, *The Other Zulus: The Spread of Zulu Ethnicity in Colonial South Africa* (Durham, NC: Duke University Press, 2012).

16.   Crawford Young, "Patterns of Social Conflict: State, Class, and Ethnicity," *Daedalus* 2, no. 3 (1982): 71–98.

17.   Vail, *Creation of Tribalism*; Eric Hobsbawm and Terence Ranger, *The Invention of Tradition* (Cambridge: Cambridge University Press, 1983).

18.   Crawford Young, *The Politics of Cultural Pluralism* (Madison: University of Wisconsin Press, 1976).

19.   Liisa Malkki, *Purity and Exile: Violence, Memory, and National Cosmology among Hutu Refugees in Tanzania* (Chicago: University of Chicago Press, 1995), 255; Benedict Anderson, *Imagined Communities* (London: Verso, 1991), 15.

20.   John Lonsdale, "Moral Ethnicity and Political Tribalism," in *Inventions and Boundaries: Historical and Anthropological Approaches to the Study of Ethnicity and Nationalism*, ed. Preben Kaarsholm and Jan Hultin (Roskilde: International Development Studies, Roskilde University, 1994), 132.

21.   Belinda Bozzoli, "Marxism, Feminism, and South African Studies," *Journal of Southern African Studies* 9, no. 2 (1983): 139–71; Cherryl Walker, ed., *Women and Gender in Southern Africa to 1945* (Cape Town: David Philip, 1990).

22.   For example, Sifiso Mxolisi Ndlovu, *The Soweto Uprisings: Counter-memories of June 1976* (Johannesburg: Ravan Press, 1999).

23.   Iris Berger, "Fertility as Power: Spirit Mediums, Priestesses and the Pre-colonial State in Interlacustrine East Africa," in *Revealing Prophets*, ed. David Anderson and Douglas H. Johnson (Athens: Ohio University Press, 1995), 65–82.

24.   Ifi Amadiume, *Male Daughters, Female Husbands: Gender and Sex in an African Society* (London: Zed Books, 1987); Oyèrónké Oyěwùmí, *The Invention of Women: Making an African Sense of Western Gender Discourse* (Minneapolis: University of Minnesota Press, 1997).

25.   Steve J. Stern, *The Secret History of Gender: Women, Men and Power in Late Colonial Mexico* (Chapel Hill: University of North Carolina Press, 1995); on mundane acts of subversion, see James Scott, *Domination and the Arts of Resistance: Hidden Transcripts* (New Haven, CT: Yale University Press, 1990).

26.   Frederick Barth, *Ethnic Groups and Boundaries* (Oslo: Universitetsforlaget, 1969); Robert Harms, *Games against Nature: An Eco-cultural History of the Nunu of Equatorial Africa* (Cambridge: Cambridge University Press, 1987).

27.   Judith Butler, *Gender Trouble: Feminism and the Subversion of Identity* (London: Routledge, 1990); Allen F. Isaacman and Barbara S. Isaacman, *Slavery and Beyond: The Making of Men and Chikunda Ethnic Identities in the Unstable World of South-Central Africa, 1750–1920* (Portsmouth, NH: Heinemann, 2004).

28.   Martin, *Catholic Women.*

29.   S. A. Sofos, "Inter-ethnic Violence and Gendered Constructions of Ethnicity in Former Yugoslavia," *Social Identities* 2, no. 1 (1996): 73–91; Prema Kurien, "Gendered Ethnicity: Creating a Hindu Indian Identity in the United States," *American Behavioral Scientist* 42, no. 4 (January 1999): 648–70; Lori Handrahan, *Gendering Ethnicity: Implications for Democracy Assistance* (London: Routledge, 2002).

30.   E. Patrick Johnson, "Race, Ethnicity, and Performance," *Text and Performance Quarterly* 23, no. 2 (April 2003): 105–6; Kelly Askew, *Performing the Nation: Swahili Music and Cultural Politics in Tanzania* (Chicago: University of Chicago Press, 2002); Laura Edmondson, *Performance and Politics in Tanzania: The Nation on Stage* (Bloomington: Indiana University Press, 2007); Isabel Hofmeyr, *"We Spend Our Years as a Tale That Is Told": Oral Historical Narrative in a South African Chiefdom* (Portsmouth, NH: Heinemann, 1993), on women's oral tradition in the everyday use versus men in public.

31.   Eric Hobsbawm, "Introduction: Inventing Traditions," in *The Invention of Tradition* (Cambridge: Cambridge University Press, 1983), 1–14; Vail, *Creation of Tribalism.*

32.   Hans Cory, *The Indigenous Political System of the Sukuma and Proposals for Political Reform* (Dar es Salaam: Eagle Press, 1954); see also Martin Channock, *Law, Custom, and Social Order: The Colonial Experience in Malawi and Zambia* (Cambridge: Cambridge University Press, 1985).

33.   George E. Brooks Jr., "The Signares of Saint-Louis and Goree: Women Entrepreneurs in Eighteenth-Century Senegal," in *Women in Africa: Studies in Social and Economic Change*, ed. Nancy Hafkin and Edna Bay (Stanford, CA: Stanford University Press, 1976), 19–44.

34.   Walter Hawthorne, *Planting Rice and Harvesting Slaves: Transformations along the Guinea-Bissau Coast, 1400–1900* (Portsmouth, NH: Heinemann, 2003).

35.   Hodgson, *Once Intrepid Warriors*, 30; Cora Ann Presley, "The Mau Mau Rebellion, Kikuyu Women and Social Change," *Canadian Journal of African Studies* 22, no. 3 (1988): 502–27; Margaret Jean Hay, "Local Trade and Ethnicity in Western Kenya," *Economic History Review* 2, no. 1 (1975): 7–12.

36.   Jean Davison, *Gender, Lineage and Ethnicity in Southern Africa* (Boulder, CO: Westview, 1997).

37. Heidi Gengenbach, *Binding Memories: Women as Makers and Tellers of History in Magude, Mozambique* (New York: Columbia University Press, 2008).

38. Carolyn Hamilton, *Terrific Majesty: The Power of Shaka Zulu and the Limits of Historical Invention* (Cambridge: Cambridge University Press, 1998); Carton Benedict, John Laband, and Jabulani Sithole, eds., *Zulu Identities: Being Zulu, Past and Present* (Pietermaritzburg: University of KwaZulu-Natal Press, 2008).

39. Gunther Schlee, *Identities on the Move: Clanship and Pastoralism in Northern Kenya* (New York: Manchester University Press, 1989); Thomas Spear and Richard Waller, eds., *Being Maasai: Ethnicity and Identity in East Africa* (Athens: Ohio University Press, 1993).

40. Isaacman and Isaacman, *Slavery and Beyond*; see also Stephan Miescher and Lisa Lindsay, eds., *Men and Masculinities in Modern Africa* (Portsmouth, NH: Heinemann, 2001).

41. Greene, *Gender, Ethnicity, and Social Change*, 13–15.

42. Tabitha Kanogo, *African Womanhood in Colonial Kenya, 1900–50* (Athens: Ohio University Press, 2005), 73–97.

43. Donna Klumpp and Corinne Kratz, "Aesthetics, Expertise, and Ethnicity: Okiek and Maasai Perspectives on Personal Ornament," in Spear and Waller, *Being Maasai*, 195–222. See also Donna Klumpp and Corinne Kratz, "Gender, Ethnicity, and Social Aesthetics in Maasai and Okiek Bead Work," in *Rethinking Pastoralism in Africa: Gender, Culture, and Myth of the Patriarchal Pastoralist*, ed. Dorothy Hodgson (Athens: Ohio University Press, 2001), 43–71; for the precolonial period on dress, see Kwesi Yanka, *Speaking for the Chief: Okyeame and the Politics of Akan Royal Oratory* (Bloomington: Indiana University Press, 1995).

44. Derek R. Peterson, *Ethnic Patriotism and the East African Revival: A History of Dissent, c. 1935–1972* (Cambridge: Cambridge University Press, 2012), 152–77.

45. For example, in southern Nigeria this argument has been made by numerous authors: Kamene Okonjo, "The Dual Sex Political System in Operation: Igbo Women and Community Politics in Midwestern Nigeria," in Hafkin and Bay, *Women in Africa*, 46–56; Amadiume, *Male Daughters, Female Husbands*, 119–23; and Sylvia Leith-Ross, *African Women: A Study of the Ibo of Nigeria* (London: Faber & Faber, 1938), 19–21; among others.

46. Hodgson, *Once Intrepid Warriors*.

47. Brett L. Shadle, *"Girl Cases": Marriage and Colonialism in Gusiiland, Kenya, 1890–1970* (Portsmouth, NH: Heinemann, 2006).

48. Hodgson, *Once Intrepid Warriors*, 92.

49. Luise White, *The Comforts of Home: Prostitution in Colonial Nairobi* (Chicago: University of Chicago Press, 1990); Kenda Mutongi, *Worries of the Heart: Widows, Family, and Community in Kenya* (Chicago: University of Chicago Press, 2007); Kanogo, *African Womanhood*; Dorothy L. Hodgson, ed., *"Wicked" Women and the Reconfiguration of Gender in Africa* (Portsmouth, NH: Heinemann, 2001).

50. Dorothy L. Hodgson, *The Church of Women: Gendered Encounters between Maasai and Missionaries* (Bloomington: Indiana University Press, 2005); Mary Wren

Bivins, *Telling Stories, Making Histories: Women, Words, and Islam in Nineteenth-Century Hausaland and the Sokoto Caliphate* (Portsmouth, NH: Heinemann, 2007).

51. Berger, "Fertility as Power."

52. Susan Geiger, *TANU Women: Gender and Culture in the Making of Tanganyikan Nationalism, 1955–1965* (Portsmouth, NH: Heinemann, 1997); E. S. Atieno Odhiambo and John Lonsdale, *Mau Mau and Nationhood: Arms, Authority and Narration* (Athens: Ohio University Press, 2003).

53. Susan Geiger, "Engendering and Gendering African Nationalism," in *In Search of a Nation: Histories of Authority and Dissidence in Tanzania*, ed. Gregory Maddox and James L. Giblin (Athens: Ohio University Press, 2005), 282–84.

54. Elizabeth Schmidt, *Mobilizing the Masses: Gender, Ethnicity, and Class in the Nationalist Movement in Guinea, 1939–1958* (Portsmouth, NH: Heinemann, 2005).

55. Schmidt, *Mobilizing the Masses*, 114.

56. See Stern, *Secret History*, for a Mexican comparison.

57. Schmidt, *Mobilizing the Masses*, 134. The larger literature on the Igbo Women's war includes Judith Van Allen, "'Aba Riots' or 'Igbo Women's War'? Ideology, Stratification, and the Invisibility of Women," in Hafkin and Bay, *Women in Africa*, 59–85.

58. Nickie Charles and Helen M. Hintjens, eds., *Gender, Ethnicity, and Political Ideologies* (New York: Routledge, 1998).

59. Charles and Hintjens, *Gender, Ethnicity, and Political Ideologies*.

60. Debbie Gaitskell, "Devout Domesticity? A Century of African Women's Christianity in South Africa," in Walker, *Women and Gender*, 251–72.

61. Julia Wells also discusses the significance of public genital display in marking out ethnic or racial boundaries in her article "Eva's Men: Gender and Power in the Establishment of the Cape of Good Hope, 1652–1674," *Journal of African History* 39, no. 3 (1998): 417–37.

62. Martin, *Catholic Women*.

Part I

Forming
Interethnic Alliances

1

Gendering the History of Social Memory in the Mara Region, Tanzania, as an Antidote to "Tribal" History

JAN BENDER SHETLER

Throughout Africa the process of ethnic identity formation has largely been predicated upon elderly men's oral traditions, which recount the origins, migration, and settlement of a group as if in relative isolation from others. This process took center stage in the colonial era, when "traditional" elders (those co-opted by a colonial administration) participated in giving form to "tribes" (defined by colonial rule) as the administrative units of indirect rule through which resources and power were allocated.[1] People in the Mara Region of Tanzania were no exception in acknowledging elderly men as the keepers of history while relegating women's knowledge to the private sphere of folktales, children's stories, and gossip.[2] In my own research in the Mara Region, I found that women themselves acquiesced to their lack of historical knowledge, defined as men's stories of communal origins and migrations. Therefore, when scholars employed oral tradition as a source for understanding the creation of ethnicity, they most easily turned to formal men's accounts, which were claimed to represent the group's history. Because oral tradition has been so entwined with the imagined ethnic community, scholarly histories using these sources struggle to produce analyses that go beyond aggregating ethnic units.[3]

Scholars have long recognized that the genius of African civilization was not in isolated "tribes" but in Africans' use of social capital and a gift economy that tied together dispersed groups in reciprocal exchange networks.[4] But capturing that in oral tradition has been more difficult. Beginning with the work of historian Jan Vansina, a methodology developed involving careful interpretation of variations, inconsistencies, off-stage comments that were not part of the formal accounts, and comparison with other kinds of sources to be able to see beyond ethnic boundaries.[5] Other scholars made it clear that oral tradition is always situated within a set of social relationships. In particular, historian David W. Cohen suggested looking at African history from "Pim's doorway," that is, from the perspective of Luo grandmothers (Pim) who taught history to the grandchildren who slept in their homes.[6]

In contrast to the "traditional" ethnic histories recounted by men, elderly women in the Mara Region took responsibility for a different kind of knowledge that grew out of another set of relationships and historical memories. Gendering social memory, that is, memory shared by a collective rather than the memory of an individual, brings into focus another way of conceiving of the region's history based on identities rooted in widespread social networks across ethnic boundaries that provide an alternative to the "tribal" metanarrative. In their narratives, women did not reject ethnicity as much as subvert its exclusivity in their embrace of a much wider set of inclusive networks and multiple identities critical for establishing and maintaining long-term regional ties. Their stories became the primary sources used in this chapter for understanding the way identity took various gendered forms in the region over time. Although male and female narratives are not entirely separate fields and vary according to individual competence and experience, women had expertise in remembering and passing on stories for which men were not responsible. An antidote to isolated and exclusive "tribal" histories is available to Mara historians through analysis of women's historical memory that provides a regional history of expanding and contracting social networks across ethnic boundaries. Constructing and maintaining these interethnic networks in their stories was critical to women's individual well-being, as well as to the public good.

Background to the Mara Region, Sources, and Methodology

The Mara Region, located on the eastern side of Lake Victoria in Tanzania, is characterized as a region of "high ethnolinguistic fractionalization" that is held together by underlying regional understandings and that presents a fascinating study of ethnic difference.[7] Eastern Nilotic Luo speakers live in the north along the lake; Southern Nilotic Tatoga speakers live on the plains to the east; and the majority, a great variety of East Nyanza Bantu speakers, live elsewhere, claiming a variety of distinct ethnic identities. Diversity also extends to the practice of circumcision (both male and female) by most of the interior ethnic groups, while those along the lake, whether Luo or Bantu speakers, did not circumcise. Mara peoples adopted a mix of matrilineal, patrilineal, and bilateral descent systems with an underlying matrifocality and various subsistence economies, including pastoral, agricultural, hunting, and mixed. Most of these geographically small clan-based ethnic communities did not coalesce into panethnic identities during the colonial period, as was often the case elsewhere in Tanzania. Colonial officers struggled to categorize and amalgamate Mara's small "tribes" (of which there were anywhere from fifteen to sixty, depending on how they were counted), few of which had chiefs. Various colonial accounts described Mara people as Bantu with "a dash of Hamitic or Nilotic blood" or "mixed with the Masai and Gaya (Luo)."[8]

Although the "tribal" histories colonial officers solicited from male elders emphasized radical difference and discrete origins, the culturally mixed nature of the region was readily apparent, if not fathomable, in the "tribal" paradigm.[9] Male elders' accounts are not particularly helpful for probing the enigma of how substantial regional interactions over the last two millennia produced underlying similarities in spite of the Mara Region's incredible diversity. Prophecy, sacred sites, generation classes, age sets, and eldership titles, to name a few, all crossed ethnic boundaries and were regionally recognized. These similarities emerged largely as a result of interethnic marriage and patrilocality, the practice of women, often from other ethnic groups, joining their husband's family homestead at marriage. Even without hierarchical chiefdoms Mara coalesced historically as an interacting region before the colonial state. This intercommunicating zone of ongoing reciprocal relationships between people who were linguistically and culturally distinct defined the geographical extent of a larger system based on common cultural understandings and interdependence.[10] Women as boundary crossers in marriage were largely responsible for the creation and maintenance of networks across vast cultural difference. They did this with knowledge that was a public asset to the community rather than being relegated to the private domain.[11]

Because women were central to that process of network formation, their accounts reflected an understanding of ethnicity and identity that was multiple and inclusive. The widespread African adage "women have no tribe" has been used to explain the loss of identity as women left their natal home at marriage but never fully became members in their husband's community. They were often seen as people "between," alliance makers and strangers in their new home.[12] The elderly women from throughout the region whom I interviewed for this study clearly identified themselves with their natal ethnic group. But, following the principle of patrilocality, many had married far from home and therefore had affiliation to other ethnic groups through the inheritance of their children, their natal ancestors, and other nonkin associates. Some of them married into ethnic groups that spoke different languages, making these women stand out even more as strangers. Depending on the lineage structure of their natal homes, some women said that they could never go back again, while others still had a voice in family affairs. A woman's networks changed over time as she had children and aged to a status of respect. Membership in and connection to a variety of ethnic groups were critical both to women's survival and to their prosperity in their husband's home village, as well as in the community as a whole.

The sources and methodology used to gain access to this view of the past are embedded in the very networks they seek to uncover. The larger study, of which this is a part, began with over ninety interviews conducted in 2010 with elderly women in six different ethnic communities in rural areas of the Mara Region, seeking to understand the regional history of gendered historical memory rather than of ethnicity itself.[13] It also builds on my ongoing research in the region over the past fifteen years, with most of the previous work in the interior, western Serengeti or Luo/Suba areas of North Mara and extensive archival work.[14] The interview sites for this study were concentrated along the lake, and interview subjects included women from the small ethnic groups of Jita, Ruri, Zanaki, Ikizu, Kuria, and Kakseru (a subsection of the larger panethnic Luo ethnic group). People with whom I had already developed relationships from my previous work in academic research and community development with the Tanzania Mennonite Church gave me a place to stay, served as local guides, and assisted in my interviews.[15] Even though most of my guides were church members, they chose a variety of women from various religious affiliations for me to interview according to their judgment of which women were knowledge-able about the past. I used Kiswahili in the interviews but always had my local guides to translate my questions into the many local languages I encountered, since elderly women were less likely to be comfortable in Kiswahili. I did not have a controlled sample of men and women from the same age groups but rather interviewed those recommended for their expertise, being aware enough of the context to know if I was missing a critical population. I was situated within particular webs of relationship in those interviews, but I soon found out that access to women's narratives was contingent upon my placement within a social network rather than my status as a "neutral" university professor. The women I interviewed trusted me or not, depending upon their relationship with the people assisting me in each community and how I was introduced.

In order to make broad regional comparisons rather than an in-depth analy-sis of one area (as I had done with men's narratives in the past), I visited communities that represented the breadth of cultural diversity in the region. For each ethnic group I interviewed about fifteen people in one or two villages, usually with a single interview for each person. The range of stories that women told me across the region was consistent enough that I felt confident I had access to at least some basic categories of gendered social memory. During my week-long stay in each community, I did as much participant observation as formal interviews and drew on my previous knowledge of living in the region and on archival and other written work for context. The questions that I used to ask men to start an interview, such as "What did you learn about the origins or history of your ethnic group?" did not work for women, so I had to find other ways to access their historical expertise. Women usually denied that they knew any history at all, as that was a category of knowledge for which men were responsible. I did not use a standard set of interview questions for each person but rather searched for forms of knowledge in which he or she had expertise, even if not classified locally as history. For clues as to where to look, I am indebted to the work of historians Heidi Gengenbach, Sandra Greene, and others who have identified women's stories about pots, tattoos, marriages, and sacred sites, among other things, as repositories of historical memory.[16] It remained a constant challenge to probe their memories with broad questions that did not determine the form of the answer. And, of course, both women and men I interviewed had a wide range of competence based on age and experience. Some women indeed knew men's stories because these women had a particular status that allowed them to sit with men, while men also heard their grandmothers' tales.[17] As time went on, I learned that questions about material culture, songs, names, childhood tales, and life experiences elicited stories that women were more comfortable telling.

In the first interviews, when I consistently began to hear individualized and very particularistic memories that lacked a larger metanarrative, I wondered whether I had misjudged. Perhaps it was true that women did not know any history and my research was in vain! The breakthrough came for me when my interviews were derailed by a funeral within the family that was hosting me. We all had to sit at the house for mourning over a three-day period. Although I was frustrated to just sit, I soon found that this was one of the venues in which women's social network memory was activated. When introducing me to other women, many of whom she had not seen in years, my host often omitted personal names, giving instead the form of relationship, both kinship and associational, between them—her aunt, her cousin, her friend from school days, the mother of her father's business partner, a church elder, the daughter of her friend's sister, and so on. For example, my host might introduce me to another woman by saying, "This is my father's sister's daughter from Butata who married the evangelist from the Chitare congregation and came to study at the Bible school." Talk among women during the hours we sat together on mats under the trees revolved around noting other people who came or went and discussing their relationships and stories, both tragic and mundane.

While popular culture minimizes this kind of talk as "gossip," I began to see how critical this setting is for constructing and maintaining social networks. Scholars have analyzed it as a "backstage performance" away from formal power venues that reaffirms group norms and boundaries or critiques those in power.[18] Anthropologist Tuulikki Pietilä's study of Kilimanjaro in Tanzania demonstrates how gossip "enables a dialogue about moral reputations and value."[19] In thinking about social memory, the semipublic performance of "gossip" serves to reactivate and invigorate social networks that cross kinship, ethnic, and social boundaries, providing a valuable resource for support on a daily basis. Women's memory was individualized and particularistic because the stories were told situationally and relationally, depending on whom they were talking to at the moment and for what purpose. Their stories were not unified as the story of any particular social group and thus could not play the role of an ethnic history, even though parts of that history were critically related to the group's past. Gengenbach characterizes women's historical knowledge in Mozambique as a "relational epistemology" that highlights the fluid, diverse, and multiple identities and experiences of women.[20] Women could tell flowing stories of particular ancestors or ritual expertise, but no two women, or even the same woman in different situations, told the same story characteristic of one ethnic group.

Women kept this kind of knowledge as a result of their common structural role throughout the region as the primary boundary crossers and alliance makers. Every community in the region, whether in a matrilineal, patrilineal, or bilateral kinship system, practiced patrilocal marriage. Whether moving to geographically close or distant in-laws, married women became strangers and outsiders. Men's mobility took the form of migrant labor, while women's was marriage. Mobility reaffirmed men's need for ethnic identity to find their own people in faraway cities or workplaces for support. But because women needed to construct a viable life for themselves and their children in a new ethnic group, they had to have intimate knowledge of all the social networks—paternal, maternal, and affinal, as well as friendship, associational, and ritual. It was not that women had not heard ethnic histories but that those histories were largely irrelevant to women's everyday needs. Instead, women needed interethnic network knowledge for negotiating their lives and carrying out their responsibility to pass on this knowledge.[21] Women performed these narratives in informal settings such as the home, where children slept in their grandmother's house;

the fields and yards, where women cooperated in their daily tasks; and communal gatherings for funerals or weddings, where women met and reconnected the webs of relationship to one another through their shared stories.

Because men remained rooted in their home communities, even if they left for education or work, their identities grew out of their own lineage, clan, and ethnic group networks. At gatherings around pots of beer, senior men told and retold the set narratives of ethnic identity in order to solve current problems. Men also told these stories in colonial settings where officials demanded the men's "tribal" expertise. Men had no problem producing "history" in an interview because they told the practiced public narratives of the collective; men used those stories in their maneuvering to gain power, prestige, and wealth. As a group without formal power in the colonial period, women exchanged narratives in off-stage performances that were not recognized as history or as *mambo ya zamani* (things of the past) by others.[22] Yet men still recognized women's area of expertise and valued it. When I was doing my original research in the region in 1995–96, I was trying to figure out relationships between the various households in the small village where I lived. The man I interviewed kept leaving the room and then coming back with the answer. When I realized that he was going out to the kitchen to ask his wife for the answers, we relocated to the kitchen!

In my interviews, I soon found that elderly women had first learned their stories of the past in the intimate setting of sleeping in their (usually paternal) grandmother's house as children. Another regional cultural constant, in addition to patrilocality, was the relationship of children to their grandparents. When children got to be about six years old, they were no longer allowed to sleep in their mother's one-room round house, where they might witness their parents' intimacy, and so the children went to stay with their grandmother, often widowed and living in her own house in the same homestead. Children of both genders heard their grandmother's stories, but girls often stayed with their grandmother until they married, whereas boys moved out before they reached puberty. Cohen credits Luo grandmothers, who also had girls from neighboring homesteads sleeping there, with transmitting a "regional consciousness and corporateness" largely responsible for the formation of a Luo "national" identity.[23] This assessment moves grandmothers' stories from the private to the public domain and gives them value for the whole community. The role of elderly women in transmitting social network memory and being responsible for interethnic relationships also affected their own sense of identity beyond ethnicity.

Whether in Luo- or Bantu-speaking communities, grandparents and their grandchildren maintained an *utani* (joking) relationship, meaning that they shared an almost peer-like intimacy and could talk about personal subjects such as sex.[24] This was in contrast to the formal respect relationship between children and their parents in adjacent generations. A grandmother often called her grandson "my little husband," or a grandfather teased his granddaughter to bring him food as "my favorite wife." When I asked women to tell me some of their grandmothers' stories, they almost always laughed and said, "Oh, you don't really want to hear those stories, do you!" intimating that their grandmothers told them stories with intimate details. They had fond memories of these sometimes scandalous times shared together.

From their grandmothers women heard stories of particular ancestors, often from distant places and ethnic groups, perhaps coming in a time of hunger and remembered because of the ancestors' expertise in healing or rain-making. It was not uncommon for women to have powerful positions as ritual specialists passed down from their grandmothers. These ancestors were located within a still-viable set of relationships out of which people visited each other for funerals and weddings, provided help in times of trouble, or carried on an utani relationship between clans because of past histories. While men told stories of clan or ethnic group founding fathers who were located in a mythical timeframe, grandmothers' stories featured named grandparents or great-grand-parents reaching back not more than a few generations. A daughter often took her name from her deceased grandmother and inherited her grandmother's bracelets in order to keep her memory alive. One woman told the story of her grandmother who disappeared into Lake Victoria and, when the family had gathered for her funeral four days later, walked out of the lake carrying medicines to begin her life as a healer. The woman who related the story practiced healing for infertility and childhood disease with her grandmother's medicines and wore her bracelets.[25] Most strikingly, I found that the women who had not slept in their grandmother's home had significantly fewer ancestral memories and more constricted social networks.

Grandmothers also told folktales that taught girls the inevitability of leaving their natal homes and the skills to survive in a strange new place. These stories, featuring animal characters and outlandish events to entertain the children before they fell asleep at night, seemed to be just for fun, but they also contained moral and practical lessons.[26] Girls were taught how to behave when they went to live with their husband's family—how to work hard, respect their in-laws, and adapt to their new home. These instructions reinforced the status quo in its most obvious form. They helped girls to accept their subordinate status, to serve and submit to the rule of their husband or, more immediately, their mother-in-law in the home. For example, one woman told a long and involved story about a girl who was sent to fetch water but was tricked by the birds into staying by the spring, entranced by their song. Her lack of attention had bad consequences for her elders, and the lesson was that you should do what you are asked.[27] A similar story tells of a girl who refused the man whom her parents wanted her to marry and instead chose her own husband. But that man turned out to be a vulture in disguise, and as soon as they married he flew away with her and took bites out of her body. The moral was not to refuse the man your parents want you to marry.[28] Thus it may be easy to dismiss grandmothers' stories as just another way to reinforce acceptance of women's subordinate role.

However, the stories also provided practical advice about how to live within and maintain the relational webs that determined a woman's life, particularly in marriage. Some stories demonstrated the help that a woman can receive from her mother-in-law if she is careful and how friendship is often stronger than kinship. These teachings parallel what historian Steve Stern referred to in his work on colonial Mexico as "contingent right and obligation." Women did not oppose the "patriarchal pact" that they made at marriage, but the fulfillment of their obligations was contingent upon their husband, father-in-law, and mother-in-law also fulfilling their obligations. Women protected their rights by finding allies, both men and women, in their new settings.[29] Girls were also taught the limits of their obligation when demands were unreasonable and how to rally support to make their case. In one story, a woman relied on her mother-in-law, who worked against her own husband to help her daughter-in-law and her son to be reunited.[30]

I also asked women to tell me their own life stories. This was often difficult, because women had not practiced this narrative in any other setting and did not see their lives as having a narrative thread. I thus had to keep asking them questions about the different stages of their lives and what they did, whom they were associated with, and what challenges they faced. Much of what women related concerned marriage and children, which were at the crux of their ability to become productive adults and the basis of their extensive networks. Most of the elderly women whom I interviewed were married during the high colonial period, in the late 1930s and 1940s. Their stories provided information on whom and how they married, if they divorced or remarried, how they made a living, how they related to children and other family members, and what their lives were like as widows. The perspective on gendered ethnic identity gained from my interviews with elderly women was influenced by their stage in life, when they could call on, and gained status from, networks built up over the years. How women used their social networks to negotiate the profound changes of the colonial and postcolonial economy provided a new perspective on this period.

What, then, do these memories, whether folktales, stories of individual ancestors, ritual expertise, gossip, or stories from their own lives, mean historically? Women do not provide an overarching historical narrative, as do men. They do not go back farther than a few generations, and they are situated within particular networks of relationships, none of which contains the same constellation of characters. Even taken collectively, these pieces, without a unifying narrative of even one life story, are difficult to use for thinking about change over time in the region. However, by comparing women's stories regionally as well as chronologically and putting them into historical context using other sources such as men's stories and colonial records, we can see a new set of patterns beginning to emerge. In examining those patterns, we must always be cognizant of the nature of these memories as individualized pieces used to construct useful relational networks. The rest of this chapter puts this theory into practice by providing three examples of how regional history is seen differently from the perspective of women's memories in terms of expanding and contracting social networks. These examples offer a view that destabilizes and subverts conventional "tribal" history and demonstrates women's multiple and inclusive sense of ethnicity.

Extensive Regional Connections in the Precolonial Past: 1870–1910

Comparing elderly women's stories of their grandmothers to those of their own lives demonstrates the large extent of precolonial interethnic networks even beyond the region. Most of these stories are set in the context of regional famine, drought, disease, conflict, and ecological collapse at the end of the nineteenth century. In contrast to men's narratives, where connections to distant peoples appeared as mythical long-ago connections, the women I interviewed told about particular, named grandparents who came from distant communities in troubled times.[31] For example, many Jita and Ruri women told of great-grandmothers coming to marry from around the lake, especially from the agriculturally productive islands of Ukara and Ukerewe in Lake Victoria just south of the region.[32] One common image was a single woman or a group of sisters accidentally leaving their home by launching out into the lake on a floating island of matted reeds until they reached a faraway shore and were adopted or married into new families.[33] The floating reeds story seems to be a trope used to dislodge these ancestors from their original families and place them firmly in the kin group of those who found them. Other great-grandmothers came as brides given for food during a time of hunger; other great-grandmothers sought refuge in a new community.[34] One woman's grandmother, named

Mugaya (meaning Luo), walked into a Kuria-Kiroba homestead from Luo areas to the north and asked to be taken in as a wife in return for her services as a rainmaker.[35] During this time of widespread insecurity, a woman might marry into another ethnic group as a way for her father to cement an alliance useful for the survival of his family or for a woman to find sanctuary for herself. Women in the colonial era continued to tell the stories of and identify with their grandmothers who came from distant places in order to sustain useful relationships.

Interethnic marriage caused profound cultural change in Mara communities, sometimes resulting in a language shift. The Kakseru ethnic group in North Mara spoke a Bantu language until the mid-nineteenth century, when they gradually began speaking Luo and adopting Luo culture. This change began when Luo-speaking immigrants came to North Mara looking for a place to settle and build their own communities. Luo men gave their daughters to marry into Bantu-speaking families as a way to make peace with the local inhabitants. Local Bantu-speaking men were eager to marry Luo women because the men had to pay less bridewealth. In addition, the men perceived connections to Luo military and ritual power as prestigious and useful.[36] One story says that the Luo girls demanded that Kakseru men stop filing their bottom teeth and circumcising if they wanted to marry them. The narrator says that was how the assimilation to Luo identity began—once a bride was exchanged, the man's family had to respect the bride's in-laws.[37] However, even in the present context, almost all of the women I interviewed in North Mara lake communities married in from other Luo-speaking communities in Kenya and North Mara outside Kakseru.[38] The women talked about accepting distant suitors who came courting because a friend or an in-law in the area had agreed to introduce the men to eligible girls. Once the woman married, there were frequent trips back and forth to visit her home area and to introduce more women from home as brides to her husband's area where she now lived.[39] Women's narratives maintained these relationships, which kept communities in contact and allowed brides to continue to be exchanged and cultures to change over time. Kakseru now identifies as a Luo territory as a result of women's work in intermarriage.[40]

In a South Mara lakeside community of Bantu-speaking Ruri people, it was women's stories that kept alive the memory of Luo grandparents who were stolen as children during the great famines and conflict at the turn of the twentieth century. Ruri fishermen went north in boats along the shore where Luo children were getting water and enticed them into boats by the promise of food. The children were then taken back to the Ruri community and adopted or married into families there.[41] These stories do not normally show up in men's histories of Ruri tradition because the men do not want to remember their ancestors as captured people. The practice of stealing children seems to be related to Ruri matrilineal descent patterns, where a man's wealth was inherited by his sister's children rather than his own sons. During this time, men were anxious to consolidate their growing wealth in the coastal trade through children who would inherit from them. The strategy of marrying a distant stranger or, better, a stolen wife (sometimes using the term for a Luo speaker, Gaya, as "slave") without kin to claim her children was a common way of circumventing matrilineal inheritance patterns.[42] When I was in Luo areas, however, I did not hear stories of Luo children who disappeared during the famine. Luo women did, however, talk about the severity of the "famine of eating goat skins," when people died because there was nowhere to go to get food.[43] Because the stolen children left no descendants in Luo communities, they were not remembered in women's stories.[44]

Women's social memory played a valued public role during the late precolonial and early colonial eras because these interethnic connections were critical for surviving the famines. Whether these stories describe women who were responsible for assimilation of a new culture when they married in distant places or children being taken forcefully in times of hunger, they demonstrate where the networks extended and how they were maintained. Although women tell these stories as those of individual grandmothers rather than of human exchange, from these accounts we can see the larger patterns. Even in extraordinarily difficult circumstances, women kept alive those connections so that their granddaughters might make use of those networks when they moved as strangers to yet other communities. While men told stories of the ethnic group in opposition to others in times of famine or conflict, the whole community benefited from the interethnic alliances and ongoing relationships that women created. Women's multiple ethnic identities were kept open and in flux as a result of these public narratives.

Colonial Ethnicity, Bridewealth, and the Constriction of Networks: 1920s–1930s

Social networks through marriage contracted within the ethnic group as the colonial government in the 1920s and 1930s imposed rigid "tribal" boundaries within which positions and resources were distributed. This resulted in fewer interethnic marriages. By marrying within the ethnic group, women could be closer to their mothers. However, with the colonial elevation of "tribal" chiefs and ethnic histories, women's ritual and social network knowledge was devalued as a private, domestic affair. In spite of that, women along the lake continued to be able to protect their rights through closer social networks. In South Mara, where various forms of both matrilineal and patrilineal systems coexisted, women still had little choice in their spouse but continued to get out of an abusive marriage by returning home, because, with little to no bridewealth exchanged, they were not held hostage to its repayment.[45] A Ruri woman said, "After marriage, you still have your parents' home and go back when the children are sick or just anytime to visit them."[46] Divorce and remarriage were fairly common in their stories, as women in these matrifocal societies exercised a certain degree of autonomy in their decisions.[47] An ethnographer of the matrilineal Kwaya concluded that a woman's emotional attachment was to her parents' home rather than her husband's.[48] In North Mara among patrilineal Luo along the lake, women reported choosing their own husband: "It was my own decision whom to marry, not my father's; even long ago it was that way."[49] Yet, although those same women returned often to visit, the kinship system did not allow them to return home permanently after they married, and they had to seek support in other networks. However, because bridewealth was low, a woman could leave a bad marriage by finding another man to repay her first husband's family.[50]

In both of these lake communities, a developing sense of in-group ethnicity is reflected in women's distinct nostalgia about the past, particularly about family relationships. Because the many small Luo-speaking groups in Kenya and Tanzania began to define themselves within a larger pan-Luo ethnic community, intermarriage continued across the national border but decreased with partners from nearby Bantu-speaking communities. Most of the Bantu-speaking Jita women I interviewed had married within the ethnic group or close geographically. Luo women spoke with affection about connections between Luo-speaking communities through marriage: "They had love between them and would visit and marry one another and help each other; they loved each other."[51] Jita women took pride in the "traditional" ways of marriage as they reminisced about the kin who surrounded them as they met their husband for the first time before marriage. Their paternal aunts covered their bodies with red earthen paint for the wedding, which involved a sequence of movements back and forth between the women's parents' and their husband's home accompanied by various relatives. Women in these areas declared that life was better in the past, when kin supported one another and the group's traditions remained strong.[52]

The contrast with women in the interior could not be any starker for the colonial period. Here, women were cut off from social networks and as a result experienced increasing domestic violence and abuse.[53] When I began talking to women in the interior ethnic groups of Kuria in North Mara and Nata, Ikoma,

Ikizu, and Zanaki in South Mara about their marriages, there was a dramatic change in the tone of the interviews to painful memories. Women consistently voiced protest against domestic violence, child marriage, and their inability to leave a bad marriage.[54] They often connected this to the rising bridewealth rates, sometimes up to forty or more cattle and other livestock, ranking as the highest rates in East Africa.[55] Women began to talk about marriage as a commodity exchange rather than a symbolic connection between families. They said their fathers treated them as capital for building wealth and sold them to the highest bidder.[56] Brides were in short supply as older men who gained cattle wealth married more wives in order to gain more labor and to assure having enough children because the prevalence of new childhood diseases and STDs increased infertility and infant mortality. Men began to "book" their potential brides, especially those from poor families, earlier and earlier. This led to the dramatic increase in child marriage, where a man gave bridewealth to take an infant girl to his homestead to be raised as a daughter by his mother or wife until she reached puberty; she was then circumcised in her natal community and then came back to the man's home to live as his wife.[57] For all the years that I spent interviewing men in this region, I never heard these stories until I spoke with women about their own experiences. Privatizing women's knowledge removed it from the realm of relevant "tribal" history.

Recent scholarship historicizes domestic violence beyond the realm of the purely personal or "traditional" and into the structural as a response to historical change. The concept of the "moral economy," often used to talk about the negotiation of reciprocal precapitalist relationships of patron/client or lord/serf even in the context of an overwhelming power differential, can be applied to marriage.[58] Men and women formed relationships based on common assumptions about their rights and obligations within a context of unequal power. As women were increasingly understood to be "bought" and disconnected from their social networks, they lost their ability to keep the level of violence within "acceptable" limits. The traditional method of coping by going for help or counsel with parents, in-laws, friends, other relatives, neighbors, and church leaders was subverted by the colonial understanding that this was a private affair of a man and his property.[59] It became clear in interviews that these patterns of abuse were relatively recent and related to the rise in bridewealth. The mothers and grandmothers of the elderly women I interviewed married with a bridewealth of one to four cattle, and men seldom took more than two wives. The switch from matriliny to patriliny and the precipitous rise in bridewealth rates and child brides happened within living memory for many.[60] The creation of colonial "tribes" gave men increased power to privatize their marriage relations as a commercial exchange.

These patterns were closely connected to the introduction of a commercial economy and colonial rule. Men from the interior recovered from the ecological disasters of the late nineteenth century by building up their wealth in cattle and raising cash crops, resulting in an increasing disparity of wealth within the community. Labor for growing cash and subsistence crops was in high demand, and wealthier men married more wives to exploit their labor. Brides were in short supply as young men turned to cattle raiding or migrant labor to earn bridewealth independently of their fathers.[61] Some men said that when Kuria, who had the most access to cash crops and cattle, began paying higher bride-wealth rates, the price went up for everyone in the region.[62] While some of the same dynamics existed along the lake, where cotton was introduced, the biggest cash earner was fishing, which depended largely on male labor. Men and women there continued to share agricultural labor, and bridewealth rates continued to be low to nonexistent.

The colonial courts contributed to further reinforcing the absolute indi-vidual rights of husbands over their wives through their payment of bride-wealth, thereby further isolating women from networks outside of their hus-band's family.[63] In the interior, colonial courts set limits on bridewealth because they were concerned that young men could not marry without resorting to cattle raiding for bridewealth. In Kuria, the first bridewealth limits were set at three cattle and then raised to ten in 1934, neither of which was enforceable.[64] On the other hand, in areas without bridewealth, the government was concerned about the frequency of divorce and the instability of marriage. As these dynamics played out, in 1945, with support from the Catholic Church, colonial officers called a meeting of Kwaya elders, who agreed to introduce an obligatory bride-wealth of fifteen cows and to end matrilineal inheritance.[65] By the 1950s the courts were full of cases in which the colonial government had codified and enforced customary law that forced women and their children back to the abusive men who had paid their bridewealth. Yet at the same time, women continued to run away from bad marriages, using their social networks to find sanctuary in the city; by the 1950s they had started using the courts to plead their own case for divorce.[66] Women in these circumstances had even less time for an ethnic "tradition" that confined them to domestic violence.

Women from the interior do not tell nostalgic stories about this period but instead relay their suffering because they lost their ability to access past social networks by the privatization of their public concerns. Many said that it was only education and law that began to make things better for them and their daughters. These women endured domestic violence because they did not want to leave their children with a co-wife who would treat them badly. The women also did not want to give up their own future security with their sons.[67] Although they were often proud of the large number of cows given in marriage for them, women connected their own abuse with high bridewealth. They said the man felt he owned the woman if he paid forty cows. Women talked about being stuck in bad marriages because their father could not pay back the bridewealth to bring them home.[68] A Zanaki woman said, "When your husband pays a large bridewealth, you are banished from your home and cannot come back for anything. It is shameful to come back with a problem, so you just put up with it."[69] In Zanaki, almost all of the elderly women I talked to had been child brides who grew up in their husband's homestead. Sadly for my own research, those women knew little about the past nor about relationships beyond their "tribal" identity, since they did not sleep in their grandmother's home and had no one to tell them the stories of their own ancestors, breaking their connections to the social networks that had sustained women in the past.[70]

Although domestic violence is now understood as a "tribal" characteristic, the historical data clearly show that the difference between domestic violence rates along the lake and the interior are connected to the way each of the sub-regions were differently integrated into the colonial economy and the differing gender roles in marriage. Stereotypes and joking relations between people in the Mara Region today reinforce ethnic patterns that developed in the colonial era. Women from the lake told me repeatedly that they would never marry a Kuria or Ikoma man (from the interior) because they would have to work too hard and be abused. And people from the interior said that Jita or Ruri women (from the lake) were promiscuous and divorced easily. Although women continued to form interethnic networks, they were also very much aware of how differently women were treated in other areas. Men did not like to marry women from the lake because those women had the reputation of not being easily controlled and would have to agree to circumcision.[71] When I told people in Dar es Salaam that I was working in the Mara Region they would look aghast and comment on Kuria abuse of women and cattle raiding.[72] A 2007 graduate-student study from the University of Dar es Salaam found the highest rate of domestic violence in the nation in Kuria areas of North Mara. Of the 140 respondents for this study, 95 percent of women said they had been abused, and 97 percent of men admitted to having beaten their wives.[73] These statistics have to be explained not as traditional timeless ethnic patterns but as historically contingent changes. It was women's stories that frequently and vehemently raised these issues, which have been marginalized out of public view.

From the perspective of women's memory, it is clear that critical changes in the colonial economy and polity precipitated devastating consequences for women directly related to their ability to access multiple social networks. Because the basic economic unit was the homestead of a man and his multiple wives with their houses, marriage patterns determined strategies that men used to gain wealth or survive drought over time, allowing us to see how larger historical changes both created new marriage patterns and were significantly shaped by existing marriage patterns. When women's networks were constricted, they suffered both physically and emotionally. They also lost their ability to tell the stories of their grandmothers and thus perpetuate the regional networks that kept the whole community healthy. By devaluing and privatizing women's knowledge, the community's ability to call on interethnic social networks was compromised. Men's definition of "tribal" ethnicity increasingly took precedence, much to the detriment of both women and the larger community.

Women's Construction of Extended Religious Networks: 1940s–1950s

Yet women were not passive in the face of difficult situations, and they used various strategies passed on by their grandmothers to subvert these constrictions and exert their agency to forge new networks and new multiethnic identities. One of the most important ways they did this was by using the church and in some places the mosque. The majority of women I talked to had some kind of affiliation with either Christianity or Islam. Their expressed reasons for joining ranged from following their peers to being called by God. Some of these elderly women only joined late in life, after they were widowed, and often on the invitation of neighbors or family.[74] Generally, women used the new networks offered by universal religions to extend their relational webs, which had been restricted during the colonial era. Both religions were associated with *ustarabu*, or "civilization" and "modernity." Many of the chiefs' families or those who wanted to succeed in business became Muslim because of their trade networks. Women valued the new names they got with baptism in the church because a Christian name marked them as modern women. The church supported women's complaints against abuse and their desire to keep their children while not supporting divorce or polygamy. The church offered another discourse for asserting women's rights that resonated with women's desire to widen their social networks.[75]

The strategy of expanding networks was obvious in some of the stories I heard in the area where child brides and domestic violence were most prevalent. One woman, supported by her Christian husband, used her church membership to defy the elders by refusing to be circumcised. When she became pregnant, the elders threatened to kill her baby, because birth by an uncircumcised woman was seen as an abomination. She ran away to a mission station along the lake for the birth. Her mother-in-law went for help to a missionary, who got the district commissioner to come and threaten the elders with arrest if the baby was harmed.[76] Another early convert wanted to marry a Christian man from the blacksmith clan whom it was taboo for her to marry. The church supported their marriage, and the woman escaped after her mother tied her down to keep her from going to the church wedding.[77]

These heroic stories of women's agency are moderated by the fact that many churchwomen understood that joining the church meant forgetting the stories of the past and discarding their grandmother's bracelets in order to accept a new identity as Christians. Many churchwomen said that they hid the bracelets because the missionaries understood them as a connection to the women's pagan past and witchcraft. Some are only now realizing that the discarded bracelets were one of the few remembrances the women had of their grandmother and her stories.[78] To join the mission church by definition meant to turn away from traditional practices, which were understood explicitly as demonic. Women found new freedom in the church, even as the male church leadership asserted another form of domination. The church encouraged interethnic relationships while discouraging ethnic practices, particularly those pertaining to religion and the ancestors.

Education in a church school was another way that women took action to change their circumstances and build interethnic networks. Women who went to the Mennonite girls' boarding school in Mugango remember fondly the community they formed together with girls from all over the region; their house mother, Rebecca Mutemwa; and the missionary woman, Miriam Wenger. They grew and cooked their own food together and learned basic reading and writing, Bible knowledge, and domestic skills. There was also a boys' section of the school, where the girls often found future husbands from other ethnic groups who had different understandings about marriage. Some of the girls were sent by their parents to school, while others made their own decision to come and defied their family's expectations for their marriages.[79] One woman in Zanaki told how the missionary had to lock the girls in a storeroom before the truck came to take them to the Mugango school so that they would not be forced to go home by their parents.[80] Women formed lifelong friendships in the schools and found church networks for support wherever they went as Christian wives. Some used their domestic science education for professions and made sure that their children got more education.[81] While boys also went to mission schools and formed long-lasting interethnic relationships there, they did not have to face the same opposition from their parents, as it was assumed the boys would return to their home communities. Girls who went to school, however, defied their parents' expectations for their marriages and bridewealth.

The East African Revival provides one of the best examples of the subversive ways that women made use of religion to build new interethnic networks. The revival began in Uganda and spread through Kenya and into Tanzania in the 1940s, with women as the majority of its supporters. The Mennonite Church, whose members constituted a large portion of my interviewees, was particularly involved in the large spiritual-life meetings and practices associated with the revival. The *balokole* (saved) characteristically practiced frequent public confession of their sins and forgiveness. They spoke about this as "walking the light" and being completely open with fellow Christians. They met in both small weekly fellowship groups and large tent meetings for testimonies, which gave these women practice in telling their life stories.[82] Of course, confession also implicated and named other people, especially men, many of whom were not happy with the public airing of sins.[83] Women, who constituted the majority of revival participants and church members, found a means to make their own struggles and pain public, as well as a new outlet for relationship formation.[84]

One significant aspect of the revival for women was becoming friends with women from other ethnic groups in tent meetings, which brought together people from all over the region and even from across national boundaries. Going to a distant spiritual-life meeting was a sanctioned way to get away from home and enjoy visiting with others. Women talked about walking for days or piling in the back of a truck to get to the meeting, staying in other people's homes, and learning to know them through their confessions. They said there was no prejudice based on "tribe" and that people loved each other in Christ. They look back nostalgically on this time of unity in the church, noting that today people have no time or money to go to spiritual-life meetings, even though they have become local rather than regional events.[85] The meaning of church membership was different for men and women and had a significant effect on their further life choices and identity. Women who joined the church early and went to its schools tended to talk almost exclusively of those relationships and their Christian identity. Men, on the other hand, continued to hold family positions in addition to their church roles, and ethnic history was an area of concern. Through the church, women were able to defy some marriage practices but became tied to others. While their relationships changed to include church members in different ethnic groups, they kept their role in maintaining relational webs. In the church and in other venues, women thus found ways for carrying out the work of forming alliances entrusted to them by their grandmothers, this time in subverting an ethnic identity to form non-ethnic networks on the basis of a Christian identity.

Conclusion

Gendering social memory in the Mara Region allows us to see a very different history organized around interethnic relations rather than discrete ethnic units. All of the women I talked to considered themselves to be part of a lineage, a clan, and an ethnic group, but they also saw themselves as a part of their husband's family, their church or mosque, women's neighborhood groups, and the kin connections made by their ancestors from distant places. Women's sense of ethnic identity in these interviews was fluid (as it changed with marriage and age), inclusive (as their lives were built around crossing boundaries and using the past to form webs of relationship that sustained them), multiple (as they managed a number of identities simultaneously and situationally), and often subversively non-ethnic (when they formed other kinds of associations). Women's historical memory, growing out of their gendered identities, is indeed a critical key to understanding the past.

A regional history of expanding and contracting networks emerges from women's historical memory. The period of disasters in the late nineteenth century sent women moving across the region to marry in distant places in order to find security for their home communities or for themselves. The connections they made endured with affinal relationships that led to more marriages and help in times of trouble. In the colonial period, these networks contracted due to the colonial emphasis on "tribe" and the rule of chiefs. Women's interethnic network role was now suspect, and their knowledge became devalued and relegated to the private, domestic sphere. In the interior, this had the most severe effect on women who married for a large bridewealth and whose social networks were cut off as marriage became a private domestic affair. Yet women in the colonial period also found ways to build new relationships through religious associations and made the connections using knowledge from their grandmothers. Women were at the center of this history, both forming those connections through their marriages and remembering and passing them on to the next generation. The sources and methodology for subverting "tribal" history and instead highlighting the regional connections of diverse people are available only if we take the time to look where we least expect to find them.

In the current context, elderly women told me that they no longer tell these stories to their grandchildren, because their grandchildren live far away in the cities and are not interested in what old people say. Yet it is still the case that their daughters are forming new kinds of families in the cities by pulling together support networks from a variety of places and coming back home to help the old people. Whether this will extend to the next generation is not yet clear. However, some in that generation are now becoming interested in their own history and assume that the ethnic history of their people is the only version of that story. Giving historical value to grandmother's stories again might help that generation to rethink the "tribal" narrative and the critical importance of interethnic social networks in the past.

The story of gendered social network memory in the Mara Region teaches us that women's practice of ethnicity is always specific to a particular context. Even within this region, women in the interior and along the lake had very different reactions to the imposition of "tribal" boundaries in the colonial period, with very different consequences for their well-being. The temporal context also matters, as women during the late nineteenth-century disasters were much more willing to open up to other identities in order to escape famine but equally willing to exclude people who were different in the colonial period. In each of these contexts, it is clear that the practice of ethnicity was certainly gendered. Men and women in each era and subregion had different experiences and roles, which influenced how they used identity in their everyday tasks. Even if people of both genders embraced a more exclusive ethnic identity in the colonial period, they defined ethnicity in different ways. By gendering ethnicity, we can begin to tell different stories about the African past that do not depend on a single ethnic metanarrative and show interethnic connection rather than exclusion. In the context of ongoing ethnic conflict on the African continent today, women's historical role as boundary crossers and memory keepers of interethnic networks is surely a valuable heritage for reassessing the role of the past in the present.

NOTES

1. Many of these elders who were put forward as "traditional" elders to tell the story of their "tribe" were chosen by the colonial authorities with a political agenda of giving the ethnic unit or "tribe" a more formal shape and fixed polity than it had in the past.

2. See Isabel Hofmeyr, *"We Spend Our Years as a Tale That Is Told": Oral Historical Narrative in a South African Chiefdom* (Portsmouth, NH: Heinemann, 1993).

3. Allusion to Benedict Anderson, *Imagined Communities* (New York: Verso, 1991).

4. See, for example, Jane I. Guyer, "Wealth in People, Wealth in Things," *Journal of African History* 36 (1995): 83–90.

5. See my work on men's ethnic histories in Jan Bender Shetler, *Imagining Serengeti: A History of Landscape Memory in Tanzania from Earliest Times to the Present* (Athens: Ohio University Press, 2007). See also Jan Vansina, *Oral Tradition as History* (Madison: University of Wisconsin Press, 1985); Elizabeth Tonkin, *Narrating Our Pasts: The Social Construction of Oral History* (Cambridge: Cambridge University Press, 1992).

6. David W. Cohen, "Doing Social History from Pim's Doorway," in *Reliving the*

Past: The Worlds of Social History, ed. Oliver Zunz (Chapel Hill: University of North Carolina Press, 1985), 191–235.

7. Daniel N. Posner, "Measuring Ethnic Fractionalization in Africa," *American Journal of Political Science* 48, no. 4 (October 2004): 849–63.

8. Otto Bischofberger, *The Generation Classes of the Zanaki (Tanzania)* (Fribourg, Switz.: University Press, 1972), 9, 12; Hans Cory, "The People of the Lake Victoria Region," *Tanganyika Notes and Records* 33 (1952): 27; Paul Kollmann, *The Victoria Nyanza: The Land, the Races and Their Customs, with Specimens of Some of the Dialects* (London: Swan Sonneschein, 1899), 175.

9. Hans Cory, *The Indigenous Political System of the Sukuma and Proposals for Political Reform* (Dar es Salaam: Eagle Press, 1954).

10. Jan Bender Shetler, "'Region' as Historical Production: Narrative Maps from the Western Serengeti, Tanzania," in *The Spatial Factor in African History*, ed. Allen M. Howard and Richard M. Shain (Leiden: Brill, 2005), 142.

11. Feminist history has long been concerned about transferring the Western assumptions of the private/public and female/male domains to other places in the world. In Africa, historians have contended that this divide did not exist before colonialism and that women's domain was public. See Merry E. Wiesner-Hanks, *Gender in History: Global Perspectives* (Malden, MA: Wiley-Blackwell, 2011), 92; Dorothy Hodgson, *The Church of Women: Gendered Encounters between Maasai and Missionaries* (Bloomington: Indiana University Press, 2005), 13, 46–62.

12. Leroy Vail, ed., *The Creation of Tribalism in Southern Africa* (Berkeley: University of California Press, 1991).

13. This chapter comes from a larger book manuscript currently in process: Jan Bender Shetler, "A Gendered History of Social Network Memory in the Mara Region, Tanzania, 1880–Present."

14. Shetler, *Imagining Serengeti*; Shetler, *Telling Our Own Stories: Local Histories from South Mara, Tanzania* (Leiden: Brill, 2003); Shetler, "Historical Memory as a Foundation for Peace: Network Formation and Ethnic Identity in North Mara, Tanzania," *Journal of Peace Research* 47, no. 5 (2010): 639–50.

15. Thanks to Perusi Kyambirya, Rhoda Koreni, Nyamusi Magatti, Pastor Katigula and his family, Pastor Musendo, Mwalimu Turfena, Pastor Marara and his family, Manyika Magotto, Pastor Nyamusika and his family, Esta Matera and her family, and Bishop Christopher Ndege at the Bukiroba Lake Diocese Office for giving me a place to stay during the research period.

16. Heidi Gengenbach, *Binding Memories: Women as Makers and Tellers of History in Magude, Mozambique* (New York: Columbia University Press, 2008); Sandra E. Greene, *Gender, Ethnicity, and Social Change on the Upper Slave Coast: A History of the Anlo-Ewe* (Portsmouth, NH: Heinemann, 1996).

17. Jan Bender Shetler, "The Gendered Spaces of Historical Knowledge: Women's Knowledge and Extraordinary Women in the Serengeti District, Tanzania," *International Journal of African Historical Studies* 36, no. 2 (2003): 283–307.

18.   James C. Scott, *Domination and the Arts of Resistance: Hidden Transcripts* (New Haven, CT: Yale University Press, 1992).

19.   Tuulikki Pietilä, *Gossip, Markets, and Gender: How Dialogue Constructs Moral Value in Post-Socialist Kilimanjaro* (Madison: University of Wisconsin Press, 2007), 6–9; see also Luise White, *Speaking with Vampires: Rumor and History in Colonial Africa* (Berkeley: University of California Press, 2000).

20.   Gengenbach, *Binding Memories.*

21.   Shetler, *Imagining Serengeti.*

22.   Shetler, *Imagining Serengeti.*

23.   Cohen, "Doing Social History," 193; see also S. H. Ominde, *The Luo Girl: From Infancy to Marriage* (London: Macmillan, 1952), 39.

24.   Ogacho-Okuttah, "Grandparent-Grandchild Utani: Its Role in Traditional Education and Socialization in the Luo Community," in *Utani Relationships in Tanzania*, vol. 3, ed. S. A. Lucas, typescript, 1975, University of Dar es Salaam, East Africana Library; Eva Tobisson, *Family Dynamics among the Kuria: Agro-Pastoralists in Northern Tanzania* (Goteborg, Sweden: Acta Universitatis Gothoburgensis, 1986), 110; interview #248, female, Jita, 2 September 2010, Bwasi. I have chosen to keep the names of my informants confidential and have listed their gender, ethnic group of origin and marriage if different, date, and place of interview in that order. The interview numbers refer to consecutive interviews in the region since my original interviews in 1995–96.

25.   Interview #249, female, Jita, 2 September 2010, Bwasi.

26.   Peter Seitel, *See So That We May See: Performances and Interpretations of Traditional Tales from Tanzania* (Bloomington: Indiana University Press, 1980).

27.   Interview #242, female, Jita, 1 September 2010, Murangi.

28.   Interview #330, female, Kuria-Kenye, 6 October 2010, Kiagata-Kwisaro.

29.   Steve J. Stern, *The Secret History of Gender: Women, Men and Power in Late Colonial Mexico* (Chapel Hill: University of North Carolina Press, 1995), 97–98.

30.   Interview #250, female, Jita, 3 September 2010, Butata.

31.   See Shetler, "Historical Memory as a Foundation," for how one male popular historian seeks to reinscribe these connections.

32.   Interview #242; interview #267, female, Ruri, 10 September 2010, Bwai; interview #268, female, Ruri, 10 September 2010, Bwai; interview #277, female, Ruri, 11 September 2010, Bwai.

33.   Interview #269, female, Ruri, 10 September 2010, Bwai; interview #271, female, Ruri, 10 September 2010, Bwai; interview #275, female, Ruri, 11 September 2010, Bwai; interview #277.

34.   Interview #267; interview #302, female, Sizaki in Ikizu, 21 September 2010, Nyamuswa; interview #308, female, Nata, 23 September 2010, Mbiso; interview #313, female, Zanaki-Butiama, 28 September 2010, Bumangi; interview #326, female, Kuria-Kenye, 5 October 2010, Kiagata.

35.   Interview #310, female, Kuria-Kiroba, 26 September 2010, Nyabange.

36.   Shetler, "Historical Memory as a Foundation."

37. Shetler, "Historical Memory as a Foundation," 644–45; for similar stories, see Zedekia Oloo Siso, *Grasp the Shield Firmly the Journey Is Hard: A History of Luo and Bantu Migrations to North Mara* (Dar es Salaam: Mkuki na Nyota, 2010).

38. Interview #279, female, Luo-Kadem in Luo-Kakseru, 13 September 2010, Shirati Kabwana; interview #293, female, Luo-Kamageta in Luo-Kakseru, 16 September 2010, Shirati Kabwana.

39. Interview #286, female, Luo-Kowak in Luo-Kakseru, 15 September 2010, Shirati Nyakina; interview #288, female, Luo-Kowak in Luo-Kakseru, 15 September 2010, Shirati Kabwana; interview #289, female, Luo-Kenya in Luo-Kakseru, 15 September 2010, Shirati Kabwana; interview #291, female, Luo-Buturi in Luo-Kakseru, 16 September 2010, Shirati Michire; interview #296, female, Luo-Kenya in Luo-Kakseru, 17 September 2010, Shirati Kuvunja Amri.

40. For another analysis of the role of women and intermarriage in causing linguistic shift in another part of Africa and in ancient times, see Jan Vansina, *How Societies Are Born: Governance in West Central Africa before 1600* (Charlottesville: University of Virginia Press, 2004), 52–60.

41. Interview #256, female, Ruri, 8 September 2010, Mugango; interview #258, female, Ruri, 8 September 2010, Mugango; interview #277.

42. H. Huber, *Marriage and the Family in Rural Bukwaya (Tanzania)* (Fribourg, Switz.: University Press, 1973), 78; interview #277; Gerald W. Hartwig, *The Art of Survival in East Africa: The Kerebe and Long-Distance Trade, 1800–1895* (New York: Africana, 1976), 265.

43. Interview #280, female, Luo-Kenya-Kamageta in Luo-Kakseru, 14 September 2010, Shirati Kabwana; interview #291; interview #292, female, Luo-Hacha in Luo-Kakseru, 16 September 2010, Shirati Michire; interview #330.

44. Interview #285, female, Luo-Ugu in Luo-Kakseru, 15 September 2010, Shirati Nyakina; interview #287, female, Luo-Kenya, 15 September 2010, Shirati Nyakina, said that "Kara" people came to raid for children.

45. Interview #235, female, Jita, 28 August 2010, Butata; interview #237, female, Jita, 30 August 2010, Butata; interview #238, female, Jita, 30 August 2010, Butata; interview #269; interview #272, female, Ruri, 10 September 2010, Bwai; interview #277.

46. Interview #260, female, Ruri, 8 September 2010, Mugango.

47. Interview #234, female, Jita, 28 August 2010, Butata; interview #267; interview #270, female, Ruri, 10 September 2010, Bwai; Wendy James, "Matrifocus on African Women," in *Defining Females: The Nature of Women in Society*, ed. Shirley Ardener (Oxford: Berg, 1993), 123–45; Pauline E. Peters, "Introduction: Revising the Puzzle of Matriliny in South-Central Africa," *Critique of Anthropology* 17, no. 2 (1997): 125–46.

48. Huber, *Marriage and the Family*, 92.

49. Interview #284, female, Luo-Kowak in Luo-Kakseru, 15 September 2010, Shirati Nyakina.

50. Interview #284; interview #286; interview #288.

51. Interview #283, female, Luo-Ugu in Luo-Kakseru, 14 September 2010, Shirati Oboke; interview #296.

52. Interview #235; interview #240, female, Jita, 31 August 2010, Butata; interview #269; interview #271.

53. Recent studies show that domestic violence increases when restraint from kin networks decreases. Emily S. Burrill, Richard L. Roberts, and Elizabeth Thornberry, "Introduction: Domestic Violence and the Law," in *Domestic Violence and the Law in Colonial and Postcolonial Africa*, ed. Emily S. Burrill, Richard L. Roberts, and Elizabeth Thornberry (Athens: Ohio University Press, 2010), 9; Stern, *Secret History*, also describes women's strategies for protecting themselves, including the appeal to multiple patriarchies, which is not possible when women's networks are cut off.

54. Interview #306, female, Ikizu, 22 September 2010, Nyamuswa; interview #307, females, Nata, 22 September 2010, Mbiso; interview #314, female, Zanaki-Butiama, 29 September 2010, Bumangi; interview #330.

55. B. A. Rwezaura, *Traditional Family Law and Change in Tanzania: A Study of the Kuria Social System* (Baden-Baden: Nomos Verlagsgesellschaft, 1985), 2.

56. Interview #303, females, Ikizu and Zanaki, 21 September 2010, Nyamuswa; interview #306; interview #315, female, Zanaki, 29 September 2010, Bumangi; interview #316, female, Zanaki, 29 September 2010, Bumangi; interview #327, female, Kuria-Kenye, 5 October 2010, Kiagata Kwisaro; interview #328, female, Kuria-Kenye, 5 October 2010, Kiagata Kwisaro; also used the metaphor of "slaves" or "dogs," interview #307; interview #311, female, Zanaki-Turi, 28 September 2010, Bumangi.

57. Interview #306; interview #312, female, Zanaki, Bumangi, 28 September 2010, Bumangi; interview #315; interview #316; interview #318, female, Zanaki, 29 September 2010, Bumangi; interview #321, female, Zanaki, 20 September 2010, Bumangi; interview #322, female, Zanaki-Busegwe, 30 September 2010, Bumangi; interview #323, male, Zanaki, 30 September 2010, Bumangi; interview #324, male, Zanaki, 30 September 2010, Bumangi; interview #329, female, Kuria-Abaasi, 5 October 2010, Kiagata Kwisaro.

58. E. P. Thompson, "The Moral Economy of the English Crowd in the 18th Century," *Past and Present* 50 (1971): 76–136; James C. Scott, *The Moral Economy of the Peasant: Rebellion and Subsistence in Southeast Asia* (New Haven, CT: Yale University Press, 1977).

59. Burrill, Roberts, and Thornberry, "Introduction"; Stern, *Secret History*.

60. Interview #315; interview #325, male, Zanaki-Turi, 30 September 2010, Bumangi; interview #327; interview #328.

61. Tobisson, *Family Dynamics*; Brett Shadle, *"Girl Cases": Marriage and Colonialism in Guisiiland, Kenya, 1890–1970* (Portsmouth, NH: Heinemann, 2006); interview #329.

62. Interview #279; interview #323; interview #327.

63. Stern, *Secret History*.

64. Tobisson, *Family Dynamics*, 18.

65. Huber, *Marriage and the Family*, 83–85.

66. Rwezaura, *Traditional Family Law*; Tobisson, *Family Dynamics*, 19.

67. Interview #286; interview #307; interview #315; interview #317, females, Zanaki-Butiama, 29 September 2010, Bumangi; interview #328.

68.   Interview #321, female, Zanaki, 20 September 2010, Bumangi; for comparison, see Burrill, Roberts, and Thornberry, "Introduction," 10; and Marie Rodet, "Continuum of Gendered Violence: The Colonial Invention of Female Desertion as a Customary Criminal Offense, French Soudan 1910–49," in Burrill, Roberts, and Thornberry, *Domestic Violence*, 81.

69.   Interview #317.

70.   Interview #305, females, Sukuma and Ikizu, 21 September 2010, Nyamuswa; interview #312; interview #315.

71.   Interview #309, female, Nata in Ikoma, 24 September 2010, Morotonga.

72.   See also Tobisson, *Family Dynamics*, 2–3, for her stories on being warned against going to the Mara Region.

73.   Happiness Stephen, "The Role of Information and Communication in Alleviating Domestic Violence among the Kurya of Tarime District, Mara Region Tanzania" (master's thesis, University of Dar es Salaam, 2007), 6, 37–39.

74.   Interview #236, female, Jita, 29 August 2010, Bwenda; interview #253, female, Jita in Kuria-Kiroba, 7 September 2010, Nyabange; interview #322.

75.   For a fuller treatment of this subject, see Jan Bender Shetler, "Historical Memory and Expanding Social Networks of Mennonite Mission School Women, Mara Region Tanzania, 1938–present," *Studies in World Christianity* 18, no. 1 (April 2012): 63–81.

76.   Interview #311.

77.   Interview #320, female, Zanaki-Turi, 30 September 2010, Bumangi.

78.   Shetler, "Historical Memory as a Foundation."

79.   Shetler, "Historical Memory as a Foundation."

80.   Interview #320.

81.   Interview #288; interview #308; interview #309.

82.   Shetler, "Historical Memory as a Foundation."

83.   Derek Peterson, "Wordy Women: Gender Trouble and the Oral Politics of the East African Revival in Northern Gikuyuland," *Journal of African History* 42 (2001): 469–89.

84.   Interview #266, female, Ruri, 9 September 2010, Kuruwaki.

85.   Interview #280; interview #281, female, Luo-Kamageta in Luo-Kakseru, 13 September 2010, Shirati Kabwana; interview #288; interview #293; interview #294, female, Luo-Kamageta in Luo Kakseru, 16 September 2010, Shirati Kabwana.

2

//

Living Ethnicity

Gender, Livelihood, and Ethnic Identity in Mozambique

HEIDI GENGENBACH

I'm called MuNwalungu, but here I'm a person of Facazisse. . . . I know that
I'm called MuNwalungu because [my paternal and maternal grandparents]
came from Nwalungwini, but me, I was born here. . . . Mmm, I'm MuChangana
[Shangaan].

Interview with Albertina Ubisse, 3 October 1995,
Facazisse, Mozambique

I was born here [in Vila da de Gorongosa]. My father is from Caia. . . . My
mother's mother had this land, then she gave it to my mother, and my
mother gave it to me because I have no children and I'm not ready to move
to my husband's home. Why? Oh! I want to know him better, otherwise I
could move today, and tomorrow I'm back with my baggage! There could be
conflict with his two other wives. Don't you think this is nice? All my friends
here prefer living this way.

Interview with Celestina (pseudonym), 24 September 2007,
Vila da de Gorongosa, Mozambique

More than thirty years of age, seven hundred miles, and a twelve-year gap
between interviews separate the two Mozambican women quoted above. Yet
their responses to an identical question about ethnic identity, while different in
detail, are strikingly similar in one respect: they reveal as much about the gendered core of "lived ethnicity" in Mozambique as they obscure about the social

content of each speaker's sense of self.[1] The first woman, Albertina Ubisse, a divorced spirit medium and commercial farmer in her midsixties when I interviewed her in rural southern Mozambique soon after the country's civil war (1976–92), claimed—and embodied—multiple ethnic affiliations. With remarkable economy of words, she juxtaposed her birth identity as MuNwalungu (a person from Nwalungwini, the Nwalungu clan homeland some 150 miles to the north of her Magude District residence) with her dual adult identities as "a person of Facazisse" (a locality of Magude) and Shangaan, the dominant cultural group in the south of the country. What her words did not convey, either in this brief excerpt or in the remainder of the session, was that she participated in the interview dressed in the clothing, wig, and beadwork of the Ndau spirit whose powers she would need for a healing ceremony later that day.[2]

The second speaker, Celestina, was interviewed in 2007 at her home on the outskirts of Vila da de Gorongosa, a bustling town on a newly improved stretch of the EN1 Highway less than fifteen miles from Gorongosa National Park in central Mozambique. A small-scale farmer, beer brewer, and (according to a male neighbor) possible commercial sex worker, or *aventureira*, Celestina (then in her midthirties) evaded the question of ethnicity altogether. Defining herself instead in terms of the livelihood and marital strategies she pursued from her tiny roadside home, a site both ancestral and transitional, she highlighted the economic safety net provided by female friends and informal matrilineal land rights (in a mostly patrilineal region) as she assessed her two-year marriage to a man she described as giving her "everything I need" while he lived with two other wives in another town. Speaking in a rapid-fire mix of Portuguese and ChiSena, the main African language of the region, Celestina so dazzled our interview team with her humor and head for numbers that we noticed only later her silence on (or rejection of) ethnic labels of any kind. In that more recent moment of Mozambique's full-speed transition to a free-market economy, with an internationally financed ecotourism project and myriad investor-driven development initiatives virtually in her backyard, Celestina's entrepreneurial support networks seemed all the group identity she needed.

These two women, somewhat unconventional members of the communities where they lived when I interviewed them at distinctly different times and places in postwar Mozambique, were not exceptional at all in their construction of a feminine ethnic identity starkly at odds with the male-centered ethnic categories prevailing in their area. Nor were they as different from one another as the circumstances of their lives might suggest. While scholars may be correct in asserting that "in relation to most other African countries, ethnicity ... plays a minor role in [Mozambican national] politics," gendered ethnic identity claims have been crucial to the everyday politics of survival for many women navigating the country's precarious livelihood landscape in the two decades since the end of the civil war.[3] Representing the relatively affluent end of the spectrum, Albertina Ubisse and Celestina illustrate successful female strategies of *living* ethnicity through gendered, relational notions of self that are not only fluid, multiple, and inclusive but also self-consciously deployed to enhance women's access to productive resources and livelihood options.[4] Not all women, of course, are so fortunate, for these strategies do not exist in a vacuum, and they can occasionally backfire. The fact that some of Albertina's and Celestina's neighbors practiced similarly creative ethnic ways yet were among the poorest women in their community cautions us against oversimplifying the causal connection between identity discourse and material well-being.

In an effort to understand this connection, this chapter explores gendered ethnicities and livelihoods in two very different research sites in southern and central Mozambique. Drawing on personal interviews, household survey data, material culture, and archival sources, the chapter argues that the multiethnic identity claims of women in Magude District (Maputo Province) and the apparent absence of ethnic consciousness among women in Cheringoma District (Sofala Province) are two sides of the same coin: where dominant ethnicities legitimize gender hierarchies that restrict women's ability to make a living, women forge alternative self-definitions that in one way or another transcend bounded notions of clan or "tribe." As both case studies show, women's living ethnicities—and the relational conceptions of identity and history on which they depend—matter as much to Mozambique's economic future as to historians' understanding of the country's past.

Ethnicity as Livelihood Asset:
Women's Identities in Post–Civil War Magude

> Zimiya, they come from over there, the land of the VaChopi. Those of the Zimiya family, they're VaChopi. [H: Are you MuChopi, then?] Mm-mm [no], I'm MuChangana. I can be MuChangana because I was born here.
>
> Interview with Favasse Zimiya, 20 October 1995,
> Tsatsimbe, Magude District

Three years after the formal end of Mozambique's civil war, when I arrived in Magude to begin dissertation fieldwork on women's forms of historical memory, the district's population still showed obvious signs of war-induced deprivation, residential insecurity, and psychosocial trauma. The region was parched by drought, and the western third of the district was still occupied by a RENAMO base camp, which government officials feared to visit and where South African rather than Mozambican currency prevailed.[5] Most returning refugees and internally displaced people relied to some extent on international relief organizations for food, seed, tools, building materials, and medical aid. The nightly drumming of healing ceremonies, most led by female spirit mediums (*vanyamusoro* in Shangaan), and daily rumors of witchcraft poisoning due to interhousehold quarrels and domestic disputes reflected deeply personal struggles to come to terms with the war's staggering toll on families, landscapes, and agrarian economies.

As I have written elsewhere, the violent uprooting of rural communities and their prolonged relocation, whether to a neighboring country, to the Mozambican capital, or simply to Magude town, did not as thoroughly destroy people's memories and historical identities as scholars writing on forced displacement elsewhere in Africa have assumed.[6] Yet the experiences of displacement and resettlement—in the broadest literal and metaphoric senses of those terms—followed distinctly gendered trajectories, further inflected by age, marital status, education, and access to critical resources, especially land. Among the women I knew as neighbors, acquaintances, friends, and interviewees in Magude District between April 1995 and December 1996, the war's most readily observable impact on identity emerged in the extreme ambiguity and fluidity in women's discourses about their own and each other's names. Whether in their everyday playful reinventions of personal names or their patterned silence—"forgetting"—about the meaning of their clan name (*xivongo* in Shangaan), women's naming practices suggested an effort to (re)construct female identity as infinitely variable and multicentered, open to multiple simultaneous social and geographic locations. This effort served women well in the uncertain circumstances of reoccupying the ravaged countryside; especially for the poorest among them, those barely scraping by on humanitarian handouts, discursive name play could generate affective ties through which vital material support—food, shelter, land—might eventually become available. The critical condition for accessing such support was a woman's ability to demonstrate, through the genealogies (formal and "fictive") implied by her names, that she belonged to a particular place and social group and thus had a legitimate claim to aid.

If women in postwar Magude exercised similar ingenuity in their ethnic self-naming, as the above quotation suggests, such material objectives tell only part of the story. The relatively recent gendered origins of southern Mozambique's dominant ethnicity, Shangaan (or Tsonga), reconstructed from archival sources and men's oral testimony by historian Patrick Harries, date to the intersection of several nineteenth-century processes: Gaza Nguni conquest of southern Mozambique by the armies of Soshangane (ca. 1830–58), from whom the term Shangaan derives; male labor migration from the lands of the Gaza

empire to the sugar plantations, diamond fields, and gold mines of South Africa
from about 1860 on; and Christian missionization, a phenomenon that began
in southern Mozambique in the 1880s and produced Swiss Presbyterian Reverend Henri A. Junod's ethnographic writings on the "BaThonga."[7] Harries's
important work, which documents Mozambican migrants' strategic mobilization of a derogatory "tribal" label to forge a masculine ethnic community in the
dehumanizing world of the mine compounds, does not examine whether or
how the womenfolk of male migrants engaged Shangaanness in their own rural
lives. (Indeed, for a region whose history has been bent in such gendered and
ethnicized ways to serve the needs of South African industrial capitalism, the
scant scholarship on men's and women's interdependence in identity formation
is rather strange.[8]) But in mid-1990s Magude, when I asked interviewees to identify their ethnic group, women's responses expressed such a consistent blend of
indifference and selective, situational attachment to being "MuChangana" that
the puzzle of gendered ethnicity increasingly drew my attention. Clearly, discursive manipulation of ethnic connections not only served women's economic
recovery needs in the wake of the war but also expressed a more fundamental
assertion about the gendered nature of historical knowledge and women's right
to contest and own it.

In their explanations for ethnic self-labeling, as in their practices of body
marking (*tinhlanga* in Shangaan) and pottery production, women in Magude
articulated female-centered affective ties that transcended, mixed, and redefined what scholars (along with other powerful interpreters of rural African
social life, such as policy makers, donors, and nongovernmental agencies)
understand as southern Mozambique's official ethnic groups.[9] While none of
the more than eighty women I interviewed identified themselves exclusively
as Shangaan, roughly half used Shangaan along with another term—the name
of a supraclan group, clan, or clan segment—as their ethnic affiliation. In all
cases, women's narratives about ethnicity, which foregrounded feminine spheres
of domestic responsibility and agrarian production, implicitly rejected the
androcentric genealogies and migration chronicles reproduced in the oral traditions told (and sometimes written down) by men in the 1990s. Emphasizing
above all the female social networks through which they have met the challenges
of patrilineal kinship, virilocal marriage, and male labor migration, women's
ethnic stories mirror representations of multiethnic selfhood present in other
past and extant forms of feminine cultural production in Magude. Changing
styles and techniques of body marking since the early 1800s reveal the determination of rural girls to inscribe inclusive standards and symbols of beauty,
learned through intervillage, intercultural, and international encounters, permanently in their skin. Designs etched into women's clay pottery (these designs

are called by the same term used for body marking, tinhlanga), an industry dating back a millennium or more, similarly document a little-known history of long-distance female travel, trade, and ethnically hybrid culture change. Oral accounts and ceramic evidence from women potters in postwar Magude belie archaeologists' typologizing of pottery styles along ethnic lines; whether recent and highly localized or persistent for centuries across wide swaths of southeastern Africa, decorative patterns on handmade clayware embody deliberate remembrance and knowledge transfer—through teaching, memory, or mimicry—among women whose paths crossed, irrespective of their ethnic affiliations.

The livelihood implications of women's multivalent approach to ethnicity in postwar Magude, hinted at in efforts to revive the pottery industry, surfaced most visibly in their work in spiritist healing and agriculture. As in the example of Albertina Ubisse, presented in the introduction to this chapter, spirit mediumship—an overwhelmingly female occupation in southern Mozambique—involved a medium's possession by, and deployment of, multiple ethnic identities to diagnose and treat physical, mental, and social afflictions. (In southern Mozambique, spirit mediums work through a minimum of two spirits, one Ndau and one Zulu, each with its own life history, costume, and repertoire of healing skills.)[10] The heightened frequency of nocturnal healing ceremonies in the mid-1990s reflected not just the lingering psychological and bodily health consequences of the civil war but also the large number of women newly eager to earn an income from this profitable line of work—what many men cynically characterized as crass opportunism ("business," or *bhisimusi* in Shangaan) in hard economic times. As in their similarly creative initiatives to use new or reactivated female friendships ("laughing kinship," or *vuxaka bya matinyo* in Shangaan) to borrow or rent plots of arable land, women were drawing on historically fluid and inclusive meanings of gendered ethnicity to enhance their economic options and reduce their vulnerability to crisis.[11] While their menfolk dwelt on reviving oral traditions of clan origins and Shangaan founding fathers, women in postwar Magude instead sought more wide-ranging and multiplex ethnic affiliations. Perhaps not surprisingly, women's efforts to activate far-reaching female support networks and assert membership in multiple communities through situational ethnic claims seemed closely and strategically correlated to the degree of hardship they faced. It was the poorest women in the district—the elderly childless widows, the single mothers, the physically disabled or infirm—who most stubbornly refused to be ethnically pinned down and whose life stories, body markings, or land acquisition methods showed the most dizzying array of ethnic allegiances. For these women especially, ethnicity was a livelihood asset, a form of social capital essential to their "means of living"—even as they "forgot," ignored, or rejected dominant versions of Shangaan ethnicity gendered male.[12]

Gender and Senaness in a Neoliberal Barter Economy

Here, we just say we're all Senas. We don't bother to ask people, What tribe are you? We call ourselves Sena. But Sena isn't a tribe, it's a place.

Leroy Vail and Landeg White, *Capitalism and Colonialism in Mozambique*

The Senas . . . are the most despised ethnic group. This is evidenced by the Ndau and Manyika usage to scold an ill-behaved child thus; "Don't be like a Sena."

Mark L. Chingono, *The State, Violence and Development*

In 2007 and 2008, as part of a multidisciplinary team including two resource economists, a forest ecologist, a tropical biogeographer, and a GIS specialist, I conducted fieldwork to investigate livelihood histories in the four administrative districts (Muanza, Nhamatanda, Cheringoma, and Gorongosa) ringing Sofala Province's Gorongosa National Park. As in Magude, gender was central to my research agenda, and ethnicity was not. Focusing on how rural households living near protected areas use natural resources to cope with political and environmental shocks, our project hoped to generate policy-relevant insights on the likely impact of climate change on resource demand, livelihood adaptation, and household welfare.[13] In addition to helping administer a socioeconomic survey to 1,780 households in the four districts, I did two rounds of interviewing in Cheringoma, where I had decided to conduct more in-depth research on livelihood change. Initially, I accepted the district government's characterization of Cheringoma as ethnically Sena ("The predominant ethnic group are speakers of the Sena or Chissena language") while also bringing my own confident assumptions, based on the Magude work, that in a province with steep rates of malnutrition, very low female literacy, and a high prevalence of HIV/AIDS, rural women would similarly be using ethnicity to access resources, create economic opportunity, and extend support networks in food-insecure times.[14] Again, though, what I witnessed of women's identity claims in Cheringoma—and of women's relationship to a dominant ethnicity gendered male—took me by surprise. Among the rural and periurban women I met, Senaness seemed mainly conspicuous by its absence. While among their menfolk Sena identity seemed alive and well, women in Cheringoma acted as though ethnic-based social ties and livelihood strategies were not worth their performative effort.

In this section, I explore the apparent unimportance of Sena ethnicity to women in Cheringoma in the context of Mozambique's current era of neo-liberal development. After an overview of the origins of Senaness as a gendered ethnic identity connected to a reorientation of rural livelihoods in sixteenth-century central Mozambique and as elaborated in Cheringoma during four centuries of protocolonial and colonial Portuguese rule, I compare the salience of Senaness for two gender-defined livelihood pursuits—men's beekeeping and women's beer brewing—that have become critical to many Cheringoma households' survival in recent years. Since my Cheringoma research had (or so I thought) little to do with ethnicity, the evidence I draw on to analyze this phenomenon is not as substantial as for the Magude case. Although in 2007 I began to notice the patterns discussed here, I did not systematically ask all interviewees about ethnicity. When I returned to Cheringoma in 2008, more alert to the puzzle of gendered Senaness, my limited fieldwork time included training three Mozambican research assistants, and our interview priorities lay elsewhere. I gathered what information I could, especially as I realized the link between gendered ethnicity discourses and livelihood pursuits, but I am aware of the gaps in what follows—and still uncertain about how one goes about finding evidence for something that is apparently not there.

Speakers of ChiSena, the dominant language of Sofala Province, derive their ethnic name from the geographic imprint of Swahili and Portuguese merchant capitalism. The town of Sena emerged in the fifteenth century as a Muslim-dominated river port on the Lower Zambezi, a key commercial link between the goldfields of the Zimbabwe plateau and the Indian Ocean coast.[15] The violent Portuguese takeover of Sena in 1571 ushered in an era of political and economic transformation fueled by thick webs of interaction among the European, Asian, and African residents of the urban settlement and its rural hinterland. This process increasingly bound the livelihoods and identities of local Tonga chieftaincies to the protocolonial society of the Lower Zambezi *prazos* (Crown estates), a system defined by multiple forms of clientship and slavery, forced resource extraction from *colonos* (tenant farmers), and interracial marriage.[16] By the seventeenth century, Portuguese documents referred to the Tonga population as "Asena" because of the latter's close ties with the Portuguese-controlled town.[17] During the eighteenth century, the expanding slave export trade from the Zambezi coast provoked ever more destructive waves of raiding, conflict, and displacement across the region, until a prolonged period of intermittent drought and famine from the 1790s through the 1830s dealt a lethal blow to the agricultural base of the prazo economy.[18] Yet the collapse of the prazo system seems to have broadened rather than undermined the appeal of Sena identity: according to historians Leroy Vail and Landeg White, the prazos' "ethnically mixed *colonos* and former *achikunda* [slave soldiers] . . . , by the middle of the nineteenth century, identified themselves as 'Sena,'" embracing a sense of cultural sameness born of their turbulent heteroethnic past.[19]

Although written sources say little about the gender content of Sena identity in the prazo era, its roots in the militarized mercantile interactions of Portuguese settlers and African communities—and its persistence through the cycles of conflict and displacement that continued through the late nineteenth and twentieth centuries—suggest that Senaness both originated in and fostered connection through primarily masculine experience. Indeed, as the work of Allen and Barbara Isaacman on the rise and fall of Chikunda ethnicity so evocatively shows, Portuguese settlement in the Lower Zambezi Valley generated conditions productive of new social identities defined through new kinds of men.[20] In the same way that the prazos' slave soldiers, responsible for the high-risk work of warfare, hunting, and long-distance trade, "made themselves Chikunda in order to set themselves apart from the local peasantry, gain leverage with owners, and lend meaning and prestige to their lives of danger," new commercial livelihoods produced through the rise of merchant capitalism may have encouraged new gendered identities tied to prazo society through the town of Sena's role in the gold and ivory export trades.[21] The likelihood that Senaness, like Chikundaness, had men's work and interests at its core is suggested by anthropologist Robert Marlin's study of reproductive illness and spirit possession in Mutarara District in Tete Province, upriver from Sena. There, according to Marlin, men threatened by a loss of social authority since Mozambique's independence in 1975 invoked Sena tradition as a strategy of patriarchal control, blaming female sexuality for everything from RENAMO brutality to HIV/AIDS. Women's resistance to this assertion of manly power through an imported form of spirit possession known as *magamba* drew on regional histories of violence four centuries deep to explain the true causes of men's grievances—industrial capitalism, labor migration, the ruling FRELIMO party's failed experiment with socialism, forced displacement during the war—while also exposing the masculine and colonial orientation of Sena ethnicity itself.[22]

Marlin's important work does not address how an identity so seemingly riven along gender lines, whose adherents have been "despised" (at least in the twentieth century) as colonial collaborators, managed to achieve such widespread staying power that roughly one and a half million ChiSena speakers still occupy a vast territory extending through four provinces in central Mozambique and into southern Malawi.[23] In the absence of archival research focused on this question, it is premature to claim that what the Isaacmans found for the Chikunda—that by the late nineteenth century, a "self-reproducing" gendered ethnicity had evolved through such mechanisms of socialization as language, initiation, body markings, dress, and storytelling—holds true for the Sena as well.[24] In particular, it is difficult to pin down the extent to which women in either group internalized prazo-derived constructions of cultural sameness, generated through men's sustained interaction with a pervasively violent "transfrontier" world.[25] Although the Isaacmans discuss Chikunda masculinity as defined in part through contrasts with femaleness (e.g., denigration of farming as women's work), neither they nor Marlin explore the possibility that a "gendered ethnicity" might mean different things to different people—not just separate gender-defined roles in a shared notion of group culture but understandings of group culture that diverge along gender lines. For a distinct ChiSena language to have endured for so many for so long, we certainly must assume some degree of female buy-in over the centuries. Without mothers' support for reproducing Senaness through early childhood education, and without an active female role in gender-segregated institutions—the adolescent *nomi* societies—that fashioned Sena women and men through training for adult life, it is unlikely that ChiSena speakers would be as numerous throughout central Mozambique as they are today.[26] And yet if women have helped to reproduce Senaness since its emergence in the Afro-Portuguese society of Lower Zambezia some four hundred years ago, their present-day silence around ethnicity in Cheringoma, a district lying within the historic heartland of prazo country, loudly begs explanation.

Situated at the meeting point of the southern end of the Great Rift Valley and the tropical humidity of the Indian Ocean, with an extraordinary variety of topographies and flora and fauna, Cheringoma has long been an object of competition among outsiders, buffeted intensely by the exogenous forces that produced a gendered Sena identity in the wider region. Between the fourth and fourteenth centuries, Tonga farming communities south of the Lower Zambezi were transformed through participation in the Swahili-dominated export trade and by the arrival of Shona-speaking Karanga migrants from the west. By the fifteenth century, the area formed part of the Karanga kingdom of Kiteve, an offshoot of the Mwene Mutapa empire.[27] Kiteve rulers formed an alliance with Portuguese traders who settled in the Zambezi Valley in the 1520s, hoping for direct access to the Mutapa's gold. When in the 1630s a succession dispute forced the Kiteve king to call for Portuguese aid, Capt. Sisnando Bayão demanded as payment the territory that became Cheringoma prazo. Under Bayão's descendants, who governed this area for the next two hundred years, Cheringoma became the largest and richest of the prazos, its highly productive agricultural economy ensuring not only a bountiful living for *prazeros* (prazo holders) and *colonos* but a regular surplus for trade.[28] According to historian Malyn Newitt, even though payments owed by prazeros to the Portuguese Crown rose steadily from 1650 through 1829, for Cheringoma those payments never exceeded 3 percent of prazeros' tribute income, calculated as a percentage of the "produce of the land."[29] Eighteenth-century tribute lists further hint at Cheringoma's prosperity and livelihood diversity. In one year, the prazero collected 1,257 arm's lengths of locally made cloth, 557 chickens, 6,000 dried fish, 5,000 bushels of sorghum, 28 pots of dried meat, 21 pots of oil, 20 balls of beeswax, and 48 pots of honey; tribute lists from other years also included rice, sesame, ivory, and buffalo hides.[30] An 1802 census reported Cheringoma having 2,120 villages of colonos divided among nineteen chieftaincies, all producing sufficiently to pay tribute, perform mandatory labor service, feed themselves, and on multiple occasions supply food to neighboring areas in times of shortage.[31]

The ecological crises of the early nineteenth century, which brought an end to the prazo system, not only failed to tarnish Cheringoma's appeal for acquisitive outsiders but also appear to have helped crystallize a gendered Sena identity in Lower Zambezia. A catastrophic period of drought and famine from 1823 to 1831, accompanied by locust and smallpox epidemics, broke the Bayão family's hold on the area.[32] From the 1830s through the 1850s, the former Bayão estate was subjected to regular slave raiding and tribute collection by Nguni rulers based near the Limpopo River to the south. Like the Indo-Portuguese warlord Manuel António de Sousa, who offered military protection to the town of Sena in exchange for control over Cheringoma, expansionist rulers viewed this area as a high-yielding place of pillage worth claiming for the long term. When the European "scramble" for Africa gathered speed in the 1880s, and Portugal was forced to prove effective occupation of the Lower Zambezi Valley, an alliance between de Sousa and Portuguese captain Paiva d'Andrade led to the founding in 1891 of the Moçambique Company, a joint stock company with jurisdiction over what are now Manica and Sofala Provinces.[33] By the turn of the twentieth century, as the political turmoil of previous decades began to subside, even recently arrived company personnel such as British consul R. C. F. Maugham could discern both a distinctive Sena identity and gender differences in Senaness, such as women's preference for local fashion and jewelry over men's for European styles:

> The influence of several centuries of intercourse with the European is extremely noticeable in the negro, his manners, his surroundings, and mode of life. . . . The Sena people are decently clad in clean calico, some even affected tailor-made coats and trousers. . . . The women also in many cases display much greater gravity and dignity than those who are found farther afield. Their clothing and

ornaments, moreover, show at times very considerable taste, the former chosen from harmonious if somewhat violent colours . . . ; *the latter, often of silver and gold, are the work of local native goldsmiths* of considerable skill.[34]

Historians of twentieth-century central Mozambique, preoccupied with African experiences of forced labor, forced cash cropping, and labor migration under Moçambique Company rule (1891–1941) and after Portugal's takeover of this territory (renaming it Beira District) in 1942, have had little to say about livelihood change, ethnicity, or gender during or after the colonial period. However, written sources indicate that throughout this period, Cheringoma sustained its anomalous position as an agricultural success story for small-holder and commercial producers alike. Although smallholder agriculture never dominated the Moçambique Company's development agenda, the in-kind tax and labor demands imposed on African populations tapped into surpluses that households were long used to generating for tribute or trade. Company officials in Cheringoma also strongly encouraged—sometimes subsidized—cash crop cultivation and gathering of forest products for export.[35] During the five decades of company rule, Cheringoma contributed a long and varied list of export commodities, including cotton, sugar, sisal, rice, maize, groundnuts, sesame, a wide range of tree fruits, coconut and lala palm, rubber, tobacco, oil seeds, beeswax, fish, mangrove bark, quarried lime, and valuable hardwoods, for which Cheringoma was especially known.[36] This productivity was an important factor in the company's decision in the 1920s to build the Trans-Zambezia Railway line connecting the port city of Beira to British Nyasa-land through the town of Inhaminga, Cheringoma's administrative capital. It is also likely the reason Cheringoma was chosen for a mid-1930s experimental development scheme, the first of its kind in Mozambique, to create agricultural villages where Portuguese farmers would have access to irrigated land on co-operative farms. A scaled-down 1940s version of this plan for African farmers, who would practice rain-fed commercial farming in special settlements called *ruralatos*, never materialized; but the proposal confirms official confidence in Cheringoma's unique agricultural potential.[37]

In fact, scholarly narratives that center on the abusive policies for which Portuguese colonizers in Mozambique are notorious sit uneasily alongside evidence of earnest official developmentalism, agronomic curiosity, and a kind of wonder—expressed most extravagantly in European hunters' accounts but evident also in the writings of European personnel stationed there—at Cheringoma householders' skilled manipulation of an environment abounding with exploitable wealth but daunting to outsiders. Published sources speak in frustratingly generic terms about the lives of Cheringoma's "native" inhabitants but wax prolific about its unhealthy climate (e.g., "one of the most fever-stricken spots on the East African coast"), its "impenetrable" landscape (e.g., "the sea of grass of the Cheringoma district"), and its aggressive wildlife (e.g., the lions' "unusual pugnacity").[38] Once in a while, however, these sources pause to note that Cheringoma's African residents still somehow managed to produce the necessities of daily life: "I saw extensive mealie fields, and, judging by the fact that I had no difficulty in bartering a supply of *ufa* (sorghum meal) from the natives for meat, and that on both occasions when I have been there I have seen several women grinding millet, I should say that they obtain large crops."[39]

Even at the height of Mozambique's forced cotton regime, when the National Cotton Company compelled African farmers throughout the colony to sacrifice food production for a labor-intensive commodity they had to sell at rock-bottom prices, most Cheringoma households continued to fill their granaries, pay their taxes, and in years of good rain have enough surplus to sell to the Indian merchants whose shops dotted the countryside. Unlike rural dwellers elsewhere in Beira District, Cheringoma residents also tended to stay put, mostly declining to migrate to neighboring British colonies or to seek employment beyond Cheringoma's borders.[40] In fact, until Portuguese rule ended in 1975, Cheringoma *imported* labor from other districts for its public works, plantations, and commercial enterprises.[41]

During the last quarter of the twentieth century, when Cheringoma was a focal point of armed conflict between FRELIMO nationalists and the Portuguese and then between the FRELIMO government and RENAMO rebels, the politics of ethnicity assumed new significance at the national level without transforming local ethnic meanings in a noticeable way—even in Sofala Province, where RENAMO has its headquarters and a leadership dominated by another area ethnicity, the Ndau. In both wars, combatants on all sides fought with particular intensity in Cheringoma and the surrounding area. The former conflict involved forced government resettlement of rural communities into "protected villages," FRELIMO sabotage of railway and water supply lines, soldiers on both sides raiding farms and granaries for food, and the use of torture by the Portuguese secret police against suspected FRELIMO sympathizers. Colonial ferocity reached new depths in February and March 1974, with the mass execution and pit burial of at least 150 African "terrorists" and napalm bombing of Inhaminga.[42] That Cheringoma residents blame FRELIMO for these vicious counterinsurgency measures may help to explain the strong support for RENAMO here during and since the postindependence war, which analysts agree was not an "interethnic" conflict.[43] When our informal conversations with Cheringoma survey respondents or interviewees turned to party politics (as often happened because of ongoing partisan violence in the district), older people recalled their willing payment of "tribute" to RENAMO forces during the war.[44] Postwar district election results showed RENAMO's continuing political sway in Cheringoma, as elsewhere in Sofala Province. Only in 2009, after FRELIMO's determined courting of pro-RENAMO voters through targeted development investments, did the ruling party enjoy a sudden surge at the polls, winning a majority in all but two of Sofala's thirteen districts.[45] Although we were not investigating voter preferences, our presence in Cheringoma in the two years prior to those elections exposed us to local discussion of the relative merits of the two dominant parties, in which ethnic claims of any kind took a distant back seat to livelihood concerns.

Indeed, in 2007–8, rural householders had good reason to be preoccupied with livelihoods, above all the contrast between their robust diversity and prosperity in the past and their fragility in recent years. With its long history of agricultural success and its remarkable ecological wealth, Cheringoma is an unlikely candidate for the severe structural poverty evident today in the district's lack of basic amenities, its skeletal transport and commercial infrastructure, and its scarce primary schools and medical services.[46] During both of our visits, abandoned cotton fields, unmovable mounds of sesame in farmers' yards, and the outrageous prices of consumer goods conveyed both the continuing high performance of smallholders and the grim reality of market-oriented production in the absence of a functioning market. The steady stream of heavy-laden bicycle and pedestrian traffic along the dirt tracks connecting rural communities to Inhaminga—and from there to the provincial capital of Beira—attested to people's resolute entrepreneurial spirit, but the economic returns for such efforts fell short of the minimum needed for household well-being. District government reports in 2005 lamented "the spectre of poverty in which the majority of the district population lives" and "poverty levels [that are] the most pronounced in the province."[47] Although district-level nutrition data are not available, we can infer from the high *average* rates of child stunting (36 percent) and wasting (7 percent) reported for Sofala Province in 2011 the grave food insecurity of most Cheringoma households.[48] Other studies confirm that the plight of Cheringoma's rural poor has likely worsened since 2007–8: according to a 2011 UNICEF report, Sofala Province showed the second largest increase in poverty incidence (more than twenty-two percentage points) between 2002 and 2010.[49]

While official explanations of poverty in Cheringoma blame the destructive impact of the civil war and postwar environmental shocks (floods in 2001–2, drought in 2002–3), the anxious conversations we heard during household visits focused instead on the national government's unpopular betterment plans for the district, which seek to develop Cheringoma's "natural" wealth and "wilderness" appeal rather than its food production potential. Plainly rejecting the area's long history of productive agrifood systems, whose success required careful management of the biodiversity from which state and private investors now wish to profit, these plans harness Cheringoma's wildlife and forest resources to a range of ecotourism ventures, "community-based natural resource management" schemes, and commercial timber and hunting concessions. The fact that by 2008 nearly 60 percent of Cheringoma's land fell within a tourism-related "protected" category and another 38 percent was in the process of being leased for commercial logging purposes makes plain the government's commitment to a nonagricultural future for the district.[50] Government rhetoric promoting this land-hungry approach to development includes such ludicrously ahistorical characterizations of Cheringoma as "not very suitable for agriculture," statements belied not only by farmers' high praise for the growing conditions of the area but also by the impressive range of food production and provisioning strategies by even the poorest households.[51] These strategies strongly resemble those documented for precolonial times: cropping systems that combine a mix of cereals, root crops, legumes, vegetables, and tree fruits on multiple, spatially dispersed plots; year-round reliance on myriad wild plant foods, gathered from the forest and from interstitial groundcover near homes and fields; and animal protein derived from goats, poultry, fish, insects, and small and large game.[52] Like official development plans, in other words, local agrifood systems—for the more than 90 percent of Cheringoma residents who still rely on rain-fed farming for survival—require access to extensive and diverse tracts of the agrarian landscape, above all the communal forests that investors are now so eager to exploit.[53]

Out of the clash between these opposing paths to rural well-being in Cheringoma, visibly under way in 2007–8, was emerging a deeply gendered livelihood response with differential consequences for men's and women's attachment to Senaness. Despite official insistence that hunting and forest concession holders and ecotourism initiatives—including Gorongosa National Park (GNP), which juts into Cheringoma's southwestern corner—respect indigenous traditions of natural resource use, an onslaught of new restrictions on residents' access to land, forests, and waterways, combined with concessionaires' de facto latitude in their treatment of the "local communities" whose livelihoods they are supposed to protect, was drastically reducing many households' ability to meet food needs through own-production.[54] The livelihood-threatening impact of these changes was exacerbated by the effects of the global food price crisis, which made purchase of food staples prohibitively expensive at a time when a negligible percentage of households had access to cash income, and a battery of new or increased user fees on public health and education services further heightened cash pressures on rural families.[55] In these unprecedented circumstances, Cheringoma residents were scrambling furiously just to get by, pursuing a wide range of new, often prohibited livelihood strategies that included sending young children into timber concessions to forage for wild plant foods, because children were less likely to be arrested if caught.[56] The district's farmers were also showing an overwhelming preference for nonmonetized exchange, ranging from ancient forms of agrarian barter (e.g., grain for homemade pottery) to new arrangements (e.g., swapping charcoal for loan of a bicycle) that reflected their determination to access critical assets in the transformed economy and their limited capacity as individuals to do so.

Because the "'scramble' for viable livelihoods" triggered by liberalization took place on social terrain long marked by a topography of gender, men and women in Cheringoma faced distinctly unequal opportunities for diversification.[57] Both male and female farmers expressed suspicion of the cash economy and greater trust in nonmonetized networks through which they could exchange locally produced goods for locally determined values. Yet while the growing popularity of barter intensified the attractiveness of diversifying into off-farm production, people's ability to diversify was both much narrower than in the past and heavily influenced by cultural traditions of gendered labor. Interviews and survey data made clear that men's options for off-farm activities generating income or barterable products were both more profitable and more highly regarded—more suitably "traditional"—than those available to women. The ubiquitous presence of dogs and the busy local trade in illegal game meat revealed men's widespread involvement in hunting, despite zealous efforts by local authorities, concessionaires, and the GNP to eliminate it.[58] Protected wetlands and forests supplied grasses, reeds, and bamboo for weaving baskets and mats, another masculine industry with readily barterable products whose aesthetic appeal was on the upswing in 2007–8.[59] In terms of cash-earning options, an illegal cross-border gold trade with Zimbabwe offered high returns for men and boys willing to chance arrest by panning for ore in rivers in the GNP and its buffer zone.[60] Most highly esteemed of "traditional" masculine pursuits were forest-based beekeeping and honey hunting, activities whose high economic importance dates at least as far back as the prazo era and whose products (honey, wax) still serve many purposes in rural households.[61] Women's off-farm livelihood choices, on the other hand, consisted mainly of ill-paid part-time work for commercial farmers; sale of homemade pottery, of which in 2007–8 we saw little; home-based brewing of maize and sorghum beer; and, among a daring few, distillation of grain alcohol.

The implications of livelihood choice for gendered ethnicity appear most vividly in a comparison of what men and women considered the most lucrative options available to them: beekeeping and home-based brewing or distilling, respectively. Honey (*uchi* in ChiSena), transported in repurposed glass bottles and jars on foot around the district or by bicycle as far away as Beira, fetched consistently high prices in cash and kind throughout the fourteen-month span of my fieldwork visits.[62] The healthy market value of Cheringoma honey reflected in part its excellent quality and its status as an indigenous product; but it also stemmed from the known heightened risks around beekeeping, above all in areas in or near the GNP and its buffer zone. Beekeeping was strictly prohibited on all protected land, mainly because GNP authorities—with government support—deemed the ring barking of trees (to make hives) and the use of controlled fire to empty hives of bees (to harvest honey) environmentally destructive. In 2007–8, tightening restrictions on residents' access to once-common forests compelled beekeepers to travel ever-greater distances from home in search of safe treetops to set their hives. Intensifying poverty made matters worse: without exception, beekeepers identified theft of honey from forest hives by unemployed young men as the most serious threat to their output and profits.[63] Beekeeping and honey sale thus demanded not only regular long treks to hive locations and residentially dispersed customers but also the presence of trusted associates at home (to prevent park rangers from finding beekeeping supplies), at forest hive sites (to prevent theft), and at points of sale (to monitor prices and competition).

Under these circumstances, men's beekeeping success depended on access to geographically extensive relational ties, which Sena identity, with its commercial and outward-looking origins and its gendered behavior codes, could do much to provide. Beekeepers spoke at length about their efforts to resurrect normative practices from the "old days" that fostered trust and cooperation among far-flung practitioners of this male-only activity, such as informal systems for apportioning communally owned forests into zones for hive placement, management of ring barking to prevent depletion of valued tree species, strict controls on fire use for the honey harvest, and collective social sanctions against theft.[64] Discussions of such practical measures, which on the surface seem unrelated to ethnicity, invariably turned at some point to the spiritual underpinnings of this hereditary skill: the father-to-son transmission of "spirits" (*hambalume* in ChiSena) that impelled young men to take up beekeeping, whether they wanted to or not, and the ceremonial offerings to ancestors to seek their help attracting bees to men's hives. Pires Faife Souce, an elderly local chief (*régulo* in Portuguese) and experienced beekeeper who identified himself to us as ethnically Sena, insisted that while beekeeping was a valuable (in times of food shortage, essential) livelihood pursuit, it was, just as importantly, "our culture, the original tradition" of the Sena people.[65] Moreover, the subterfuge and risk increasingly required for this proscribed activity prompted nostalgic comments about the "manly" occupations of the precolonial past and pride in a resurgent—and newly outlaw—Sena masculinity that defied legal restrictions, Western conservationist discourse, and the emasculating impact of neoliberal development at the same time.[66]

Home-based brewing and distilling, on the other hand, offered women in Cheringoma neither the high exchange value of honey, the social capital of a tradition under fire from an unpopular state, nor the incentive to activate ethnically defined relational networks far from home. Like honey, home-brewed maize and sorghum beer (kabanga and bwadwa in ChiSena, respectively) have ancient religious and political functions in the cultures of this region, in addition to their utility as nutrition supplement, social lubricant, and currency exchangeable for labor, household necessities (e.g., food, firewood), or cash. And like beekeeping, home-based brewing involves gender-specific interhousehold cooperation: in interviews, women described coordinating with other brewers to avoid glutting the market, along with cooperative production and marketing strategies such as sharing utensils, pooling cash to buy sugar, helping one another with the brewing process, and spreading the word when a friend's batch was ready for sale.[67] Yet in terms of time and resources invested, the returns on beer brewing for women were substantially lower than those for beekeeping, while the potential loss was greater, since home-brewed beers are difficult to preserve, and spoilage can occur. For this reason, in 2007-8, some bolder brewers in Inhaminga and its periurban neighborhoods were experimenting with home-based distilling of more potent grain-based liquor known as nipa in ChiSena. Despite its higher input costs and labor requirements, nipa had a wider profit margin than kabanga and bwadwa, especially if women used granulated (purchased) sugar instead of raw sugar cane.[68] This livelihood adaptation, a deliberate effort to compete with the cheap manufactured spirits flooding Inhaminga since privatization, may have raised a few women's income, but it was also earning female brewers a bad name due to mounting local concern about alcoholism among youth and adult men. (Interestingly, social criticism of nipa producers was not enough to deter some men from crossing a once-inviolable gender boundary to take up home-based distilling—a phenomenon about which several female interviewees complained heatedly.)[69]

The most significant differences between beekeeping and brewing or distilling, however, stem from their dramatically different geographies of production and exchange and the impact of these spatial realities on men's and women's attachment to Senaness. Just as production and consumption of kabanga, bwadwa, and nipa took place in women's open-air kitchens and household yards, so the forms of interhousehold cooperation that alcoholic beverage production entailed were strictly, unavoidably local. With their responsibility for family food provision, childcare, and domestic work, women were rarely in a position to venture far from home in any case; and their ability to channel portions of the household grain supply into brewing or distilling depended on close attention to crop planning, harvest management, and food stocks over the course of the year. In these circumstances, women had little incentive to embrace an ethnic identity rooted in geographically wide-ranging commercial and social ties. Senaness served little purpose if one was tethered to the household while—in a distinct departure from precolonial and colonial patterns— fathers, husbands, and sons took up livelihoods that required them to spend protracted periods and seek ethnic kinfolk long distances away from home. Indeed, in a somewhat ominous development, even while men we interviewed acknowledged women's eagerness to diversify income sources, they drew restrictively gendered boundaries around off-farm pursuits, implying that as men traveled farther in search of products to barter or sell, women were more obligated to stay home. According to Souce, "My wives would like to gather honey too, but it's very hard work. The bees are dangerous. Honey, in Sena tradition, that's just for men."[70]

In none of the household visits and interviews we conducted with women in 2007–8 did the phrase "Sena tradition" or words to that effect occur in a conversation about kabanga or bwadwa production. Although home-based beer brewing in Cheringoma, as elsewhere in southern Africa, is as iconically "traditional" a feminine skill as beekeeping is a masculine one, interviewees explained their success—in brewing flavorful beer, in income earned in cash or kind— not in terms of inherited cultural knowledge, "spirits" transmitted from mothers and grandmothers, or ritual intercessions with ancestors but as the result of individual hard work and "luck."[71] If nostalgia for gendered tradition surfaced at all in women's accounts, it was in recollections of now-defunct uses of homebrewed beer for ritualized social purposes, such as serving one's husband specially prepared bwadwa to "cool his heart" and express thanks for his labor during the harvest.[72] Unlike earlier times, when women in Cheringoma were as likely as women in Magude to travel on foot outside their community seeking grain in exchange for homemade clay pots, by 2007–8 new restrictions on land access, a blossoming barter economy, and surging cash needs for which women were primarily responsible left them with few off-farm livelihood alternatives beyond home-based brewing and distilling.[73] For these pursuits, the only relational ties that mattered were quotidian, face-to-face networks among neighbor brewers and their local customers—spatially contracted social circuits in which ethnic identities in general and Senaness in particular were largely irrelevant.

Conclusion

The foregoing discussion of gendered ethnicity in two temporally and spatially distant, and culturally distinct, areas of post–civil war Mozambique sidesteps two important issues: the likely diversity in men's experiences of ethnicity in Magude and Cheringoma Districts, and the role of ethnicity discourses in the constitution of gender itself, in meanings of femininity and masculinity that change, always in relation to other dimensions of identity, over time. As the writings of Patrick Harries, Elizabeth MacGonagle, and especially Allen and Barbara Isaacman have shown, masculinity and ethnicity are just as interdependent in Mozambican history as they are embedded in men's own ways of making a living; for Mozambican men too, the dynamic relationship between identity and work—between identity and livelihood—affirms historian Sandra Greene's insight that African ethnicities are mutable, rooted in local power contests, and always constituted through and constrained by the politics of gender.[74] Much work remains to be done on the intertwined politics of masculinity and ethnicity in Mozambique, not least because the spiraling impact of neoliberal development policies, dependence on foreign donors and investors, and dissatisfaction with the country's de facto one-party state will have gendered repercussions at the local and national levels, as in the resurgence of partisan violence in Sofala Province in 2012, and RENAMO's resumption of "low-level armed struggle" the following year.[75]

This chapter's focus on rural women's strategies of living ethnicity in southern and central Mozambique highlights the fluid, adaptive, and relational character of feminine notions of ethnic selfhood not to suggest that women's experience of ethnicity is unique or more important than men's but to shed light on the power of gendered ethnic discourses to enable some livelihood options and suppress others. This distinction has extreme, sometimes life-or-death significance for the more than 60 percent of rural Mozambicans, the majority of them women, still living in poverty today.[76] If women in Magude District in 1994–96 found Shangaanness conducive to survival only to the extent that they could combine this originally masculine ethnic identity with other ethnic claims or redefine Shangaanness in female-centric terms, women in Cheringoma District in 2007–8 turned away from Senaness for reasons equally related to its altered capacity to contribute to their own and their families' well-being. An artifact of mercantile capitalism and protocolonialism, of a time when African men might form profitable alliances among the ethnically and racially diverse, and economically outward looking, inhabitants of Lower Zambezia, Sena ethnicity made little sense to women whose spatially constricted livelihood options narrowed their relational networks to the social world literally outside their door.

NOTES

My thanks to Jan Bender Shetler, Allen Isaacman, and Eric Allina for helpful comments on earlier drafts of this chapter.

1. The term "lived ethnicity" is borrowed from Bonnie J. Clark, "Lived Ethnicity: Archaeology and Identity in *Mexicano* America," *World Archaeology* 37, no. 3 (2005): 440–52.

2. Elizabeth MacGonagle creatively explores Ndau identity and history in *Crafting Identity in Zimbabwe and Mozambique* (Rochester: University of Rochester Press, 2007).

3. See, for example, Tony Vaux, Amandio Mavela, João Pereira, and Jennifer Stuttle, "Strategic Conflict Assessment: Mozambique," unpublished report for the UK Department for International Development, 2006 (http://siteresources.worldbank.org /INTMOZAMBIQUE/Resources/DFID_governance_0406.pdf, accessed 2 April 2013), 10.

4. I use the term "living ethnicity" instead of Clark's "lived ethnicity" to highlight that these strategies are ongoing in the present and to emphasize my reading of Mozambican women's expressions of ethnic self as inherently contingent and dynamic.

5. Resistência Nacional Moçambicana (RENAMO), the rebel army that sought to overthrow the government of Mozambique in the country's sixteen-year civil war, is now the largest Mozambican opposition party.

6. See Heidi Gengenbach, "Naming the Past in a 'Scattered' Land: Memory and the Powers of Women's Naming Practices in Southern Mozambique," *International Journal of African Historical Studies* 33, no. 3 (2000): 523–42.

7. Patrick Harries, *Work, Culture, and Identity: Migrant Laborers in Mozambique and South Africa, c. 1860–1910* (Portsmouth, NH: Heinemann, 1994); see also Harries, *Butterflies and Barbarians: Swiss Missionaries and Systems of Knowledge in South-East Africa* (Athens: Ohio University Press, 2007). The classic ethnographic work on southern Mozambique is Henri A. Junod, *The Life of a South African Tribe*, 2 vols. (London: Macmillan, 1927).

8. The key exceptions are David Webster, "Abafazi Bathonga Bafihlakala: Ethnicity and Gender in a KwaZulu Border Community," in *Tradition and Transition in Southern Africa*, ed. Andrew D. Spiegel and Patrick A. McAllister (New Brunswick, NJ: Transaction, 1991), 243–49; and Jeff Guy and Motlatsi Thabane, "Technology, Ethnicity, and Ideology: Basotho Miners and Shaft-Sinking on the South African Gold Mines," *Journal of South African Studies* 14, no. 2 (1988): 257–78.

9. This paragraph and the next summarize arguments presented in Heidi Gengenbach, *Binding Memories: Women as Makers and Tellers of History in Magude, Mozambique*, Gutenberg-e Electronic Book (New York: Columbia University Press and the American Historical Association, 2005).

10. Alcinda Honwana, "Undying Past: Spirit Possession and War Memory in Southern Mozambique," in *Magic and Modernity: Interfaces of Revelation and Concealment*, ed. Birgit Meyer and Peter Pels (Stanford, CA: Stanford University Press, 2003), 60–80; Henri P. Junod, "Les cas de possessions et l'exorcisme chez les VaNdau," *Africa* (1934): 270–99.

11.   See Heidi Gengenbach, "'I'll Bury You in the Border!': Women's Land Struggles in Post-war Facazisse (Magude District), Mozambique," special issue on Mozambique, *Journal of Southern African Studies* 24, no. 1 (1998): 7–36.

12.   Although the literature on livelihoods is vast and conceptually far from homogeneous, I here understand "livelihood" as "the capabilities, assets (including both material and social resources) and activities required for a means of living" (Robert Chambers and Gordon Conway, *Sustainable Rural Livelihoods: Practical Concepts for the 21st Century* [Brighton, UK: Institute of Development Studies, 1991], 6).

13.   The project, run by Woods Hole Research Center in Falmouth, Massachusetts, was funded by a Human and Social Dynamics grant from the National Science Foundation (2007–10). See Gregory Amacher, Richard Howarth, and Maria Bowman, "Buffering Stochastic and Efficiency Shocks: The Importance of Natural Resources Access to Rural Subsistence Households in Sofala Mozambique" (unpublished manuscript, 2012).

14.   The text quote is from Administração do Distrito de Cheringoma, "Distrito de Cheringoma: Plano distrital de desenvolvimento," October 2005, 31 (my translation). On malnutrition, see Ministério da Saude, Instituto Nacional de Estatística, and ICF International, *Moçambique inquérito demográfico e de saúde 2011* (Calverton, MD: MISAU, INE e ICFI, 2011), 156. According to the World Bank, Sofala's adult female illiteracy rate in 2003 was 72 percent, compared to the national rate of 68 percent (http://web.worldbank.org/WBSITE/EXTERNAL/COUNTRIES/AFRICAEXT/MOZAMBIQUEEXTN/0,,contentMDK:20585288~pagePK:141137~piPK:141127~theSitePK:382131,00.html). A 2009 Mozambique Ministry of Health survey found that 15.5 percent of adults aged fifteen to forty-nine in Sofala Province were HIV-infected (Kenneth Sherr et al., "Strengthening Integrated Primary Health Care in Sofala, Mozambique," supplement, *BMC Health Services Research* 13, no. 2 [2013]: 2).

15.   Malyn Newitt, *A History of Mozambique* (Johannesburg: University of the Witwatersrand Press, 1995), 141.

16.   Allen F. Isaacman and Barbara Isaacman, *The Tradition of Resistance in Mozambique: The Zambesi Valley, 1850–1921* (Berkeley: University of California Press, 1976); M. D. D. Newitt, *Portuguese Settlement on the Zambesi: Exploration, Land Tenure, and Colonial Rule in East Africa* (New York: Africana Publishing Company, 1973).

17.   António Rita-Ferreira, *Fixação portuguesa e história pre-colonial de Moçambique* (Lisbon: Junta de Investigações Cientificas do Ultramar, 1982); Robert Marlin, "Possessing the Past: Legacies of Violence and Reproductive Illness in Central Mozambique" (PhD diss., Rutgers University, New Brunswick, NJ, 2001), 19ff.

18.   M. D. D. Newitt, "Drought in Mozambique 1823–1831," *Journal of Southern African Studies* 15, no. 1 (1988): 15–35.

19.   Leroy Vail and Landeg White, *Capitalism and Colonialism in Mozambique: A Study of Quelimane District* (Minneapolis: University of Minnesota Press, 1980), 69.

20.   Allen F. Isaacman and Barbara Isaacman, *Slavery and Beyond: The Making of Men and Chikunda Ethnic Identities in the Unstable World of South-Central Africa, 1750–1920* (Portsmouth, NH: Heinemann, 2004).

21.   The text quote is from Allen Isaacman and Derek Peterson, "Making the Chikunda: Military Slavery and Ethnicity in Southern Africa, 1750–1900," *International Journal of African Historical Studies* 36, no. 2 (2003): 258.

22.   FRELIMO is the acronym for the Frente de Libertação de Moçambique (Mozambique Liberation Front), the country's ruling party since independence in 1975. Marlin notes that Sena identity has also connoted a close relationship to Portuguese power, as evidenced in Sena leaders' refusal to join the anticolonial Barue revolts of 1902 and 1917 (Marlin, "Possessing the Past," 180). On the Portuguese loyalties of "the Sena" through the early twentieth century, see Isaacman and Isaacman, *Tradition of Resistance*, 165; and Vail and White, *Capitalism and Colonialism*, 174. However, Isaacman and Isaacman suggest that Sena "peasants" may have been more receptive than political elites to the Barue cause.

23.   The word "despised" is from Mark F. Chingono, *The State, Violence and Development: The Political Economy of War in Mozambique, 1975–1992* (Aldershot, UK: Avebury, 1996), 48. According to Ethnologue, there are 1,340,000 ChiSena speakers in Mozambique (2006) and 270,000 in Malawi (2001) (http://www.ethnologue.com/language/seh, accessed 17 September 2010). Though an imperfect metric for Sena ethnicity, language persistence at least indicates some enduring cultural connection. In contrast, Chikunda identity lives on only in "backwater regions along the Mozambican-Zambian-Zimbabwean frontier" (Isaacman and Peterson, "Making the Chikunda," 281).

24.   Isaacman and Isaacman, *Slavery and Beyond*, chap. 2.

25.   On the prazos as a transfrontier society, see Allen Isaacman and Barbara Isaacman, "The Prazeros as Transfrontiersmen: A Study in Social and Cultural Change," *International Journal of African Historical Studies* 8, no. 1 (1975): 1–39.

26.   Marlin, "Possessing the Past," 40–41; Vail and White, *Capitalism and Colonialism*, 71–72.

27.   For an overview of the early history of this area, see Newitt, *History of Mozambique*, chap. 2.

28.   M. D. D. Newitt, "The Portuguese on the Zambezi: An Historical Interpretation of the Prazo System," *Journal of African History* 10, no. 1 (1969): 77.

29.   Newitt, *Portuguese Settlement*, 164; Newitt, "Portuguese on the Zambezi," 76.

30.   Allen F. Isaacman, *Mozambique: The Africanization of a European Institution* (Madison: University of Wisconsin Press, 1972), 31; Vail and White, *Capitalism and Colonialism*, 10.

31.   Newitt, *Portuguese Settlement*, 238; Isaacman, *Mozambique*, 117.

32.   Newitt, *Portuguese Settlement*, 164–68; Newitt, "Drought," 31–33.

33.   Eric Allina, *Slavery by Any Other Name: African Life under Company Rule in Colonial Mozambique* (Charlottesville: University of Virginia Press, 2012), 29–30.

34.   R. C. F. Maugham, *Zambezia: A General Description of the Valley of the Zambezi River, from Its Delta to the River Aroangwa, with Its History, Agriculture, Flora, Fauna, and Ethnography* (London: J. Murray, 1910), 75 (emphasis added).

35.   Gustavo de Bivar Pinto Lopes, *Respostas ao questionário etnográfico: Apresentado pela secretaria dos negócios indígenas em Lourenço Marques acérca da população*

indígena da província de Moçambique: Parte referente ao território da Companhia de Moçambique (Beira: Imprensa da Companhia de Moçambique, 1928), 68.

36. Maugham, *Zambezia*, 120–25; Lopes, *Respostas*, 65–71; Mario Augusto da Costa, *Do Zambeze ao paralelo 22°* (Beira: Imprensa da Companhia de Moçambique, 1940), 133–44. Da Costa reported that Cheringoma had the largest area devoted to forest concessions in company territory (126). The company's keen interest in the timber resources of Cheringoma is evident in "Notes on the Country and Trees from Villa Machado to Tambarara," *Agricultural Journal of the Mozambique Company* 1, no. 2 (1911): 60–64.

37. José Negrão, "How to Induce Development in Africa? The Case of Mozambique" (unpublished manuscript, http://www.sarpn.org/documents/d0000091/P94_Negrao.pdf, accessed 18 March 2013), 3. The Cheringoma experiment predated the better known *colonato* scheme in the Limpopo Valley.

38. For the quotes on climate and landscape, see Frederick Roderick Noble Findlay, *Big Game Shooting and Travel in South-East Africa; an Account of Shooting Trips in the Cheringoma and Gorongoza Divisions of Portuguese South-East Africa and in Zululand* (London: T. F. Unwin, 1903), 13, 164; for wildlife, see F. Vaughan Kirby, *Sport in East Central Africa: Being an Account of Hunting Trips in Portuguese and Other Districts of East Central Africa* (London: Rowland Ward, Ltd., 1899), 321.

39. Findlay, *Big Game Shooting*, 95.

40. Lopes, *Respostas*, 69.

41. Malyn Newitt and Corrado Tornimbeni, "Transnational Networks and Internal Divisions in Central Mozambique: An Historical Perspective from the Colonial Period," *Cahiers d'études africaines* 192, no. 4 (2005): 39.

42. Fathers J. Martens, A. Verdaasdonk, J. van Rijen, A. van Kampen, and J. Tielmans, "Diary of Inhaminga," *Issue: A Journal of Opinion* 10, nos. 1 and 2 (1980): 53.

43. Although RENAMO's leadership has been dominated by Ndau speakers from central Mozambique, its "middle- and lower-level cadres . . . were completely multiethnic," and there is no evidence of strong ethnic patterns in its postwar electoral performance. See Michel Cahen, "Nationalism and Ethnicities: Lessons from Mozambique," in *Ethnicity Kills? The Politics of War, Peace and Ethnicity in Subsaharan Africa,* ed. Einer Braathen, Morten Bøås, and Gjermund Sæther (New York: St. Martin's Press, 2000), 163–87.

44. Relevant incidents of partisan violence included the August 2004 shooting death of a police officer by armed RENAMO supporters in Inhaminga and a wave of arson attacks against homes of FRELIMO members in Maringue District in September 2007.

45. In 1994, the year of Mozambique's first multiparty democratic elections, RENAMO won a "landslide victory" in all districts of Sofala Province (Cahen, "Nationalism and Ethnicities," 176). In 1999, RENAMO's Alfonso Dhlakama won 86 percent of Cheringoma District's vote and then 63 percent in 2004 against Armando Guebuza, the country's current president. See Domingos M. do Rosário, *From Negligence to Populism: An Analysis of Mozambique's Agricultural Political Economy*, Future Agricultures Working

Paper no. 34, April 2012 (http://www.future-agricultures.org/component/docman/doc_details/1541-from-negligence-to-populism-an-analysis-of-mozambiques-agricultural-political-economy, accessed 12 March 2013), 14.

46. In 2008, the vast majority of rural residents lacked access to electricity, potable water, paved roads (or motorized transport), and basic health care. See Administração do Distrito de Cheringoma, "Plano Distrital de Desenvolvimento" (unpublished report, October 2005), 62–66, 82; and Instituto Nacional de Estatística, *Estatísticas do distrito: Cheringoma 2008* (Maputo: Instituto Nacional de Estatística, 2010), 10.

47. Administração do Distrito de Cheringoma, "Plano distrital," 108, 116.

48. Ministério da Saude, Instituto Nacional de Estatística, and ICF International, *Moçambique inquérito demográfico e de saúde 2011*, 156.

49. United Nations Mozambique, *Child Poverty and Disparities in Mozambique 2010* (Maputo: UNICEF, 2011), 4, 16, 57.

50. The same holds true for Sofala Province as a whole. In 2008, Sofala boasted not only Gorongosa National Park (the country's largest national park) but also three forest reserves, a buffalo reserve, and eight of the country's thirteen sport-hunting concessions, totaling nearly 45 percent of the province's land area. See Administração do Distrito de Cheringoma, "Plano distrital," 53–54. Commercial timbering is officially considered Cheringoma's "principal economic activity" (54). See also Direcção Provincial para a Coordenação da Acção Ambiental (DPCA)–Sofala, Departamento de Planeamento e Ordenamento Territorial, "Zoneamento ambiental do Distrito de Cheringoma" (unpublished report, DPCA, Beira, 2007), 38–41.

51. Administração do Distrito de Cheringoma, "Plano distrital," 45.

52. Widespread occurrence of tsetse fly limits cattle ownership in Cheringoma.

53. Commercial forest concession seekers in Cheringoma and elsewhere in central Mozambique—predominantly Chinese and Brazilian nationals—have not been deterred by the cumbersome and decidedly nontransparent application process. For a strong critique, see Catherine Mackenzie, *Forest Governance in Zambézia, Mozambique: Chinese Takeaway!* (Quelimane: Forum das Organização Não–Governmental da Zambezia [FONGZA], 2006).

54. About 5 percent of GNP and another 64,000 acres of the GNP's "buffer zone" lie within Cheringoma District (Administração do Distrito de Cheringoma, "Plano Distrital," 24). GNP is a twenty-year public-private partnership between the government of Mozambique and the Gorongosa Restoration Project, a US nonprofit organization founded by American entrepreneur-philanthropist Greg Carr.

55. In 2007–8, the price of maize increased by 87 percent in Mozambique, one of the first African countries to experience rioting due to the global food price crisis (Julia Berazneva and David R. Lee, "Explaining the African Food Riots of 2007–2008: An Empirical Analysis" [unpublished paper, Charles H. Dyson School of Applied Economics and Management, Cornell University, 2011, http://www.csae.ox.ac.uk/conferences/2011-EdiA/papers/711-Berazneva.pdf, accessed 30 November 2013). Less than 4 percent of Cheringoma survey respondents in 2007 reported *any* wage income from formal employment for the preceding year. Average annual income for these households was just US$41.

56.   Sara João, interview by the author, 25 July 2008, Dimba, Cheringoma District.

57.   Deborah Fahy Bryceson, "The Scramble in Africa: Reorienting Rural Liveli-hoods," *World Development* 30, no. 5 (2002): 725.

58.   Most men were reluctant to admit to hunting until the survey team assured them of confidentiality and anonymity. Strict GNP rules prohibiting residents from killing animals within the park and buffer zone are an ongoing source of conflict between park staff and local residents, and several survey respondents reported having been detained, fined, and/or beaten by park rangers over minor violations of "antipoaching" rules. For a critique of illegal hunting and the bush meat trade as constraints on "sustainable wildlife-based tourism," see Peter Lindsey and Carlos Bento, *Illegal Hunting and the Bushmeat Trade in Central Mozambique: A Case Study from Coutada 9, Manica Province* (Harare: TRAFFIC East/Southern Africa, 2012).

59.   Xikita Kalikoka, interview by the author, 2 August 2008, Tsotse, Cheringoma District.

60.   Conversation with a survey respondent who requested anonymity, 27 September 2007, Machisso, Gorongosa District.

61.   Forest-based beekeeping involves placement of homemade hives in treetops in ritually protected areas of the forest, an activity noted for this area in David Livingstone, *Narrative of an Expedition to the Zambesi and Its Tributaries, and of the Discovery of the Lakes Shirwa and Nyassa 1858–1864* (London: John Murray, 1865), 439.

62.   Pires Faife Souce, Marcos Sozinho Gunda, and Matias Vicente, interview by the author, 22 July 2008, Tsotse, Cheringoma District; Victor Miguel, interview by the author, 24 July 2008, Chite, Cheringoma District; Jose Jase, interview by the author, 29 July 2008, Chite, Cheringoma District; and António Felipe, interview by the author, 31 July 2008, Chite, Cheringoma District.

63.   For example, Jase, interview.

64.   Miguel, interview; Felipe, interview; Ernesto Tangata Manuel Torcida, interview by the author, 1 August 2008, Muanandimae, Cheringoma District.

65.   Souce, interview.

66.   This sense of forest beekeeping as a "traditional" masculine skill with counter-hegemonic political import in the neoliberal era emerged most clearly from a lively group discussion about changes in men's income sources in Muanandimae, a community within GNP that in 2008 was still resisting government and park pressure to relocate to the buffer zone. Joao Charombo Branco (*régulo*), Felix Dinis, Joaquim Ernesto Brumo Nota, Isaquiel Felix Dinis Nota, Joao Manuel Tennis, Manuel Catique, Ricardo Arnance Campira, and Paulino Mines, interview by the author, 28 July 2008, Muanandimae, Cheringoma District.

67.   Kalikoka, interview; Ines Londe and Maria António, interview by the author, 2 August 2008, Tsotse, Cheringoma District; Maria Munisia Kilampi, interview by the author, 4 August 2008, Tsotse, Cheringoma District.

68.   Kilampi, interview.

69.   Women reputed to brew especially potent and flavorful beverages were spoken of with disdain by some members of their community, especially self-identified Christians.

70. Souce, interview.

71. Kalikoka, interview; Kilampi, interview.

72. Kalikoka, interview.

73. For a description of women's pottery production and sale in early colonial Sofala Province, including among Sena women, see Lopes, *Respostas*, 77.

74. Sandra E. Greene, *Gender, Ethnicity, and Social Change on the Upper Slave Coast: A History of the Anlo-Ewe* (Portsmouth, NH: Heinemann, 1996).

75. Although significant sources of disagreement remain, the FRELIMO-led government and RENAMO signed a ceasefire in August 2014 to halt this violence ahead of the October 2014 presidential election (Al Jazeera, "Mozambique's Government and Renamo Sign Truce," 25 August 2014 [http://www.aljazeera.com/news/africa/2014/08/mozambique-rebels-government-sign-truce-201482563950966537.html, accessed 28 August 2014]).

76. Benedito Armando Cunguara, "Pathways out of Poverty in Rural Mozambique" (MS thesis, Department of Agricultural Food and Resource Economics, Michigan State University, 2008), 2. According to a more recent (2009) source, the incidence of poverty is 58 percent in Sofala Province and 67.5 percent in Maputo Province (http://www.undp.org.mz/en/MDGS-GOAL/Goal-1-Eradicate-Absolute-Poverty-and-Hunger/Reducing-Absolute-Poverty-Situation-and-Trends, accessed 11 December 2013).

Part II

Constructing New Forms of Identity

3

Re-reading the 1835 "Fingo Emancipation"

Women and Ethnicity in the Colonial Archive

POPPY FRY

It is a well-worn joke about historians that our approach to research is often like that of the drunk who searches for his keys under the streetlight, not because that is where he left them but because that is where the light is. Historians regularly enjoin their students, both graduate and undergraduate, to "follow the sources" as they undertake research. Indeed, without adequate source material to illuminate questions about the past, there can be no historical narrative. There is a fine line, though, between being led by sources and being misled by sources. The "archive fever" described by Jacques Derrida implies not only intoxication with the archive's possibilities but also an irrational faith in its truthfulness and omniscience.[1] Absolute acceptance of the archive's authority is particularly problematic for historians studying African women's history. The colonial archive—overwhelmingly the product of European men—would appear to be doubly uninterested in, or perhaps hostile to, African women.[2] Yet women appear in the colonial archive. At every turn there are hints and clues about women's lives. There are sources as tantalizing as they are thorny. Might it be possible to tease from the archive narratives very different from those intended by their authors?

In evaluating the possibilities of the colonial archive, this chapter takes as its case study the so-called Fingo Emancipation of 1835. The term refers to the movement of nearly twenty thousand men, women, and children from Xhosaland

into the Cape Colony. In 1835, the border between British colonial territory and
the indigenous Xhosa chiefdoms lay in present-day South Africa's Eastern
Cape in a region that would come to be known as the Ciskei. In the years leading
up to the "Emancipation," conflict had been simmering among the Xhosa. The
demands and opportunities of having the colony as a neighbor highlighted
long-standing political and social divides. By 1835, a particular group of people
found themselves at the center of this conflict. Both Xhosa informants and
colonial observers described these people as Fingo, and these informants and
observers characterized Fingoness as representing an emphasis on agriculture
over pastoralism and a disregard for established systems of authority (particularly chiefship).[3] Witchcraft accusations, the classic mechanism for punishing
the antisocial, proliferated.[4] Although they were Xhosa speakers, those identified
as Fingo challenged the basic elements of Xhosaness. The two identities became
increasingly irreconcilable.

When the petty violence of the frontier blossomed into full-blown warfare
between the Xhosa and the Cape Colony in 1834 and 1835, the attendant upheaval
caused a decisive break between Xhosa authorities and a large group of Fingo
people. Thousands of individuals migrated into the colony in a process that
colonial governor Benjamin D'Urban grandly labeled an emancipation. D'Urban
considered that these people had been freed from savagery and from the witchcraft accusations of envious neighbors. He also believed—wrongly, as it turned
out—that they would soon convert to Christianity and become docile subjects
of the British Empire. D'Urban could not fathom the possibility that the Fingo
had their own agendas and ambitions, in particular, the development and pro-
liferation of a distinct ethnic identity. Women, especially, used the war and the
"Emancipation" as an opportunity to critique or reject the moral economy of
Xhosa ethnicity and to imagine something else in its place.

Although Fingo identity would come to be associated with masculinity and
patrilineality, a close reading of the colonial archive shows that the migration
into the colony—the act that "made" the Fingo a distinct and coherent group—
was driven, both directly and indirectly, by women. During the 1834–35 war, at
least, Fingoness represented the possibility of an identity grounded in agriculture rather than pastoralism and in female agency rather than patrilineality. In
a variety of ways, women moving into the colony sought to renegotiate ethnic
belonging, and, in doing so, they sketched out the contours of a new ethnicity.

Why Study the "Emancipation"?

As an object of historical study, the "Emancipation" is both tantalizing and
treacherous. It was a remarkable transformation during which questions of

identity seem to have been up for negotiation. As Premesh Lalu notes in a book that takes as its starting point the 1834–35 war in the Eastern Cape, it is the job of historians to find and interrogate those moments in the archival record "where another story might have taken place" in addition to or instead of the one explicitly recorded. The "Emancipation" represents just such a moment in the history of British-Xhosa relations. Its simultaneous political and cultural significance also allows a reconsideration of the relationship between those two spheres. Given the central role political authorities played in the creation of the "Emancipation," it is not surprising that the colonial archive tends to posit politics as the primary driver of history. The "Emancipation" offers the opportunity to ask, as Dror Wahrman does, "whether there is something to be gained from treating politics as an arena of culture, rather than culture as an arena of politics."[5] The kind of refocusing that Wahrman suggests would have significant ramifications for the study of the early nineteenth-century Cape Colony, an area where masculine, authority-centered narratives continue to loom large. Considering the "Emancipation" less as a political event and more as a marker of cultural conflict and change allows us to consider all the possible actors involved, not just those men who figure most prominently in the archive.

The "Emancipation" appears in the archive as an event overwhelmingly recorded by men and surrounded by masculine rhetoric. In the early nineteenth-century Eastern Cape, the most ubiquitous (and best-recorded) discourse of ethnicity—whether among the Xhosa, the Khoikhoi, or the British—took place within the idiom of masculinity. Different ethnic identities were frequently represented as competing ideals of manhood. In the Eastern Cape, at least, men spent a great deal of time, energy, and ink extolling their own models of masculinity and denigrating those of other groups. Report after report of frontier conflict reveals claims of manliness. Attacks against traders and settlers were frequently accompanied by loud declarations that the Xhosa were men and their enemies were "old maids," or women of some other variety.[6] Since these raids frequently focused on the capture of cattle, such exclamations further reinforced the connection between cows, men, and power. The fact that such cries were widely reported by Europeans, even though the noise may have compromised the security of raiding parties, suggests that the Xhosa actively sought to assert their conception of masculinity against that of their neighbors. In the war of 1835, colonial troops on the field of battle faced not only spears but also taunts: "[The Xhosa] invited them to advance nearer if they were men; but, said they, 'You are not men, but children; we are warriors and chiefs.'"[7] Immediately preceding the same war, a Xhosa chief told a visiting missionary that violence against the Cape Colony was necessary for the preservation of masculine political authority—the Xhosa paramount chief "would not rule," he said, "over the followers of those who think him a woman." The missionary, although unconvinced of Xhosa grievances against the colony, approved of the statement as "a manly remonstrance."[8] At first glance, archival sources seem to indicate that the public conversation around group identities was not only dominated by men but explicitly about masculinity.

The predominance of masculinity in documents does not mean, however, that the archival record is useless in sketching out women's relationship to ethnicity. Recognizing the subtexts and implications of "tribal" or ethnic identities for Xhosa and Fingo women requires a certain amount of "reading against the grain"—interrogating sources in creative ways. This use of documentary evidence to sketch out cultural systems has been pioneered by scholars of the medieval and early modern periods. Working primarily from terse inquisitorial records, scholars have pieced together the ideas and beliefs of both individuals and communities so ably that the basic premise of their method—that "even meager, scattered and obscure documentation can be put to good use"—has been widely accepted in their fields. The approach to sources developed by Emmanuel Le Roy Ladurie, Carlo Ginzburg, and Natalie Zemon Davis (among others) moves away from positivist concerns about objectivity and bias, recognizing the human frailty of scribe and subject alike.[9] Although the administrators, missionaries, soldiers, and settlers whose observations dominate the colonial record clearly wrote with particular political, cultural, and personal agendas in mind, as historical "informants" they are not necessarily any more problematic than other sources. The colonial archive must be read not as *the* definitive account but rather as a jumble of information in which a range of patterns, stories, and perspectives may be discerned. For historians seeking to write about African ideas and experiences, the judgments and claims of the archive's authors are of less interest than the details of description, minor anecdotes, and moments of confusion. This is certainly true in the case of the "Fingo Emancipation"—the clues to understanding Fingoness are hidden in plain sight within a bland and sometimes unreliable narrative.

The "Emancipation" is not unique in providing a glimpse of ethnicity in flux, but it does offer an example of how women's experience or understanding of ethnic identity might be manifested in liminal moments and of how historians can situate women as driving agents in identity shifts. The paradigm of emancipation emphasized—at least for British observers—the centrality of free male wage labor. Indeed, over the coming years it would be the demonstration by the Fingo of a particular sort of liberal agricultural masculinity that would endear them to the British and underpin their claim to a shared ethnicity. This situation, however, was a result, not a cause, of the move into the colony. In 1835,

Fingoness represented less a fully formed ethnic structure and more a set of possibilities marked out in contrast to Xhosa understandings of gender and belonging. In her study of the archives of Kohler, Wisconsin, Katherine J. Oderbeck writes of the importance of unbuilt blueprints as records of how individuals and communities imagined themselves.[10] Women's conceptions of Fingoness during the 1834–35 war were blueprints for a new identity, a vision for a kind of Fingo ethnicity that would ultimately remain largely unbuilt.

Gender and Agriculture

The difference between the Xhosa and the Fingo—the conflict that precipitated the latter's move into the colony—centered on the place of agriculture in household production. Within the moral economy of Xhosaness, a clearly defined, and supernaturally charged, division of labor kept farming secondary to pastoralism. The care and milking of cattle was an exclusively male domain and was linked to a distinctive Xhosa masculinity, while farming was explicitly women's work. The precedence of pastoralism over agriculture is indicated by oral traditions outlining extensive transhumance and by early accounts that describe the Xhosa as living a "nomade [sic] life" in which "habitations [were] so often changed."[11] Movement was directed by the grazing needs of cattle and therefore fell under the control of men. In the context of the "Emancipation," it is worth noting that migration outside of the cyclical changes of pasture constituted a rejection of cattle and, by extension, men as the determinants of communal behavior.

The connection between pastoralism and authority stretched beyond the logistics of seasonal migration. Cattle symbolized the spiritual health of the community—they were charged with layers of social meaning. Waxing nostalgic about a better time, a Xhosa councilor insisted, "Our fathers were MEN; they loved their cattle; their wives and children lived upon milk."[12] Milk, not agricultural produce, was the defining feature of prosperity. In the mid-nineteenth century, a Xhosa prophetic movement would explicitly dismiss crops as "only horse food"—not an appropriate foundation for a human diet.[13] The centrality of cows in the Xhosa social imagination was reflected in a metaphoric equivalence between women and cattle. This relationship was most obviously referenced in the payment of cows as bridewealth, but it cannot be reduced to an exchange of resources. The movement of cattle and wives between households wove individuals and families into a coherent community. The reproductive capacity of women and cows provided the foundation for civilization itself, and mastery over that capacity formed the basis of male claims to power.[14] Those who identified as Fingo problematized the relationship of cattle to political authority both through the prioritization of agriculture over pastoralism and through the participation of men in agricultural labor.

Fingoness as an ethnic identity was grounded in agriculture as a defining mode of production and as a male, as well as a female, pursuit. Given the powerful connotations of pastoralism, it is tempting to assume that male farmers were driven solely by material desperation, but pre-1835 reports do not reveal a pattern of prosperous Fingo men rejecting agriculture as their central pursuit.[15] Rather, it appears that men's participation in farming reflected something deeper and more complex than immediate nutritional needs. Certainly it need not have indicated any greater status or power for women—in fact, the movement of men into agriculture might well have been seen as usurpation. At the same time, it may have meant an end to the tension between transhumance and farming, as well as a shift in the household balance of power. As early as 1826, missionary William Shrewsbury noted the initial enthusiasm of Xhosa women toward the plow—a reasonable reaction in light of its implicit demand that cattle, the symbol of male authority, be literally yoked within the female sphere of agriculture.[16] Despite this apparent interest, however, plows did not become commonplace in Xhosaland until the 1860s. In 1835, Jeremiah Goldswain argued that the inevitable acceptance by Xhosa women of British farming techniques would necessarily undermine the labor requirements driving polygamous marriages.[17] Goldswain, too, seems to have miscalculated either the willingness or the ability of Xhosa women to reshape agricultural production—the changes he predicted did not come to pass. The overall continuity of agricultural practices highlights how unusual and potentially radical Fingo men's move away from pastoralism and into farming truly was.

Interpreting the Archive

In the early nineteenth-century Eastern Cape, disagreements about the significance of agriculture were necessarily disagreements about the role of women, whether in individual households or in wider society. The Fingo-Xhosa divide was thus inherently an issue for and about women—and yet it has not been considered as such either by contemporary observers or by historians. Close readings of a number of documents around the "Fingo Emancipation" suggest that the absence of women as central actors in the historical narrative has far less to do with their actual actions and words and more with the way those actions and words were interpreted—and frequently dismissed—by colonial officials, settlers, and missionaries, as well as by historians. To recover women's role in the "Emancipation" requires mapping out their actions and then "try[ing] to discern the pattern in those actions, as a way of inferring the shared understanding which sustains them."[18] In other words, any plausible claim regarding women's understanding of Fingoness must adequately account for women's actual behavior.

In his widely read essay "Unmasking the Fingo," Alan Webster argues that the "Emancipation" was, in fact, the cover story used to justify the expropriation of women and children from Xhosaland to meet the labor demands of white settlers in the Cape Colony.[19] While admirable in his willingness to question established narratives, Webster approaches the colonial archive with such skepticism that his rejection of documents' simplest meanings is as complete as earlier historians' embrace of those meanings. One totalizing assumption—that British writers' claims fully reflect the historical reality—is replaced by another—that British writers' intent is to hide, rather than record, actual events. Webster's theory has been largely debunked, in particular by Alan Lester in his study of settler society, but it is worth noting that one of Webster's central pieces of evidence is the predominance of women and children among those who moved from Xhosaland into the colony.[20] By Webster's count, only 12 percent of the newly arrived Fingo were adult men. Given the desirability of women and children as domestic workers in the Cape Colony, he claims this disparity reveals the mercenary agenda of the British and thus the coerced nature of the migration.[21] Leaving aside the fact that a significant number of Fingo men joined British military forces rather than immediately moving to the colony, this line of argument entirely ignores the gendered component of the Xhosa-Fingo divide and the possibility of agency on the part of Fingo women. It replicates the biases and assumptions of Webster's sources, even as he repudiates the truthfulness of those sources.

Webster's interpretation not only disregards the realities of the frontier but also strips the migrants of agency. The British military on the Eastern Frontier of the Cape Colony in the 1830s had limited means to carry out even the most conservative of its objectives, and even the addition of civilian settler levies during periods of open violence did not produce a fighting force capable of consistently and unequivocally defeating the Xhosa forces. Moving thousands of people through hostile territory and across the border against their will would have been nearly impossible. Webster's scenario makes sense only if the actors in the story are limited to male settlers, male colonial officials, and male Xhosa chiefs. Once the women and children are envisioned as individuals with interests and agendas rather than as household property incapable of moving independently, the disparity Webster notes becomes not sinister but intriguing. It suggests that more women than men found the prospect of rejecting Xhosa ethnicity and claiming Fingoness sufficiently attractive to undertake the journey into the colony. Concerns about women leaving Xhosa communities during wartime existed at least as far back as 1828, when settler Jeremiah Goldswain apparently observed warriors attacking women who were attempting to cross the battlefield and reach British lines by "nocking out thear brains [*sic*]."[22]

If women were, in fact, migrating independently and potentially against the wishes of their husband or father, it indicates that the intrahousehold dynamics of ethnic identification were less straightforward than has previously been assumed—women and children were not simply subsumed by the ethnicity of the male head of the household. The "Emancipation" may have presented an opportunity for women to define their own ethnicity and the ethnicity of their children. In an 1852 court case, a witness named Klaas Mafee answered the question "Are you a Fingo?" with "Yes, and my father was also a Fingo."[23] If Fingoness passed through the male line, the latter portion of his statement would not have been necessary. The ethnic identity Mafee claimed was apparently not the inevitable result of his father's ethnicity—it derived from his own identification, his mother's ethnicity, or both. If Fingoness could even partially decenter the senior male as the definer of a household's identity, it is not difficult to imagine how threatening it might have seemed to those for whom ethnicity, masculinity, and power were linked—namely, Xhosa chiefs.

British settler Caesar Andrews's diary of the 1835 war offers a tantalizing hint of the ways in which Fingoness could challenge patriarchal authority. He reports that a large group of Fingo arrived in the British camp led by "a queen of huge dimensions" who "had two splendidly formed young Fingoes as her A.D.C.'s."[24] Most other accounts of significant women in the 1834–35 war refer to them as wives of chiefs and frame their actions in terms of their role as their husband's agents. While Andrews's choice of the word "queen" may have been a misunderstanding, it seems that this woman exercised authority over the other people with her, including her "splendidly formed" aides-de-camp, whose gender was not specified, and at least some men. Col. Harry Smith—not a man known for his feminism or his respect for Xhosa authority—negotiated with her directly, rather than addressing her as the representative of a male authority, in working out the details of her people's move into the colony. The queen's name is never mentioned, and she does not appear in other accounts, but Andrews's account suggests that in at least some cases, women claimed positions of authority not just within the nascent Fingo community but on the basis of Fingo identity itself. If women were indeed migrating into the colony without their adult male household members and in part as a rejection of those men's claims on them, it seems reasonable to expect to see women as the leaders of migrant groups.

That the negotiation between female leaders and British officials coincided so closely with the "official" migration into the colony led by male authorities, furthermore, raises questions of causation. The initiative of the "Fingo chiefs" in organizing and overseeing the move can be read less as a coherent political strategy and more as an attempt on their part to assert control over a diffuse and female-dominated migration already under way. Andrews noted "numerous bodies of the Fingo tribe" arriving behind British lines nearly a month before the actual "Emancipation," while Thomas Holden Bowker recorded Fingo "deputations" around the same time.[25] The explicitly political narrative of the "Emancipation"—self-proclaimed male leaders negotiating with colonial officials and agreeing on a dispensation—could well have been the result, rather than the cause, of large-scale migration into the colony.

Women and the Language of Violence

The role of women in defining both Xhosa and Fingo ethnicity continued to be an issue in the 1834–35 war, even after the "Emancipation." In his memoir of the war, Maj. Gen. John Bisset discusses a number of Xhosa practices and rituals, focusing particularly on the ceremonial slaughter of cattle. In careful, detached prose, he outlines how the cow's lower chest was cut open and its trachea severed.[26] Several pages later, however, any pretense of scholarly objectivity vanishes when he discovers the bodies of several Fingo women attacked and killed by Xhosa forces. In a display of "atrocious" barbarism, he writes, "the young women had their bosoms cut out," their chests opened, and their tracheas severed.[27] In inflicting violence upon these female Fingo bodies, Xhosa forces (presumably men) mimicked the mechanism of cattle killing, reinforcing male power over social and economic resources. The mutilation, furthermore, focused on the breasts, a body part associated with reproduction and with femininity. This attack can be read as a defense of the essential connection between women and cattle that underpinned Xhosa order. Xhosaness was violently inscribed upon flesh in a statement about the control of women's bodies—but this registered for Bisset only as broad, abstract savagery. As Jill Lepore has noted in the North American context, "ritual cruelty is a symbolic language that can be 'read'"—although neither Bisset nor other British observers seem to have been able to do so.[28] The failure of colonial officials to comprehend the specific meanings attached to violence means that, in order to get at those meanings, historians must extrapolate, think imaginatively, and situate the events of the 1834–35 war within larger historical patterns.

The gendered violence of the 1834–35 war foreshadows later accounts of Xhosa men forcing Fingo women to act out their equivalence to cattle.[29] It also echoes earlier patterns of hostile behavior. Bowker's account of Xhosa men "butcher[ing]" Fingo suggests no understanding either of the aptness of his word choice nor of the fact that the cutting off of a Fingo woman's ears and nose might indicate something more than mindless cruelty.[30] Yet in the years preceding the war, Xhosa raiding parties had mutilated those colonial livestock they were unable to take with them. In at least one instance, this mutilation included ears "cut off close to the socket."[31] The precision of Xhosa violence remains—for the moment, at least—only partly legible, but it points in the direction of a brutal "conversation" regarding the relationship between women and ethnic identity.

Women themselves certainly participated in this conversation. Bowker wrote of an incident that took place near Fort Beaufort in early June 1835, only a few weeks after the "Emancipation": "Alarm at the Fingo huts. The men run out of the fort to help. It turns out to be a family broil. One of the Fingoes was only giving his wife a hiding upon which she began to squall out 'Kaffeli' (i.e., Kaffirs) [a colonial term for the Xhosa]."[32] The woman apparently believed that her identification as Fingo, as distinct from and opposed to Xhosa, offered her some protection from domestic violence. She seems further to have expected the British to enforce her understanding of the implications of Fingoness. Bowker doesn't seem to have taken seriously this implicit claim, but despite his dismissive attitude, the arrival of white men on the scene may well have diffused the conflict or distracted the abusive husband, at least temporarily. The unique position of the Fingo in the Cape Colony meant that British colonial authority became a potential factor in intrahousehold disputes, a fact that might have made migration an appealing prospect for women.

It is possible, furthermore, that the choice to call out "Kaffeli" was not simply a matter of drawing the attention of British soldiers. The woman may in fact have been describing her husband as a "Kaffir," meaning his behavior was something associated with the patriarchal strictures of Xhosaland, or at least with a particular articulation of Xhosaness against which the British were fighting. She must have been aware, too, of the derogatory and emasculating tone of the word "Kaffir" when deployed by white men against African ones. Settler Arthur Phillips wrote in 1823 that "[Kaffir] is an Arabian word for Infidel or Bad Man, and they themselves frequently so apply it."[33] Given the woman's apparent expectation that white men should protect her from domestic violence, her use of their epithet might be read as mocking or calling into question the manhood of her husband and the British soldiers alike. This anecdote suggests that the move to the colony might have seemed like an emancipation to some women, although a kind of emancipation very different from the one Benjamin D'Urban and his British compatriots had in mind. Sadly, it also hints at the extent to which women's expectations regarding Fingo identity and its implications would be disappointed in coming years.

Conclusion:
Women's Agency in the "Emancipation"

These sources on the "Fingo Emancipation" demonstrate both the challenge and the potential for writing women into early nineteenth-century ethnicity. Against the loud and potentially overpowering discourses of masculinity, evidence of female agency and experience seems to be hidden in plain sight, at least in moments of transition. There can be little doubt that women and their roles in family and production were at the very center of what it meant to be Xhosa or Fingo in 1835 and in the following decades. This is evidenced by women's centrality in the migration into the colony, by the emphasis on agriculture in Xhosa/Fingo conflict, and by the gendered ritual violence that sometimes arose from that conflict. Despite the assumptions, expectations, and agendas of male chroniclers, the colonial archive can be used to sketch a narrative its authors may never have imagined.

Ethnic communities in the early nineteenth-century Eastern Cape depended upon female bodies—as wealth, as labor, as symbols. The meanings of Xhosaness and Fingoness hinged on the question of how women fit into networks of economic and political power, even as African and European men alike understood them as incapable of wielding such power. Yet women were not the passive vessels or victims of ethnicity and its associated conflicts. Their actions, and the resulting reactions, not only appear in the colonial archive but also appear often enough and in enough detail to suggest a pattern. The archival extracts analyzed here point to the conclusion that women pursued their own agendas in and around the "Emancipation." Women were key agents—perhaps *the* key agents—in the creation of Fingo ethnicity as a distinct identity.

NOTES

1. Jacques Derrida, *Archive Fever: A Freudian Impression* (Chicago: University of Chicago Press, 1995).

2. Lynn Schler, "Writing African Women's History with Male Sources: Possibilities and Limitations," *History in Africa* 31 (2004): 319.

3. This essay uses "Fingo" instead of the more common "Mfengu" to highlight the constructed and contingent nature of this ethnic identity. Mfengu has been associated with anthropological attempts by both the colonial and the apartheid state to define the group as a genealogically connected "tribe."

4. Poppy Fry, "Siyamfenguza: The Creation of Fingo-ness in South Africa's Eastern Cape, 1800–1835," *Journal of Southern African Studies* 36, no. 1 (March 2010): 25–40; Richard Moyer, "A History of the Mfengu of the Eastern Cape, 1815–1865" (PhD diss., University of London, 1970), 516.

5. Premesh Lalu, *The Deaths of Hintsa: Postapartheid South Africa and the Shape of Recurring Pasts* (Cape Town: Human Sciences Research Council, 2009), 62; Dror Wahrman, *The Making of the Modern Self: Identity and Culture in Eighteenth-Century England* (New Haven, CT: Yale University Press, 2004), 306.

6. An important example at the beginning of the 1834–35 war can be found in the war diary of Thomas Holden Bowker, transcribed by Mary Layard Mitford-Barberton and published in Ivan Mitford-Barberton, *Cmdt. Holden Bowker: An 1820 Settler Book Including Unpublished Records of the Frontier Wars* (Cape Town: Human and Rousseau, 1970), 99.

7. Basil Le Cordeur, ed., *The Journal of Charles Lennox Stretch* (Cape Town: Maskew, Miller, Longman, 1988), 46.

8. Thomas Pringle, *Narrative of a Residence in South Africa* (Cape Town: C. Stuik, 1966), 287.

9. Carlo Ginzburg, *The Cheese and the Worms: The Cosmos of a Sixteenth-Century Miller* (Baltimore, MD: Johns Hopkins University Press, 1980); Emmanuel Le Roy Ladurie, *Montaillou: The Promised Land of Error* (New York: Braziller, 1978); Natalie Zemon Davis, *The Return of Martin Guerre* (Cambridge, MA: Harvard University Press, 1983).

10. Katherine J. Oderbeck, "Archives of the Unbuilt Environment: Documents and Discourses of Imagined Space in Twentieth-Century Kohler, Wisconsin," in *Archive Stories: Facts, Fictions, and the Writing of History*, ed. Antoinette Burton (Durham, NC: Duke University Press, 2005), 270–71.

11. J. B. Peires, *The House of Phalo: A History of the Xhosa People in the Days of Their Independence* (Berkeley: University of California Press, 1981), 8–9; Henry Lichtenstein, *Travels in Southern Africa in the Years 1803, 1804, 1805, and 1806*, trans. Anne Plumptre (Cape Town: Van Reibeeck Society, 1928), 369.

12. Pringle, *Narrative*, 285 (capitalization in original).

13. Una Long, ed., *The Chronicle of Jeremiah Goldswain* (Cape Town: Van Reibeeck Society, 1946), 193.

14. Nancy Jacobs, "Environment, Production and Social Difference in the Kalahari Thornveld, c. 1750–1830," *Journal of Southern African Studies* 25, no. 3 (September 1999): 361, 372.

15. Fry, "Siyamfenguza."

16. Hildegarde H. Fast, ed., *The Journal and Selected Letters of William Shrewsbury 1826–1835, First Missionary to the Transkei* (Johannesburg: University of the Witwatersrand Press, 1994), 11.

17. Long, *Goldswain*, 101–2.

18. Inga Clendinnen, *Ambivalent Conquests: Maya and Spaniard in Yucatan, 1517–1570* (Cambridge: Cambridge University Press, 1988), 132.

19. Alan Webster, "Unmasking the Fingo," in *The Mfecane Aftermath: Reconstructive Debates in Southern African History*, ed. Carolyn Hamilton (Johannesburg: University of the Witwatersrand Press, 1995), 241–76.

20. Alan Lester, *Imperial Networks: Creating Identities in Nineteenth-Century South Africa and Britain* (London: Routledge, 2001).

21.   Alan Webster, "Land Expropriation and Labour Extraction under Cape Colonial Rule: The War of 1835 and the 'Emancipation' of the Fingo" (master's thesis, Rhodes University, 1991), 154. For the most widely circulated version of Webster's argument, see Webster, "Unmasking the Fingo."

22.   Long, *Goldswain*, 63.

23.   *The Trial of Andries Botha* (Cape Town: Saul Solomon and Company, 1852), 14.

24.   Caesar Andrews, *Reminiscences of the Kafir War 1834–1835* (Port Elizabeth, 1877), 40.

25.   Andrews, *Reminiscences*, 23; Mitford-Barberton, *Bowker*, 121.

26.   The sacrificial process is described in J. B. Peires, *The Dead Will Arise: Nongqawuse and the Great Xhosa Cattle-Killing Movement of 1856–57* (Johannesburg: Ravan Press, 1989), 105. Jeremiah Goldswain also includes a detailed, if not terribly articulate, account of ritual slaughter in his *Chronicle*. Recorded in Long, *Goldswain*, 104.

27.   Maj. Gen. John Bisset, *Sport and War, or Recollections of Fighting and Hunting in South Africa from the Years 1834–1867* (London: John Murray, 1875), 19–21.

28.   Jill Lepore, *The Name of War: King Philip's War and the Origins of American Identity* (New York: Vintage Books, 1999), 118.

29.   F. Lucas, report, 12 May 1842, LG 440; and William Elliot to the Civil Commissioner, Uitenhage, 27 November 1843, LG 592, both in Cape Archives, Cape Town.

30.   Mitford-Barberton, *Bowker*, 129.

31.   Arthur Keppel-Jones, ed., *Phillips, 1820 Settler, His Letters* (Pietermaritzburg: Shuter and Shooter, 1960), 136.

32.   Mitford-Barberton, *Bowker*, 141.

33.   Keppel-Jones, *Phillips*, 200.

4

New African Marriage and Panethnic Politics in Segregationist South Africa

MEGHAN HEALY-CLANCY

"How can we build Africa when we regard each other as aliens?" In early 1942, a journalist posed this question to readers of the *Bantu World*, a Johannesburg newspaper with a national circulation. This question did not emerge in front-page reporting on a political convention. Nor did it appear in an editorial treatise against "tribalism." It was not posed by a prominent political leader like Dr. Alfred Xuma of the African National Congress (ANC), a frequent contributor on similar themes. Rather, this big question appeared in the newspaper's "women's pages" in a column by "Miss Rahab S. Petje," an urbane young writer who would soon be attracted to the African National Congress Youth League in Johannesburg.[1] Her column focused on a more immediate challenge than building Africa: "why we modern girls find it so very difficult to get married." She blamed "barbarism and backwardness in our parents, and worse still, segregation": she complained that parents, particularly "uneducated" parents, discouraged otherwise ideal unions between young women like herself, "an educated Mosotho lady," and eligible young men who were "Zulu B.A.'s, Xosa B.A.'s, etc."[2] She urged parents to accept interethnic pairings between "educated" youth so that their daughters might become proud "mothers of Africa" rather than "old maids" or "fallen girls."[3]

Scholars of South African political history have paid much attention to contemporary discourses of panethnic (often called pan-"tribal" at the time) unity staged at political conventions and in newspaper editorials—discourses usually issued by men.[4] Indeed, scholars have characterized women as marginal to

African nationalist politics before the 1943 formation of the African National Congress Women's League.[5] Political histories have generally neglected to explore the political interpolation of private life in public culture that was also characteristic of the 1930s and 1940s, which Petje's writing exemplifies. Scholars of gender history have likewise foregrounded other crosscutting issues uniting or dividing women—particularly race and class—without paying sustained attention to gendered modes of claiming (or rejecting) ethnicity, as Jill E. Kelly's chapter in this volume discusses.[6]

Building on the revisionist insights of this volume, this chapter explores how mission-educated men and women broadcast marital narratives as panethnic political discourses of race making and nation building. I first situate this complicated class of writers and readers within segregationist South Africa, where they were known as "New Africans." I elucidate the stakes of Petje's writing about interethnic marriage by examining the racial, gendered, and class politics of New African public culture, particularly of the women's pages of the *Bantu World*. I then turn to the marital memoirs of a consummate New African couple, the ANC activist Zachariah Keodirelang Matthews and his educator wife, Frieda Bokwe Matthews. Composed, revised, and published between the early 1950s and the mid-1990s, these memoirs reveal a prominent New African woman's authority in mediating ethnic affiliations to create and write about a New African family. For both Petje and Matthews, writing about interethnic marriage enabled them to assert that the making of racial consciousness was a project in which women were integral.

New African Men and Women
in Segregationist South Africa

The prototypical New African, who was referred to by that name in the African press at least as far back as 1928, had a Christian mission education, cosmopolitan interests, and a sense of racial consciousness. This racial consciousness united people categorized as "native" or "Bantu" from across the Union of South Africa as *Africans*. These Africans claimed ties to other Africans across the continent and in the diaspora at the same time as they made specific rights claims on the basis of their belonging in the Union of South Africa. The New African was connected to the visions of a "New Negro" summoned by the African American intellectual Alain Locke and his colleagues in the mid-1920s, which heralded a "renaissance" of black cultural expression that would enable both collective political empowerment and individual psychological liberation from racism.[7] The "talented tenth" of educated black leaders invoked by Locke's colleague W. E. B. Du Bois did not have a serious equivalent in South Africa, as I will discuss. The New Negro thus entered South Africa as a figure from another "temporality": the tiny and tenuous class of mission-educated black South Africans looked to Locke's New Negro as a vision of their future selves.[8] Marcus Garvey's Universal Negro Improvement Association was also a vector for the translation of a more militant New Negro into black South African public culture. In 1926, the organ of the Cape branch of the ANC, the *African World*, claimed that "the UNIA created the New Negro. . . . The New Negro is a problem to those who do not understand him. They do not know what to do with him. But he knows what to do with himself. He is going to blast his way to complete independence and nationhood."[9]

The New African, like the New Negro, emerged as a multivalent icon that linked cultural, psychological, and political struggles. R. V. Selope Thema, a journalist who had cut his teeth on the ANC's *Abantu Batho* before becoming the editor of the *Bantu World* in 1932, first described the New African as a cosmopolitan thinker in the Johannesburg newspaper *Umteteli wa Bantu*: "Although the colour line is at present fenced with racial barbed wires yet there is no racial bar which prevents the mind of the new African from appropriating the intellectual and spiritual heritage of civilised mankind," he contended.[10] To indicate what he meant by "civilised mankind," he notably quoted Du Bois: "Across the color line I move arm in arm with Balzac and Dumas."[11] In his own "humble residence" in inner-city Johannesburg, Thema added, he had recently "enjoyed the company of Tagore the Indian Poet, Koo the Chinese social reformer, and Kagawa the Japanese Author. It is wonderful, this mental fellowship with men of other races and other lands—And who can prevent it?" But Thema emphasized that "the awakening of the African is not only seen in the field of learning" but also seen "in the ordinary occupations of life; in the farming and mining industries, in the factories and in the workshops. The New African is a creature that is emerging from oppression with vigour and vitality. He looks the white man in the face, and laughs at his puny efforts to fight against God's scheme of Creation. . . . The African has a force which conquers the chains of slavery and the iniquity of oppression, and that force is contained in the sunshine of his smile."[12] In his shift from the pleasures of cosmopolitan texts to the pleasures of antiracist struggle, Thema exemplifies the ambiguities of the New African as an avatar of racial modernity: bookish but populist, forceful but smiling, appealing to *Umteteli*'s predominantly black readership without terrifying its white owners at the Chamber of Mines.

The New African developed over the next decade as a figure that combined ethnic pride, and sometimes even ethnic chauvinism, with a commitment to panethnic unity in daily living and in politics. Zulu history and identity particularly appealed to many New Africans, especially in Natal.[13] But as historian

Shula Marks has emphasized, it was hardly the case that these mission-educated people sought "an unconditional return to 'tribal' life."[14] Far from it. While ethnic consciousness could facilitate cultural pride and stave off intraethnic class tensions while making the most of segregationist policies for black communities in the short term, New African leaders argued that "tribalism" was ultimately inimical to liberation from white domination. As the leaders of the panethnic All-African Convention put it in 1937, "The Africans are urged to close their ranks and pool their intellectual and material resources for the emancipation of their race from the thralldom of European oligarchy.... Your salvation depends on the unity of all the tribes."[15] As the next chapter in this volume describes in East Africa in the same period, African racial consciousness clearly emerged not as an inevitable point of commonality in a context of ethnicized colonial administration but as a strategic mode of affiliation. Anton Lembede, who became the first president of the ANC Youth League in 1944, stressed in 1945 that "all Africans must be converted from tribalism to African Nationalism which is a higher step or degree of self-expression and self-realisation of the African spirit."[16] That same year, the journalist and public intellectual Herbert Dhlomo thus described the New African in distinction to the "Tribal African" or the "Neither-Nor African": while the "Tribal African" eschewed racial solidarity, the latter neither took pride in his heritage nor understood the possibilities of African national politics. In sharp contrast,

> the New African knows where he belongs and what belongs to him; where he is going and how; what he wants and the methods to obtain it. Such incidents as workers' strikes; organised boycotts; mass defiance of injustice—these and many others are but straws in the wind heralding the awakening of the New African masses. What is this New African's attitude? Put briefly and bluntly, he wants a social order where every South African will be free to express himself and his personality fully, live and breathe freely, and have a part in shaping the destiny of his country; a social order in which race, colour and creed will be a badge neither of privilege nor of discrimination.[17]

Dhlomo's invocation of the "New African masses" reveals the fundamentally transformative ambitions of the tenuous cultural class of educated Africans to which he belonged: he sought not just unity among elites but rather a just society.

The prominent New Africans discussed have all been male. But women also harbored gendered versions of these transformative ambitions. Charlotte Maxeke, the American-educated leader of the Bantu Women's League and the National Council of African Women, brought models of African American women's achievements onto South African shores; she also initiated the historic union between an independent South African church movement and the

African Methodist Episcopal (AME) Church.[18] Lillian Tshabalala followed Maxeke's path to the United States and an AME school in Ghana, returning to Natal in 1930 to launch the Daughters of Africa as a national women's club movement based on African American models. The organizing work of such New African women also encouraged women to think broadly about their place in South Africa and the world and to transform that world. But New African women's public authority issued pointedly from their domestic authority. In a 1936 *Bantu World* piece, Tshabalala characteristically argued, "The typical clubwoman is a home woman who has found that she cannot isolate her home from her community, government and social [life], and that health conditions also invade its sanctuary, and that in order to protect her brood she must go out from its walls for part of her time and do her best to make government and social order and physical conditions as fine as possible, that they may upbuild and not destroy."[19] In meetings with domestic workers, teachers, and nurses around rural and urban Natal and Johannesburg in the 1930s and 1940s, the Daughters of Africa promoted "communications that are extensive of the home," as members summoned their domestic authority to build nursery schools, develop savings schemes, and protest injustices, from pass laws to high transport fares.[20]

Scholars have highlighted how New African nationalist organizing excluded women. Most usefully, historian Natasha Erlank has pointed out that while African politics had historically been rooted in patriarchal relations, the liberal tradition on which early African nationalist politics drew was predicated on a "fraternal contract" between men. While the first tradition subordinated women, the latter had historically excluded them.[21] Erlank focuses on how men's patriarchal and fraternal ideals legitimated women's marginalization from male-led politics. But she neglects to explore the political consequences of the space that New African men ceded to New African women in engaging domestic issues in public culture.

Precisely because men saw women's roles as "managers of the house" as a key sign of racial modernity, they had to support women's expanding authority over homes and the community institutions emanating from them.[22] Dhlomo emphasized that "the civics of any country begin in the home," urging women to engage with "self-improvement" societies to nurture proud, self-sufficient families.[23] Comments such as "the question of happy marriage is of supreme importance to a civilised nation, because peace and prosperity of nations depends on happy homes" were not uncommon in the press.[24] A *Bantu World* letter on girls' education highlighted New African men's encouragement of women's domestic authority as an indicator and force of progress:

A girl is more clever than a man, and if she has been highly educated she becomes the greatest asset to the man that she marries, for a girl with a trained mind knows well how to manage her household, to take care of the husband and the children. . . . When a girl is uneducated she is the greatest drawback in the family, and the family retrogrades, instead of progressing and generally the family does not attain any highest civilization as the case would be if she had been an educated girl. . . . Girls must be highly educated even above education which a man has, because she has great work to do in the family, more important than of a man. . . . The girls are in reality involved in a great drama of human improvement.[25]

New African women, of course, often used their education precisely to escape their "great work" at home, but they authorized their public engagements in terms of racial service. For instance, a recent college graduate named Pumla Ngozwana spoke before a panethnic group of high school girls in 1935 in an address that the *Bantu World* reproduced in full. "Before the emancipation of women who ever heard of a woman leaving her home and going about giving lectures?" she said of her own engagement. "That was an unknown thing. Her place was the home and nowhere else. Yet we have good examples of Bantu women who are devoting their lives to the service of their people." Through service such as delivering uplifting lectures, she urged, "race consciousness is another of the qualities we have to develop. . . . We must work for a time when we shall all be just Africans or Bantu people without being too conscious of our various groups."[26] Women did not see their efforts to build "the race" as ancillary to the unifying work of male-led and male-dominated groups like the ANC but rather as central. In a Johannesburg meeting of the Daughters of Africa in 1942, for example, "Mrs. W. M. J. Nhlapo, B.A.," gave an address titled "Women in the Centre of Things." In this address, which also appeared in the *Bantu World*, she stressed that "the African woman" should focus on "emancipating herself from the age-long inferiority complex born of the age-long idea . . . [that] her place is that of remaining and toiling in the home." But she should also take on the "task of seeing in the home, not an institution of a menial character, but the anvil on which men and women are to be shaped. Destroy the homes, you have destroyed the very life of a people."[27]

New African marriages, as partnerships between men and women with gendered ideas of sociopolitical transformation, were accordingly also in a state of transformation. Marriage, prior to the coming of colonial capitalism in southern Africa, had been the foundation of an economy premised on homestead-based agricultural production and pastoralism: it was far from a private or individualistic institution. It was through marriage gifts of cattle—known variously as *lobolo*, *lobola*, *bogadi*, *bohali*, or bridewealth—that men brought wives into their new homesteads, and it was through women's labors as mothers and agricultural workers that these homesteads survived.[28] As historian Jeff Guy has stressed, "This control and appropriation of the productive and reproductive capacity of women was central to the structure of southern Africa's precapitalist societies. It was *the* social feature upon which society was based."[29] Marriage was a socially integral institution predicated on the unions of not only families and homesteads but also polities. As historian Paul Landau has pointed out, "Agrarian South Africa before the mid-nineteenth century was built not by tribes, but by active pioneers and state-makers," and these "pioneers and state-makers" expanded their influence through ties of marriage.[30] Landau's study reminds us that the "nation-building" work of New African marriages was not a new thing but rather a new chapter in a long history of "popular politics" in which people shifted their political allegiances in pursuit of land, power, and well-being for themselves and their kin, deploying strategies that centrally included marriage.

Nonetheless, the forms of marriage that New Africans pursued and their social meanings represented a significant historical shift. Nineteenth-century missionaries had urged converts to see marriage as a union of two individuals, uniting on their own volition and creating a sanctuary from the world in which to raise Christian children.[31] Yet missionaries, in their expressed ideals and in their own models of monogamy, could not present marriage as a *strictly* private institution. For Christian social transformation to occur, missionary and convert couples had to serve, first and foremost, as radiant models: the family as sanctuary was valuable to the Christian mission not only because each family cultivated their own relationships with Christ but also because these families would inspire other women and men to follow their lead.[32] Ironically, then, missionaries' fetishism of private domesticity was accompanied by an evangelical commitment to publicizing forms of monogamous, God-fearing family life that they termed "civilized." All of this occurred in a context in which African Christians' claims to civilization fueled their self-awareness as a class and prompted some of the earliest organization under "national" banners. The private, modern family was therefore quite public at its inception.

As Christianity grew deeply rooted over the first half of the twentieth century, Africans selectively contested, took up, and reinvented missionary ideals and practices of home. This was a defensive response to the constraints of racialized land policies and restrictions on urban residence, to be sure. But it was also a creative effort to maintain some of the core relations of precolonial homesteads, which combined productive and reproductive activities and included extended kin. Upon marriage, New African women sought to lead what we might call public-private homes. New African families sought new forms of privacy, particularly against an overreaching state, but they also opened their homes to their communities and extended kin as they embraced new ideals of public service. Some even ran clinics, schools, and other social institutions out of their houses.[33] This was the context of change to which Petje's call for interethnic marriage spoke.

The Politics of Writing about Marriage in the *Bantu World*

To understand more specifically the audience to which Petje spoke, we must consider the *Bantu World* and its women's pages more closely. From its 1932 advent, the *Bantu World* had published pieces on ideals and practices of family; this content found a home in a "women's supplement" called "Marching Forward" in November 1935. As historian Les Switzer has described, the *Bantu World*'s founding heralded white advertisers' rising interest in African consumers.[34] By 1945, the white-controlled Argus group operated ten African-oriented newspapers under its Bantu Press division, including pioneering publications such as *Ilanga Lase Natal* (Natal sun) and *Imvo Zabantsundu* (Native opinion), founded by mission-educated African men in the late nineteenth and early twentieth centuries. By the transition to apartheid in 1948, *Inkundla ya Bantu* (Bantu forum, 1938–52) was the only African-owned newspaper with a national audience.[35] But the editorship of the other newspapers remained black, and their content remained multilingual. The *Bantu World* characteristically published most of its content in the mission-school lingua franca of English, but it also included translated and original content in Zulu, Xhosa, Sotho, Tswana, Venda, Tsonga, and Afrikaans. Despite what Switzer has called their "captive" position under white control, these newspapers remained sites of rich debates over race and nation—and these debates increasingly occurred in seemingly "nonpolitical" sections. In part, this was an ironic consequence of the commercial ownership structure: to attract readers and thus advertisements, these newspapers became more mass-oriented publications, including more images and reportage on social life from the 1930s.[36] The *Bantu World*'s women's pages reflect this push; letters from readers suggest that it provoked popular interest, attracting advertisers hawking a new range of gendered goods.[37] While newspapers were not a mass phenomenon in this period, they did tap into a population that was aware of the power of texts. The African literacy rate increased from 12 to 20 percent between the mid-1930s and mid-1940s: by the mid-1940s, some twenty-four thousand copies of the *Bantu World* sold each week; and staff claimed that at least five people read each issue and, significantly, that they shared its contents with nonliterate neighbors and kin.[38]

Indeed, we should be careful not to caricature this audience as too elite. Readers lacked significant economic, political, or cultural power, as the very ownership structure of the press in this period reflects. In a context in which factory or domestic workers could command higher incomes than journalists or teachers, the class histories of families and individuals were often highly varied.[39] Many black women in this period went from school to at least a spell in domestic service.[40] Some of these educated domestic workers, like the future unionist and Federation of South African Women activist Lucy Twala, wrote for the *Bantu World*. Moreover, as anthropologist Karin Barber has pointed out in her discussion of the politics of literacy across Anglophone Africa, few in this "educated elite" were as educated as they would have liked: "Literacy embodied aspiration, and aspiration was founded upon lack—a sense of personal inadequacy associated with an education perceived as incomplete."[41] Education beyond the primary level remained rare for African men in this period, and rarer still for African women, in South Africa as throughout the continent. *Bantu World* writers and readers were defined less by occupation or income than by a shared culture, defined by these formative if incomplete experiences of mission education. They were rooted in what one 1940 editorial termed "The Book World," a world in which texts and ideas mattered as indicators and engines of racial progress. "Before Africans can take their place in the league of progressive nations, our people must be taught to read," this editorial contended. "Reading makes a people rediscover themselves and the world round them, impels them not only to progress, but to expression—to live more abundantly."[42] This text assumed an existing "our people" who must "be taught to read" (by educated Africans and their allies). Literacy would enable them to "rediscover" an identity as "a people" and join "the league of progressive nations." Above all, the *Bantu World* depicted its writers and readers as part of an *uplifting* class. This self-conception reflected and reinforced the politics of proximity accompanying segregationist policies in the urban areas from which most writers and readers came. Although the *Bantu World* writers routinely evinced a sense that they were culturally superior to uneducated neighbors, they are better understood as an *evangelizing* class than an exclusive elite. The scope of their ambition and the limits of their success—in the face of challenges from both a racialized state and those in their communities who rejected their visions of progress— emerge acutely in the *Bantu World*.

The *Bantu World* is a challenging source, befitting its complicated class of writers and readers. This difficulty is enhanced by writers' common use of pseudonyms, a technique that seemed to appeal less to their desires for anonymity than to stylistic play.[43] Brothers Herbert and Rolfes Dhlomo, the most prolific journalists of this era, mastered the art of multiple monikers. One of Rolfes

Dhlomo's key noms de plume was female: when he came to the *Bantu World* in his early thirties, he took on the role of "Editress" of the women's pages. This publication was therefore "predicated on fictions of racial and gendered autonomy": black run but white owned, even its women's section was under male control.[44] These fictions make it difficult to unearth women's voices from layers of representation, suggesting why scholars have generally not looked to press sources to understand gendered relations.[45]

In this compromised context, we can nonetheless see that Petje and other young women articulated ideas that placed pressure on men—although they couched these demands in the language of patriarchy, reflecting the constraints of the discourse in which they wrote. Petje, for instance, called men out for disrespectful conduct, appealing to chivalry: "Woman is and has to be the centre of admiration and respect. . . . We see today women disgraced, degraded, shunned and neglected, and even robbed of their lives by so called gallants of today," she contended in "Do Women Deserve Inconsideration?"[46] In her 1933 piece "Husbands Should Encourage Their Wives to Take Interest in Life," Miss Maria C. T. Piliso criticized any man who subordinated his wife's career interests to her domestic responsibilities, demonstrating his desire to control his wife's labor in the mode of a traditional head of homestead: "As lovers, [men] were full of generous impulses [and] talked of the equality of the sexes, and a wife's right to lead as free an existence as her husband, but the marriage ceremony is hardly over before tradition asserts itself, and out comes the old, old catch phrase—sometimes disguised by modern slang—'A woman's place is in her home.'" Behind modern marriages predicated on choice, she suggested, lurked patriarchy. She argued that such restrictions were a vestige of a tradition that should be cast off in the march of modern progress: "A good many of husbands in their hearts would agree with me that, in this modern world and judged by modern standards, it is utterly fallacious." Men persisted in trying to control their wives, she suggested, because they feared that if they do not, "they themselves may very well wake up one day to find that they have been dislodged from their position—a courtesy position, assigned to them by custom, seldom won in fair fight—as head of the household." Yet as soon as Piliso suggested the possibility of a new domestic order in which authority would be premised on merit rather than gender, she acknowledged that this order would emerge only through the agency of men in their current roles as heads of household. "My husband must insist on me continuing my career. Because if I do, I will be so much more sympathetic about his work," she contended. "Moreover, my being a worker myself, my own mind will be so attuned, my brain so organised to understand and cope with modern problems, that in moments of crisis he shall be able to ask my advice." In closing, she avowed, "I hope my husband will do everything in his power to help me in the pursuit of my career, broadening of my experience, the development of personality. Whatever other accusations I may be in a position to lure at my husband's head, I shall not be able to accuse him of being a tyrant, chaining me all day long to our home's front door. I shall belong to myself, not him, nor to my home, nor again my children, but entirely and absolutely to myself. I shall be free."[47] While at first glance her claim to freedom was startlingly redolent of liberal individualism, it was imbricated within an assumption that women still must convince their husbands of women's right to work, as men still mediated between women and the world of wage labor. The type of women's labor ideal for New African families was implied in the accompanying photograph of "Mrs. R. W. Msimang, Orlando district nurse," the paradigmatic profession of racial service.[48] Whether these narrative strategies most fully reflected Piliso's own views or were limited by the vision of the "Editress," their effect was to underscore the contestations in which New African marriage was enmeshed—debates that would deepen over the next decade as women's urban settlement and public presence increased.[49]

At least some men were clearly embracing ideals of companionate marriage over the course of the 1930s: one reader's 1937 "New Marriage Pledge" for men began, "I Promise: That I will adjust myself to the new status of woman and treat my wife as a partner and not as a chattel!" The vows concluded with a confirmation of marriage as a profession: "That I will look on marriage not as a lottery or a necessary evil or convenience of living but as a splendid art which it is every man's privilege to practice. That I will work for success of my marriage as I would for a career and not expect result in a minute or triumph in a DAY."[50] Petje was one of many women to endorse this vocational construction of marriage: in her "Civilisation and Matrimony," for instance, Petje made an "appeal to African women who are single like me," urging her readers to see that "marriage is a job. It requires brains and stamina from both parties. It does not mean a soft place for the woman, and a fool's paradise for the man. It needs strength, generosity and honesty, and human understanding." She affirmed that women bore particular responsibility for making companionate marriages work, as "women are the integrity of home, while men are just big babies that still have to be nursed and petted; not only in the sentimental point of view, but also in the economical point of view."[51] The endurance and reinvention of patriarchy within companionate marriage manifested more plainly in contributions from men. In a typical 1937 letter to the editor, one Eccles B. Mathabathe warned that youth were entering into marriage too lightly—a common complaint among male and female writers. He affirmed that modern marriage should be "a business run by two partners—wife and husband." But he emphasized women's contributions to this partnership most heavily: "Less time than before marriage should be spent in amusements and more time devoted to the improvement of her home. She should attend to or supervise household affairs, stitch her hubby's torn shirts and trousers, mend his socks and then and only then will she find that she has little or no time for gossip and amusements."[52] As Mathabathe's pedantic tone suggested, New African men could still regard themselves as the ultimate authorities atop a domestic hierarchy, despite women's invocations of their management of the house to justify their public engagements.

Over heated discussions of love, sex, and marriage lurked racial questions—not only political and cultural questions of what historian Lynn Thomas has called "racial respectability" but also questions animated by *eugenic* anxieties.[53] Concerns about failed motherhood were often rendered in biological terms, as "Editress" Rolfes Dhlomo's writings typify. Under the alias "X.Y.Z." in 1939, for instance, Dhlomo argued, "A woman must be chaste, for by her chastity she insures well for the future of her progeny, and hence for the social and moral uplift and advance of her nation. If a woman fails to do this, then she spells ruination for her people, and hence she's a murderer and a traitor." He was warning not only that women's reproductive health would shape the biological fitness of her children (and "her nation") but also that women's conduct would shape the moral fiber of her children (and "her nation"). He claimed that "a woman who indulges in foul talk" is "slaying her race, and has no business to be alive"; she "is sure to produce an offspring of swearing reprobates and brigands." Women's smoking and acting "too modern" should also be "stamped out ruthlessly," for such a mother would "ruin her race." He emphasized that women's "natural responsibility over their offspring and race" gave them an "unalterable influence" in shaping model youth or in "sowing the seeds of savagery in the poor innocent offspring."[54] In Petje's warning about stunted interethnic courtships leading to women's "degeneration," we see how her writing similarly naturalized the politics of marriage as a politics of racial salvation.

The article in which Petje asked, "How can we build Africa when we regard each other as aliens?" bore a revealing title: "Segregation and Unsociable Mothers and Fathers." Conversations about unmarried women in the *Bantu World* often accused these "modern girls" of being "too independent" to pursue marriage seriously.[55] But Petje suggested that the "many old maids found about town"—"most" of whom were "fallen girls" heading for "degeneration"—really did not "want to be degenerates." The problem, she claimed, was instead that "uneducated" parents did not trust their daughters to pursue uplifting New African marriages. She walked readers through a nightmare courtship scenario between a "very prominent and outstanding Zulu B.A." who was humiliated by the parents of his Sotho girlfriend "for the simple reason that he is a Zulu." Petje complained, "They actually have no pride in their daughters and they even have no thought that the Zulu ogre may in other ways raise them to the standard they could never have reached had she married a Mosotho drunkard. The same thing happens even amongst Zulus, Xosa parents, etc., who regard Basutos as aliens and therefore are not fit to marry their daughters or sons." She particularly urged mothers not to see themselves as part of a "more advanced nation" than their daughters' suitors, emphasizing that the "pride and salvation of a mother depends on a daughter's sound marriage."[56] To create New African families, Petje suggested, youth who had been educated at pan-ethnic mission schools and socialized in diverse urban spaces needed to educate their parents to see "the nation" in more expansive terms. That is, Petje wanted parents to see education as a more distinctive marker of status than lineage—against the inclinations of even many Christians toward older patterns of prestige, as chapter 6 in this volume discusses for the Ndebele. Petje argued that women—both daughters and mothers—were central to this process of building an African consciousness because they were central to biological and social reproduction: it was young women who "would one day be mothers of Africa," and it was their mothers who must ensure that their daughters raised children with "prominent and outstanding" New African men. Although the print culture in which she worked was multiply constrained, writing about inter-ethnic marriage enabled Petje to make space for a gendered vision of New African politics in which domestic hierarchies should be more flexible and empowering to young women as a matter of racial progress. But how did women navigate domestic hierarchies to build New African families? Memoirs of a New African marriage address this complex question.

The Politics of Marital Memoirs:
Frieda and Z. K. Matthews

In a 1935 speech at Adams College outside of Durban, Z. K. Matthews addressed the "tribal" spirit among educated South Africans. He stressed that reports of African "detribalization" had been exaggerated, as elements of "the old political organization of the tribe" endured in mission-educated Africans' homes—in relationships of respect and hierarchy in families, and especially in courtship and marriage practices. Matthews underscored that national consciousness would be attained not by the erasure of ethnic consciousness but by the incorporation of ethnic pride into a broader racial movement: "Hence the growing movement among educated South African natives for the promotion of a larger unity which will give full place to the peculiar traditions of each tribe and yet make possible co-operation between different tribes for their mutual benefit.

Education, properly conceived, far from being a detribalizing instrument, could be made the chief integrative factor between natives of all types, rural and urban, educated and uneducated, tribal and non-tribal."[57]

To understand where Matthews's national vision came from, we might look to his professional biography. He was born in 1901 near the diamond-mining center of Kimberley. His parents were Tswana-speaking Christians from modest economic backgrounds—his father worked on the mines then as a shop clerk, and his mother was a domestic servant. But the family had strong connections to nationalist politics—founding member of the ANC Sol Plaatje was Matthews's cousin. Matthews attended high school at Lovedale Missionary Institute, the bastion of New African schooling in the Cape.[58] He was the first African to earn a bachelor's degree in South Africa, graduating from the South African Native College at Fort Hare in 1923. He then became the first African head of the high school at Adams College in 1925. In 1930, he became the first African to complete the bachelor of laws degree from the University of South Africa, which he followed with a master's degree from the program "Race Relations and Culture Contact" at Yale and then a year's study with Bronisław Malinowski at the London School of Economics. In 1936, he was appointed a lecturer in law and anthropology at Fort Hare. He was also active in nationalist politics as a force behind the All-African Convention in the mid-1930s and then as ANC provincial president for the Cape in the late 1940s and early 1950s; in 1956, along with his son Joe and 154 other leading anti-apartheid activists from diverse backgrounds, he would stand in the famous Treason Trial. After his acquittal, he resigned from Fort Hare to protest its classification as an apartheid institution for Xhosa-speaking students.

Matthews's personal life also shaped his vision of education as a force for panethnic unity: his schooling led directly to his own marriage to a woman raised in a Xhosa-speaking home. His paternal line hailed from the Bamangwato chiefdom in present-day Botswana, which his grandfather and namesake Zachariah Keodirelang Matthews left following a succession dispute to settle with the related Barolong chiefdom in Thaba Nchu, near the politically vibrant city of Bloemfontein. His maternal line was Barolong royalty. When he was a boy, his mother "would tell us story after story about people in our family and Barolong history." At Lovedale, he remained connected to that heritage, as there he forged a lifelong friendship with his classmate, future Bamangwato regent Tshekedi Khama.[59] But also, he explained,

as I look back on it now, it seems that the most valuable experience at Lovedale was the intimate contact it provided among boys and girls from different groups and different parts of the country. This contact rubbed away whatever I still had of the strange notions one grows up with about members of groups with different languages and customs. I got to know some of these languages, Xhosa and Zulu. I made fast friends with boys of these other peoples and learned through them that my own Tswana were not the only true humans in the universe.[60]

Students made these connections despite their residence halls and sports teams, which school leaders structured by language group—a reflection of missionaries' tribalizing tendencies, despite the connections that their institutions also structured.

One of the most important relationships of Matthews's life was forged across these boundaries. "If anybody had told me when I entered Lovedale that I would marry a Xhosa-speaking girl, I would have said he was talking nonsense. But that is precisely what I did," he recollected.[61] He met the young Frieda Bokwe, also a Lovedale and then a Fort Hare student, through her older brother, Rosebery. The Bokwe family had been deeply rooted at Lovedale since its founding. Frieda and Rosebery's father was the remarkable composer and minister John Knox Bokwe, whose forebears had been among the first Christian converts in the region.[62] Their mother was a teacher of Mfengu origins. Matthews and Rosebery Bokwe became close friends at Lovedale. "Rosebery and I shared classes and studies and we even shared the one pair of long pants which he acquired and which—great day—I too would wear, taking turn for turn with him," Matthews recalled. He fell in love with Frieda Bokwe at a picnic on her seventeenth birthday, in 1922, but their families urged them not to rush into anything: "The customary age for marriage among Africans of our kind was much beyond that. Moreover the completion of our schooling had to come first."[63] They married in December 1928, after a three-year engagement. She was then twenty-three and held a teacher's diploma, and she was teaching at the Inanda Seminary for girls outside of Durban.

Significantly, Matthews's reflections on courtship and marriage were edited by his wife and by their friend the anthropologist Monica Hunter Wilson, a white woman raised at Lovedale. Between 1952 and 1953, Matthews recounted his memories of his youth; after his death in 1968, Frieda Bokwe Matthews and Wilson supplemented these early recollections with their accounts of his later career. The result appeared in 1981 as an unusually collective memoir: *Freedom for My People: The Autobiography of Z. K. Matthews, Southern Africa 1901 to 1968*, was billed as a "memoir by Monica Wilson," its editor. But Frieda Bokwe Matthews provided most of the narrative of their engagement and marriage in her husband's "autobiography": in brackets before this section in *Freedom for My People*, Wilson notes that "no account of his marriage was given by Z. K. in his autobiography and the following passage is taken from his wife's journal," and so Matthews's autobiography moves into Frieda's voice for the next several pages.[64] She went into more detail about their marriage in her own memoirs, which she composed for her grandchildren and then published in 1995 as *Remembrances*. In her representation of this betrothal in her memoirs and those of her husband, Frieda Bokwe Matthews positioned herself as central in mediating ethnic affiliations to create a New African family.

Growing up, Frieda Bokwe's strongest identification was with the cosmopolitan African Christian community around Lovedale and Fort Hare, as she recalled her childhood as being passed in "happy afternoons at my mother's house when young people from all parts of southern Africa would spend an hour or two to enjoy something of the homeliness which mother gave, and we girls fussed around, making tea and passing scones we all agreed were the best ever made."[65] Among their many guests was future Bamangwato regent Tshekedi Khama (14–16). She also recalled her grandmother's stories of their Mfengu heritage, but Frieda's sense of a specifically ethnic identity seems to have been subordinated to a strong African Christian identity (3). Despite the diverse home in which she was raised, she recalled the "puzzled, rather antagonistic attitude" of her kin to the arrival of Matthews's father to request Frieda's hand in marriage on his son's behalf (10). As her father had died when she was an adolescent, her uncles were in charge of these negotiations. "My mother had had to call them together to report that a visitor was coming from the land of the Tswana to take one of their daughters. One old man wanted to know where the sons of well-known Xhosa men were that a daughter of Knox/Bokwe should be married to a foreigner," she recalled. He fretted, in Frieda's presence, that she would be "thrown away to people whose ways and customs were not known" (10).

Her uncles' hostility was such that Frieda decided to stay during the negotiations to mitigate tensions. Z. K. Matthews translated between Tswana and Xhosa. The uncles nonetheless attacked the Matthews men over their English surname, which they explained derived from the missionaries who had converted Z. K. Matthews's grandfather. Then the uncles asked for the Matthewses' *isiduko*, or clan name, which alarmed Frieda: "I had never asked Zac this. We had become somewhat detribalised in our quest, as students in a brand new college, for education and a western way of life. So such questions were never asked except by the newcomers who would be laughed at and treated with scorn if heard. I knew my *Siduko*, 'MaRila' of the Bamba clan in the Ngqika tribe of the Xhosa nation, but had never been sure whether the Tswana had such traditions as ours." Much to her relief, her future father-in-law replied easily, "I am Phuti of the Ngwato tribe of Bechuanaland." She recalled that her uncles relaxed immediately, as "although this man came from a town, and although he carried a white man's name, he was an ordinary country man, knowing his past and his tribe." Her brother subsequently dismissed Frieda from the negotiations, which culminated in a plan for a small sum of *bogadi/lobola* and a "Western engagement ring" for Frieda (11–12).

Frieda Bokwe Matthews found that her husband's sense of ethnic identity was much more pronounced than her own. She reported being miffed when, after her Christian wedding ceremony on the Lovedale campus, she encountered, "seated on the green grass in front of my brother's house, crowds of traditionally dressed, in ochre-coloured robes, men and women whom I did not know. My brother told our expected guests that he had invited 'relatives' from the villages at Ncera. This is where our family had originated and where the missionaries had laboured for twenty years, trying to convert the Xhosa, but whose labours had been in vain except for the first eleven who moved with the missionaries"— her paternal ancestors (18). This historical engagement with Christianity, which introduced cleavages between "red" and "school" Xhosa, was quite different from that of the Bamangwato, whose chief Khama III had become an enthusiastic Christian two generations earlier.[66] But Frieda Bokwe Matthews emphasized that she came to accommodate their differences, seeing positive elements in her Tswana, Xhosa, and African Christian affiliations. She came to regard her "real home-in-law" as Serowe, from which the Matthews family originally came, and she settled in Botswana after her husband's death (9). She gave all of her five children both Tswana and English names in deference to her husband's concern that "their true nationality should not be obliterated. Already the surname 'Matthews' was a handicap" (21). But she also nourished her children's Xhosa and Christian identities. At home, she wrote that the "children became more Xhosa than Tswana in speech," while she and her husband spoke English to each other (27). As her friend Phyllis Ntantala tellingly remembered Frieda, "Of the African women I know, there are none as African and aware of their great African heritage as she is. And yet, on the surface, she is so English."[67]

In addition to providing insight into the ethnic negotiations of a prominent New African couple, Frieda Bokwe Matthews's memoir depicts the politics of marriage beyond her family. She expressed great interest in the marriage of Tshekedi's nephew Chief Seretse Khama to a British woman, for which he would be forced out of his chieftainship. In 1966, Seretse Khama would become independent Botswana's first president, with his wife, Ruth Williams Khama, by his side; Z. K. Matthews would serve as Botswana's ambassador to the United States. "The irony of it for me," Frieda recalled, was that shortly before the announcement of Khama's marriage, "Chief Tshekedi had read a letter to us from one of our important Xhosa chiefs, who suggested that the four great nations of southern Africa, the Tswana, Sotho, Zulu, and Xhosa, should draw closer together by intermarriage between the heirs to the thrones of each. This chief had four daughters, and he felt that the eldest should marry Seretse when he came back from England. According to African custom this was not an unusual suggestion" (26). But Chief Tshekedi refused, affirming his nephew's right to choose his wife. "I daresay he had not reckoned with the possibility that Seretse would want a white girl," Frieda noted (26). She also mentioned, in passing, her role in contracting one of the more prominent transnational New African marriages. After Christopher Kisosonkole of Uganda came "especially to us to help him find a wife, an educated one, who would be a companion and not merely a wife," she recalled, she set him up with her close friend Pumla Ngozwana (31). Their 1939 pairing anticipated ANC president Alfred Xuma's 1940 marriage to the African American teacher and clubwoman Madie Hall, whom Xuma had similarly pursued in hopes of a companionate marriage through which he could lead "the race."[68] Frieda Bokwe Matthews's marital narrative thus bolsters a broader narrative of marriage as integral to the expansion of political communities.

Conclusion

Frieda Matthews's marital narrative reads as a mirror image of Rahab Petje's nightmare courtship scenario, with which we began. While Petje complained of African families unable to bridge ethnic difference to "build Africa," Matthews depicted her marriage as a model navigation of ethnic difference, which placed her at the helm of a New African family that would take leading roles in anti-apartheid politics. In both cases, women's marital narratives wrote a politics of home firmly into African nationalism. This chapter thus contributes to a growing concern in African studies to understand the private and public politics of writing in colonial Africa.[69] This perspective has shed new light on gender historians' broader effort to understand "the term 'political' far beyond direct organized action against the colonial state and its functionaries."[70] It has shown how the effort to "build Africa" was hardly confined to the halls of male-led political organizations but was rather wrapped up in women's navigations of domestic hierarchies to assert new space for themselves in private and public. In particular, the New African women's writing explored here asserted women's *central* role in mediating ethnic difference within families to build a panethnic political community. When we reevaluate the development of New African identities through these gendered navigations of ethnicity, we see that women were as essential to the construction of racial consciousness as men. But while New African men generally worked through idioms of public community building, women focused on more intimate navigations of difference. The implications of these gendered strategies for African nationalist politics in the apartheid years demand further consideration.

NOTES

1.   Minutes and List of Those Present, 2 March 1944, file La2.3, Records of the African National Congress, Historical Papers, University of the Witwatersrand, Johannesburg.

2.   Here "Mosotho" refers to Sotho speakers in present-day South Africa and Lesotho, while Zulu and "Xosa" refer to speakers of the southern African Nguni languages Zulu and Xhosa. All of these people were then classified as "Native" or "Bantu" in South Africa.

3.   Rahab S. Petje, "Segregation and Unsociable Mothers and Fathers," *Bantu World*, 21 March 1942, 8.

4.   See, for example, Peter Limb, *The ANC's Early Years: Nation, Class and Place in South Africa before 1940* (Pretoria: Unisa Press, 2010); Richard Rive, "The Early Years," in *Seme: The Founder of the ANC*, ed. Richard Rive and Tim Couzens (Braamfontein: Skotaville, 1991), 9–35; Alan Cobley, *Class and Consciousness: The Black Petty Bourgeoisie in South Africa, 1924 to 1950* (New York: Greenwood, 1990); Tim Couzens, *The New African: A Study of the Life and Work of H. I. E. Dhlomo* (Johannesburg: Ravan, 1985); and Peter Walshe, *The Rise of African Nationalism in South Africa: The African National Congress, 1912–1952* (Berkeley: University of California Press, 1971).

5.   See, for example, Natasha Erlank, "Gender and Masculinity in South African Nationalist Discourse, 1912–1950," *Feminist Studies* 29, no. 3 (Fall 2003): 653–71; Anne McClintock, *Imperial Leather: Race, Gender, and Sexuality in the Colonial Contest* (New York: Routledge, 1995), 380; and Cherryl Walker, *Women and Resistance in South Africa*, 2nd ed. (Cape Town: David Philip, 1991), 26.

6.   This neglect of the politics of interethnic marriage in this period may reflect a foundational unease with ethnicity as an analytical category in the 1980s and 1990s, when feminist historiography began to flourish in South Africa. See Saul Dubow, "Ethnic Euphemisms and Racial Echoes," *Journal of Southern African Studies* 20, no. 3 (September 1994): 363.

7.   See Couzens, *New African*, 110–13; Ntongela Masilela, "The 'Black Atlantic' and African Modernity in South Africa," *Research in African Literatures* 27, no. 4 (Winter 1996): 88–96; and Alain Locke, *The New Negro: Voices of the Harlem Renaissance* (New York: Albert and Charles Boni, 1925).

8.   Laura Chrisman, "Black Modernity, Nationalism and Transnationalism: The Challenge of Black South African Poetry," in *Beyond the Black Atlantic: Relocating Modernization and Technology*, ed. Walter Goebel and Saskia Schabio (London: Routledge, 2006), 31.

9.   Quoted in Robert Trent Vinson, *The Americans Are Coming! Dreams of African American Liberation in Segregationist South Africa* (Athens: Ohio University Press, 2012), 100.

10.   A Wayfarer [R. V. Selope Thema], "The New African," *Umteteli wa Bantu*, 21 July 1928, 3.

11.   W. E. B. Du Bois, *The Souls of Black Folk* (Chicago: McClurg, 1903), 109.

12.   A Wayfarer, "The New African," 3.

13.   See especially Paul La Hausse, *Restless Identities: Signatures of Nationalism, Zulu Ethnicity and History in the Lives of Petros Lamula and Lymon Maling* (Pietermaritzburg: University of Natal Press, 2000).

14.   Shula Marks, "Patriotism, Patriarchy and Purity: Natal and the Politics of Zulu Ethnic Consciousness," in *The Creation of Tribalism in Southern Africa*, ed. Leroy Vail (Berkeley: University of California Press, 1989), 221.

15.   A. B. Xuma and H. Selby Msimang, "The Leaders' New Year Message," *Bantu World*, 2 January 1937, 1.

16.   Quoted in Couzens, *New African*, 260.

17.   H. I. E. Dhlomo, "African Attitudes to the European," *Democrat*, 1 December 1945, 21, 24.

18.   See James T. Campbell, *Songs of Zion: The African Methodist Episcopal Church in the United States and South Africa* (New York: Oxford University Press, 1995); and Heather Hughes, "Lives and Wives: Understanding African Nationalism in South Africa through a Biographical Approach," *History Compass* 10, no. 8 (August 2012): 562–73.

19.   C. L. Tshabalala, "What Is the Club Woman?," *Bantu World*, 4 April 1936, 12.

20.   Tshabalala, "What Is the Club Woman?" See also Meghan Healy-Clancy, "Women and the Problem of Family in Early African Nationalist History and Historiography," *South African Historical Journal* 64, no. 3 (September 2012): 450–71; John Nauright, "'I Am with You as Never Before': Women in Urban Protest Movements, Alexandra Township, South Africa, 1912–1945," in *Courtyards, Markets, City Streets: Urban Women in Africa*, ed. Kathleen Sheldon (Boulder, CO: Westview, 1996), 259–83; and Catherine Higgs, "African Women's Self-Help Organizations in South Africa, 1927–1998," *African Studies Review* 47, no. 3 (December 2004): 119–41.

21.   See Erlank, "Gender and Masculinity."

22.   I borrow the term "managers of the house" from Afsaneh Najmabadi, who has explored a similar process of women's association with domestic authority as a signal of modernist nationalism in late nineteenth-century and early twentieth-century Iran. See Afsaneh Najmabadi, *Women with Mustaches and Men without Beards: Gender and Sexual Anxieties of Iranian Modernity* (Berkeley: University of California Press, 2005). See also Susanne M. Klausen, *Race, Maternity, and the Politics of Birth Control in South Africa, 1910–1939* (New York: Palgrave Macmillan, 2004); and Lisa Pollard, *Nurturing the Nation: The Family Politics of Modernizing, Colonizing, and Liberating Egypt, 1805–1923* (Berkeley: University of California Press, 2005).

23.   H. I. E. Dhlomo, "Bantu Womanhood," *Umteteli wa Bantu*, 10 May 1930, 3.

24. Solomon J. S. Lehana, "Can Marriage Be Successful without Love?," *Bantu World*, 21 August 1937, 12.

25. S. H. D. Lee Mnyandu, "An Appeal for Educated Girls," *Ilanga Lase Natal*, 16 May 1936, 9.

26. P. E. Ngozwana, "Emancipation of Women," *Bantu World*, 18 and 25 May 1935, 13.

27. "African Women and Organisation," *Bantu World*, 1 August 1942, 8.

28. See Adam Kuper, *Wives for Cattle: Bridewealth and Marriage in Southern Africa* (London: Routledge, 1982); and Monica Wilson, "Xhosa Marriage in Historical Perspective," in *Essays on African Marriage in Southern Africa*, ed. Eileen Jensen Krige and John L. Comaroff (Cape Town: Juta, 1981), 133–47.

29. Jeff Guy, "Gender Oppression in Southern Africa's Precapitalist Societies," in *Women and Gender in Southern Africa to 1945*, ed. Cherryl Walker (Cape Town: David Philip, 1990), 40.

30. Paul S. Landau, *Popular Politics in the History of South Africa, 1400–1948* (New York: Cambridge University Press, 2010), 2.

31. See Jean Comaroff and John L. Comaroff, "Homemade Hegemony," in *Ethnography and the Historical Imagination: Selected Essays*, ed. John L. Comaroff and Jean Comaroff (Boulder, CO: Westview, 1992), 265–95; Lynn M. Thomas, "Love, Sex, and the Modern Girl in 1930s South Africa," in *Love in Africa*, ed. Lynn M. Thomas and Jennifer Cole (Chicago: University of Chicago Press, 2009), 31–57; and Isaac Schapera, *Married Life in an African Tribe* (New York: Sheridan House, 1941). See also Kristin Mann, *Marrying Well: Marriage, Status and Social Change among the Educated Elite in Colonial Lagos* (New York: Cambridge University Press, 1985); and David Parkin and David Nyamwaya, eds., *Transformations of African Marriage* (Manchester: Manchester University Press, 1987).

32. See Meghan Healy-Clancy, *A World of Their Own: A History of South African Women's Education* (Pietermaritzburg: University of KwaZulu-Natal Press, 2013).

33. Mwelela Cele, "*Eposini Elidala*: A Modern *Umuzi*," in *Ekhaya: The Politics of Home in KwaZulu-Natal*, ed. Meghan Healy-Clancy and Jason Hickel (Pietermaritzburg: University of KwaZulu-Natal Press, 2014), 247–59. See also Leslie J. Bank, *Home Spaces, Street Styles: Contesting Power and Identity in a South African City* (Johannesburg: Wits University Press, 2001).

34. Les Switzer, "*Bantu World* and the Origins of a Captive African Commercial Press," in *South Africa's Alternative Press: Voices of Protest and Resistance, 1880s–1960s*, ed. Les Switzer (New York: Cambridge University Press, 1997), 189–212.

35. See Ime Ukpanah, *The Long Road to Freedom: "Inkundla ya Bantu" (Bantu Forum) and the African Nationalist Movement in South Africa, 1938–1951* (Trenton: Africa World Press, 2005).

36. Ukpanah, *Long Road*, 7.

37. See Lynn M. Thomas, "The Modern Girl and Racial Respectability in 1930s South Africa," in *The Modern Girl around the World: Consumption, Modernity, and Globalization*, ed. Alice Weinbaum et al. (Durham, NC: Duke University Press, 2008), 96–119.

38. See Ukpanah, *Long Road*, 6; Thomas, "The Modern Girl," 97.

39. See Hughes, "Lives and Wives"; Limb, *ANC's Early Years*.

40. See Healy-Clancy, *World of Their Own*, 111–12.

41. Karin Barber, "Introduction: Hidden Innovators in Africa," in *Africa's Hidden Histories: Everyday Literacy and Making the Self*, ed. Karin Barber (Bloomington: Indiana University Press, 2006), 5.

42. "The Book World," *Bantu World*, 7 December 1940, 4. See also Bhekizizwe Peterson, "The *Bantu World* and the World of the Book: Reading, Writing, and Enlightenment," in Barber, *Africa's Hidden Histories*, 236–57.

43. See also Stephanie Newell, *The Power to Name: A History of Anonymity in Colonial West African Newspapers* (Athens: Ohio University Press, 2013).

44. See Healy-Clancy, "Women and the Problem," 463.

45. Strong exceptions are Thomas, "Love, Sex, and the Modern Girl" and "The Modern Girl"; Jon Soske, "Navigating Difference: Gender, Miscegenation and Indian Domestic Space in Twentieth-Century Durban," in *Eyes across the Water*, ed. Pamila Gupta, Isabel Hofmeyr, and Michael Person (Pretoria: University of South Africa Press, 2010), 197–219; and M. J. Daymond et al., eds., *Women Writing Africa: The Southern Region* (New York: Feminist Press, 2003).

46. Rahab S. Petje, "Do Women Deserve Inconsideration?," *Bantu World*, 4 April 1942, 8.

47. Maria C. T. Piliso, "Husbands Should Encourage Their Wives to Take Interest in Life," *Bantu World*, 20 May 1933, 10.

48. See Shula Marks, *Divided Sisterhood: Race, Class, and Gender in the South African Nursing Profession* (Johannesburg: University of the Witwatersrand Press, 1994).

49. See Thomas, "Love, Sex, and the Modern Girl" and "The Modern Girl"; Marijke Du Toit, "The General View and Beyond: From Slum-Yard to Township in Ellen Hellman's Photographs of Women and the African Familial in the 1930s," *Gender and History* 17, no. 3 (November 2005): 593–626; and Ellen Hellman, *Rooiyard: A Sociological Survey of an Urban Native Slum* (Cape Town: Oxford University Press, 1948).

50. F. S. Haiyan, "The New Marriage Pledge," *Bantu World*, 20 February 1937, 12.

51. Rahab S. Petje, "Civilisation and Matrimony," *Bantu World*, 7 March 1942, 8.

52. Eccles B. Mathabathe, "Marriage—a Partnership," *Bantu World*, 4 September 1937, 12.

53. Thomas, "The Modern Girl."

54. X.Y.Z. [Rolfes Dhlomo], "Failure of Responsibility," *Bantu World*, 14 October 1939, 9.

55. Thomas, "The Modern Girl"; see also Dorothy L. Hodgson, ed., *"Wicked" Women and the Reconfiguration of Gender in Africa* (Portsmouth, NH: Heinemann, 2001).

56. Petje, "Segregation."

57. Z. K. Matthews, "The Tribal Spirit among Educated South Africans," *Man* 35 (February 1935): 26–27.

58.   Donovan Williams, "African Nationalism in South Africa: Origins and Problems," *Journal of African History* 11, no. 3 (July 1970): 373–74.

59.   Z. K. Matthews, *Freedom for My People: The Autobiography of Z. K. Matthews, Southern Africa 1901 to 1968* (Cape Town: David Philip, 1981), 11, 16.

60.   Matthews, *Freedom for My People*, 35.

61.   Matthews, *Freedom for My People*, 36.

62.   See Grant Olwage, "John Knox Bokwe, Colonial Composer: Tales about Race and Music," *Journal of the Royal Musical Association* 131, no. 1 (2006): 1–37.

63.   Matthews, *Freedom for My People*, 40, 70.

64.   Matthews, *Freedom for My People*, 89.

65.   Frieda Matthews, *Remembrances* (Bellville: Mayibuye, 1995), 7. Hereafter cited in the text.

66.   See Paul S. Landau, *The Realm of the Word: Language, Gender and Christianity in a Southern African Kingdom* (Portsmouth, NH: Heinemann, 1995).

67.   Phyllis Ntantala, *A Life's Mosaic: The Autobiography of Phyllis Ntantala* (Berkeley: University of California Press, 1992), ix.

68.   See Iris Berger, "An African American 'Mother of the Nation': Madie Hall Xuma in South Africa, 1940–1963," *Journal of Southern African Studies* 27, no. 3 (September 2001): 547–66.

69.   For particularly strong recent work on writing and community formation in colonial Africa, see Andreana C. Prichard, "'Let Us Swim in the Pool of Love': Love Letters and Discourses of Community Composition in Twentieth-Century Tanzania," *Journal of African History* 54, no. 1 (March 2013): 103–22; Isabel Hofmeyr, *Gandhi's Printing Press: Experiments in Slow Reading* (Cambridge, MA: Harvard University Press, 2013); Jonathon Glassman, *War of Words, War of Stones: Racial Thought and Colonial Violence in Colonial Zanzibar* (Bloomington: Indiana University Press, 2011); and Susan Z. Andrade, *The Nation Writ Small: African Fictions and Feminisms, 1958–1988* (Durham, NC: Duke University Press, 2011).

70.   Jean Allman, Susan Geiger, and Nakanyike Musisi, introduction to *Women in African Colonial Histories*, ed. Jean Allman, Susan Geiger, and Nakanyike Musisi (Bloomington: Indiana University Press, 2002), 7.

5

Women and Non-ethnic Politics in East Africa, 1934–1947

ETHAN R. SANDERS

Several chapters in this volume have demonstrated that women in Africa often performed and utilized ethnicity to create advantages in local contests of power. At the same time, however, women in Africa have also found it expedient to downplay or discard ethnic identities, especially when organizing politically. The most prominent example of this is the large number of women who joined nationalist organizations in the 1950s and 1960s that intentionally reached across ethnic groupings, partially out of a desire for national liberation.[1] But during the colonial period in Africa, the political imaginations of African women were both larger and smaller than either territory or ethnicity.[2] Many of the women in this study appear uninterested in territorial issues, for instance, and were more invested in local concerns that were not intrinsically ethnic in nature. Some women, therefore, explored alternative identities that would provide them with greater agency in finding solutions to their various problems.

This chapter examines a group of women activists from Tanganyika and Zanzibar who embraced a wider and more encompassing African identity by joining the explicitly non-ethnic and non-territorial African Association of East Africa (AA) during the 1930s and 1940s. Founded in Dar es Salaam in the 1920s, the association was open to any black-skinned African regardless of territory, ethnicity, religion, wealth, education, or gender, and the leaders vehemently opposed letting any of these identities cause members to disassociate from one another. The male founders of this organization had come to conceive of Africa as a field of action and of Africans as a political community worthy of investment. They imagined an African nation to which all black-skinned people

123

of the continent belonged. The African Association not only foregrounded an African identity by opening its membership to Africans of any territory or tribe but also actively attempted to establish branches all over the continent. By the mid-1940s, it had opened dozens of chapters throughout Tanganyika and the Zanzibar Protectorate and also had a chapter in both Kenya and Uganda. A central aim of its leadership was to establish the organization as "the voice of the Africans" by creating communication links that would allow Africans, as Africans, to share their voices and opinions with colonial authorities and with other Africans. By claiming African status and joining the African Association, many African men and women were able to bypass the ethnically focused structures of British colonial rule and communicate directly with colonial authorities. For women, this feature was particularly salient and attractive, as it gave them a new outlet for solving their problems. By embracing an African identity and joining the organization, women gained a voice in the male-dominated world of colonial politics—a sphere that many historians have seen as largely closed off to women during this period.[3]

Thus, the women who joined the African Association chose to look beyond ethnicity to a larger racial construct of Africanness, and they used this identity to empower themselves in their dealings with colonial governments in their different locales. Their participation did not preclude them from a sense of belonging to an ethnic identity. Indeed, many of these women undoubtedly embraced ethnic loyalties to varying degrees and may have found such identities useful for other areas of their lives. Conversely, even though many of these women joined a community that embraced an "African" identity and conducted its politics along racial lines, this did not mean that the women were predetermined to think of themselves as Africans (this identity too had to be constructed), and their African identity may have been downplayed or discarded at other points in their lives if they felt it lost its purchase. Even though women did not have to abandon one identity for another, there were times when it was advantageous to choose to foreground a particular identity or categorical group with which women could claim commonality or connectedness. They often did this in order to increase their chance of procuring material or nonmaterial benefits (e.g., social acceptance, prestige, etc.). Such decisions were usually made with some level of awareness of the machinations of colonial politics, which implies that ethnicity and identity for women was largely situational and strategic in certain cases.[4]

The case of the women of the African Association is useful not only because it shows how and why women might choose a non-ethnic identity for empowerment but also because it illustrates how the men and women of the AA used this interethnic organization in different and gendered ways. Certainly many men embraced the African identity for similar reasons as the women—the opportunity to have their voices heard in local affairs—but the organization also provided a platform for some of the male members and leaders to promote or enforce certain gender roles based on their own conceptions of African identity. Some men wanted to use the organization to mold women according to their own vision of African womanhood. However, some of the prominent female activists of the AA publicly emphasized certain strands of the organization's ideology of gender-inclusive African unity to oblige male leaders to assist women in issues important to them, even when the male leadership was uncomfortable doing so. Thus the women of the AA used the product of the male founders' intellectual labor in constructing a particular identity of Africanness in ways different from what some of those leaders might have conceived. They did this through claiming a non-ethnic identity in circumstances that were beneficial particularly to women.

The story of the female members of the African Association has largely been invisible from the record, in spite of the fact that much has been written about the organization. Scholars have largely been silent about the scores of women who joined the organization in the 1930s and 1940s.[5] The archival material on these women and their activities is admittedly sparse, and the sources that remain are fairly androcentric, dominated by the writings of the male secretaries.[6] However, we are still able to gain an understanding of who some of these women were, how many joined, and why some of them may have wanted to take part in the organization by carefully examining the Swahili-language files kept by the organization, which included membership application forms and lists, as well as minutes of meetings. The voices and concerns of the AA's women can also be obtained through letters written at their request to colonial officials and, in very rare cases, letters that were drafted by women themselves.[7] Drawn together, these various strands provide a unique glimpse into African women's own perspective on the usefulness of ethnic—or in this case, non-ethnic—identity in colonial East Africa. Furthermore, this chapter demonstrates that the women of the African Association who embraced a non-ethnic identity were able to gain a political voice in matters important to them and that the interethnic identity espoused by the leaders of the AA was sometimes practiced in gendered ways as some male and female members utilized the organization's platform to push their own gender-specific agendas.

The African Association's Recruitment of Women

The male founders of the organization had two major motivations for including women in the organization, one ideological and the other more practical. First, the African Association saw itself as a group where all Africans could come together in unity regardless of their differences. In the words of Paul Seme, an important ideological leader of the organization, the purpose of the African Association was to "put together in one group the sons and daughters of Africa."[8] Or, as stated at an association-wide conference, the aim was for "African sons and daughters [to] endeavor to see that their Mother Africa regains her . . . glory."[9] This egalitarian strand in the organization's ideology led to the provision for allowing women to attain full membership on an equal basis with men. The equality of the sexes was laid out in the constitution, which declared that men and women "all have the same rights."[10] Such equality did not always play out in actuality, as will be demonstrated below. Beyond notions of equality and the ideological purposes for a mixed-gender organization, the men had more practical reasons for the inclusion of women in the association. The AA sought to add women to its actual constituency because AA members thought doing so would increase their political authority in the eyes of colonial policy makers. More comprehensive and encompassing membership lists gave further credence to AA male leaders' claims of representing the African community as a whole.

As a result of these motivations, there was an active campaign to recruit women starting at least as early as the foundation of the chapter in Zanzibar Town in 1934. During the organization's years of expansion in the mid-1930s, Seme explained the need for recruiting women to other nascent branches. In response to one of his letters in 1936, the new Dodoma chapter in central Tanganyika invited five women to attend a meeting to learn about the AA. These women agreed to join, and they were encouraged to go out and recruit more women, who would then be brought to the secretary to fill out membership forms and sign the register.[11] Edward Mwongosi, the secretary of the Dodoma chapter, in turn asked the leader of the new Mpwapwa branch the following year if he was acquainted with any women in the town who could join the organization. Mwongosi went on to admonish him to behave politely toward women so that they would have no hesitations in joining.[12] Later, after the opening of the rural Bahi branch in 1944, the male leaders there inquired of the headquarters at Dodoma how many women were *really* supposed to be in the association, and the response was that "women can join the Association just as men." This was reinforced by a trip to Bahi by the chief advisor of AA Dodoma, Hassan Suleiman, who made sure women were registered. He also let the women know that they should attend the AA meetings, just as the female members in Dodoma did.[13]

Not only did the African Association explicitly seek out women members, but it also added the incentive of reduced fees to entice them to join. According to the constitution, women had to pay an entrance fee of only two shillings, while men had to pay three.[14] Moreover, monthly subscription fees for men were double what they were for women (one shilling versus half a shilling).[15] Even though the female members paid lesser rates, they still played a significant role in raising funds for the AA through paying their membership dues and, in other cases, through participating in fund-raising campaigns. From the financial records that remain, it appears as though many women members regularly contributed financially, and there is no indication that they were either better or worse at paying dues than their male counterparts.[16] During a fund-raising drive in 1943, one of the wealthier women of AA Dodoma, Asha Mwinyi, gave a voluntary contribution of three shillings, which was larger than several of the contributions of male members.[17] The following year, many women in the Dodoma chapter were praised for their fund-raising efforts by Salahe Juma of AA Zanzibar.[18]

The association's attempt to recruit female members seems to have produced fairly substantial results, particularly given the lack of women in other East African political associations at the time.[19] The bulk of the AA's membership was male, but records indicate that around 10 percent of the members of most chapters were female. From the very beginning, four of the first thirty-three members of the Zanzibar Town chapter (12 percent) were women.[20] There were similar numbers for the early years of the chapters in Tanganyika's Central Province, as 12 percent of Kondoa's membership were female in 1937, while Mpwapwa recorded 14 percent for that same year.[21] In 1936, AA Dodoma's female ranks stood at 13 percent, and eight years later the male secretary of the branch boasted that sixty-two women had formally signed the registration book, had paid their entrance fee, and were active members of the chapter.[22] Outside of Central Province in Tanganyika, the numbers were a little smaller, with records indicating that 10 percent of the Tabora branch were women in 1946, while only 4 percent of Bagamoyo's membership and 6 percent of the Ujiji branch were women at around the same period.[23] Even though formal membership records do not exist for other chapters, there is evidence that there were women members in the chapters of Bahi, Bukoba, Manyoni, Moshi, and Mwanza in Tanganyika, as well as Wete in the Zanzibar Protectorate.[24]

Like the men of the African Association, the women of the AA were drawn from a broad range of occupations, and female membership cut across class lines and levels of education.[25] Some held respected positions in their communities, like Zanzibar teacher Evelyn Kingango, who was literate in English, as well as Fatima Mwaji Mkasu, a hospital worker in Dodoma, and Mwavita Kasongo, who was given the honorary title *kwinyi*, meaning "owner" or "proprietor." Other women were beer brewers and sellers, and there were also quite a few women whose membership forms reported that they had no formal work.

While certain occupations were more prominent than others, the female members seemed to have cut across social lines. These activists were not just from the educated elite.[26]

Importantly, the women were also drawn from a large number of ethnicities, and one of the most common factors connecting them was the fact that they lived outside of their "indigenous areas," to use colonial terminology.[27] In indirect rule, Tanganyika administrative districts were drawn to correspond to perceived "tribal boundaries." All Africans living within a demarcated "tribal area" were thus subject to the traditional laws of the dominant ethnicity, regardless of whether or not they belonged to that tribe. The reality was not nearly so neat on the ground as colonial mapmakers believed, however, as thousands of Africans in Tanganyika found themselves living outside their "home areas" and subject to the laws and authorities of another ethnic group. Therefore, a political group whose entrance qualifications were not based on ethnic affinity but on a shared racial identity held great appeal for such individuals. While the evidence for the African Association's trend of attracting outsiders is clearest from the more voluminous documentation on the men of the organization, we can see that the trend seems to have also held true for the women.[28] For instance, in Dodoma, not a single female member who listed an ethnicity on her membership application claimed to belong to the Gogo "tribe," the dominant ethnicity of the district. Instead, women in this area claimed to belong to ethnic groups such as the Sandawi, Manyema, Nyakyusa, Mkimbu, and Rangi, which were all deemed not "native to the district."[29] The racial camaraderie of the African Association provided a sense of belonging to men and women from across the social spectrum, to those who may have fit uncomfortably into an ethnically structured colonial society, or to those who had emigrated over long distances from the place of their birth, such as Fatima Mwaji Mkasu, who came to Dodoma from Songea in the far southwestern corner of Tanganyika.[30] Moreover, racial organizations in colonial towns provided opportunities that could not always be met by ethnic affiliations.

Activities of Women Activists in the AA

Many of the women who joined the African Association were quite active and got involved in a number of ways in order to promote the advancement of women within their communities and their own agendas within the organization. Some women rose to positions of leadership in the African Association. Even though the AA was somewhat progressive for the time by promoting a certain amount of integration of leadership between the sexes, this did not always equate to full equality in practice.[31] Theoretically, "a woman could be given the chance of being appointed to be President of the Association if she was well educated," according to a letter Paul Seme wrote to AA Dodoma.[32] Seme went on to explain that there should be several leadership positions reserved for female members: an Assistant Secretary for Ladies who had her own female Sub-Assistant, as well as a ladies' Assistant and Sub-Assistant treasurer.[33] However, female leaders were given an extra hurdle to obtaining these special seats, as they were required to be able to read and write a European language ("Kizungu") in order to understand the correspondence with governments.[34] It is apparent that men were not always held to this educational standard, as many male officeholders did not have such abilities.[35] Clearly, then, the women who gained positions of influence were to be restricted to certain kinds of women, those with education and a knowledge of the modern world. Moreover, it seems that these women were placed in these roles as a strategy to separate them from the mainline power structure of the organization by limiting their responsibilities "to doing the work of her fellow women."[36] Although these female leaders were somewhat relegated to "women's affairs," it did not stop them from bending the organization to their own desires when trying to bring about benefits to the women of their communities.

Not all of the activities of the AA were completely segregated, however, as many of the rank-and-file female members seem to have participated in the association in ways similar to those of most ordinary male members. Attending the association's meetings was the most common form of involvement. There is ample evidence that women often attended the general meetings, which were open to all members. In Dodoma, these meetings were usually attended by several dozen to two hundred members, and women often made up 15 to 24 percent of the crowd. A broad range of issues were addressed at these meetings, but the anonymity of most minutes makes it unclear how much women participated in discussions.[37] We are left to wonder if influential members, such as Mwavita Kasongo, who attended these meetings, would have spoken up on issues that they felt passionate about.[38] Occasionally, women's opinions at general meetings were intentionally sought on specific issues.[39]

The women of the AA often took a more proactive role in the organization by bringing their concerns directly to the smaller meetings of a chapter's managing committee.[40] Female leaders were in theory supposed to be present at all of these gatherings, although minutes indicate that the day-to-day operations of the chapters were largely a male-only affair, presumably because the male leaders preferred it this way.[41] Sometimes women were invited to these meetings, but most often women's involvement with the managing committee came when women leaders initiated special meetings with the committee to make their voices heard on specific issues of importance to them.[42] In Dodoma, these meetings often concerned the selling of *pombe*, a locally made alcoholic beverage, or women's property rights, and when such issues were discussed, women members usually made up the majority of the attendees.[43]

Like the men, the women of the African Association also took political trips on official AA business, possibly to make a name for themselves in the organization or even to elevate their status in the wider community. In 1937, female members of Dodoma were sent as delegates to the inauguration of the Kondoa chapter, traveling by truck with other male members.[44] At the opening ceremony in Bahi in 1943, Martha Chunga, a longtime member of AA Manyoni, was in attendance to present a crown she had made for the new president of the Bahi branch at the climax of the ceremony. The chronicler of the event pointed out that the act would "not be forgotten as long as the AA lives," because "she is a famous woman who left her work and took a long journey to please the name of the black people (African Association)."[45] Chunga was treated with great respect and given the honorary title of *bibi*, even though she was still fairly young and had not yet married.[46]

Chunga was not the only important female traveler of the AA. In 1937, the first Zanzibar assistant secretary for ladies, Evelyn Kingango, traveled with AA member Mrs. Batigwaga to Kwimba on official business, possibly to try and get women involved in that chapter. Even though Mrs. Batigwaga's husband accompanied the women on the first leg of their journey, they next traveled on to Mwanza and Dodoma on their own. Arrangements had been made for the two women to meet with Edward Mwongosi when they reached Dodoma. This interview lasted for about an hour, during which time they likely exchanged information about the affairs of the different chapters.[47]

Female members acted in a number of other ways that demonstrated a desire to assist fellow women in their communities and create dialogue about the challenges facing women in their societies. In Zanzibar, the women members organized a donation box to be displayed at gatherings so that those attending could donate small change for the women of the association who ran into periods of difficulty.[48] In the early 1940s, the women of this chapter also had a number of meetings with Lady Pilling, the wife of the British Resident, and a number of other women seemingly to discuss issues affecting women in wartime Zanzibar.[49] In Dodoma, female member Fatima Musafiya got involved by helping in the creation of an AA store where food would be sold to African women in the town at fair prices.[50] In another unique example, women took part in a night of performances put on by AA Dodoma on 8 June 1943. Seventeen skits were performed, followed by two dances. Some of the skits had potentially politically charged messages. One performance by Asha Hamisi had the provocative title "A native woman demanding a divorce because of maintenance," while two others dealt with the sensitive issue of female beer brewers.[51] By using drama, women employed a medium that was possibly more conducive for making statements about pertinent issues for the women of their community in a relaxed atmosphere. The women of the AA thus got involved in the organization in a number of ways, often to help empower the women of their communities.

Finding a Voice in Male-Dominated Politics

The most significant appeal of the African Association for many of the female activists was the opportunity to represent their concerns to local authorities. In a world where colonial governments were most interested in listening to the views of chiefs, male elders, and appointed headmen, there was little room for female voices in the halls of colonial *bomas*. Because the AA saw itself as a forum where all Africans could share their ideas and concerns and then act as mediators to convey some of those thoughts to the governing authorities, it gave women opportunities to promote their opinions in a political sphere that was otherwise largely closed off.[52] The most practical way that the mediational intentions of the African Association were implemented was in situations where members sought the assistance of the AA's leaders in order to obtain help in their legal court cases. Many potential members, both men and women, perceived that the AA would be able to give them greater influence in tribal or district courts or would help to serve as a conduit to bypass local courts and native authorities altogether. According to the AA's leaders, the association's right to circumvent the colonially instituted ethnic reporting structures derived from the association's claim to act as the representatives of all Africans of any ethnicity, and therefore it would be improper for the AA's petitions to come through the channel of a single ethnic headman. Thus residents who did not identify with the ethnic group of the area could send their requests to the colonial government through the auspices of the AA by staking their claim in an African identity. The organization's role of mediator was what attracted many women to become involved in the association. For instance, Martha Chunga, mentioned earlier, first approached the AA in 1937 when she was looking for help with her court case.[53] The most common legal cases that the leaders of the AA decided to take up on behalf of women involved quarrels over land and property rights.

The African Association also intervened in cases dealing with men's property rights, but a greater number of the cases concerned women, who held fewer rights than men in "traditional courts" and were thus in greater need of finding other avenues to solve their problems.[54] In both Zanzibar and mainland Tanganyika, the African Association intervened in both local and colonial courts to help female property owners fight for their land. In a rural area on Unguja Island, the AA was approached by Fatuma Abdulla, who complained that she had bought a *shamba* (field) from Stambuli Kitoroni for 310 shillings but was not given a legal document of conveyance. She was told to see the local headman about the matter, which she allegedly did, but she never received a response and continued to be harassed by the (former) owner of the shamba. The secretary of AA Zanzibar wrote a letter to the senior commissioner on her behalf, and he recommended that she take the case to the civil court to claim the deed from the seller, which the AA assisted her in doing.[55] In the Buhaya region in northwestern Tanganyika, the association took a local headman to court for destroying the property of a female squatter who was a member of the AA.[56] In this instance, the AA won its case, and the woman received payment for damages.[57]

In the urban areas, property rights were particularly important to the many female property owners who came to the towns to take part in the urban economy. Many of these landladies were single women and did not have recourse to eject their tenants by force. Instead, they chose to utilize the political clout of the AA in the towns to try to get their way. In 1943, the African Association petitioned the Rent Restriction Board of Dodoma Township on behalf of two female landladies, Tausi binti Adam and Hadija binti Ramadhani. Tausi binti Adam had rented out a room to a Mr. Yusufu, who occupied it for four years but vacated without notice and then gave the key to his son. According to Adam, Yusufu junior did not live in the room but only kept it "for his own private affairs" and did not use it in the ways "a proper man" should. What she was implying about his usage was not clear, but she was certain that the room was falling into disrepair because of its lack of a full-time occupant. When she discovered white ants coming from the room, she tried to break the padlock to get in and was beaten for this action by Yusufu junior, who caught her in the act. He refused to pay after this incident, and after three months without receiving any rent, she asked the AA to intervene. Hadija binti Ramadhani similarly had male tenants whom she claimed treated her property poorly by breaking the door and purposely damaging a wall so as to get her in trouble with the Township Authority for not having her premises up to standard. She maintained that they would not let her into the room to make the proper repairs, and, similar to Adam, she reported that they ill-treated her. Both of the owners had the AA request that the tenants be removed from the premises.[58]

The African Association had some success in helping these women in colonial courts in part because they produced arguments about good citizenship and hygiene that found resonance in the ears of colonial administrators. AA member Mwamini Kayumba had received a notice that her house in Dodoma was to be demolished because it was considered "unfit for human habitation." Kayumba had been fixing the roof of her house in preparation for the rainy season, and an inspector considered this to be an unfinished major structural alteration. According to a number of AA members, the unnecessary demolition of houses by the Township Authority was becoming widespread during the fall of 1942, and this was brought to the attention of the AA's executive committee. The male leaders of AA Dodoma decided to intervene on behalf of Kayumba by asking the president of the Township Authority to personally go and view Kayumba's home. He was promised that he would find it in good condition and not needing to be pulled down. Moreover, the association's leaders pointed out that Kayumba paid her annual house tax and always kept her premises clean, while more generally the members of the AA "cooperate with Government on all matters of public welfare, and do always endeavor to induce people in maintaining the sanitation of the township to the satisfaction of the Health Department." By using the language of cleanliness and good citizenship, the AA hoped the Township Authority would be more inclined to treat Kayumba with leniency.[59]

At this time in Dodoma, however, the largest issue that preoccupied the energy of the women of the African Association was the brewing and marketing of alcoholic beverages.[60] Local brews had been sold for cash in East Africa since the 1890s, and it was one of the few industries of the colonial cash economy that was open to women.[61] In fact, most of the brewers and sellers of alcohol in colonial towns were women, and it was one of the most lucrative pursuits for female entrepreneurs at this time, although profits were not always stable, and sellers were often vulnerable. Nevertheless, some of the most successful urban female brewers who owned and operated their own businesses achieved respect and status in their communities.[62] Several of these female brewers joined AA Dodoma in the late 1930s and utilized the organization to push the agenda of the women brewers within the district government.

Unlike in Kenya, where for many years during this period women were not allowed to sell alcohol, the 1923 Tanganyika Native Liquor Ordinance allowed for a highly regulated system of sale and was open to sellers of either gender. The territory-wide ordinance put all of the licensing power in the hands of the district officer, who controlled the registration process without the help of a licensing board in his district. Many female beer brewers had the choice of defying the laws and running the risk of fines or submitting to the burdensome regulations and licensing system.[63] The women of the AA were largely in the latter camp and appear to have wanted to make their changes by working within the governing system and trying to get the regulations modified in ways that were more advantageous to their businesses.

The first petition related to beer brewing sent to the local colonial authorities by the African Association came in response to a reduction in the number of tins that brewers were allowed to brew per day from twelve to six. Female members of the AA who owned breweries met with the managing committee of AA Dodoma in February 1939 to ask them to send a memorandum to the district officer of Dodoma. This letter was typed and signed by Secretary Mwongosi, and while the opening and closing paragraphs explained that the petition had the support of the leadership, the six statements were the words and arguments of the female brewers themselves.[64] The first section pointed to the scarcity of lawful work open to women in colonial towns, pleading, "As we (women) are not able to find work as traders and as there are very few who can consider a woman to be a worker, we have found that we should only stick to making pombe. This trade helps us much in paying our hut tax, and also we help our husbands who have no work as well as ourselves and our children."[65] The sentiments conveyed in this passage were trying to win the favor of the colonial authorities by demonstrating the women's submission to the colonial laws and their desire to be good citizens and pay the hut tax. Furthermore, the petition may have illustrated notions of female honor that saw providing for families through economic opportunities as more important than domesticity.[66]

The petition went on to complain about the cost of a license, which worked out to be around fifty-seven shillings a month, while retail shop owners selling various dry goods only had to pay one hundred shillings per year. The women requested permission to brew twelve tins a day instead of six, an increase in the amount of hours brewers were allowed to sell in the market, and improvements in the facilities in the market hall, as the roof leaked, and sellers were not supplied with water or seats. The underlining point was that these problems were seriously inhibiting the women's businesses and livelihoods, and the women asked the government help them out on the specific points raised or lower the license fees to previous levels. The committee reemphasized the point that these women brewers were in "serious difficulties" and noted that the women had the right to claim such assistance from the government.[67]

The response from the district officer came a week later and was not as generous as the AA had hoped. The district officer noted that there would be no change in the cost of a license. He insinuated that there was no shortage of others willing to pay the rate and that if the women brewers of the AA were not happy with the financial benefits of the profession, their places could be filled by others more eager to try. He further disagreed that there were "any hardships of the nature" suggested by the AA that were "suffered by Licensees." He did agree to take the condition of the market structure into consideration.[68]

After a meeting to discuss this response, the male leaders of AA Dodoma decided to reply to the district officer to explain that the women really did suffer hardships and that the "keenness to obtain . . . a Native Liquor Licence [was] aroused because of the scarceness of getting work in Dodoma" and not because large profits were being made. The AA leaders went on to elucidate the volatility of the brewing business by explaining that women had to give samples to entice customers, who might arbitrarily reduce the price if they felt the brew did not meet their expectations. The AA leaders also explained that pombe spoiled easily and did not last more than a day. If a batch was spoiled, the women were not allowed to remake it once they had made six tins and were therefore often not able to sell all six tins' worth of pombe. Again the rhetoric of good citizenship was used to point out that it was right for any citizen to ask for assistance from the government when in need. The AA thought the district officer had possibly misunderstood the women's desires in the first message and clarified succinctly that they wanted either permission to brew twelve tins a day, which had been the rule the previous year, or a reduction of the monthly permit fee to twenty shillings, which was the rate before 1930.[69] The district officer's response was even more concise. He reaffirmed that there were to be no alterations to the conditions of the native liquor license.[70] Undeterred, the prominent female leaders and pombe sellers sent two more letters through the AA to the district officer in July of that year. The responses on both counts were terse and negative.[71]

In early 1942, the AA had more luck with a new district officer (now called district commissioner), who was more favorably inclined to work with the AA and the female brewers.[72] This good fortune was short-lived, however, when later that year yet another district commissioner was installed and used the wartime shortages and famine-like conditions as an excuse to ban the brewing of alcohol in the district altogether. The new district commissioner thought he was taking care of two problems with a single solution, as at this time the insobriety of Africans in Central Province, Tanganyika, was seen as a perennial problem by Europeans.[73] In an emergency general meeting of the AA in November 1942, it was decided to send a letter of complaint to argue that the majority of Africans "on earth" had been in the habit of drinking pombe since childhood and regarded native beer not only as an enjoyment but also as a domestic food. The AA members were here trying to reverse the language of the ban to their own advantage. Whereas the government said that the making of pombe was taking away from the Africans' diminished food supply (because ingredients usually included millet or maize), the Africans argued that pombe itself was a type of food in their eyes. The AA therefore asked that pombe could at least be sold on the weekends and special holidays or that kangara could be brewed instead. This latter native brew only used inedible cornhusks and honey, which were not then in short supply, and a precedent was cited from Tanga Province.[74]

The argumentative innovation of the AA male leaders in conjunction with the female members met with some success. While the district commissioner disagreed with some of the sentiments that seemed to imply that Africans worked best when they were a little drunk—confirming in his mind that Africans in Dodoma had a real problem with alcoholism—he was now at least open to dropping the ban if the food supply situation changed.[75] He was also willing to consider the idea of allowing kangara to be brewed so long as it was not very intoxicating and there were no cases of drunkenness. He asked for a representative of the brewers to come and talk to him more about the brewing process of kangara. Aziza Abdallah was selected, as she was both an elected women's leader of the AA and a beer brewer herself.[76]

Abdallah's trip appears to have been successful, as the district commissioner decided to allow the brewing of kangara under the regulation of licenses. An elder of the city lauded the efforts of both the women and the drinkers of Dodoma for pleading with the AA to get involved. He heralded it a major triumph that the government modified the ban to allow women to produce beer again at the request of the AA.[77] It was not long, however, before Aziza Abdallah and Mama Bilali, another prominent AA women's leader, were again before the committee, imploring them to make further requests on their behalf. They explained that, unlike the former pombe permits, which were obtained through the district commissioner's office, the licensing of the new kangara permits was done by a Mr. Fedha, who was accused of issuing licenses unfairly, hinting at corruption. The leaders of the AA sent a letter to the district commissioner complaining about the irregularities of issuing permits.[78]

The women's sustained insistence on having the male leaders continue to promote new causes concerning drinking regulations began to cause tension with some of the male leaders, particularly when it became clear that the women brewers of the AA were not following the law. In the fall of 1943, more and more women brewers were caught brewing pombe and not the legal kangara, and they were fined. At a special meeting held on 18 January 1944, the executive committee, joined by a leader of AA Zanzibar, met with twenty-four female members to discuss the issue of brewing and selling. The male leaders said that they were disappointed with the women because several of them had broken rules, such as selling pombe, selling from their houses, and selling to those who were already drunk. The women stated that they did not see such things as offensive, but they promised not to do them again.[79] The men were anxious that these women demonstrate to the colonial authorities that the members of their African community were following the path of good citizenry.

At the meeting, however, women raised concerns about their livelihoods, showing a greater concern for their roles as mothers and providers for their families than for following every facet of colonial laws. A female member named Fatina Selemani admitted that the rules had been broken and promised to keep them in the future, but she was apprehensive that such limitations would make it hard for women to find enough money for food. She complained that she was planting as the government had instructed her to do but that it was not enough—possibly because of the poor harvests. A couple of male members suggested that they needed to figure out how the women could legally sell the most amount of kangara possible. There was then a discussion about asking the government to create a central beer market where all kangara would be sold and regulated. Another male leader said that women should accept such a solution and asked them if they would like for the AA to recommend the beer hall idea to the government. The minutes noted that the women agreed that it should be done straight away, but it is not clear if they truly desired the creation of a beer hall or if they just felt obligated to agree to such an arrangement. Women's concerns were glossed over with the encouragement to continue planning according to government recommendations while a legal solution could be found to make them more money. It appears that the idea of allowing women to continue selling whatever, whenever, and wherever so that they and their families could have enough to eat was not entertained and that the male members wanted more control to regulate the relations between their recalcitrant female members and the colonial administration.[80]

The underlying tension is illustrated in the minutes of an executive committee meeting the previous summer when the female leaders were absent. The male leaders pondered the possibility of the government totally banning beer brewing (pombe and kangara), which was a rumor then circulating. After the discussion it was decided that the AA would not interfere if the government decided on a final, total ban. The leaders came to this conclusion not because of a Zanzibar rule that forbade members from drinking alcohol—which seems to have been discreetly ignored in most chapters throughout the period—but because they felt the women brewing beer had "started to disrespect the council."[81] The women had done this by making accusations that the committee was not doing as much as they should to help out their fellow Africans. The male leaders, furthermore, did not like that the illegal actions of their female members were reflecting poorly on the organization in the eyes of the colonial government at a time when the AA felt its legitimacy depended on being good citizens and complying with the laws and legal structures of the land. "In view of this, the elders felt that it was not a good idea to help the women in any way."[82]

By the end of 1944, this tension was beginning to come out in the open as some women quietly began questioning the male leaders' commitment to the organization's egalitarianism. Tausi binti Ali Kangomba lamented in a letter that the sons of Mother Africa were forgetting her daughters who were in need. A member of the AA, Kangomba had been sentenced to a four-month prison term.[83] She complained to the leaders of AA Dodoma by saying that even though she was guilty of breaking the law, she felt she had been abandoned by her "fellow African brothers" who were aware of her situation: "At the beginning of the trial and at the end of the case or even when I was released there was none, not even a brother or an elder who empathized with me from my African Association community."[84] Kangomba utilized the association's language of African familyhood to shame the male leaders of the organization for not taking care of their duties as African brothers to help their African sisters in need. In this particular case, the executive committee agreed to apologize for their actions and sent a letter of sympathy to Kangomba. The committee also notified women's secretary Aziza Abdallah of their actions.[85] That the male leaders felt the need to redress their failure to help Kangomba and that they also continued to intervene on behalf of the female brewers in 1944 despite the fact that they had a clear desire not to—and may have done so begrudgingly—demonstrates that the women were effective in using the interethnic African identity and ideology of the African Association to oblige the men to assist them in the name of African unity.

The attitudes of the male leaders of Dodoma also illustrate, however, that they felt these women were not acting in ways that African women should— they were breaking the government's laws and disrespecting the male elders. The subtle desires for patriarchal control by the male leaders of the AA manifested themselves in several other ways that show that they occasionally used the African Association to try and shape the identity of African womanhood by protecting their modesty and reforming their manners.[86] Like other male-dominated groups of the period in East Africa, the men of the AA were particularly concerned over the sexual mores of women and made efforts at controlling them.[87] The issue of prostitution was often a topic of discussion at AA meetings, although, unfortunately, few of the conversations were recorded for us to know exactly what both the men and women were saying about it.[88] In one case in Dodoma in 1944, a general meeting was convened to "resolve the issue of eradicating or avoiding three illnesses destroying and causing stress to our [African] nation: gonorrhea, syphilis and yaws." The moral and physical cure for these diseases, which were seen as primarily transmitted sexually, was to monitor the single women of the town by drawing up a list of every unmarried girl or woman who had reached the age of sexual maturity and submit the list to the district administration. Six AA volunteers—all male—were chosen to carry out the task of going door to door to compile the list of single women.[89] Thus the male members were putting their bureaucratic skills to use in keeping track of the sexual mores of the women in their town.

The men of the AA also felt it was their duty to protect the modesty of African women. One major issue that several chapters of the AA pursued centered on the treatment of women in colonial hospitals. One concern was the failure to seclude women in an appropriate manner. For instance, after receiving a letter from the AA in Bagamoyo, the director of medical services informed the association that he did not agree with its view that it was deplorable for women to be seen by male orderlies and surgeons. He told the AA that "it is usual in Europe for women in confinement to be attended by Medical Officers of either sex" and that until recently in Bagamoyo "nearly every European woman was attended by a man."[90] However, the male leaders did not accept this reasoning and felt that this was one European social trait that did not agree with their desires for African women. The AA in Dodoma similarly complained to the town's Hospital Welfare Committee that injections given to African women should be done by a religious sister or *ayah* (an African or East Indian female nurse) because "it is unlawful from [the] African point of view for a man to touch [a] woman's buttock."[91] This issue of having women patients seen by female nurses was a salient issue in a number of chapters and was discussed at the association-wide conference of 1946.[92]

Many male members joined the African Association for similar reasons as women, such as the benefits of embracing a non-ethnic identity in an ethnically organized colonial society and leveraging this African identity to help solve their problems in local courts.[93] However, there were also specific gendered dimensions, as some male leaders used the interethnic association to promote a particular type of African womanhood and even envisioned women's roles in shaping the African nation in gendered terms.[94] On the other hand, men's attempts to establish patriarchal control did not stop the women from attempting to assert their agency in pushing their own agendas. Women members were able to utilize the ideology of African unity to their advantage by pressuring male leaders into assisting the women in accomplishing their objectives and gaining a voice in the male-dominated world of colonial politics.

Conclusion:
Alternative Identities and Practical Solutions

Even though there were no known ideological luminaries among the female members of the AA, this did not mean that entrepreneurial women were kept from using the political space opened up to them by the AA's egalitarian ideology and utilizing the representational opportunities that the organization provided. Unlike certain male leaders, the women of the AA do not appear to have been as motivated by grand visions of African unity, though it is possible that some of the women who joined found liberating the sentiments of leaders like

Mtumwa Zaidi, who said that men and women must stand united "together, shoulder to shoulder."[95] The single most important reason why women joined the African Association, however, seems to have been access to the colonial government and a greater ability to make their voices heard on issues important to them. While notions of equality, progress, and belonging to an imagined African nation may have been significant contributing factors, it appears that the promise of the AA to hear women's claims and make representations on their behalf to the appropriate authorities was the most prevalent incentive for women to join.

What emerges in the case of the female activists of the African Association is that the attraction to a non-ethnic political organization was largely due to these innovative women's belief that claiming a more encompassing identity had the potential to create several practical advantages not otherwise available through ethnic affiliation. These women did not wholly discard their ethnicities, but they were not so invested in them that they were unable to consider fore-grounding an alternative identity that held out practical advantages. The pragmatic impulse in their politics is most clearly seen in the fact that the initiatives that most inspired the female members of the AA to act were related to their occupations and livelihoods. As Claire Robertson, Heidi Gengenbach, and others have shown, the threat to employment was often at the heart of women's collective action in colonial and postcolonial Africa.[96] Time and again, women utilized the African Association when their access to income was under challenge. For instance, the women of Wete, Pemba, turned to the AA when their food stalls were closed down due to a failure to meet hygiene and sanitation standards.[97] As has been shown, women landlords sought the help of the AA when they saw no other recourse to obtain rent and compensation from tardy and abusive tenants, while female brewers sought to gain better working conditions and advantages by using the AA to voice their opinions to the township authorities. These women activists seemed less interested in the AA's vision of African unity than in its pledge to be the voice of Africans by using bureaucratic skills to serve as mediators between Africans and governing authorities. Thus, as both individuals and as collective groups, AA women utilized the organization to solve problems in their personal lives and the lives of other women at the local level.

The case study of the women of the African Association is also useful because it serves as an example of women activists who were uninterested in methods of resistance and who were also willing to work in collaboration with men in order to pursue their political goals. Most previous studies on women's political activism during the mid-twentieth century have concentrated on demonstrating how women were resistors, either to colonial rule or to patriarchal dominance in their societies, and have primarily focused on women-only groups.[98] But the women of the AA were not overtly opposed to men and were willing to work with the male leaders whose access to the colonial authorities gave the women new opportunities to see their objectives achieved. But they also acted in more subversive ways by drawing on their African identity to pressure men into fulfilling their duties and obligations under the egalitarian ideology of African familyhood. Women practiced this non-ethnic identity, an identity first constructed by male visionaries, in gendered ways to pursue their own agendas, often in a manner male leaders may not have anticipated. Whether it was to find acceptance as outsiders in an ethnically dominated colonial society or to gain greater access to governing authorities, the women of the African Association perceived that an African identity would be more useful and valuable than their ethnicity in the political arena.

NOTES

1.   While there have been several studies on women and nationalist movements in Africa, surprisingly few have specifically looked at the intersection of gender and ethnicity in such movements. One exception is Elizabeth Schmidt, *Mobilizing the Masses: Gender, Ethnicity, and Class in the Nationalist Movement in Guinea, 1939–1958* (Portsmouth, NH: Heinemann, 2005), 113–15, 146. See also Healy-Clancy (chapter 4) for a study of how New African women organized across ethnic lines.

2.   This idea was first put forth in Frederick Cooper, "Conflict and Connection: Rethinking Colonial African History," *American Historical Review* 99, no. 5 (December 1994): 1519, and was given further discussion in the East African context in Ethan R. Sanders, "The African Association and the Growth and Movement of Political Thought in Mid-Twentieth Century East Africa" (PhD thesis, University of Cambridge, 2012).

3.   On the AA idea of an African nation, see Sanders, "The African Association"; and on colonial politics being a sphere closed off to many African women, see Jean Allman, Susan Geiger, and Nakanyike Musisi, "Women in African Colonial History: An Introduction," in *Women in African Colonial History*, ed. Jean Allman, Susan Geiger, and Nakanyike Musisi (Bloomington: Indiana University Press, 2002), 1.

4.   Daniel N. Posner, *Institutions and Ethnic Politics in Africa* (Cambridge: Cambridge University Press, 2005), 1–12. See also Frederick Cooper, *Colonialism in Question: Theory, Knowledge, History* (Berkeley: University of California Press, 2005), 59–90.

5.   In the most thorough treatment of the African Association, John Iliffe's *A Modern History of Tanganyika* (Cambridge: Cambridge University Press, 1979), there is no mention of female members in the organization, while Susan Geiger, the foremost scholar on women and politics in Tanganyika, has denied that women ever took part in the African Association, arguing that "women were notably absent from the ranks of leadership *or membership* in TAA [*sic*]" and that it was not until the founding of TANU "after years of all-male membership" that the TAA called for the participation of

women. Susan Geiger, *TANU Women: Gender and Culture in the Making of Tangan-yikan Nationalism, 1955–1965* (Portsmouth, NH: Heinemann, 1997), 113, 68–69 (emphasis added). It should be noted that Geiger, like others, incorrectly used "TAA" (Tanganyika African Association) when talking about the years between 1929 and 1948. At this time the organization solely went by "African Association" or one of its Kiswahili equivalents. In 1948, the organization split along territorial lines, and the branches in Tanganyika renamed their organization the Tanganyika African Association. Many scholars, most interested in telling the story of territorial nationalism, have wrongly assumed that the organization had a territorial focus from the start and thus referred to it as "the TAA." When speaking of the Zanzibar Town chapter of the AA, Jonathon Glassman in passing mentions that "the association had a women's branch from the start," which is partially correct, as it does not appear that the women were separated into a distinct branch. Glassman, however, gives no discussion of who these women were, why they joined, or even what they did in the association. Jonathon Glassman, *War of Words, War of Stones: Racial Thought and Violence in Colonial Zanzibar* (Bloomington: Indiana University Press, 2011), 111.

6.   This is a perennial problem for historians writing African women's history for the colonial period. See Susan Geiger, "Women in Nationalist Struggle: TANU Activists in Dar es Salaam," *International Journal of African Historical Studies* 20 (1987): 3–4; Tabitha Kanogo, *African Womanhood in Colonial Kenya, 1900–1950* (Oxford: James Currey, 2005), 10.

7.   The largest single collection of documents pertaining to the African Association are the Hassan Suleiman Papers, housed in the Tanzania National Archives (TNA) in Dar es Salaam (accession #571). There is also information on some of the women members of the Zanzibar chapter of the African Association held in the Secretariat Files of the Zanzibar National Archives (ZNA).

8.   Paul Seme was the secretary of the chapter in Zanzibar Town from 1934 to 1939 and the primary architect of the organization's largest program of expansion; he was also the drafter of the 1934 constitution. See Sanders, "The African Association," chap. 2. The Kiswahili original of the text quote reads, "muwaweke kundi moja wana na binti za Africa." TNA 571/46/AA/101/45, AA Zanzibar to Gen. Sec. AA Dodoma and Kondoa Irangi, 9 March 1940.

9.   TNA 19325/II/67a, minutes of the Fifth East African Conference of the African Association held at Zanzibar on 7 April 1947. There are other appearances of the phrase "sons and daughters of Mother Africa" in the private papers of John Iliffe (hereafter cited as PJI [Papers of John Iliffe]), notes of TNA 46/A/6/3/I/15, Augustine Ramadhani, A. Benjamin Boyd, and P. A. P. Seme Sindi to AA Dodoma, 22 April 1937; ZNA AK 1/73/nf (no folio), "The African Association's Motto Fund Appeal May 7th 1938 Zanzibar, East Africa."

10.   Part 2, section 9, "Kanuni na Sheria za Chama Cha Umoja wa Watu wa Afrika," African Association Constitution, Zanzibar, 28 January 1935, manuscript held in the Africana Collection of the University of Dar es Salaam Library.

11.   TNA 571/35/09, African Association, Dodoma, 25 May 1936, meeting minutes.

12.   TNA 571/16/AAB/M/06, Edward Mwongosi to Thom ——, Mpwapwa, 11 May 1937.

13.   TNA 571/6/AA/38/47, AA Bahi to AA Dodoma, 13 June 1944; TNA 571/6/AA/38/52, AA Dodoma to AA Bahi, 21 September 1944; TNA 571/6/AA/38/51, "The African Association Central Province Dodoma: Safari ya Bahi."

14.   "Kanuni na Sheria."

15.   TNA 571/35/10, Mkutano wa African Association, Dodoma, "Tarehe 21/5/36"; PJI, notes of TNA 46/A/6/3/I/6, Superintendent of Police Dodoma to Commissioner of Police, Dar es Salaam, 17 October 1936; TNA 571/12/AA/70/2, minutes of the dance meeting held on 2 May 1943.

16.   See, for instance, the record lists of fees paid, such as TNA 571/44/AA/25/52, "Wanawake hawa walio wanachama wa African Association, Dodoma"; TNA 571/24/113, dues-paid list for AA Kondoa Irangi, January and February 1938.

17.   TNA 571/53/136, list of those who gave a voluntary contribution to an unknown cause, 7 September 1943.

18.   TNA 571/53/44, AA Dodoma, "General Meeting, 9.9.1944," 9 September 1944.

19.   Many political groups in East Africa in the 1930s and 1940s were vocally opposed to women joining. See, for instance, the comments of a leader of the Bataka Party of Uganda, CO 537/3593/67, Semekula Mulumba to Rubamabansi Omugabe of Ankole, ca. 27 May 1948, National Archives of the United Kingdom. Some groups, such as the Kikuyu Central Association in Kenya, had separate wings for women, but women could not obtain full membership or leadership positions in the organization. See Cora Ann Presley, *Kikuyu Women, the Mau Mau Rebellion, and Social Change in Kenya* (Boulder, CO: Westview, 1992), 107–8.

20.   ZNA GC 1/18, "Historia Fupi ya Chama Cha African Association Zanzibar Mwaka 1923 mpaka 1929" (A short history of the African Association of Zanzibar, 1923–1929 [*sic* 1933–1939]).

21.   TNA 571/24/75–76, "Orodha ya malipo ya mwezi wa marchi 1937"; TNA 571/16/AAB/M/23–24, list of members of AA Mpwapwa, ca. August 1937.

22.   PJI, notes of TNA 46/A/6/3/I/6; TNA 571/13/AA/83/05–09, AA Dodoma to Combined Dancing Club, Tabora, 18 March 1944.

23.   TNA 571/13/AA/83/76–77, list of AA Tabora members, ca. 1946; TNA 180/A6/1/nf, "Orodha na Majina ya Wanachama wa Tanganyika African Association"; TNA 7/3/2/24, "African Association: Wanachama Bagamoyo, 21 August 1944."

24.   For Bahi, see TNA 571/6/AA/38/51; for Bukoba, see TNA 571/25/BA/AAD/41–46, AA Nshamba to AA Bukoba, 3 August 1939; for Manyoni, see TNA 571/27/49, AA Dodoma to Miss Martha Chunga, 10 October 1937; for Moshi, see S. W. Frederick, "The Life of Joseph Kimalando," *Tanzania Notes and Records* 70 (1969): 24; for Mwanza, see Geiger, *TANU Women*, 136–37, 142; TNA 19325/II/202, TAA Moshi to Chief Secretary, AA Dar es Salaam, 28 May 1952; for Wete, see ZNA AK 1/73/nf, AA Chake Chake to J. D. Robertson, senior medical officer in Zanzibar Protectorate, 12 November 1951; ZNA AK 1/73/nf, District Commissioner Pemba to AA Pemba, memorial, 19 November 1951. Interestingly, there is no record of female members in the Dar es Salaam headquarters.

Women may have been involved in Dar es Salaam and the evidence is just lacking, or it may have been that women were not allowed in the more stratified and clerk-dominated Dar es Salaam chapter, which never seemed quite as committed to implementing the ideological principles of the association as the branches connected to the Zanzibar and Dodoma headquarters were. The lack of evidence of women in the Dar es Salaam branch may also be a reason behind the dearth of historical writing on women in the AA for the reason that many histories of the AA have been largely Dar focused, due to a greater reliance on the English-language secretariat files.

25.   For an examination of the occupational and social background of male leaders, see Sanders, "The African Association," 117–23.

26.   TNA 571/3/AA/12/53, AA Zanzibar to AA Dodoma, 30 March 1937; TNA 571/53/102–3, "AA Dodoma, agenda, general meeting, 30 August 1943"; TNA 571/30/189, application form for Fatima binti Mwaji Mkasu. See the other application forms in TNA 571/30.

27.   TNA 571/30.

28.   For more on the documentation of the male members, see Sanders, "The African Association," chap. 3.

29.   See the application forms in TNA 571/30.

30.   Songea is about 440 miles south and slightly west from Dodoma; see TNA 571/30/189.

31.   Groups like the Kikuyu Central Association had a separate women's wing, but the women were not allowed to attend the meetings. In the AA, women could attend meetings, and, as will be demonstrated presently, they were theoretically supposed to have positions of leadership on the main committees of the organization—though this did not always work out in practice. On the women of the KCA, see Presley, *Kikuyu Women*, 118.

32.   TNA 571/3/AA/12/03, AA Zanzibar to AA Dodoma, 17 March 1936. No woman ever became president of the AA.

33.   TNA 571/3/AA/12/03. While many branches had female members, there is only evidence that the headquarters of Zanzibar and Dodoma had enough qualified women to be elected to these special offices. Such positions may have been inspired by the prominent roles of women in the women's wings of Beni dance societies or in church administrations such as the Women's African Advisory Committee of the Universities' Mission to Central Africa. T. O. Ranger, *Dance and Society in East Africa: The Beni Ngoma* (London: Heinemann, 1975), 22–24; A. G. Blood, *The History of the Universities' Mission to Central Africa*, vol. 2, 1907–32 (London: Universities' Mission to Central Africa, 1957), 214.

34.   Part 1, section 38, "Kanuni na Sheria."

35.   While it was deemed essential that male secretaries could read and write English, the other positions did not require education, and many male leaders throughout the organization's chapters were illiterate or lacked formal education. See Sanders, "The African Association," 118–19.

36. TNA 571/3/AA/12/03; TNA 571/53/35, committee meeting, 19 November 1944; TNA 571/41/26–28, AA Dodoma to the Acting District Officer of Dodoma, 25 February 1939; TNA 571/53/120, "Minutes za Mkutano wa tarehe 8 May 1943 katika nyumba ya Ag. President."

37. TNA 571/35/10, "Mkutano wa African Association, Dodoma, Tarehe 21/5/36"; TNA 571/53/82, AA Dodoma, general meeting, 15 October 1943; TNA 571/53/56, AA Dodoma, general meeting, 26 February 1944; TNA 571/53/51, minutes of the general meeting, 15 April 1944; TNA 571/53/52, general meeting, 15 April 1944; TNA 571/53/44.

38. TNA 571/53/102–3. On the same meeting, see TNA 571/53/99, AA Dodoma, general meeting, 30 August 1943.

39. TNA 571/35/10, "Mkutano wa African Association, Dodoma, Tarehe, 21 May 1936"; TNA 571/53/44.

40. Also referred to as the executive meeting.

41. Even though these committees were supposed to be "full with the presence of women," according to Seme, it is clear that this was seldom the case. See TNA 571/3/AA/12/03; TNA 571/28/26, list of committee members, AA Dodoma; TNA 571/37/06, "Majina ya wakuu wa African Association Dodoma-Kondoa-Irangi." In 1952, TAA Moshi had two female members on the executive committee. See TNA 19325/II/202, TAA Moshi to CS Dar es Salaam, 28 May 1952.

42. See, for instance, a case when women were invited to a committee meeting in Zanzibar to discuss issues sent by the new Dodoma branch: TNA 571/3/AA/12/22, Ali Ponda to AA Dodoma c/o AA Zanzibar, 22 June 1936. Occasionally, these meetings were meant to facilitate the election of women officeholders: TNA 571/53/44.

43. TNA 571/53/62–63, "Special meeting, Government Village School, [Dodoma] 18 January 1944"; TNA 571/53/128, special meeting, Dodoma, 6 March 1943; TNA 571/53/120.

44. TNA 571/24/62–63, "Kufungua African Association-Kondoa-Irangi, 7 March 1937."

45. He went on to praise the value of the crown. See TNA 571/6/AA/38/27–33, "Ufunguo wa Tawi la African Association, Bahi, 7 November 1943."

46. *Bibi* translates into English as "lady" or "grandma." When she later moved to Dodoma, she was elected Ladies' Secretary of the chapter in 1944. See TNA 571/53/44.

47. TNA 571/3/AA/12/44–46, AA Dodoma to AA Zanzibar and Pemba (Zanzibar Town), 1 May 1937; TNA 571/3/AA/12/53, AA Zanzibar to AA Dodoma, 30 March 1937.

48. TNA 571/53/62–63.

49. TNA 571/46/AA/101/91, Saleh Juma, AA Zanzibar, to Lady Secretary, AA Dodoma, 29 October [1944].

50. They believed Indian merchants were charging Africans exorbitant rates. See TNA 571/53/121, "Standing Committee Meeting, 4/5/1943" [Dodoma].

51. TNA 571/36/17, "Programme and its Events."

52. Allman, Geiger, and Musisi "Women in African Colonial History," 1.

53. TNA 571/27/49.

54. For cases where the African Association was involved in helping men with their property rights, see TNA 571/6/AA/38/53, Rajab Sudi (Bahi) to District Commissioner, Dodoma, 3 November 1944; Frederick, "Joseph Kimalando," 23. For good studies on the dynamics of women and "traditional courts" during the colonial period, see Martin Chanock, *Law, Custom, and Social Order: The Colonial Experience in Malawi and Zambia* (Cambridge: Cambridge University Press, 1985); Richard Roberts, *Litigants and Households: African Disputes and Colonial Courts in the French Soudan, 1895-1912* (Portsmouth, NH: Heinemann, 2005).

55. It is unclear, however, whether or not she and the AA were successful in pleading her case before the courts. See ZNA AK 1/73, AA Zanzibar to Senior Commissioner, 15 May 1949; ZNA AK 1/73, Senior Commissioner to Hon. Secretary AA Zanzibar, 19 May 1949.

56. Göran Hydén has previously pointed out that the AA very early on got involved with women's land rights. See Hydén, *Political Development in Rural Tanzania: TANU Yajenga Nchi* (Nairobi: East African Publishing House, [1969]), 109.

57. TNA 571/25/BA/AAD/41–46, AA Nshamba to AA Bukoba, 3 August 1939.

58. TNA 571/44/AA/25/56, AA Dodoma to the Chairman, Rent Restriction Board, Dodoma Township, 1 November 1943.

59. TNA 571/34/21, AA Dodoma to the President, Township Authority, Dodoma, 24 October 1942; TNA 571/34/15, The African Association, Dodoma, "Mkutano wa Committee Members," 30 October 1942.

60. This was also a significant issue with which the Moshi chapter of the AA got involved. See Frederick, "Joseph Kimalando," 26. Similarly, in Dar es Salaam, Erica Fiah's Tanganyika African Commercial Welfare Association also supported female brewers. See Marjorie Mbilinyi, "'This Is an Unforgettable Business': Colonial State Intervention in Urban Tanzania," in *Women and the State in Africa*, ed. Jane L. Parpart and Kathleen A. Staudt (Boulder, CO: L. Rienner, 1989), 118–22.

61. For an interesting comparison to the way in which beer brewing still has a gendered dynamic to it in contemporary East Africa, see Gengenbach (chapter 2).

62. Justin Willis, *Potent Brews: A Social History of Alcohol in East Africa, 1850-1999* (Oxford: James Currey, 2002), 100, 104; Mbilinyi, "'This Is an Unforgettable Business,'" 115–16; Geiger, "Women in Nationalist Struggle," 10.

63. Willis, *Potent Brews*, 99, 102, 130–31.

64. It is unclear whether this wording was meant to give the memorandum more force by having it come directly from the female brewers or if it was meant to distance the leadership of the organization from the comments, despite the repeated claim that the women had the support of the executive committee.

65. TNA 571/41/26–28.

66. John Iliffe, *Honour in African History* (Cambridge: Cambridge University Press, 2005), 263, 272–73.

67. TNA 571/41/26–28.

68. TNA 571/41/30, District Officer, Dodoma, to AA Dodoma, 2 March 1939.

69. TNA 571/41/35–36, AA Dodoma to District Officer, Dodoma, 21 March 1939; TNA 571/41/26–28.

70.   TNA 571/41/3?, District Officer, Dodoma, to AA Dodoma, 30 March 1939.

71.   TNA 571/41/52, AA Dodoma to District Officer, Dodoma, 4 July 1939; TNA 571/41/54–55, AA Dodoma to District Officer, Dodoma, 18 July 1939; TNA 571/41/56, District Officer, Dodoma, to AA Dodoma, 20 July 1939; TNA 571/41/57, District Officer, Dodoma, to AA Dodoma, 20 July 1939.

72.   TNA 571/41/138, AA Dodoma to District Commissioner, Dodoma, 17 February 1942; TNA 571/41/140, District Commissioner, Dodoma, to AA Dodoma, 17 February 1942.

73.   TNA 46/2/6/32, annual report, Dodoma District, 1942; TNA 46/a.2/1/1942/34, annual report, Central Province, 1942; Gregory H. Maddox, "Narrating Power in Colonial Ugogo: Mazengo of Mvumi," in *In Search of a Nation: Histories of Authority and Dissidence in Tanzania*, ed. Gregory H. Maddox and James L. Giblin (Oxford: James Currey, 2005), 94–96.

74.   TNA 571/41/238–39, AA Dodoma to Provincial Commissioner Dodoma, 25 November 1942.

75.   While the district commissioner chafed at such sentiments by the AA, Gregory Maddox and Earnest Kongola have effectively shown how beer was an integral part of agricultural production in this part of the territory because it both served as a form of payment and helped to create social bonds between communities due to the near-ritual style of consumption during harvesting. Maddox, "Narrating Power," 94–96; Gregory H. Maddox with Ernest M. Kongola, *Practicing History in Central Tanzania: Writing, Memory, and Performance* (Portsmouth, NH: Heinemann, 2006), 129–31.

76.   TNA 571/41/243, District Commissioner, Dodoma, to AA Dodoma, 1 December 1942; TNA 571/41/244, AA Dodoma to District Commissioner, Dodoma, 4 December 1942.

77.   In actuality, this was just a concession. See TNA 571/53/64, "General Meeting, held on 1 January 1944 at Government Village School, Dodoma."

78.   It is not clear who this Mr. Fedha was, and it is possible that this was not his actual name, as *fedha* in Kiswahili can mean "currency" or "money," possibly alluding to a corrupt African official who took bribes. See TNA 571/53/120.

79.   TNA 571/53/111, "Minutes za Mkutano wa tarehe ya 19 June 1943 katika nyumba ya President" (thanks to John Shabaya for his help in translating this document); TNA 571/53/62–63.

80.   TNA 571/53/62–63.

81.   TNA 571/53/111; item 24, "Kanuni na Sheria."

82.   TNA 571/53/111.

83.   It is unclear what offense Kangomba had been convicted of. It was possibly for repeated violations of the regulations concerning the brewing and selling of alcoholic beverages.

84.   TNA 571/37/138, Tausi binti Ali Kagomba to AA Dodoma, 14 November 1944 (thanks to John Shabaya for his help in translating this document).

85.   TNA 571/53/35.

86.   Patriarchal control is a recurring theme in colonial African women's history. See Cooper, "Conflict and Connection," 1523; Kanogo, *African Womanhood*, 1–10;

Pamela Scully, "Race and Ethnicity in Women's and Gender History in Global Perspective," in *Women's History in Global Perspective*, vol. 1, ed. Bonnie G. Smith (Urbana: University of Illinois Press, 2004), 209; Claire C. Robertson, *Trouble Showed the Way: Women, Men, and Trade in the Nairobi Area, 1890–1990* (Bloomington: Indiana University Press, 1997), 3–5; Iliffe, *Honour in African History*, 274–75; Nancy Rose Hunt, "Placing African Women's History and Locating Gender," *Social History* 14 (1989): 364.

87.   For studies on African male concern over women's sexuality and attempts to control it, see Scully, "Race and Ethnicity," 209; Kanogo, *African Womanhood*, 7–10; Robertson, *Trouble Showed the Way*, 239–40; Geiger, "Women in Nationalist Struggle," 6–7; Iliffe, *Honour in African History*, 274–75; John Lonsdale, "The Moral Economy of Mau Mau: Wealth, Poverty and Civic Virtue in Kikuyu Political Thought," in *Unhappy Valley: Conflict in Kenya and Africa, Book Two: Violence and Ethnicity*, ed. Bruce Berman and John Lonsdale (Oxford: James Currey, 1992), 340; Luise White, *The Comforts of Home: Prostitution in Colonial Nairobi* (Chicago: University of Chicago Press, 1990), 190–94; Lynn M. Thomas, *Politics of the Womb: Women, Reproduction, and the State in Kenya* (Berkeley: University of California Press, 2003); Derek R. Peterson, *Ethnic Patriotism and the East African Revival* (Cambridge: Cambridge University Press, 2012), chap. 7.

88.   TNA 571/53/102–3; TNA 19325/II/41c, "Territorial Conference of the African Association, April 1946"; TNA 215/1921/I/19–25, "The African Association Provincial Conference, Lake Province, Mwanza, 17th–18th May 1947."

89.   TNA 571/53/45, "General Meeting, held on 14/5/1944."

90.   TNA 7/3/2/59, Director of Medical Services, Bagamoyo, to AA Bagamoyo, 16 May 1946.

91.   TNA 571/40/154, AA Dodoma, 13 November 1941, "Suggestions for discussion of next meeting of the Dodoma Hospital Welfare Committee."

92.   TNA 19325/II/41c, "Territorial Conference of the African Association, April 1946." These are the minutes taken by a Tanganyikan government observer, who calls it a territorial conference when it was actually an association-wide conference.

93.   For instance, a number of male landlords also got the association to intervene on their behalf. See ZNA AK 1/73/32, AA Zanzibar and Pemba to Provincial Commissioner Zanzibar, 16 February 1939; ZNA AK 1/73/nf, AA Zanzibar to District Commissioner, Zanzibar, 4 August 1941; TNA 571/43/AA/43, H.M. High Court Dar es Salaam to AA Dodoma, 31 May 1943.

94.   This was sometimes in the guise of clearly gendered language, as seen in the address of Saleh Juma of AA Zanzibar to the women of Dodoma when he thanked them "for being the leaders of our nation. [The women of Zanzibar] have big expectations that you will unite together and succeed to carry our small baby which is the AA, though most of you have already thrown away those baby carriers." TNA 571/46/101/91, Saleh Juma, Secretary, AA Zanzibar, to Lady Secretary, AA Dodoma, 29 October [1944].

95.   The Kiswahili reads, "tushikane bega kwa bega." TNA 571/46/AA/101/86, Mtumwa Zaid, AA Zanzibar to AA Dodoma, 5 March 1944 (thanks to John Shabaya for his help in translating this document). Geiger has argued that this rhetoric of women

and men working "side by side" was begun for utilitarian reasons during the beginning of TANU in the mid-1950s. This quote from 1944 shows that the rhetoric was deployed at least a decade earlier, and while similarly used for reasons of recruitment, it also points to a more ideological basis for the sentiment. Geiger, "Women in Nationalist Struggle," 22–23.

96. See Gengenbach (chapter 2); Robertson, *Trouble Showed the Way*, 3–5; Jean F. O'Barr, "Making the Invisible Visible: African Women in Politics and Policy," *African Studies Review* 18 (1975): 21; Mbilinyi, "'This Is an Unforgettable Business,'" 125.

97. ZNA AK 1/73, AA Pemba (Chake Chake) to J. D. Robertson, Senior Medical Officer, Zanzibar Protectorate, 12 November 1951.

98. For studies examining the themes of militancy, resistance, or women in anti-colonial nationalist movements, see Hunt, "Placing African Women's History," 362–64; Aili Mari Tripp et al., *African Women's Movements: Changing Political Landscapes* (Cambridge: Cambridge University Press, 2009), xiv, 32, 35–36, 44; Schmidt, *Mobilizing the Masses*, 113–14; O'Barr, "Making the Invisible Visible," 24; Jean O'Barr and Kathryn Firmin-Sellers, "African Women in Politics," in *African Women South of the Sahara*, 2nd ed., ed. Margaret Jean Hay and Sharon Stichter (Harlow, Essex: Longman, 1995), 197; Iris Berger and E. Frances White, *Women in Sub-Saharan Africa: Restoring Women to History* (Bloomington: Indiana University Press, 1999), 44; Allman, Geiger, and Musisi, "Women in African Colonial History," 2–3, 6–7; Gisela Geisler, *Women and the Remaking of Politics in Southern Africa: Negotiating Autonomy, Incorporation and Representation* (Uppsala: Nordiska Afrikainstitutet, 2004). For an overview on colonial women-only movements, see Tripp et al., *African Women's Movements*, 14, 42–43; Andrew Roberts, "African Cross Currents," in *The Colonial Moment in Africa: Essays on the Movement of Minds and Materials, 1900–1940*, ed. Andrew Roberts (Cambridge: Cambridge University Press, 1990), 253–54; Hunt, "Placing African Women's History," 362–64; Robertson, *Trouble Showed the Way*, 245–48. For other women-only groups in East Africa, see Margaret Strobel, *Muslim Women in Mombasa, 1890–1975* (New Haven, CT: Yale University Press, 1979), 182–95; Jean O'Barr, "Pare Women: A Case of Political Involvement," *Rural Africana* 9 (1976): 121–34.

Part III

Promoting Gendered Domains of Ethnicity

6

Gender and the Limits of "Ndebeleness," 1910–1960s

Abezansi *Churchwomen's Domestic and Associational Alliances*

WENDY URBAN-MEAD

The Ndebele Kingdom reigned over what is today western Zimbabwe from the 1830s until colonial conquest in the 1890s. The founding king, Mzilikazi Khumalo, and his closest relatives and supporters came from what is today KwaZulu; this group formed the ruling core of the kingdom. The precolonial kingdom had a centralized government with hierarchically arranged social strata that came from linguistically and culturally distinct groups successively incorporated into the kingdom as it moved north, first to the Highveld of South Africa and then on across the Limpopo River into Zimbabwe by the 1830s. These waves of incorporation created an ethnically layered polity. This chapter is a case study of members of the Brethren in Christ Church (BICC), a Protestant mission church that up to the 1950s was exclusively located in the rural areas of western Zimbabwe, the former territory of the precolonial kingdom. Tracking the selection of marital partners of BICC members between 1898 and the 1960s indicates that the precolonial social strata remained salient, in spite of the BICC's special emphasis on the notion of the radical equality of believers, expressed in their phrase, "God is no Respecter of persons," rendering the persistence of intramarriage according to the precolonial status categories noteworthy. Thus, although Ndebele converts of the BICC were Christians in a

153

church that emphasized the concept of equality before God, in fact, many families chose to ignore that aspect of the mission church's teaching when it came to whom their children ought to marry. For example, out of a total of forty-one church weddings performed in the BICC in 1940, only one can be said to be a cross-stratum union.[1]

Both women and men of the highest precolonial social stratum, the *abezansi*, actively participated in encouraging their children to marry other abezansi throughout the first half of the twentieth century. Oral interviews with elder members of the church reveal a pattern that senior men were genealogically motivated, keen to preserve abezansi "purity," while for senior abezansi women, the motivation came from household-level concerns. Whether welcoming daughters-in-law into their homes or sending daughters away to live in their husband's families, marrying within the precolonial caste groups helped ensure successful integration of brides into patrilocal family groups. It is also clear, with motivations that are not related to their abezansi identity, that Ndebele BICC women proved capable of forming lasting church-based alliances with other members of the lower social strata. The two trends, one subethnic, micro-, and family-based and the other more broadly determined and not ethnically inflected, are discernible in the lives of abezansi BICC women (and their families) in Matabeleland over the course of the first half of the twentieth century. Both trends, however, open questions about whether Ndebeleness is a useful category for analysis of gendered ethnicity for the people of western Zimbabwe in the early and mid-twentieth century.

The pace of modernizing change quickened after World War II. After 1959, the church moved into the regional capital, Bulawayo, and then into the colonial capital, Salisbury (now Harare), changing the rural nature of the church's membership base. As urbanization, nationalist politics, and the formation of an African middle class touched more people, a more generalized Ndebele ethnic identity was embraced, particularly in urban Bulawayo. Correspondingly, after the 1960s, the precolonial strata became increasingly less important and less common a factor in the selection of marriage partners. Women of abezansi families were motivated, for purposes of harmonious relations among the non-agnate kinswomen of a homestead, to exert what influence they could to retain abezansi intramarriage for their children through at least the 1950s and in some instances even longer. There was an ethnic element to this, but it was what I am calling a "subethnic" identity, because being abezansi was a linguistically and culturally inflected identity that existed within what from the outside looked like a general "Ndebele" category. For matters beyond the domain of marriage and homestead functioning, these same women were nonetheless able to cross the precolonial strata when it came to building and participating in associational alliances within the church.

Lomapholisa Khumalo:
A Case Study in Abezansi Intramarriage

The case of Lomapholisa Khumalo, descended from the Ndebele royal house, and her son Samuel Mlotshwa illustrates one devout BICC abezansi woman's marital priorities for her son. In the 1930s, Lomapholisa Khumalo and her husband, Masikwa Mlotshwa, were the parents of a large and growing family in the village of Mayezane. The people of Mayezane were plow-using, literate African Christians in what is today known as Matabeleland South Province in Zimbabwe. They had managed to navigate the traumas of the Ndebele Kingdom's destruction and colonial conquest in the 1890s. MaKhumalo and Mlotshwa had made a home at Mayezane in the 1910s, having left their family's homesteads in the Matopos Hills just to the north due to the displacing arrival in the late 1890s and early 1900s of white settlers, including agents of the BICC. (A woman whose father's praise name, or family name, was Khumalo would be called MaKhumalo. After she had a child, she would be referred to as the mother of that child; for example, Lomapholisa Khumalo's first child was named Samuel, so she was also known as NakaSamuel, mother of Samuel.)

MaKhumalo's firstborn child, a son named Samuel, was among the first to graduate from the Teacher Training School at the Brethren in Christ's Matopo Mission. By 1937, Samuel was a teacher at a primary school in the Filabusi District and ready to marry. He had fallen in love with a girl whose praise name was Dube, a name that was most commonly found among members of the lowest precolonial social stratum, the *abantu bakaMambo* (people of the *mambo*, or king). It was clear that the formidable Lomapholisa Khumalo did not approve of MaDube as a suitable wife for her son. Samuel recalled that his mother suggested, "Why don't you consider MaMatshazi?" Matshazi is a praise name connected to the abezansi. Young Mlotshwa and MaMatshazi had recently met at the wedding of another relative. Samuel Mlotshwa's respect for his family, and his mother in particular, proved a guiding principle. He heeded MaKhumalo's redirecting of his attentions. After many letters in which Samuel Mlotshwa professed his love for MaMatshazi, she consented to become his wife.[2] After the wedding, Samuel returned to his teaching post many miles to the east, while MaMatshazi stayed at Mayezane with MaKhumalo, her mother-in-law. After a period of time unspecified in Samuel's interview, when MaKhumalo was satisfied that her daughter-in-law had mastered the ways of the Mlotshwa family's household, she decided that her daughter-in-law could have "her own fireplace," allowing her to cook for Samuel and herself, which meant the young couple's married life together could begin. "After a woman got married she had to hang out with her mother-in-law to learn the ways of doing things until the mother-in-law released her to move on."[3] This quote conveys the importance of the mother-in-law in forming a functional relationship with her daughter-in-law, a relationship on which both of their futures depended, suggesting why a mother would have such a stake in deciding whom her son married.

Much of this story was told in 2006 by eighty-eight-year-old Samuel Mlotshwa to his niece. It is clear that the mother, Lomapholisa Khumalo, emerges as the pivotal character. Oral testimonies reveal that both senior men and women in abezansi families acted to preserve intramarriage, although women's reasons for doing so were often specific to their gender roles as mothers and wives. The ethnic element in the preference for intramarriage is that abezansi sons marrying into one of the lower strata would have meant that the new bride spoke a different language (such as TjiKalanga—see below) and observed different patterns of deference, and her unchurched relatives likely had different religious practices from unchurched abezansi. Because of the language, religious, and cultural differences among the strata, even though these differences were in some instances quite subtle, the focus on intramarriage has an ethnically inflected element to it that women actively supported for their own household-level reasons.

The Ethnically Layered Strata of the Nineteenth-Century Kingdom

Under colonial rule in present-day Zimbabwe, the Ndebele were configured as an ethnic group distinct from the Shona. Historian Terence Ranger and others have detailed the ways that these ethnic categories were "invented."[4] The Mlotshwa case study demonstrates that the likelihood that a young person from an abezansi family would also marry among the abezansi remained high until after World War II, a longer period than Ranger's earlier studies had assumed.[5]

Scholarship on the nineteenth-century Ndebele polity emphasizes its multi-peopled character: three strands of people with different languages hierarchically arranged, but all loyal to the central figure, Mzilikazi Khumalo, and, later, his son Lobhengula. In the nineteenth century, the Ndebele formation was a polity not strictly defined by ethnic unity. Historian Paul Landau shows that there was a distinct pattern of polity formation across precolonial southern Africa centered on the gathering of people around a powerful individual who would be fashioned a chief. Thus understood, a chiefship on the southern African Highveld "was an incorporative institution, and its success lay in bridging differences among varied constituencies." Mzilikazi Khumalo came to the Highveld in the 1820s with a band of warriors who then gathered a varied following around themselves based on their successes in war against other chiefdoms, which brought to his followers captive women, children, and cattle. As Landau put it, "Mzilikazi created a mobile capital which eventually ruled over a largely Sechuana-speaking infrastructure in the Transvaal, . . . [and] [d] espite his ferocious reputation his dominion did not differ greatly from other Highveld kingdoms."[6] The core traits of Ndebeleness in the nineteenth century were political loyalty to the Ndebele royal family and king, speaking isiNdebele, adopting Ndebele dress, and slitting the ears (the prefix *isi* indicates language; thus, isiNdebele is the language of the Ndebele people).[7] The Ndebele under the Khumalos thus were a political entity, a kingdom that began in the 1820s in present-day South Africa, eventually finding a permanent home in what are today the Matabeleland provinces of Zimbabwe.

Scholars as diverse as Julian Cobbing and Enocent Msindo agree that the nineteenth-century precolonial Ndebele Kingdom had a three-layered society.[8] The layers maintained their distinctiveness by marital endogamy. The first tier was comprised of the elite abezansi (people from downstream, i.e., from the south), who came from South Africa's KwaZulu region. Members of the abezansi were the only ones permitted to marry into the Khumalo royal family. Kin connection and proximity to the royal family ensured their highest status. In the early twentieth century, several decades after the end of the Ndebele Kingdom, the abesanzi families referred to a version of isiNdebele that reflected their forebears' abezansi origins in KwaZulu. Members of the second tier, or *abenhla* (people from upstream, meaning from the north), mainly married other abenhla, although occasionally abenhla were permitted to marry into abezansi families. The abenhla were the Sotho- and Tswana-speaking peoples whom the Ndebele Kingdom had incorporated when it was located on the South Africa Highveld in the 1820s and 1830s near present-day Pretoria, South Africa.[9] Additional Sotho and Tswana people joined the Ndebele polity in the following decades as a result of raids for cattle and children, and they also came in as abenhla.

After 1838, under pressure from attacks by the Zulu war parties under Shaka and his successors and from mounted gunmen belonging to white and mixed-race groups vying for dominance on the Highveld in today's South Africa, King Mzilikazi Khumalo moved the Ndebele nation to present-day Zimbabwe, north of the Limpopo River. There they found—and conquered—the Kalanga, Nyubi, and Venda peoples. These were the *abantu bakaMambo* (people of the Mambo).[10] The abantu bakaMambo, members of the lowest layer of society, were sometimes loosely referred to as the "slaves" of the Ndebele.[11] Msindo emphasizes that the caste system existed to provide the "superior classes moral authority over lower castes." Lower groups adopted a new political identity as they took on Ndebele "cultural, linguistic, and social practices," even though these adoptions did not make upward mobility possible.[12]

Msindo's insights make it imperative that we distinguish between the broader Ndebele polity, which encompasses all the caste groups, and Ndebele in the narrowest sense of the top tier of abezansi, who strove to retain elements of "purity" through enforcing their version of the language, which was closely related to the Nguni language spoken in KwaZulu, and preserving the purity of the bloodline through marital endogamy. As members of the lowest caste, the abantu bakaMambo, the Kalanga people were active agents from the late nineteenth century to the present in shoring up the importance of Kalanga chiefs and retaining the Kalanga language (TjiKalanga) and various cultural practices even while acceding to Ndebele rule up to the end of the kingdom in 1893. The Kalanga people's efforts to retain their language continued into the colonial period, since the colonial government did not recognize TjiKalanga for use in government communications or school texts. By emphasizing the cultural differences between the abezansi and the Kalanga people and their resilience in maintaining their distinct ethnic identity, Msindo reminds us that although it is easy to collapse all of the subgroups under the precolonial Ndebele Kingdom into the colonial-era Ndebele identity, in fact, Ndebele had more of an administrative and political designation than a cultural, linguistic, or religious one. Msindo's study is not focused on women or gender, however; a fruitful topic for future research beyond this study could investigate what role Kalanga women had in these efforts at preserving a separate Kalanga identity.

In addition to the status divisions within the Ndebele Kingdom between abezansi, abenhla, and abantu bakaMambo, there were divisions based on wealth and gender. The wealthiest were the male family heads from all strata, who controlled large herds of cattle and enjoyed the rank and capacity to function hospitably that were afforded by multiple wives and children. Poorer members of the kingdom lived either near the king's central settlement under the patronage of the king or the other leading men or at the periphery of the kingdom. Gendered understandings of work in the kingdom meant that women constructed and maintained houses, took care of children, and cultivated as many crops as possible, given the fact that the kingdom was on the move in its formative years. Wives of prominent men also had an important role in hosting and feeding the guests and clients of the household.[13] Generally, men herded the cattle and other livestock, trained and served as warriors, practiced artisanal crafts such as ironwork and the preparation of hides for clothing, and participated only briefly in the cultivation of crops at the key moments of breaking sod and harvest. Compare Heike I. Schmidt's chapter, "Shaming Men, Performing

Power," in this volume, which points to Ngoni identity in Tanzania, a primarily male phenomenon exemplified by individuals with enough military prowess that they could supply war booty to the king (*nkosi*). The parallels are not surprising, given that the Ndebele Kingdom and the Ngoni polities of Tanzania both emerged from Nguni-speaking leader-warriors dispersing out of what is today KwaZulu in the 1820s and after.

Very little scholarly attention has been given to the experience of women in terms of understanding Ndebele ethnicity, one exception being the indication that many women joined the Ndebele Kingdom as captives: they were taken from neighboring peoples during *impi* (warlike raids). An increasingly large proportion of the kingdom's subjects had joined as captives or as refugees. With full membership in Ndebele society reserved for adult men who had proved themselves as warriors and had matured into married heads of homesteads, many captured men and virtually all captured women were kept in a position that prevented any sense of full belonging. Unlike members of those chiefdoms who voluntarily submitted to Ndebele overrule and therefore were permitted to retain their own chiefs, captives were entirely cut off from their families and homes of origin and were thus subject to greater insecurity because of their lack of kin.[14] What did this mean for the young captives? For men, future survival lay in their capacity to assimilate use of isiNdebele and to prove themselves worthy as warriors in the Ndebele army. Captive children of both sexes were taken in by families as foster children/servants. Boys could look forward to a childhood of goat and cattle herding. Around age eighteen young men would become *amajaha*, unmarried warriors, joining the regiments associated with their new family or being chosen to join a newly formed regiment.[15] If they survived warfare, they might aspire to become *amadoda*, mature married men who wore the head ring.

Female captives were married to men of similar status selected for them by their adoptive abezansi or abenhla father. In unusual instances, as mentioned above, the female captive might marry her adoptive father, although historian Pathisa Nyathi says this was rare and not generally approved, since it violated the preferred pattern of intramarriage within status groups.[16] In patrilineal African societies in which some form of bridewealth is exacted, women have tended to find authority more through their roles as mothers of sons, as daughters, and as sisters than as wives.[17] Captive women were cut off from their lives as daughters and sisters and left only with the servant-like condition as wives, as daughters-in-law, and as sisters-in-law. If an abezansi woman ascended to become one of King Lobhengula's many wives, she might be given a large outpost homestead, at which she served as the king's eyes and ears; in this position, she could exercise significant derivative power. King Lobhengula's highest-ranking wife, Lozikeyi Dlodlo, played a vital role in the 1896 rising against the rule of the British South Africa Company (BSAC). Her determination to see the conflict come to war helped focus the people in the wake of the king's 1893 disappearance during the first military conflict between the Ndebele warriors and the BSAC.[18]

In the course of my oral history research in the 1990s and early 2000s, I discovered that when I asked isiNdebele-speaking informants "What makes an Ndebele man?" most answered polygyny, a love of meat, an attachment to beer, and a certain "hardness" of heart that made men less open to teachings about Christianity than women were.[19] Similar questions put to women about what makes an Ndebele woman yielded few answers, feeding my sense that Ndebele identity was chiefly a masculine one. The salient elements of ethnicity in this study focus on the abezansi women of the BICC. I argue that their actions after colonial conquest in the first half of the twentieth century supported abezansi continuation through intramarriage because of a subethnic sensibility centered on household concerns regarding family harmony.

In sum, Ndebele identity is fluid and elusive: it changed over time, it was originally more of a political than an ethnic designation, and it has meant different things to different stakeholders. Ethnicity-related elements overlap with political elements that are really not ethnic at all, if ethnic means things like language, religious practices, and customs. This fluidity makes it quite challenging to write about Ndebeleness, gendered or not, coherently. Ndebeleness conceived of as an ethnicity is a poor tool for understanding the women featured in this study. Working with the abezansi subcategory provides a more traceable phenomenon from which to puzzle out gendered elements in that identity—at least for the first half of the twentieth century.

Endogamous Elite Marriages, Women, and Abezansi Ethnic Expression

Colonial conquest meant the end of the Ndebele Kingdom (by the mid-1930s, hopes for a restoration of the Ndebele monarchy were effectively dead), and church teaching emphasized that reinforcing the caste boundaries of the nineteenth-century kingdom was not a Christian aim. Yet the official marriage records of the BICC show that converts continued to marry within their precolonial status categories well into the twentieth century. The colonial government discouraged making meaning in the kingdom's caste distinctions. In fact, they "made much of the equality enjoyed in the eyes of the law by 'the Matabele and their former slaves.'"[20] Among other things, for example, the colonial government refused to support the kingdom-derived ban on intercaste marriages. Nonetheless, influential Ndebele elders of both sexes, including committed members of the BICC, exercised their influence to keep the precolonial status groups intact. While for senior women there may have been an element of a larger national vision shared with the menfolk—a yearning to retain the salience of the narrowly defined Ndebele royal caste—the discussion of MaKhumalo's case above demonstrates that her concerns seemed chiefly to be at the household level.[21]

The abezansi are identifiable through a distinct set of praise names associated only with their stratum. It is possible—through a cross-referencing of the marriage records, which record the brides' and grooms' praise names, and an analysis of oral history interviews—to track abezansi BICC members' decisions about marriage across several decades in the twentieth century. In many southern African societies, individuals did not conduct courtship *as* individuals; instead, spouses were chosen with the approval of both families, and multiple members of the family helped to conduct courtship. As one BICC elder remarked, "It's one thing to marry an individual. . . . But his whole family—you don't marry for the individual. You marry the whole family. If their ways are different, it's very difficult."[22] The key phrase in this remark is "their ways," which refers to differences in matters associated with ethnicity, such as the interrelated elements of language, specific patterns of deference within the family (which directly affected how a new bride would enter her husband's homestead in a rural area), and religion.

Lomapholisa Khumalo's assertiveness regarding her son's choice of spouse is significant. She did not want the Dube girl as a daughter-in-law. As noted above, members of the abezansi, including the Mlotshwa family, originated from KwaZulu in South Africa.[23] Dube was a surname frequently found among the abantu bakaMambo. As such, MaKhumalo did not consider a girl from a Dube family an acceptable choice for a young man descended from the royal family and its associated elite families.

Although I believe MaKhumalo's opposition to the girl named Dube was motivated by a strong stance that a girl from the lower stratum was an unsuitable choice for her son, Samuel's own testimony avoids stating directly that his mother wanted to retain abezansi endogamy. He said, "My mother did not care for the Dube girl very much. I did not try to find out why." This polite evasion on Samuel's part reflects the changing sensibilities about abezansi identity and the culture of the church. By 2006, the time of this interview, strict adherence to intramarriage within the precolonial Ndebele Kingdom's castes had largely died away. The woman conducting the interview was Mlotshwa's niece, who herself had married into the lowest stratum during the 1970s. The elder Mlotshwa would have found it rude to speak on abezansi elitism in that time and with that interviewer.

For several decades into the twentieth century, both older women and men from abezansi families found it advantageous in their different sets of interests to promote endogamy. With the migrant labor patterns of the colonial era pulling men away from the homestead, it was as relevant as it had been during the era of the kingdom, if not more important than ever, for a mother-in-law to get along well with her daughter-in-law. Therefore, abezansi women had an incentive to participate in maintaining abezansi marital endogamy; a mother of sons at a rural homestead would be more likely to get along well with her daughters-in-law if they came from families of a similar background, language, and culture.

Ranger's work on the history of Matabeleland has argued that the narrower abezansi, Ndebele royalty–based chauvinism was markedly at play in the first years after the colonial conquest, especially in the efforts of the last Ndebele king's descendants and their allies to have the monarchy restored. Ranger identified an Ndebele identity that emerged in Matabeleland during the 1930s and 1940s that "transcended and ideally abolished caste distinctions," while at the same time new class and material distinctions, in which the majority were illiterate and poor and based their agricultural practices on the guidance of the regional rain deity, emerged. The minority was educated and progressive, following the teachings of agricultural demonstrators trained by the colonial government. In the latter category, there were also storekeepers and wealthy chiefs who owned thousands of cattle.[24] Ranger noted that Ndebele consciousness had broadened by the 1950s and 1960s into a wider understanding of politically meaningful Ndebeleness that subsumed and essentially moved beyond the caste system as part of the struggle against Rhodesian colonial rule. Nationalist leader Joshua Nkomo's identity, for example, emerged in concentric layers from his Kalanga-speaking home in the Matopos to a regional, Matabeleland-based "Ndebele" identity and on out to a pan-Zimbabwe African identity.[25] This study shows, however, that the precolonial social strata continued to be important for abezansi families in the BICC past the 1940s, with the mothers and grandmothers at the forefront encouraging their children to marry other members of the abezansi. The fact that these efforts occurred at the household level and not as formally organized political movements may be why this trend eluded Ranger's periodization of the continuing relevance of the precolonial caste system.

Well into the 1950s (and later for some), abezansi families continued to stress that their children grow up speaking what they called "pure" Ndebele, which meant a variation of the language that retained the grammar and vocabulary that originated in the royal family's area of origin in KwaZulu, South Africa. Recollections from Huggins Msimanga, a man of abezansi origin, on his childhood in Matabeleland South in the 1950s underscore the continued close linkage between abezansi (which he termed Nguni) purity and the emphasis on intramarriage:

> We were not allowed to speak broken Ndebele. Every time we used vocabulary that was not Ndebele we would be rebuked. . . . The way you put emphasis in a sentence they would correct you; they were strict with their language. It was mainly Kalangas around our homestead. . . . So yes, we are surrounded by Kalanga. . . . So part of our vocabulary had to kind of merge. And our parents didn't like to see that happening. Overall it was understood, when an individual was grown up enough to get married, they would have to be selective to marry within that Nguni tribe. . . . There was a lot of marriage within the group.[26]

It is worth also noting that in the Msimanga homestead, the cooperation between Huggins's grandmother and his daughters-in-law marked the functionality and harmony in his home and family; the men were often away due to migrant labor and were occupied with male associational work of drinking beer and political organizing when they were home. It was the "mothers" who kept the household running and who raised, fed, churched, and schooled the children.[27] In this kind of home setting, where a daughter-in-law lives in the same homestead with her husband's mother, the senior mother's opinions about the suitability of a bride were of consequence. The cases examined in this study thus suggest that instead of *erasing* precolonial status distinctions, abezansi Christians of the BICC, while willing to worship, go to school, and serve as coworkers with those of lower precolonial status, with a very few notable exceptions, preferred to keep abezansi endogamy even while they pursued the newer forms of status.

The Exceptions:
Examples of Cross-Caste BICC Marriage

While there were very few cases prior to 1960 in which two people of different strata were married in the BICC, it did happen in rare instances. In the Sibanda-Nsimango case highlighted below, the family cited their conscious embrace of Christian egalitarianism for justifying their choices. Such matches that did cross precolonial status groups often reinforced new forms of status found in education and a progressive Christian identity. The fact that these marriages were exceptional highlights the typicality of intramarriage for most others. The only obvious case of cross-group marriage in 1941, Sibanda-Nsimango, was between two teachers, a fact that is not insignificant. A small but growing number of BICC members discerned that status could be acquired by new means, means not defined by one's family or "tribal" status but by educational level or Christian identity, even while most others both within and outside the church continued to adhere to the endogamous marriage patterns. It was not an overwhelming shift at this time but was rather more like a discernible crack in the prevailing marriage patterns, a crack that grew wider in the next two generations. The Sibanda-Nsimango case marks the beginning of a transition in how elements such as Christian piety, colonial meritocracy, and precolonial aristocracy affected marital choices during these decades among Ndebele Christians of the BICC. Thus, in families where the male suitor either did not have a mother or lived away from his parents' homestead, cross-stratum marriages were easier to enact.

In 1941, Mangisi Sibanda married a woman who carried higher status according to both new and old definitions. Sibanda was a young teacher-pastor at a BICC outstation with a standard 4 (grade 6) education when he prayed for a wife sometime around 1940. According to one account, he wrote a letter to God asking for help in finding a wife, indicating that a woman's Christian character, more than her looks, was what mattered to him.[28]

Sibanda's Venda origins marked him as a member of the abantu baka-Mambo.[29] Born in 1914 near Inyathi, he was named Mangisi (white) because of the presence of white people in the area at the time of his birth.[30] He had come to Tshalimbe to be raised by his father's brother after the death of his parents in the influenza epidemic of 1918. Sibanda attended the school at Tshalimbe, headed by Mnofa Nsimango, as a teen in the late 1920s.[31] It was while listening to Nsimango preach that Sibanda was moved to confess his sins and become a Christian.[32]

Hannah Nsimango was among the first women of the Brethren in Christ Church in Southern Rhodesia to qualify as a professionally trained teacher. The BICC Matopo Teacher Training Institute first admitted women in 1934, and Hannah Nsimango completed the two-year course in 1938 with a primary teaching certificate.[33] Hannah Nsimango's own parents' marriage exemplifies the complexities of understanding the strata of the precolonial kingdom. Hannah's father, as Nsimango, was of the abezansi; her mother was Ntombiyaphansi "Sixpence" Ndlovu. Was MaNdlovu from the abezansi or not? The lack of clarity is fed by the fact that the Ndlovu praise name, meaning "lion," could be found in all three of the Ndebele Kingdom's social strata. This is an instance in which the praise name does not provide an indicator of status. One clue that this Ndlovu family was of high status is found in a missionary's anecdote given about Hannah's uncle Matshuba Ndlovu, Ntombiyaphansi's brother: "His father, Mpisa [Mjobhiza], had been one of the most trusted witch doctors of the King, and had been held in great respect by all of the natives in that part of the country. The boy was very eager for school, and the first morning he and Mapita's girls begged us to allow only the Matabele to attend school, and not the Amahole, or subject races [abantu bakaMambo]. This furnished an excellent opportunity of teaching them that God is no Respecter of persons."[34] Ntombiyaphansi Ndlovu married Mnofa Nsimango in the 1920s; Nsimango was directly related to King Lobhengula's paramount wife, making him definitively of the abezansi.[35] The fact that Hannah's elder sister, Sithembile, noted that their father, Mnofa Nsimango, had set the example of marrying into a lower stratum because he "didn't follow the abezansi way" (i.e., endogamous marriage) suggests, however, that this Ndlovu family was not from the top stratum. This then leads to the conclusion that the Ndlovu family into which he married was of the next stratum down, the abenhla, who were held in much higher regard than the abantu bakaMambo. The daughters remembered their parents' match as a cross-caste marriage, and Hannah's sister explained that their willingness to do this was due to their faith: "It was a different view of Christians."[36]

As an orphan, Sibanda did not have a mother to whom he would have to bring his abezansi bride. By contrast, consider Samuel Mlotshwa's case: MaKhumalo redirected Samuel's attention away from a girl named Dube in favor of a girl of abezansi heritage and then took the preferred bride, Ma-Matshazi, into her home for a period of time for training in Mlotshwa family ways. If Sibanda were living in his parents' homestead, might his mother have tried to influence his choice of bride away from a girl with the Nsimango praise name? Would she have been willing to take a girl of higher-status origin into her home for training in Sibanda family ways? These questions are, if unanswerable, worth considering, especially in light of the discussion of Zama Ncube's case below, where a cross-stratum marriage was also eased due to the lack of necessary cohabitation with in-laws.

Sibanda did marry Hannah Nsimango, daughter of the man who had been his teacher and pastor in his home of Tshalimbe. Sibanda's marriage to MaNsimango created a lasting partnership in Christian leadership; she embraced her role as the wife of an ordained minister. As a mission school–educated daughter of a pastor, MaNsimango knew the other church leaders and their families well and had her own flair for leadership and community outreach, which only enhanced her husband's influence in the BICC's Wanezi District, where they served until she died in the 1970s.

While Mangisi Sibanda and Hannah Nsimango did marry across the social strata, as stated above, their marriage was the exception. Most people, including Christians, continued to marry within their social stratum in the early and middle decades of the twentieth century. An abenhla woman remarked in a 1999 interview how her mother, MaMguni, married within the abenhla caste in the late 1910s, indicating that in her mother's time people knew to which caste they belonged and expected their marriage partner to come from within that caste.[37] Another notable example of the persistence of this practice is seen in the family of another prominent churchman, who happened to be Mangisi Sibanda's predecessor, Manhlenhle Kumalo.[38] Kumalo's children were age-mates to Sibanda and Nsimango, and he exerted tremendous influence over his children's choice of spouses in order to preserve their status as members of the elite abezansi stratum.

Kumalo was a nephew of the former Ndebele king Lobhengula. One mission source's starstruck praise for Kumalo conveys some worldly awe at his elevated status: "He ranked high in the Royal Family, and the blood of the proud Matebele [a now-outdated term for Ndebele people] flowed thru his veins. The power of the Gospel of Jesus Christ humbled Kumalo."[39] The fact that for a time Manhlenhle Kumalo served under the supervision of Nyamazana Dube was hailed in an article in the BICC's North American newspaper, the *Evangelical Visitor*, as a triumph of Christian egalitarianism and humility over royal arrogance:

> Dube's first wife was of a higher tribe: Dube was a slave of the slaves by natural birth.... At one time in Bishop H. P. Steigerwald's day, Dube was in charge of the Swazi outschool. Manhlenhle Kumalo (later, Overseer), his brother-in-law, whose royal standing was in sharp [contrast] to Dube's low birth, was there as a helper under Dube. When Bishop Steigerwald told them that he would have to shift one, as either of them were able to take charge of a school, they both answered in about the same breath, "We would be glad to stay right on as we are now." As Bishop Steigerwald remarked through his tears later, it was a real demonstration of what the Gospel does for people; for according to native custom—and to human nature—the one of royal lineage would want to be at the head.[40]

Dube's marriage to an abezansi woman was made so much of precisely because it was still rare for anyone else in the African membership to have crossed that divide at that time. The BICC, like many of the mission churches in colonial southern Africa, was very slow to ordain African men as ministers. Thus, by 1959 only six men had been ordained, among them Nyamazana Dube, Manhlenhle Kumalo, and Mangisi Sibanda. Both Dube and Sibanda were men of the abantu bakaMambo stratum who had, very exceptionally, married abezansi women.[41] Nonetheless, Kumalo's willingness to serve in the church under the supervision of his Kalanga brother-in-law, Dube, did not mean that he was willing to allow his children to pick spouses from among the abantu bakaMambo.[42]

The story of another cross-caste marriage illustrates a crucial aspect of the transition from the continued importance of endogamy among the abezansi and the new priorities of an urbanizing and modernizing African middle class: the marriage between Zama Ncube (MaKhumalo) and her husband, Ncube.[43] Born in the 1920s to Mawogelana Khumalo (the brother of Lomapholisa, mentioned earlier) and his wife, MaDlodlo, Zama had two abezansi parents with close kinship links to the Ndebele royal family. Both of her parents were early converts to the BICC, and Zama was raised a devout member of the church. When she met and fell in love with a man of the family name of Ncube (of the Kalanga group), her father was not happy about it, according to Zama. Her father's objections centered on the fact that he wanted to ensure that among his offspring there would be someone to carry forward a "pure" abezansi lineage:

> He called his brothers to talk about it. Then it was my uncle who really encouraged [my father] and told [him] that I was grown up enough to decide to choose whatever I wanted to. [My father] said, "No, I won't let my daughter marry a Kalanga. My only daughter. You Makanyas have got four daughters. If one of them marries a Kalanga, perhaps these three would marry their own tribe; not so with me." They talked over and over until at last he gave in. And [we] got married in September 1960, yeah, and I came to live in town with him. I have been here since then. Happily married. And afterwards he [my father] was happy about it too.[44]

The fact that Zama moved to town to live with her husband at the time of her marriage is important here. She was not going to have to live with a mother-in-law of the Kalanga people. The newly married couple were free to live a modern, more broadly defined Ndebele identity in Bulawayo's Mpopoma Township, the type of life articulated by Ranger in *Voices from the Rocks*. Zama Ncube's husband was active in the anticolonial nationalist party, the Zimbabwe African People's Union (ZAPU). Later, her son joined ZAPU's armed wing, the Zimbabwe People's Liberation Army (ZIPRA), during the liberation war. Zama's own agency centered on her work among BICC youth at the vibrant, African middle-class congregation in Mpopoma, where abezansi and abantu baka-Mambo mixed much more freely than in the rural areas. Her Ndebele sensibility by the late 1990s, when I interviewed her, was very much a pan-Ndebele nationalist political identity, not that of the narrower, nineteenth-century-looking abezansi kind.

As noted above, a crucial factor in the viability and success of the Nsigmano-Sibanda and Khumalo-Ncube marriages is that in both instances, the bride did not have to enter the homestead of her mother-in-law. For the Khumalo-Ncube union, the fact that the young couple could earn their living in town, away from the rural home, gave them more space to endure MaKhumalo's father's objections until he relented. There is little doubt that the Khumalo father's motivations were ethnically inflected to retain abezansi "purity" of lineal descent. His daughter was less concerned about it; her ethnic sensibility had shifted into the more homogenized, urban-based "Ndebele" identification. Times had changed, and for her, marrying a Ncube was not a point of shame. And, being based in town, she did not have to worry about moving in with a Ncube mother-in-law. For the Nsimango-Sibanda couple, who married more than twenty years earlier, although their lives remained rurally based at the rural mission station, the church's official teaching that "God is no Respecter of persons" supported their union, as well as the fact that abezansi Hannah Nsimango came from a family that had already consciously broken with abezansi exclusivity in her parents' generation. As stated above, the Nsimango-Sibanda 1941 marriage, although occurring earlier in the timeline as an exception, serves as a harbinger for the trends that flourished by the time Zama Ncube was getting married in Bulawayo in the 1960s.

Beyond Subethnic Identification: Women Forging Cross-Group Alliances

Even from the beginning of the colonial period and the first conversions to the BICC, abezansi Christians worked closely, for purposes of the church's mission, with members of the other status groups. Before Lomapholisa MaKhumalo was married, she had also participated in two long-distance evangelistic initiatives with her close friend Sitshokupi Sibanda, another young, unmarried female convert but from the lowest stratum, the abantu bakaMambo.[45] She and Sitshokupi Sibanda joined the 1911 effort led by BICC missionary Levi Doner to expand the BICC presence to the east in Chibi, Mashonaland.[46] In 1911, MaSibanda and MaKhumalo were both about twenty-one years of age. They were not merely laborers who had come along to haul water or cook, although they also did these things.[47] African elders in the church today instead emphasize that MaSibanda and MaKhumalo were evangelistic "pioneers": "They were the first people to go to Chibi, these two women."[48] Lomapholisa's son Samuel recalled that his mother and the Africans with her, including Sitshokupi Sibanda, were motivated to join Doner's group because they wished "to go and preach the Word of God, preach the Gospel of Jesus Christ."[49]

The mission to Chibi was closed down shortly after it began due to the death of Doner.[50] Oral tradition among African church members states that MaSibanda and MaKhumalo were unhappy with the central mission authorities' decision to discontinue the Chibi Mission. Still desiring to preach the Gospel in foreign places, the two embarked on an evangelistic journey on foot across the

Zambezi to the Tonga people in Northern Rhodesia (Zambia). Because the women lacked the sponsorship of any missionaries, the costs were borne by the young women themselves and those who hosted them as they traveled.[51] Macha Mission's 1914 annual report to the BICC General Conference in North America noted that "Sr. Setyokupi of Mapane" (Sister Sitshokupi) had arrived at Macha.[52] The oral testimonies indicate that Lomapholisa Khumalo was there with her, at least for a time; it is not known whether the two returned to Matabeleland together or separately. The partnership of these two women was fostered by their common experiences as young converts of the BICC missionaries' first years in western Zimbabwe. Although each woman hailed from a different stratum of the precolonial kingdom, the two shared commitment to the new faith and knew many people in common. Being the same age and unmarried also allowed them to form a cooperative bond. Their shared yen for evangelistic adventures far from home was more important than the fact that one was from the abantu bakaMambo and one from the abezansi. Abezansi women's advocacy for marital endogamy was not a relevant factor in MaSibanda and MaKhumalo's shared work on behalf of the church.

Thus, while MaKhumalo acted to protect her family's elite-stratum interests by influencing Samuel's (and perhaps his brothers') choice of a spouse, she also made enduring and significant working partnerships with other BICC Christians who came from other social strata. She was a committed Christian; she established and taught the first Sunday school at Mayezane, where she interacted with and mentored people from all the social strata.[53] Other abantu baka-Mambo BICC members specifically remembered the hospitality and Christian mentoring they received from MaKhumalo at the Mlothswa homestead in Mayezane.[54] The fact that MaKhumalo formed significant bonds of coopera-tion and association with women of all precolonial social strata in her church work shows an opposite impulse that was not motivated by a significantly dis-cernible ethnic agenda. By looking at MaKhumalo's life from more than one angle, therefore, we see how she both acted to preserve the status of her abezansi family and forged lasting, cross-caste working relationships with other African women in the BICC church. Her abezansi ethnic priorities were expressed at the household level and were not relevant in the associational work of her wider church life.

In the 1960s, Hannah Sibanda also enacted cross-caste cooperation in the interests of the church's evangelistic and associational aims. She encouraged and supported the calling to evangelism experienced by Maria Tshuma, a member of the abantu bakaMambo.[55] Maria Tshuma's home of Mbaulo was in the BICC's Wanezi District, where Hannah Sibanda's husband, the Reverend Mangisi Sibanda, was the overseer, with responsibility for over thirty BICC congregations. After teaching primary school for the BICC for many years, Maria Tshuma was forced to retire around age fifty in 1962. Hannah Sibanda chose Maria Tshuma to build the network of congregation-based women's groups all over the district. With plenty of energy and many kin and church connections throughout the Wanezi District, Maria Tshuma took to the work readily and effectively. Hannah Sibanda and the wife of another ordained minister, Joyce Khumalo, later in the 1960s worked together with the wife of missionary bishop Alvin Book, Thata Book, to start a pan-BICC women's group called the Omama Bosizo (Women Who Help).

The churchwomen's associational strength across the precolonial status categories that Hannah Sibanda and Maria Tshuma had built in the Wanezi District was one of several important precedents for the successful launching of the Omama Bosizo. Monogamously married women in good standing in the church constituted the membership of the Omama, and, as in women's groups in other mission churches, the leaders were wives of prominent churchmen. Blending piety, propriety, and the teaching of homemaking skills, Omama Bosizo branches were modeled not only after the women's meetings of the BICC and the uniformed women's *manyanos* of the Methodists and other denominations but also after the secular women's clubs.[56] Secular women's clubs were devoted to teaching homecraft, performing philanthropy, or serving as women's auxiliaries to the trade unions or nationalist political parties. The Omama Bosizo quickly became a crucial arbiter of female status and propriety within the BICC and displayed a complex urban-rural dynamic not significantly affected by the status dynamics from the precolonial social strata.[57] The Omama Bosizo up to the time of writing remains a vital force in the BICC. The women in Omama Bosizo came from all of the precolonial strata; when the organization was established in the late 1960s, the newer status categories connected to church membership, education, and middle-class professions were more important than membership in the abezansi. Even for those women of the Omama Bosizo who still cared about abezansi intramarriage, those subethnic household concerns did not interfere with their ability to participate in the work and associational benefits of the Omama.

Conclusion

Nineteenth-century Ndebele ethnic identity was easily identified for its male qualities of loyalty to the king and the capacity to perform well in the war parties to raid for cattle and subject people. For women in the kingdom, Ndebeleness was an elusive quantity; it was easier to identify gendered ethnicity according to the hierarchically arranged social strata, each of which had its own ethnic inflection. This pattern carried into the twentieth century, after the kingdom had been conquered by the British and turned into the colony of Rhodesia, and after the arrival of Christian missionaries, including agents of the Brethren in Christ Church.

Africans in present-day Zimbabwe responded to, adapted to, and appropriated for their own purposes the Christian teaching that came in the wake of colonization in the 1890s. Thus, although Ndebele converts were Christians in a church that emphasized the concept of equality before God and one might think they would stop observing intramarriage customs, in fact, many families chose to ignore the mission church's teaching when it came to whom their children ought to marry. Exhaustive analysis of the BICC's marriage certificates reveals that marital endogamy according to the caste structure of the nineteenth-century Ndebele Kingdom remained a resilient practice even among these modernizing, literate Christian Africans who had joined the BICC, a mission church that placed particular emphasis on the teaching that "God is no Respecter of persons." Both men and women—fathers and mothers—cared about the continuance of abezansi intramarriage. The oral testimonies suggest that the reasons why this is so for men and women were different. All the women at a rural homestead would have come from different families when they married into their husband's family. Senior women found it easier to incorporate daughters-in-law from the same precolonial stratum. Senior men were used to making bridewealth deals and alliances with men of the same stratum and were concerned to see abezansi lines continue as such into the next generations.

The colonial dispensation and the BICC had separate reasons behind their common interest to discourage continued salience of the nineteenth-century caste system. Nonetheless, abezansi women supported the goal of intramarriage, if for no other reason than the fact that the population was still largely rural based, with brides coming to live in the homesteads of their mothers-in-law. Successful integration of young women into their husband's family's homesteads was eased when there were not cultural and religious differences to add to the usual challenges of marriage. Thus, abezansi mothers wanted their sons to marry abezansi girls and their daughters to marry into abezansi families.

It becomes clear, after consideration of a range of cases of Ndebele male and female individuals and families affiliated with the BICC over the course of the period of colonial rule up to the 1950s, that the term Ndebele is less useful than the ethnically inflected social strata that existed under that umbrella term. Msindo's history of Ndebele-Kalanga relations, which foregrounds Kalanga perspectives and the Kalanga's efforts to retain their distinctive ethnic identity, supports investigation into the distinctive ethnic elements within the different segments/layers of the broader Ndebele category. In this chapter, the lens has

been narrowed to consider the elite abezansi caste; the subethnic identity was
noticeably expressed in the choice of marriage partners. In the first half of the
twentieth century, abezansi women and men of the BICC urged, coaxed, or
required their children to marry other abezansi. As articulated by an abezansi
female elder in 1999: "It wasn't because of 'ooh, Khumalos, royal family. . . .'
No. It was more a matter of cultural differences, different traditions. People
kept that line. There are still those who keep it to today. It's hard to marry
across the line. You wouldn't want your daughter to marry of the Mambo
people. There are so many different customs."[58] It was Zama Ncube's father
who had the prominent place in the story of reinforcing (or attempting to reinforce) spousal choices in favor of keeping the abezansi from mixing with the
Ndebele-affiliated ethnic groups of lower social strata. In Samuel Mlotshwa's
case, it was his mother who advocated for the same. Huggins Msimanga, who
grew up in an abezansi homestead that reinforced the use of "pure" isiNdebele,
was most influenced by his grandmother. His grandmother and the various
wives of his father and his father's brothers were a cooperative unit running the
homestead. The Msimanga homestead's women's subethnic homogeneity (all
from the abezansi) was an advantage. We see from this small set of examples that
both women and men—elders of both sexes—in abezansi families were motivated to see their descendants also marry abezansi, albeit for different reasons.
By the 1960s, urbanized, middle-class Ndebele young people of abezansi origin
were far less likely to heed their parents' urgings for intramarriage.

In the interests of advancing the church's work, isiNdebele-speaking members of the BICC worked across the nineteenth-century social strata to build
associational strength and to advance evangelistic goals. The twentieth-century
transformations seen with urbanization, nationalism, postcolonial nationhood, and, most recently, diaspora expanded the likelihood that women would
forge wider associations, such as the Omama Bosizo, to the point that abezansi
marital endogamy remains a high priority in very few families by now, while
the cross-group, church-based associations keep growing.

The political organizing for African rights that occurred after World War II
along with the rise of an African middle class and urbanization led to yet more
shifts in understanding what made a person, man or woman, Ndebele. The
social strata of the precolonial kingdom had the most relevance in the rural
setting. As increasing numbers of people built their livings, identities, and
religious expression on urban wage labor, Western-style education, or the
Christian deity (one of universal rather than familial proportions), the rural
social categories came to matter less. In terms of the lives of women and the
domestic-level concerns of mothers, urbanized life meant it was far less likely
that a new bride would need to live with her husband's family and have to

learn how to get along intimately with her mother-in-law. This also lessened abezansi families' motivations and need for such a concerted effort to promote intramarriage.

In light of the individual cases highlighted here and the broader changing understandings of Ndebele identity explored here, it is plausible to regard Ndebele as a shifting, layered, even problematic term of limited use for consideration of questions of gendered ethnicity. This study, for reasons of necessary brevity, has focused on the subethnically inflected abezansi members of the BICC. Research into early twentieth-century marriage partner choices among the other castes and among people who belonged to other churches would valuably extend the analysis. In addition, further investigation into the precise nature of the "different ways" (e.g., the varying modes of ancestor veneration practiced in the different precolonial strata) that female family heads were reluctant to have to deal with from outsiders who married their children would enhance the depth of understanding behind these choices.

NOTES

1.   See the table in Wendy Urban-Mead, "Women, Religion, and Gender in the Brethren in Christ Church, Matabeleland, Zimbabwe, 1898–1978" (PhD diss., Columbia University, 2004).

2.   The story of the depth of Mlotshwa's filial piety and the wedding celebration for him and MaMatshazi has been detailed in Wendy Urban-Mead, "Negotiating Plainness and Gender in the Creation of an Africa Rural Elite: Christian Weddings in Matabeleland, 1913–1944," *Journal of Religion in Africa* 38, no. 3 (2008): 209–46.

3.   Samuel Mlotshwa, interview by Hlengiwe Sibanda (MaMlotshwa), 4 June 2006, North End, Bulawayo, Zimbabwe.

4.   Terence Ranger, *The Invention of Tribalism in Zimbabwe* (Gweru, Zimbabwe: Mambo Press, 1985); Terence Ranger, "Missionaries, Migrants, and the Manyika: The Invention of Ethnicity in Zimbabwe," in *The Creation of Tribalism in Southern Africa*, ed. Leroy Vail (Berkeley: University of California Press, 1991), 118–50.

5.   Terence Ranger, *The African Voice in Southern Rhodesia 1898–1930* (Evanston, IL: Northwestern University Press, 1970); Terence Ranger, *Voices from the Rocks: Nature, Culture and History in the Matopos Hills of Zimbabwe* (London: James Currey, 1999). However, Arthur J. B. Hughes's 1956 ethnographic study of the "Rhodesian Ndebele" noted a continued adherence to intracaste marriages: "Much is made of the modern tendency for intercaste marriages to occur, but investigations suggest that this type of union is far rarer than one would imagine from the lamentations of the more conservative Zansi and Enhla" (*Kin, Caste and Nation among the Rhodesian Ndebele* [Manchester: Manchester University Press, 1956], 59).

6.   Paul S. Landau, *Popular Politics in the History of South Africa, 1400–1948* (Cambridge: Cambridge University Press, 2010), 11.

7.   See Julian Raymond Dennis Cobbing, "The Ndebele under the Khumalos, 1820–1896" (PhD diss., University of Lancaster, 1976); and Pathisa Nyathi, *Traditional Ceremonies of Amandebele* (Gweru, Zimbabwe: Mambo Press, 2001).

8.   Cobbing, "The Ndebele"; Hughes, *Kin, Caste and Nation*; Enocent Msindo, *Ethnicity in Zimbabwe: Transformations in Kalanga and Ndebele Societies, 1860–1990* (Rochester, NY: Rochester University Press, 2012).

9.   Hughes, *Kin, Caste and Nation*, 9.

10.   Mambo was the title of the king of the Rozvi polity, which ruled in central and western Zimbabwe prior to the arrival of Mzilikazi and his people. The Mambo people included a variety of different groups: the Venda, Kalanga, and Nyubi peoples were historically, linguistically, and culturally distinct. Thus, the reference in this chapter to abantu bakaMambo is, not unlike use of the term *Ndebele*, more of a political description and not a unified ethnic designation.

11.   A fictional reimagining of the British conquest of the Ndebele Kingdom bemoaned the loss of Ndebele sovereignty over the abantu bakaMambo, pejoratively known as the *amahole*: "Amahole women and children are no more our slaves. Instead, the Amandebele [Ndebele] have become the Amahole—the slaves of the whiteman" (Stanlake Samkange, *On Trial for My Country* [London: Heineman, 1967], 11).

12.   Msindo, *Ethnicity in Zimbabwe*, 49.

13.   Leroy Vail and Landeg White, *Power and the Praise Poem: Southern African Voices in History* (Charlottesville: University Press of Virginia, 1991), 84–111.

14.   Ngwabi Bhebe, *Christianity and Traditional Religion in Western Zimbabwe, 1859–1923* (London: Longman, 1979), 10.

15.   Pathisa Nyathi, based on his interviews with a senior male Khumalo, indicated also that captive children taken into Nguni families would be given "another surname, any local surname, such as Sibanda, Tshuma, Moyo or Dube," because otherwise allowing the captive to take on an Nguni surname "would be disastrous for intermarriage" (Pathisa Nyathi, interview with the author, 14 August 2000, Bulawayo, Zimbabwe).

16.   Bhebe, based on evidence gleaned from an oral history interview, argued that it was common for adoptive fathers to marry their captive female children (*Christianity*, 10). Pathisa Nyathi disagreed, citing the social stigma. He said such unions were characterized as "I have had sex with a rock rabbit/dassy. . . . If a Dlodlo impregnates a local girl, her pregnancy would be assigned to a local man, a Moyo" (Nyathi, interview).

17.   See Wendy Urban-Mead, "Dynastic Daughters: Three Royal Kwena Women and E. L. Price of the London Missionary Society, 1853–1881," in *Women in African Colonial Histories*, ed. Jean Allman, Susan Geiger, and Nakanyike Musisi (Bloomington: Indiana University Press, 2002), 48–70; Iris Berger, "'Beasts of Burden' Revisited: Interpretations of Women and Gender in Southern African Societies," in *Paths towards the Past: African Historical Essays in Honor of Jan Vansina*, ed. Robert W. Harms, Joseph C. Miller, David S. Newbury, and Michele D. Wagner (Atlanta, GA: African Studies Association Press, 1994), 123–41; Martinus Daneel, *Old and New in Southern Shona Independent Churches*, vol. 1, *Background and Rise of the Major Movements* (The Hague: Mouton, 1971), 47–48.

18. Marieke Faber Clarke with Pathisa Nyathi, *Lozikeyi Dlodlo: Queen of the Ndebele* (Bulawayo, Zimbabwe: AmaGugu Press, 2011).

19. See Wendy Urban-Mead, *The Gender of Piety: Intersections of Faith and Family in Matabeleland Zimbabwe since 1900* (Athens: Ohio University Press, forthcoming).

20. Hughes, *Kin, Caste and Nation*, 56.

21. See Msindo, *Ethnicity in Zimbabwe*; Sabelo J. Gatsheni Ndlovu, *The Ndebele Nation: Reflections on Hegemony, Memory, and Historiography* (Amsterdam: UNISA Press, 2009); Ranger, *African Voice*; and Ranger, *Voices from the Rocks*, for more on efforts to revive the Ndebele Kingdom and the history of both protonationalist and backward-looking groups such as the Matabeleland Home Society. Hughes also notes that the women of the abezansi families were particularly loath to welcome a bride from a lower stratum, especially of the abantu bakaMambo (*Kin, Caste and Nation*, 61).

22. Nellie Mlotshwa (Maduma), interview by the author, 27 June 1999, Bulawayo, Zimbabwe.

23. For a list of family or praise names associated with the abezansi, abenhla, and abantu bakaMambo groups, see Neville Jones, *My Friend Kumalo* (Bulawayo, Zimbabwe: Books of Rhodesia, 1972).

24. Ranger, *Voices from the Rocks*, 149.

25. Ranger, *The African Voice*; Ranger, *Voices from the Rocks*.

26. Huggins Msimanga, telephone interview by the author, 17 December 2008.

27. Huggins Msimanga, telephone interview by the author, 18 January 2001 and 17 December 2008.

28. Barbara Nkala, ed., *Celebrating the Vision: A Century of Sowing and Reaping* (Bulawayo, Zimbabwe: Brethren in Christ Church, 1998), 160.

29. Sibanda said that some of his forebears came up with Mzilikazi, while others, also Venda, came up "later," presumably later in the nineteenth century (Mangisi Sibanda, interview by the author, 26 May 1999, Tshalimbe, Zimbabwe). David Beach explains that there were many different waves of Venda moving across the Limpopo into what is now Zimbabwe between the sixteenth and nineteenth centuries. The Venda are linguistically and religiously very close to the Kalanga (David Beach, *The Shona and Zimbabwe 900–1850: An Outline of Shona History* [Gwelo, Zimbabwe: Mambo Press, 1980], 211–12).

30. Sibanda, interview.

31. The Tshalimbe village outstation was opened in the 1920s by Mnofa Nsimango and his wife, Ntombiyaphansi (NakaSithembile).

32. Sibanda, interview.

33. J. N. Hostetter, "Mission Education in a Changing Society: Brethren in Christ Mission Education in Southern Rhodesia, Africa, 1899–1959" (Ph.D. diss., SUNY Buffalo, 1967), 207.

34. H. Frances Davidson, *South and South Central Africa: A Record of Fifteen Years' Missionary Labors among Primitive Peoples* (Elgin, IL: Brethren Publishing House, 1915), 66–67. Revised spelling of *Mpisa* from Sithembile Nkala (MaNsimango), interview by the author with Musa Chidziva interpreting, 15 August 2000, Bulawayo, Zimbabwe.

35.   Mnofa was descended from the original members of Lobhengula's queen Xhwalile's *umthimba*, or marriage procession, from Gaza. Nkala, interview. See Urban-Mead, *Gender of Piety*, for a profile of Mangisi Sibanda's sister-in-law, Hannah Nsimango's sister, Sithembile.

36.   Nkala, interview.

37.   "Mrs. Moyo" (pseudonym at request of interviewee), interview with the author, 9 April 1999, Bulwayo, Zimbabwe.

38.   "Kumalo" is an older spelling of the name "Khumalo."

39.   Brethren in Christ Church, *Handbook of Missions: Home and Foreign of the Brethren in Christ Church* (1935), 1.

40.   Walter O. Winger, "The Memory of the Just Is Blessed" (obituary for Nyamazana Dube), *Evangelical Visitor*, 2 December 1957, 5.

41.   Hughes points out that among the rare instances of an abezansi–abantu baka-Mambo marriage, it was far more common for an upper-caste woman to marry into the lower group because of the way that in-laws were ranked. The lower-caste family, being on the husband's side, would have to give cattle to the abezansi family, the bride-supplying side. This meant that the cattle receivers (the wife's family) would be of higher rank in the configuration of in-laws, thus rendering their union more acceptable than had it been the other way around (*Kin, Caste and Nation*, 62).

42.   Confidential material given in personal communication with a church elder. See also Grace Holland, interview by the author, 7 December 1999, Grantham, PA.

43.   Zama Ncube (MaKhumalo), interview by the author, 24 and 27 May 1999, Bulawayo, Zimbabwe.

44.   Ncube, interview.

45.   Nellie Mlotshwa (Maduma), interview by Eliakim Sibanda, 6 August 1987, cited in Eliakim Sibanda, "The Brethren in Christ in Southern Rhodesia, 1898–1980: A Historical Study of Its Contributions towards the Promotion of Human Rights" (Ph.D. diss., Iliff School of Theology, University of Denver, 1998), 253; H. Frances Davidson and L. B. Steckley, "General Report from Macha Mission," in minutes from the General Conference of Brethren in Christ, 19–22 May 1914, 39, Archives of the Brethren in Christ Church, Messiah College, Grantham, Pennsylvania.

46.   "News from the Chibi Reserve," *Evangelical Visitor*, 13 November 1911, 12.

47.   Missionary Sadie Book noted that Lomapholisa Khumalo was gathering firewood and that "they" (presumably both Lomapholisa and Sitshokupi) gathered water; both water and wood were carried on the head ("God's Beautiful Creation," *Evangelical Visitor*, 25 December 1911, 14).

48.   Mlotshwa (Maduma), interview by Sibanda, cited in Sibanda, "Brethren in Christ," 244.

49.   Samuel Mlotshwa, interview by the author, 22 May 1999, Mayezane, Zimbabwe. Mlotshwa recalled that others who went on the mission to Chibi were four African men: Mantshi Moyo, Mahutsha Mafu, Lomapholisa's brother Mawogelana Khumalo, and Mafa Baloyi. Lomapholisa's daughter corroborates the evangelistic motivations of her mother: Joyce Khumalo recalled that Lomapholisa "was one of those girls who

was interested in evangelizing" (interview by the author, 27 August 1997, Bulawayo, Zimbabwe).

50.   The Chibi Mission at Mandanabgwe was taken over by the Dutch Reformed Church (DRC) (Sibanda, "Brethren in Christ," 288).

51.   Mlotshwa (Maduma), interview by Sibanda, cited in Sibanda, "Brethren in Christ," 244–45, 253n420.

52.   Minutes from the General Conference of Brethren in Christ, 38.

53.   Sunday schools were not places to teach Bible stories to children; they were where the adult faithful gathered each Sunday before the worship service to study the Bible under the direction of a lay leader, who was influential in their spiritual formation.

54.   Orlean Ndlovu (MaNkala), interview by the author, April 1999, Bulawayo, Zimbabwe.

55.   See Urban-Mead, *Gender of Piety*, for Maria Tshuma's story, which goes over the details of her schooling, teaching career, and evangelistic work.

56.   Mia Brandl-Syrier, *Black Woman in Search of God* (London: Lutterworth Press, 1962); Deborah Gaitskell, "'Wailing for Purity': Prayer Unions, African Mothers and Adolescent Daughters 1912–1940," in *Industrialisation and Social Change in South Africa: African Class Formation, Culture and Consciousness 1870–1930*, ed. Shula Marks and Richard Rathbone (London: Longman, 1982), 338–57. For more on the secular women's clubs, see Sita Ranchod-Nilsson, "'Educating Eve': The Women's Club Movement and Political Consciousness among Rural African Women in Southern Rhodesia, 1950–1980," in *African Encounters with Domesticity*, ed. Karen Tranberg Hansen (New Brunswick, NJ: Rutgers University Press, 1992), 195–97.

57.   See Urban-Mead, "Women, Religion, and Gender," chap. 6.

58.   Mlotshwa (Maduma), interview.

7

"Women Were Not Supposed to Fight"

The Gendered Uses of Martial and Moral Zuluness during uDlame, 1990–1994

JILL E. KELLY

As Zulu historian John Laband has recently pointed out, the isiZulu-speaking people of South Africa continue to hold the Western imagination as the epitome of the noble, courageous warrior.[1] This image of Zulu martial masculinity pervades the nineteenth-century accounts of southeastern Africa's first trader-adventurers and the recorded oral testimonies of isiZulu speakers conquered by the nascent Zulu Kingdom; the numerous twentieth-century films, mini-series, and popular books on King Shaka and the Zulu battles with the British; and the more recent heritage tourism ventures such as Shakaland, a resort built on the set of the *Shaka Zulu* miniseries.[2]

This Zulu martiality and masculinity also dominated the international media coverage of South Africa's transition from apartheid to democracy. As South African president F. W. de Klerk lifted the ban on the African National Congress (ANC), the Pan-Africanist Congress, the South African Communist Party, and other liberation organizations on 2 February 1990, internecine conflict plagued the provinces now known as KwaZulu-Natal and Gauteng. Between 1985 and 1996, nearly twenty thousand people died as a result of this devastating regional civil war, known in isiZulu as uDlame.[3] Tensions began to run high in the KwaZulu-Natal Midlands, the focus of this chapter, in 1983 with the formation of the United Democratic Front (UDF), an umbrella organization of grassroots movements against apartheid ideologically aligned with the ANC. Violence escalated dramatically after a divisive 1985 strike outside of Pietermaritzburg and erupted into civil war in the townships. Supporters of Inkatha Yenkululeko Yesizwe, a Zulu nationalist cultural movement turned political party that was intimately tied to the apartheid system of separate development, and the ANC/UDF struggled for control of the city's townships and rural areas in competition over who would represent Zulu interests. In 1990 the war spread from KwaZulu-Natal to the Pretoria-Witwatersrand-Vereeniging (PWV) area, now part of Gauteng Province. State-organized covert networks often referred to as the Third Force instigated and sponsored the conflict as a counterrevolutionary strategy.

The international media labeled this kind of violence "black-on-black" and "tribal," especially in Gauteng, where reporters often simply described the conflict as one between the Zulu nationalist Inkatha and the Xhosa-dominated ANC under Nelson Mandela. Headlines such as "Tribal Feuds Won't Let Up in South Africa" and "In South Africa, Violence Takes on Tribal Overtone" dominated the global press.[4] In KwaZulu-Natal, where the violence pitted Zulu versus Zulu, the contemporary media portrayed Zuluness as an ethnic identity bound up with "tradition," martial culture, and patriarchy. Scholarly analyses of the conflict focused on the political violence as the product of a crisis of masculinity related to the long-term decline of African patriarchal power, generational tensions between male juniors and elders, and the manner in which Inkatha president Inkosi (Chief) Mangosuthu Buthelezi drew upon and manipulated heritage and custom to mobilize Zulu men as both workers and warriors.[5]

Women were not absent in the contemporary media and scholarly coverage of uDlame, but where they appeared they did so as "innocent victims" fleeing the conflict and living in refugee camps or as "peacemakers" marching against police inaction and favoritism. These images of victims and peacemakers are part of cultural notions about warfare that use and maintain a gendered construct in which soldiers go to war to uphold an image of social order that is symbolized by "womenandchildren" (as stated by feminist writer Cynthia Enloe) as "the protected" and "the defended."[6] While many women did indeed suffer from and mobilize against the violence, these depictions of the "protected" and the "peacemaker" highlight Zuluness as a male domain and obscure women's own constructions and uses of ethnicity during a tumultuous time marked by martial masculinity, violence, and rapid social change.[7] While the dominance of the image and analyses of Zulu martial masculinity might suggest that women cannot be or are not Zulu, as is demonstrated in Heike I. Schmidt's contribution to this collection on the Ngoni, the women interviewed here saw themselves as Zulu.[8] They not only promoted Zuluness, in particular martial masculinity, through gendered performances but also utilized both martiality and a sense of moral ethnicity as resources to inform decision making and to create coping strategies in the midst of war.

During the war and the transition from apartheid to democracy, isiZulu-speaking South Africans experienced an era of unprecedented cultural and political change. The dismantling of apartheid and promise of equal rights led some rural Zulus, as anthropologist Jason Hickel has argued, to violently resist the egalitarian project of democracy, which contrasted with their cultural imperative of collective well-being.[9] Fears abounded about what fate the democratic dispensation would bring for Zulu hierarchical social relations, traditional leadership, and migrant labor. The historian John Lonsdale described this violence where Zulu killed Zulu as a conflict in which the internal debate on civic virtue, or moral ethnicity, was linked to the new question of who—Inkatha or the ANC—was best qualified to represent Zulu interests in the new democratic dispensation.[10] Philippe Denis, historian of religion, also found that the Inkatha- and ANC-affiliated communities at conflict in rural Nxamalala (to the west of Pietermaritzburg) came to be labeled as both politically and culturally different. While these communities both spoke isiZulu, the Inkatha-aligned wards called their ANC-aligned neighbors "Indians" and "comrades" rather than Zulus. ANC areas labeled Inkatha communities in a manner denoting their stricter adherence to Zulu practices.[11] This was a war in which these labels—though more political than ethnic—had deadly impact.[12] During this era of violence and unprecedented change, Zuluness served not only as something to fight for but also as a resource men and women could use to make informed decisions, defend themselves, and mourn.

Generally, uDlame heightened and disturbed Zulu practices undertaken by both men and women, but gendered spheres of action within Zuluness shaped individual responses to war. This chapter looks at several of these domains, including martiality and moral ethnicity (in particular, spiritual beliefs and funeral customs), in which the different roles of men and women contributed to a shared but gendered sense of ethnicity. After a brief review of theory and methods, the first section examines women's support for and subversion of Zulu martial masculinity. Inkatha and its leadership drew upon the Zulu past to call for an enhancement of martial masculinity. Many men responded to appeals to their Zulu warrior inheritance with alacrity, while women ideologically and practically supported or subtly subverted the Zulu conception of war as a male realm. Women used this gendered understanding of Zuluness to inform their decisions not to fight. They supported their husbands, sons, and fathers in war through ululation and a practice of inversion intended to protect warriors. But women also subverted Zulu martial masculinity to protect their husbands and sons, sometimes overtly and other times more subtly. The second section turns to women's use of moral ethnicity, the spiritual weapons women wielded as the aspect of their Zuluness available to them. When martiality as a male domain closed opportunities for women to take up arms, women turned to religion, both Christian and Zulu, to protect themselves and their families. The last section turns to gendered aspects of moral Zuluness, particularly those disrupted by the civil war, *ukuhlonipha*, and funeral practices. The breakdown of order and ukuhlonipha, a practice of respect employed by youth and women toward elders and males, during an era in which youth were the vanguard of the struggle may have caused many mothers and fathers to retreat into Zuluness. While the laments about youth co-option of funeral practices suggest both women's and men's desire for the order promised by ukuhlonipha, women complained about their inabilities to perform gendered mourning practices. When women made claims about what the war prevented them from doing, they highlighted their participation in the process of reification of Zuluness and revealed their investment in ukuhlonipha, a gendered hierarchical order that recognized their roles as mothers. The end of apartheid and its accompanying violence saw both Zulu men and women look to Zuluness, but the ways in which they wielded it to respond to war, cope, and mourn were based upon gendered access to martiality and moral ethnicity.

Gendering Zuluness:
Theory, Historiography, and Methods

The chapter is premised on the theory that Zuluness is a malleable but lived construct functioning through linguistic and cultural norms. As the historian Jabulani Sithole noted, *ubuZulu bethu* (our Zuluness) is an idiom that captures the shifting, hybrid, and even contradictory meanings and practices of Zuluness. It provides an analytical lens through which to examine the many ways in which individuals and groups utilized language, culture, and historical events to construct a useable ethnicity.[13] Zuluness is thus used here both as a category of everyday social practice and as a category of analysis.[14] During the civil war of South Africa's transition from apartheid to democracy, mothers, wives, and daughters across the political spectrum had stakes in the construction of Zuluness and used gendered components of Zuluness, including martiality and moral ethnicity (here including religion, ukuhlonipha, and funeral customs), to make decisions, defend themselves and their families, and cope.

These cultural aspects of Zuluness must be understood as a rich resource used selectively by different social agents in various social projects within specific power relations and political discourse. Not only gender but also age and ability affect access to and availability of ethnicity as resource.[15] As well, it must be kept in mind that the cultural stuff of "custom" and "tradition" can be real or invented but not fixed. The historian Eric Hobsbawm has called attention to the more frequent "invention of tradition" during a rapid transformation of society.[16] In the midst of the negotiations for a transition from apartheid to democracy, the countrywide revolt of youth, and civil war, women's laments about the absence of cultural practices should be seen also as evidence of their efforts to make a place for themselves as Zulu women in the changing South Africa.

While this chapter largely focuses on the cultural aspects of ethnicity as employed by rural Zulu women, I recognize that ethnicity or Zuluness cannot be reduced to "culture." Culture is just one component, alongside history, language, and politics, through which a collective sense of likeness can be constructed and communicated. But particularly because access to and availability of resources are gendered, the rural women interviewed here had few political, economic, or historical resources to wield. While men responded to Inkatha calls to political ethnicity, a shared history as warriors, and a common experience as workers, woman constructed and used what Lonsdale calls "moral ethnicity," which he defines as "the common human instinct to create out of the daily habits of social intercourse and material labour a system of moral meaning and ethical reputation within a more or less imagined community."[17] Unaffiliated, Inkatha-supporting, and ANC-supporting women believed that the warrior past, weaponry, and conflict were the realm of men, and the women reinforced this with their decisions to not fight, to flee, and to assist their husbands. Women also employed a moral ethnicity, including spiritual aspects, ukuhlonipha, and funeral practices, that was available to them as females. This resonates with Ndubueze L. Mbah's chapter in this collection, where he shows the way in which Ohafia-Igbo women both reinforced militant masculinity and challenged the masculinist image of ethnicity through the promotion of matriliny. IsiZulu-speaking mothers, wives, and daughters were invested in the construction of Zuluness. They complemented Zulu martial masculinity with performances and turned to components of moral ethnicity, including religion and custom, to make choices, protect their families, and manage the traumas of war.

While the reification of Zuluness was and continues to be a social process in which men and women, the elite and the masses, have taken part, the historiography of Zulu ethnicity largely assumes a male-centered discourse. These studies show Zuluness as intimately tied to gender and class but fail to treat women as ethnic subjects who might identify with, construct, or use ethnicity. From the rise of the Zulu Kingdom under Shaka in the early 1800s onward, Zulu males, chiefs, and the colonial and apartheid state used a gendered ethnicity to order society. King Shaka used the *amabutho* (regiment) system to obtain economic and military labor and to control fertility, or more specifically women's reproduction and cultivation. According to the historian Jeff Guy, this organization was based upon the accumulation by adult men of the labor power of women and children via marriage.[18] Patriarchy gave power and prestige to kings, chiefs, and homestead heads and "synchronized powerfully with a martial masculinity that was at the heart of Zulu cultural expression."[19] Under colonialism in Natal, these gender divisions of labor continued as the containment of women as productive and reproductive agents became a point of collusion between colonial and African patriarchs.[20]

But Shaka's consolidation of power did not immediately produce a unified sense of Zuluness, and it was only in the late nineteenth and twentieth centuries that Zulu began to expand as an identity. The early kingdom's elite had made a clear social and political distinction in order to justify the subordination of peoples on the periphery of the growing Zulu Kingdom.[21] Ordinary young African men in the late nineteenth century were responsible for the spread of Zulu ethnicity beyond the kingdom into colonial Natal and the goldfields via migrant labor and culminating in the Zulu rebellion of 1906.[22] In the early twentieth century, Christian Zulus known as *amakholwa* (believers) turned toward their cultural roots as a means of asserting political rights. Men of more middle-class origins articulated ideas about Zulu nationalism via lectures and sermons that sparked public and private debates.[23] Then, in the 1920s, Zulu Christian businessmen and community leaders formed a cultural movement, Inkata kaZulu, connected to the Zulu king as a means to facilitate their economic goals and resist white consolidation of power.[24] During South Africa's transition from apartheid to democracy, the Zulu nationalist movement Inkatha Yenkululeko Yesizwe and its leadership mobilized men on the basis of a Zulu warrior heritage and attracted the rural, traditional elite.[25] Scholars clearly show the manner in which male royals, politicians, writers, and rebels constructed and reified a sense of Zuluness. Women were central to this male reification as rural mothers and agriculturists, but they are not examined as ethnic agents who identified with or used Zuluness.

Despite the strong recent literature on women and ethnicity in Africa, the topic remains understudied in South Africa, where the growing historiography on women rarely overlaps with studies of ethnicity.[26] This gap likely reflects not only the sources available but also contemporary ideologies.[27] Women's subordination—and their role in maintaining patriarchal systems, such as that of Zulu society—may not be an attractive topic for progressive historians. The historian Meghan Healy-Clancy too has suggested this in her theorization of African nationalism in South Africa, which highlights the ideological and practical implications of women's attention to the family, body, home, and community for the creation of an African body politic. She notes how scholars generally dismissed women's groups as essentially stabilizing and conservative influences, relegating them to the footnotes.[28]

It has indeed been Zulu women's subordination that dominates the historiography on Zulu women. Earlier studies of precolonial Zulu women have been broadly referred to as the "gender oppression school" for their conclusion that a clear and rigid division of labor and of male and female spheres subordinated Zulu women.[29] They argue that indigenous patriarchal structures and colonialism, or, as the sociologist Belinda Bozzoli labels it, a "patchwork of patriarchies," caused systemic gender inequities.[30] This school of thought has been critiqued by Africanist scholars who contend that, while social controls delineated women's place, gender relations were characterized by cooperation in the interests of maintaining a collective, if hierarchical, society. Often through examinations of royal women, such as King Shaka's aunt Mnkabayi, these scholars suggest that gender relationships offered both males and females channels to influence and power.[31] But as the historian Sean Hanretta has shown, these schools collapse the diversity of women's positions into a single, homogeneous class in which women are oppressed or content without recognizing the different conditions, experiences, and constructions of gender.[32]

Consideration of more contemporary Zulu women continues to suggest them as non-ethnic subjects. Both the political scientist Shireen Hassim and the historian Thembisa Waetjen have considered women affiliated with the Zulu nationalist movement Inkatha. Hassim's study of the female branch of the movement, the Inkatha Women's Brigade, highlights how the group promoted the role of women in development while simultaneously limiting them with entreaties to maternal responsibility, obedience to husbands, and commitment to church. Hassim shows how Inkatha succeeded with this message in organizing women not in spite of its conservative, patriarchal, hierarchical, and essentialist discourse but precisely because these constructions resonated with women's daily experiences.[33] Waetjen's study of masculinity and Zulu nationalism echoes that of Hassim concerning women. Inkatha directed appeals to Zuluness, Zulu history, and Zulu "tradition" mainly to men, as workers and warriors. Its leaders called women to political action on the basis of their identities as Christians, South Africans, and the backbone of family and community life.[34] As Hassim points out, it would be wrong to assume that women saw these roles as oppressive. Women's Brigade leaders themselves promoted understandings of women as wives, mothers, and Christians as an integral part of their lives. These studies suggest that women joined the Inkatha as Christians and as the mothers and wives of Zulus.

But the isiZulu-speaking women interviewed about the transition years of uDlame did identify as Zulu, and they used their gendered understandings of Zuluness as a resource in the midst of war. There is a need to reevaluate women's roles not only during uDlame but also in the historical constructions of Zuluness. As the historian Eva Jackson has recently pointed out, analyses that focus on the constructions of gender can be especially mindful of, rather than dismissive of, deeply embedded understandings of gender that may be tied to systemic gender inequalities.[35] By focusing on Zuluness and gender as constructs, scholars can examine the ways in which individual women experience these constructs and use their understandings of them to make decisions about performing, rejecting, or subverting ethnicity.

Carefully listening to women's testimonies reveals the manner in which women had stakes in and used gendered constructions of Zuluness as decision-making, defense, and coping strategies during a time of war. Oral history has gained a prominence in enabling women's voices and worldviews to be heard by a wider audience. However, oral history is still a methodology molded by the researcher. The historian Susan Geiger has argued that one of the objectives of feminist oral history methodology should be the acceptance of women's own interpretations of their identities, experiences, and social worlds. It follows, then, that the framing of the researcher's questions must be done in a manner that allows women's own interpretations to be voiced.[36]

It is thus that I need to insert myself and my own oral history methodology into the analysis. The examination below is based on oral history interviews conducted by me (with oral history methodology training and four years of isiZulu language study) and an accompanying female Zulu research assistant with over sixty male and female current and former residents of the rural Table Mountain region of Pietermaritzburg, which includes the Maphumulo and Nyavu chiefdoms.[37] Table Mountain was recognized until early 1990 as a haven of peace in a region in turmoil. The inkosi of the Maphumulo at Table Mountain, Mhlabunzima Maphumulo, earned a reputation as "the peace chief" for his efforts to quell the violence that had engulfed Pietermaritzburg's townships. But as the inkosi vocally critiqued the South African police and joined the UDF-aligned and ANC-friendly Congress of Traditional Leaders of South Africa, he began to attract the ire of the state and Inkatha at both the local and national levels. Over the weekend of 26–28 January 1990, conflict broke out between the Maphumulo and the neighboring Inkatha-aligned Nyavu, sparking a cycle of violence that would last through South Africa's first democratic elections in 1994.

The men and women interviewed included supporters of both Inkatha and the ANC/UDF, as well as a few who maintained no affiliation. I set out interested in women's experience of uDlame and their understanding of what it meant to be Zulu during a time of such unprecedented turmoil. I had prepared a list of questions to guide the interviews but set them within the larger framework of life history to enable individuals to tell me about their lives. I wanted to know what it meant to them to be Zulu, how they learned to be Zulu, and how they taught their children to be Zulu. Were these life lessons and the ability to practice Zuluness impacted by the years of uDlame? How did people protect themselves, sustain themselves, and mourn?

Over the course of twelve months of fieldwork, I was repeatedly frustrated by challenges both anticipated and unexpected. My research coincided with local municipal elections and thus heightened community tensions. There was sensitivity to discussing so recent a civil war. There was gendered resistance to interviewing women, where men failed to understand why I wanted to talk to women. One male community elder exclaimed at an Inkatha meeting I attended, "Women did nothing at the time; it was the men who were fighting!"[38] Another male community elder who lost several children in a massacre was adamant that I would not speak to his wives. Whether or not he was concerned about the pain such an interview might revive or what they might reveal, he did not ask them so that they could make the decision for themselves.

But perhaps what was the most surprising was my own initial failure to *hear* what women were telling me.[39] Most women agreed with the men. They did not take part in the civil war. They did not fight or carry weapons. They did not go to political meetings. They cared for their families and often fled. They could not pray or mourn properly because of the dangers of war. But what I could not hear at first was that, through these conversations and complaints, these rural Zulu women were making claims on Zuluness, about how they employed it or wished they could have during a time of turmoil. Women relied on gendered spheres of Zuluness to inform their decisions. The Zulu conception of war spurred men to battle and suggested women should not fight but support their husbands and children. Women used this understanding of martial masculinity as well as moral ethnicity, including Zulu custom and spiritual beliefs both traditional and Christian, for physical and emotional survival. Their complaints about their inability to rely on spiritual and mourning customs reveal their participation in and promotion of alternate but also complementary gendered Zulu practices of martial masculinity and moral ethnicity.

"Sasibaleka!": Women and Martial Zuluness at Table Mountain

In January 1990, uDlame erupted at Table Mountain. When it did, gendered spheres of action characterized Zulu responses to war. Men answered the call to battle, but women too took action based on their understandings of martiality as a male domain. The isiZulu-speaking women interviewed here performed Zuluness in a manner that complemented Zulu martiality. Most chose not to fight, and some chose to flee, as they believed it was a man's duty to fight and to protect his family and a woman's responsibility to support life. Women thus supported their fathers, husbands, and sons with ululation, childcare, and daily feedings and launderings. Some women also chose to subvert the clear delineation of gender roles in war, hoping to protect their families from violence. Most subverted the gendered spheres of action in a manner that still promoted martial masculinity, describing their own violence as only in support of their husbands or dressing their sons as girls to help them escape the expectations that men participate in battle. In the realm of Zulu martiality, we see men and women constructing gendered ethnicity in relation to one another. Women not only build concepts of female ethnicity based on their experiences as mothers but also contribute to the promotion of Zulu masculine martiality.

At the time of uDlame, some of the women interviewed supported Inkatha or the UDF/ANC, though the majority claimed they had not joined either or were simply "doing what was happening in our place" when it came to politics.[40] Several of them still assert no affiliation. Few of them had attended any political party meeting or heard local or national political figures speak. None knew of any efforts by these leaders to speak to or organize women in their area. There was no local branch of the Inkatha Women's Brigade or ANC Women's League. The calls to be "mothers of the nation" by Inkatha and the ANC/UDF in speeches and literature did not reach these women.[41] The majority of those interviewed understood uDlame as a conflict about "politics" and "meetings" and between two chiefs (Maphumulo and Nyavu) over land. They felt the war was different from previous violent conflicts they had experienced, such as *izimpi zezigodi* (section wars). The widow of a prominent headman and Inkatha leader, Thombi, explained that conflict during uDlame "was not the usual fight like war between wards. . . . It was coming while you were not aware."[42] In other clashes, the enemy and battles were more clearly defined.

Women's understandings of Zulu martiality as gendered male informed their decisions not to take up arms. They all agreed that violence was a male (both young and old) domain. Thombi explained that "it was a must for a man to be part of the war, because a man was supposed to protect his family and the nation. Once a man ran away from his home, who was going to look after his family?" She further stated that women did not take up arms because it was their responsibility to look after the children while men were in battle.[43] In a society in which women play important roles as productive and reproductive agents, many believed that it was because they were mothers that they should not take part in war. Most asserted, "Women were not supposed to fight . . .

because they are parents . . . because women know how to give birth."[44] Another explained, "I do not think a mother can do what was happening there at the time [referring to the violence]."[45] Still another, when asked whether or not women should fight, incredulously responded, "A mother, who gave birth, carrying a weapon? Mothers know about labor pains."[46] Thobekile, the first wife of the Table Mountain inkosi Mhlabunzima Maphumulo, moved to the rural community from a township after her marriage. She suggests that rural women such as those at Table Mountain were unlikely to subvert gendered roles in war. She explained, "Women from rural areas, they only know this, that the only person who is supposed to protect the home is the head of the house. It is rare to find women in rural areas having guns and other weapons. They believe that if there is a problem, a man of the house must be always in the front."[47]

Women's understandings of Zulu martiality as masculine also influenced their choices to flee their homes rather than take up arms, running to local places of safety and later leaving the region altogether. One woman laughed as she explained, "Sasibaleka! [We were running!] We were not even able to cook, because it might happen that you would leave the pot before the food was ready."[48] The women expressed that it was always their decision to flee. Many husbands, fathers, and brothers were migrant laborers or were gathered in camps for both offensive and defensive purposes. The headmen were also fighting. So when conflict broke out, the women took their own actions. They found refuge in camps, the nearby forests, or the chief's courthouse or at the school under the protection of the police or the South African Defence Force (SADF). Others fled to safer areas, staying with family or employers either indefinitely or permanently. Many former Table Mountain residents now live in a newly constructed township closer to the city, Haniville.

While gendered understandings of Zuluness may have prevented some women from taking up arms, it also informed their decisions to promote martial Zuluness and support men at war. The practice of ululation echoes that described by Mbah in his chapter on Ohafia-Igbo identity where women celebrated warrior *ufiem* (masculinity, but also a status of superiority). *Ukukikiza*, or ululation, is a practice specific to women through which they expound and uphold Zulu norms and values. Ululation occurs when women are moved to express their feelings and in evocations of the *amadlozi* (ancestors). It is most commonly associated with joy and excitement at marriage and spiritual ceremonies and in encouragement during dance. But it also occurs during dangerous situations such as war and confrontation. During conflict, women ululated to motivate men and to call upon the amadlozi to protect them. Women also ululated to encourage men to be brave and to celebrate their success. Both Doris and her daughter shared that women helped their husbands by coming out to ululate.[49] Another young woman recalled women ululating to celebrate the men's success, the retreat of the enemy.[50] According to isiZulu scholar Eugenia Lindiwe Sikhosana, ululation can serve as a "power which makes men forget themselves and look at the common goal."[51] While war may have been a masculine domain, women shaped Zulu martiality through their encouragement of brave deeds.

Women were not the only ones who were aware of the significant role of female support for martial masculinity. Zulu men also instructed women to practice a long-held custom believed to protect warriors, an inversion of attire.[52] One young KwaNyavu woman, Philisile, recalled such an instance. She related, "Our mothers were told to wear their dresses inside out and not to wear scarves on their heads." The same KwaNyavu men who would have informed the women to do this participated in the Seven Days War, a particularly devastating week during uDlame to the east of Pietermaritzburg in March 1990. Father Tim Smith, a Catholic priest stationed in the region under attack during the Seven Days War, received reports that on the day of the KwaNyavu men's arrival, the women turned their clothes inside out as the men prepared to attack.[53] The practice has evolved to reflect women's recent attire, but oral testimonies from the early twentieth century suggest that this was then a protective exercise. The Zulu elder Nsuze kaMfelafuti told the oral archivist James Stuart that during battles, women in hiding would turn the top rolls of their *isidwaba* (leather skirt) inside out in order to avert danger and so that men would be safe during the fighting.[54] The anthropologist Eileen Krige noted in her 1936 study that this inversion of the skirt was part of women's general careful behavior during wartime; it was intended to prevent misfortune for men at war.[55] Krige cites A. T. Bryant's dictionary entry on *qunga*, a verb once meaning "to discolor" but also referring to a process of self-fortification against evil consequences.[56] This reversal is one of several kinds of inversions prevalent in Zulu society. The first is a complementary opposition of the sexes, where women are associated with the left and men with the right (in seating arrangements, rituals, and the like), and a second is the opposition of good/light and evil/dark. The third and of most interest here is that which the anthropologist Axel-Ivar Berglund refers to as funerary inversions, where ordinary custom and procedures are reversed. These are associated with birth, puberty, marriage, and death, stages in which persons are integrated into new age sets. A widow might turn her skirt inside out on the occasion of her husband's death.[57] Philisile's mother suggested that the women's inversion may have been related to expectations about death. "That was another way of mourning," she stated. "You were mourning before somebody died?" we queried. "Yes, they said they were mourning because a war was happening."[58] Here the inversion of attire could indicate a man's passage into battle, marked by his wife's protection and concern for his life.

This clear, gendered division of action during war within Zuluness with men as warriors is by no means unchallenged in Zulu history or during uDlame. Testimonies preserved in *The James Stuart Archive of Recorded Oral Evidence Relating to the History of the Zulu and Neighbouring Peoples* suggest that women fought in amabutho during King Shaka's reign over the Zulu Kingdom.[59] Also, several scholars have examined the participation of Zulu women in these regiments and other conflicts, ranging from Shembe women's 1939 murder of Mdolomba Nkabinde to the Durban women's beer hall protests.[60] Scholars have also examined female membership, some Zulu, in the UDF, the ANC underground, Umkhonto weSizwe (the ANC's external military wing), and the SADF.[61] While there are of course exceptions, during the violence most of these interviewed mothers, wives, and daughters believed their roles were to look after children and cook and wash for their families and the fighters.

While most women promoted and participated in ethnically defined gendered practices of war during uDlame, some openly or subtly subverted masculine martiality, placing their love for family members over promotion of Zulu martiality. One woman joked about challenging martial masculinity by encouraging her husband to flee with her to the farm where he worked for safety. She recognized that according to custom her husband should stay in the community and fight, but she was happy he did not. She exclaimed, "I was married to a coward, but I prefer a coward to a fearless person because they die!"[62] Another woman also challenged the gendered responses to war, attempting to persuade her father to subvert the role of men as warriors. Ntombi had lost her brother during the conflict, but her father refused to flee with his wife and children. She chose to remain behind with him until she could convince him to seek safety.[63] Ntombi's mother described her daughter's bravery: "If ever my husband were to die, Ntombi was also going to die. Gunshots were everywhere, but Ntombi never left her father. She was there to protect him."[64] Love for their family led some women to openly challenge the dominant martial norms.

Other women subverted Zulu masculine martiality more subtly, using gendered spheres of action to protect their sons or describing their own warring activities in a way that suggested they had not acted improperly as Zulu women. Some women used martial masculinity to shield their sons, dressing them up as girls so they could escape the conflict. Theni lost her eldest son in the war. If martial masculinity required her sons to fight, she would disguise her youngest son as a girl: "I gave him my dress to wear and a hat so that no one would recognize him as a boy. Then we ran with my daughters."[65] This construction of Zuluness, which delineates war as a masculine sphere, may also have impacted women's oral history testimonies. Women may have picked up weapons in offense or defense but chose not to share this in their interviews, as they thought it would not be proper for Zulu women to do so. Even those who admitted that females did participate in the conflict positioned these women as transgressors or as not taking on primary roles in battle. Khethi, an Inkatha supporter, believed that women who carried weapons or got involved were doing so because "they were big-headed women" who wanted political positions. She described them as acting "like men."[66] Doris, a proud ANC member, set up women as secondary participants: "They carried bush knives. Their husbands were shooting, and the women would come and finish you with bush knives while you were lying down helpless."[67] In her description, men took the offensive, while women supported them. These women used conceptions of Zulu martiality to subtly challenge the gendered realms in both the practice and description of their subversions, but they did so in ways that still reaffirmed gendered notions of Zulu martiality.

These women's testimonies reveal how they used gendered realms of Zuluness to inform their actions in the context of violence. Women employed this gendered Zulu martiality to decide whether or not to fight and bear arms. Women also encouraged men to perform bravely in their roles as fighters. They aided their husbands, sons, and fathers in both practical and inspiring ways, providing meals and forging the men's bravery with ululation and a practice of inversion. They used gendered Zuluness subversively in attempts to protect their sons by dressing them up as girls before they fled. Even those who reported female participation in the violence worded their testimonies so that these violent women were unusual or merely assisting the men. During uDlame, women supported and reaffirmed martial Zuluness as a gendered construct.

"So That the Bullet Can't Hit You": Moral Ethnicity and Spiritual Weapons

With martiality defined within Zuluness as a masculine realm in which women played only supporting roles, women turned to other aspects of their ethnicity to protect themselves and their families. Gendered spheres of action during war prevented women from picking up arms. Instead, they wielded spiritual weapons, and moral ethnicity became a tool with which women could ascribe meaning and order to the experience of violence. Women employed a range of religious beliefs, both Zulu and African Christian, to sustain themselves during the violence. While these moral aspects of Zulu culture are available to both men and women, during uDlame women sought resources beyond the masculine weapons, the guns, machetes, and assegais, to protect their families. One of the most prominent responses from those interviewed regarding how women protected themselves and their families during uDlame involved faith and spirituality. Whether they spoke of using *izintelezi* (a protective or preventative potion made from herbs) or *muthi* (a medicinal charm), calling upon amadlozi, praying to the Christian God, or the manner in which the conflict prevented them from practicing, women revealed the significance of their religious beliefs as coping and protective strategies during uDlame. This is not surprising nor limited to Zulu women. Several Africanist scholars have examined how spirituality serves as a site for the negotiation of gender and ethnic identities and religion becomes a source of personal, political, and collective empowerment for women.[68]

This section specifically builds upon Denis's argument that spiritual beliefs, both African traditional and African Christian, enabled survival and resilience during the conflict.[69] In research based on interviews with twenty-three men and women in the rural Nxamalala area (Pietermaritzburg), Denis attributed the lack of resentment so soon after uDlame to the religious faith of the interviewees. Asked by fieldworkers associated with the School of Religion and Theology of the University of KwaZulu-Natal about the role of religious beliefs in traumatic situations, interviewees expressed a "conviction that the conflict, as painful as it might have been, had been wanted by God." Denis further pointed to the varying overlap of "African traditional religion" and Christian practice. Denis found that while many interviewees normally adhered to Zulu religious customs, war disrupted their ability to perform rituals to the ancestors because there was not the time nor a safe space to do so in the midst of violence.[70]

The dangers of war prevented the performance of rituals, but women did employ prayers to both the Christian God and their Zulu ancestors as protective and coping strategies. These entreaties became a particularly important tool for a woman dealing with death and seeking protection for her family when her husband was about to leave for camp or when the woman herself was on the run, hiding in the forest or gathering with other women for protection by the SADF at the local school. One woman described women's religious practices as based on gendered expectations of war: "Every night before we went hiding and our husbands left for their spot, we prayed."[71] Thombi described nights at the school where the women sought safety: "Life was not good. Everyone was always complaining about the situation we were living under. Sometimes we would hear that somebody had passed on, and we would pray hard."[72] Another woman explained their prayers: "We were praying to get strength for what was happening in our land."[73] But these spiritual coping strategies were not always limited to prayers to the Christian God. Women also made pleas to their Zulu ancestors, despite the difficulties of performing spiritual rituals, and they sought out Zulu healers to protect their families. While prayers to the ancestors would usually accompany the use of *impepho* (the plant ritually burnt as incense), during war women called on their predecessors even if the women could not burn impepho. Thombi related, "We were praying while we were standing; we were always running. We could not kneel down or burn incense to talk to our ancestors. We were talking to our ancestors on our way running."[74] The women were not supposed to fight, but they wielded spiritual weapons, praying for their families' security, for the passing of their neighbors and loved ones, and for the fortitude to survive the war.

Women's testimonies regarding these and other Zulu spiritual practices reveal a gender and generational divide among Zulu users of muthi and izintelezi. Women saw men as more likely to use izintelezi for their own protection and often at the instruction of a chief prior to a conflict. One woman described it thus: "Our children were informed to come to the chief's place. . . . They were targeting young men. The young men were told to bring their weapons because they were making izintelezi at the chief's place."[75] One woman suggested that her family's reliance upon prayer to protect themselves was a decision made in the absence of her husband. "I did not use muthi. We were praying," said Nikiwe. "My husband was not staying at home," she said, suggesting that, had he been home, their strategies for spiritual protection might have changed.[76]

Fewer women spoke about the hope that they placed in traditional healers and medicines to protect themselves, their families, and the warriors. There were some, though—such as Busisiwe, who lived in Msinga during uDlame and whose mother was a *sangoma* (diviner) trained in the preparation and use of izintelezi—who employed these beliefs. Busisiwe related, "Those who were fighting were using izintelezi for their protection. We were also using i[zi]ntelezi in our homes to sprinkle our yards [for protection]."[77] One female Nxamalala resident, Nompumelelo, described the extraordinary power of a woman with muthi who instructed a small group of Inkatha men to defend their area. Nompumelelo described the attack on her neighborhood, largely affiliated to Inkatha, by several buses of ANC supporters.

One day buses of ANC people came to attack, a big crowd, [ANC] people from a different district. This woman sprinkled muthi at [the small group of local Inkatha men]; there were only five of them. We were all watching, standing on a hill. She told [the five Inkatha men] to go and fight. She advised them that they shouldn't look back. What they did there that day shocked everyone. They were only five, but they killed a lot of [ANC] people. . . . I am telling that what happened there is indescribable. . . . [The Inkatha men] had guns and knives. I know two of them, although now they are mentally disturbed. They fought and killed, and they came back.[78]

Even women who did not usually call upon an *inyanga* (healer) related, "You would hear that so and so was helping over there, and you would also go there to protect yourself . . . to protect the whole family so that the bullet can't hit you."[79] In the context of war, women sought out any resources available to them that would contribute to their safety and the safety of their families, including Zulu traditional medicines more likely to be used by their husbands.

But within this use of traditional medicines there is also the hint of a generational divide, where the senior women were more likely than their daughters to rely upon such Zulu practices. Busisiwe, the daughter of a sangoma mentioned above, explained that, since women were not supposed to fight, their mothers instructed the women to put muthi in their hair to prevent injury to the men. "They were saying it would protect the fighters from getting hurt. . . . We did not do that, although our mothers were telling us to do it. We were questioning ourselves about this. Our mothers were widows, but they still believed that using the muthi would help us, although it did not work for them."[80] While an older generation of mothers believed in the protective powers of izintelezi and muthi, the daughters were skeptical and less likely to employ these medicines for protection.

The Zulu gendered spheres of action during war prevented women from joining their husbands, fathers, and sons in violent clashes, but they wielded their own spiritual weapons. They employed moral ethnicity to protect themselves and their families and assuage the trauma and fears of war. They called upon both the Christian God and their Zulu ancestors to give them strength even when they could not kneel or could not burn the incense that welcomed the ancestors. Some believed in the power of traditional medicines such as muthi and izintelezi and attempted to shelter their families with visits to the inyanga. The women's testimonies reveal that the use of these Zulu healers and medicine was gendered and generational, but during war many women were willing to employ whatever resources they could.

"We Were Mourning, but There Was No Respect": The Disruption of Gendered and Generational Funeral Practices

During uDlame, men and women relied upon gendered spheres of action within Zuluness to inform their decisions. Men took up arms while women supported them, promoting martial masculinity and performing duties expected of wives, mothers, and daughters. They could not protect themselves with weapons, but instead used moral ethnicity, including spiritual beliefs, to protect themselves and cope with the violence. But uDlame also significantly disrupted other Zulu practices normally available to women, such as the performance of ukuhlonipha, an aspect of Zuluness invested in by both men and women, and gendered funeral rites. Complaints about what women were *not* able to do also reveal the gendered realms of Zulu funeral rites and women's investment in the Zulu practice of ukuhlonipha. War constrained their abilities to properly mourn. Unsafe at burial sites and in their homes, women felt unable to carry out funeral roles expected of them in Zulu culture. Woman after woman commented on the intrusiveness of guns, police, and soldiers and the youthful control of the burial services, a practice usually overseen by elders. Women could not wear proper attire, sit in mourning for the usual amount of time, or even attend funerals in other areas due to the danger and politicization of territory. The stress of violent conflict, displacement, injury, and death was traumatic. But the inability to properly mourn or bury a loved one furthered the distress. Mourning customs in Zulu society, according to Krige, serve as "the means by which the social sentiments of the survivors are slowly reorganized and adapted to the new conditions produced by the death."[81] The people were mourning, but there was no respect for custom, thus magnifying the sense of turmoil. During uDlame, elders and women could not perform the funeral roles expected of them according to the gendered and generational realms of Zuluness.

Both men and women experienced the disruption of the practice of ukuhlonipha during uDlame. The code of ukuhlonipha in its broadest sense is a custom of deference that regulates family and clan relationships in the interests of peaceful coexistence. It requires that any young person practice rituals of deference in behavior, speech, and general conduct to any older person irrespective of sex. These rituals can include avoidance of physical or eye contact and the substitution of alternative words for certain respected names, places, or objects. The code is primarily observed by children in relation to elders and women in relation to men, for instance, a newly betrothed woman to her father-in-law. This generational order was shaken after the 1976 revolt of schoolchildren in Soweto as youth led the resistance to apartheid.

The transition-era violence made funerals not only dangerous, as the war continued unabated during burials, but also sites for youth to assert themselves and their vision for a new South Africa. Ntombi, who lost her older brother to the conflict, related the co-option of funerals by the more militant younger generation: "We were mourning, but there was no respect . . . There were funerals, but they were not dignified. They used to sing *iziqubulo* [war-related songs] and shoot guns, because if you die by the gun, at your funeral they would be shooting in the air. Youth were taking care of the funeral. As far as I know, people who used to take care of the funeral are old people, but at the time it was the youth."[82]

Another woman echoed Ntombi's description of funerals dominated by weaponry: "If a person died by a gun, [the youth in control of the burial] would shoot guns at the funeral."[83] Nikiwe related that warring parties failed to respect funeral customs by harassing mourners and preventing travel. She expressed the disappointment that many felt when relatives from other wards or regions could not attend the funerals: "You were supposed to be brave, because you had to do things accordingly. But our relatives could not attend the funerals, since the place was a no-go area."[84] Here, these women not only lament the invasive presence of martiality at funerals but also express dismay about the absence of ukuhlonipha among funeral goers and organizers.

These women's complaints attest to women's investment in ukuhlonipha and provide evidence for another aspect of uDlame and the wider liberation struggle: generational tensions.[85] Both women and men criticized the youth's control of funerals in contrast to the values and desires of their elders. These grievances resound with recent arguments by historians Thokozani Xaba and Mxolisi Mchunu about KwaZulu-Natal's civil war. Xaba contended that young ANC affiliates were impatient with their more tolerant elders.[86] Mchunu locates this tension as particularly emanating from culture change, or two different views on manhood held by youth and elders accentuated during conflict.[87] Bozzoli argued that this youthful usurpation of "an unquestionably acceptable ceremonial ritual" transformed funerals into "political theatre" in Johannesburg's Alexandra Township during the rebellion.[88] Whereas Bozzoli highlights the willingness of most families concerned to adopt the redefinition of their deceased loved ones as "children of the township" and to participate in political funerals, the rural women interviewed in Table Mountain and Nxamalala indicated dismay at the idea of youth taking control of the funerals and at the presence of soldiers, guns, and iziqubulo. "Funerals were truly painful," said one Nxamalala woman. "We walked on guard. . . . We walked with weapons about us, and here is the grave; you have to bury someone. . . . Yes, funerals were an ordeal, truly difficult."[89] The women's complaints about a lack of ukuhlonipha on the part of the militant youth reveal their investment in this gendered and hierarchical aspect of Zuluness.

Women also made claims on Zulu practices through laments about the difficulties of properly performing gendered functions of funeral practices while under assault. These attacks included the use of guns and petrol bombs. Florence explained, "There was no time because you would not know if they got into the house what they would do. . . . If there was a funeral, we were supposed to make it fast and leave the place before havoc starts."[90] Another woman, Eunice, described her family's flight to the home of her husband's employer, a nearby farmer, because the violence prevented proper mourning: "We could not [sit in] mourning in our places. It was possible to get hit by petrol bombs inside the house."[91] Eunice's complaint speaks to women's frustrations as chief mourners or as the company of the bereaved. These female mourners were expected to withdraw from the community and be confined to the house after a death, a responsibility nearly impossible to fulfill when one is not safe at home or when one is sleeping in group camps or in the forests. Bonangani furthered these complaints, lamenting women's inability to wear proper black mourning attire: "Yes, we were mourning, but we were running with a black cloth. We used to mourn for one week, but it was no longer working accordingly. Even when your husband passed on, you were not mourning as we used to, because we were always on the run."[92] While Bonangani showed no concern about the wearing of black during mourning, others complained that they could not wear mourning clothes because of the affiliation of particular colors with political parties. Khethi "mourned [for her son], but at the end it was not happening, because you were judged by the dress code and particular colors. If you wore a black skirt, that meant you were in a particular organization. . . . Inkatha used to wear black skirts."[93] While both men and women mourned, women were aggrieved by their inability to perform the gendered roles of funeral rites.

Other women expressed concern about fleeing their communities and leaving their sons behind to fight during uDlame because of their mourning-related responsibilities as Zulu women. Alzina related that many women in Nxamalala were encouraged by "the whites" to leave their areas for safer ones. But when considering whether or not to run away, "our children cried, if you leave us, who is going to close our eyes when we die?"[94] When an unmarried child dies, it is the mother who serves as the chief mourner. It is her responsibility to close the eyes and mouth of the dead, wash the body, and straighten the limbs in preparation for burial, as well as sit in mourning, covered in a blanket, on the bare floor. After burial, the mother continues in mourning until she is ritually released, much later than other members of the family. The passage of the deceased's spirit is effected through the mother, a married woman.[95]

Through these complaints about what they were *not* able to do, women reveal their investment in the gendered hierarchy of ukuhlonipha and their participation in gendered responsibilities of mourning. They wanted to wear proper mourning clothing and sit in seclusion for the recommended period of time. They promoted their roles as Zulu women, mothers, and chief mourners. Their laments about the co-option of funerals by youth also reveal how they shared with men an expectation that Zulu life should be ordered according to age and the practice of ukuhlonipha.

Conclusion:
Gendered Realms of Martial and Moral Zuluness

While the dominant images of uDlame focus on Zulu martial masculinity and women as non-ethnic victims or peacemakers, this analysis of oral history interviews with rural isiZulu-speaking women indicates the ways in which they made claims on ethnicity and utilized their Zuluness, particularly gendered notions of martial and moral ethnicity, to inform decision-making, defensive, and coping strategies. Their grievances about what they were *not* able to practice highlight their investment in Zulu ethnicity during an era of unprecedented change and turmoil. They used the discourse of martial masculinity to make choices about fleeing the violence or supporting their husbands both physically and emotionally. Some also used this gendered norm subversively in attempts to protect their male loved ones. While Zulu martial masculinity suggested that women should not take up arms, they used Zulu religious beliefs as cultural weapons to protect themselves and cope with the traumas of war. They prayed to the Christian God and their Zulu ancestors even when they were unable to do so properly by burning incense. Some sought the powers of Zulu healers and medicines for protection "so that the bullet can't hit you." They complained about the interference of war and the lack of ukuhlonipha at funerals, as well as their inability to wear proper mourning attire and sit in seclusion for the appropriate period of time.

In these discourses, women not only assert their claims on Zuluness but also reveal gendered uses of martial masculinity and moral ethnicity as resources during an era of unprecedented turmoil and social change. This echoes the essays of Urban-Mead and Mbah in this collection, where women used aspects of ethnicity as a tool to ensure smooth marriages or to promote women's power. While Schmidt presents a case of women within Ngoni communities who found ethnicity unavailable to them, and several others (Healy-Clancy, Gengenbach, and Sanders) suggest that women chose other identities or crossed borders to achieve their goals, the Zulu women interviewed here were proud of their ethnicity and made clear the ways in which it helped them to order their lives. As Mbah's contribution to this collection also suggests, militant masculinity does not preclude women from ethnic identities. Women support men's martial ethnicity through performance and use it to make decisions about their own actions. Women not only construct concepts of their own ethnicity and then wield it as a resource but do so in relation to men.

NOTES

Here, I use English translations of interviews conducted in isiZulu. Please see my dissertation for the original isiZulu quotes. All interviewees signed oral consent forms, but due to the sensitivity of the violent subject, I include only their first names in publication unless they were individuals of significant standing in the community. See Jill E. Kelly, "'Only the Fourth Chief': Land, Conflict, and Chiefly Authority in 20th Century KwaZulu-Natal, South Africa" (PhD diss., Michigan State University, 2012).

Special thanks to Jan Bender Shetler, Lauren Jarvis, Peter Alegi, Peter Limb, and participants in the 2011 Southern African Historical Society Biennial Conference and the North Eastern Workshop on Southern Africa for constructive feedback.

1. John Laband, "'Bloodstained Grandeur': Colonial and Imperial Stereotypes of Zulu Warriors and Zulu Warfare," in *Zulu Identities: Being Zulu, Past and Present*, ed. Benedict Carton, John Laband, and Jabulani Sithole (Scottsville: University of KwaZulu-Natal Press, 2008), 168–76.

2. For more on the historical invention and mythology surrounding King Shaka and the Zulu, see Carolyn Hamilton, *Terrific Majesty: The Powers of Shaka Zulu and the Limits of Historical Invention* (Cambridge, MA: Harvard University Press, 1998); Dan Wylie, *Myth of Iron: Shaka in History* (Oxford: James Currey; Athens: Ohio University Press; Pietermaritzburg: University of KwaZulu-Natal Press, 2006); John Wright, "Reflections on the Politics of Being 'Zulu,'" in Carton, Laband, and Sithole, *Zulu Identities*, 35–43. On the commodification of Zulu ethnicity, see John L. Comaroff and Jean Comaroff, *Ethnicity, Inc.* (Chicago: University of Chicago Press, 2009).

3. The noun *udlame* now translates simply as "violence" but has a semantic history that conveys the savagery and chaos that disrupted every aspect of daily life during the transition era. Udlame literally translates as "the use of savagery in achieving aims" and implies the resultant chaos, such as that which might result from an elephant storming through one's home. I use uDlame as a proper noun to refer to the war. C. L. Sibusiso Nyembezi, *AZ: Isichazimazwi Sanamuhla Nangomuso* (Pietermaritzburg: Reach Out Publishers, 1992).

4. Christopher S. Wren, "Tribal Feuds Won't Let Up in South Africa," *New York Times*, 25 February 1990; Roger Thurow, "In South Africa, Violence Takes on Tribal Overtone," *Wall Street Journal*, 20 August 1990.

5. Mzala (Jabulani Nxumalo), *Gatsha Buthelezi: Chief with a Double Agenda* (London: Zed Books, 1988); Gerhard Maré and Georgina Hamilton, *Appetite for Power: Buthelezi's Inkatha and South Africa* (Johannesburg: Ravan Press, 1987); Daphna Golan, "Inkatha and Its Use of the Zulu Past," *History in Africa* 18 (1991): 113–26; Catherine Campbell, "Learning to Kill: Masculinity, the Family and Violence in Natal," *Journal of Southern African Studies* 18, no. 3 (1992): 614–28; Daphna Golan, *Inventing Shaka: Using History in the Construction of Zulu Nationalism* (Boulder, CO: L. Rienner, 1994); Hamilton, *Terrific Majesty*; Thokozani Xaba, "Masculinity and Its Malcontents: The Confrontation between 'Struggle Masculinity' and 'Post-struggle Masculinity' (1900–1997)," in *Changing Men in Southern Africa* (Pietermaritzburg: University of Natal Press, 2001), 105–24;

Thembisa Waetjen, *Workers and Warriors: Masculinity and the Struggle for Nation in South Africa* (Urbana: University of Illinois Press, 2004); Mxolisi Mchunu, "Culture Change, Zulu Masculinity and Intergenerational Conflict in the Context of Civil War in Pietermaritzburg (1987–1991)," in *From Boys to Men: Social Constructions of Masculinity in Contemporary Society* (Cape Town: Juta and Company, 2007), 225–40.

6.   Jacklyn Cock, *Colonels and Cadres: War and Gender in South Africa* (Cape Town: Oxford University Press, 1991); Nira Yuval-Davis, *Gender and Nation* (London: Sage Publications, 1997); Cynthia Enloe, "Womenandchildren: Making Feminist Sense of the Persian Gulf Crisis," *Village Voice*, September 25, 1990.

7.   For an examination of women's protests against the violence, see Debby Bonnin, "Changing Spaces, Changing Places: Political Violence and Women's Protests in KwaZulu-Natal," *Journal of Southern African Studies* 26, no. 2 (2000): 301–16.

8.   Elsewhere, Thembisa Waetjen has argued that Zulu nationalism was explicitly a politics for the recruitment of men. The focus here is not on political ethnicity but on other ways in which ethnicity was shaped and used by women in the context of war. See Waetjen, *Workers and Warriors*, 66.

9.   Jason Hickel, "Democracy and Sabotage: Moral Order and Political Conflict in KwaZulu-Natal, South Africa" (PhD diss., University of Virginia, 2011).

10.   John Lonsdale, "Moral Ethnicity and Political Tribalism," in *Inventions and Boundaries: Historical and Anthropological Approaches to the Study of Ethnicity and Nationalism*, ed. Preben Kaarsholm and Jan Hultin (Roskilde: International Development Studies, Roskilde University, 1994), 140.

11.   Philippe Denis, Radikobo Ntsimane, and Thomas Cannell, *Indians versus Russians: An Oral History of Political Violence in Nxamalala (1987–1993)* (Dorpspruit: Cluster Publications, 2010).

12.   John Aitchison, "They Just Give You Labels and Then They Come and Kill You: A Failed Search for Ethnicity in the Natal Midlands Violence" (paper presented at the Conference on Ethnicity, Society and Conflict in Natal, September 14–16, 1992), Alan Paton Centre (hereafter cited as APC), Pietermaritzburg, PC 14/2/6/5.

13.   Carton, Laband, and Sithole, *Zulu Identities*.

14.   Rogers Brubaker and Frederick Cooper, "Beyond 'Identity,'" *Theory and Society* 29, no. 1 (February 2000): 1–47.

15.   Yuval-Davis, *Gender and Nation*, 43.

16.   Eric Hobsbawm and Terence Ranger, eds., *The Invention of Tradition* (Cambridge: Cambridge University Press, 1983).

17.   Lonsdale, "Moral Ethnicity," 132.

18.   Jeff Guy, "Gender Oppression in Precapitalist Societies," in *Women and Gender in Southern Africa to 1945* (Cape Town: David Philip Publishers, 1990), 33–47.

19.   Robert Morrell, John Wright, and Sheila Meintjes, "Colonialism and the Establishment of White Domination, 1840–1890," in *Political Economy and Identities in KwaZulu-Natal*, ed. Robert Morrell (Durban: Indicator Press, 1996), 57.

20.   Jeff Guy, "An Accommodation of Patriarchs: Theophilus Shepstone and the Foundations of the System of Native Administration in Natal" (seminar paper, Colloquium: Masculinities in Southern Africa, University of Natal, Durban, 1997).

21.   Carolyn Hamilton and John Wright, "The Making of the AmaLala: Ethnicity, Ideology and Relations of Subordination in a Precolonial Context," *South African Historical Journal* 22 (1990): 3–23; John Wright, "The Thukela-Mzimkhulu Region of Natal," in *The Mfecane Aftermath: Reconstructive Debates in Southern African History* (Johannesburg: Witwatersrand University Press, 1995), 163–83; Morrell, Wright, and Meintjes, "Colonialism."

22.   Michael R. Mahoney, *The Other Zulus: The Spread of Zulu Ethnicity in Colonial South Africa* (Durham, NC: Duke University Press, 2012).

23.   Paul La Hausse, *Restless Identities: Signatures of Nationalism, Zulu Ethnicity, and History in the Lives of Petros Lamula (c. 1881–1948) and Lymon Maling (1889–c. 1936)* (Pietermaritzburg: University of Natal Press, 2000).

24.   This Inkata is to be distinguished from the latter-day Inkatha Yenkululeko Yesizwe. Nicholas Cope, *To Bind the Nation: Solomon kaDinuzulu and Zulu National-ism, 1913–1933* (Pietermaritzburg: University of Natal Press, 1993); Shula Marks, *The Ambiguities of Dependence in South Africa: Class, Nationalism, and the State in Twentieth-Century Natal* (Baltimore, MD: Johns Hopkins University Press, 1986); Shula Marks, "Patriotism, Patriarchy and Purity: Natal and the Politics of Zulu Ethnic Conscious-ness," in *The Creation of Tribalism in Southern Africa* (Berkeley: University of California Press, 1989), 215–40.

25.   Maré and Hamilton, *Appetite for Power*; Gerhard Maré, *Brothers Born of Warrior Blood: Politics and Ethnicity in South Africa* (Johannesburg: Ravan Press, 1992); Waetjen, *Workers and Warriors.*

26.   For literature on both Africa and South Africa, see this collection's suggestions for further reading.

27.   Nancy Rose Hunt, "Placing African Women's History and Locating Gender," *Social History* 14, no. 3 (1989): 359–79.

28.   Meghan Healy-Clancy, "Women and the Problem of Family in Early African Nationalist History and Historiography," *South African Historical Journal* 64, no. 3 (2012): 451.

29.   John Wright, "Control of Women's Labour in the Zulu Kingdom," in *Before and After Shaka: Papers in Nguni History*, ed. J. B. Peires (Grahamstown: Rhodes Univer-sity, 1981), 82–99; John Wright and Carolyn Hamilton, "Traditions and Transformations: The Phongolo-Mzimkhulu Region in the Late 18th and Early 19th Centuries," in *Natal and Zululand: From Earliest Times to 1910*, ed. Andrew Duminy and Bill Guest (Pieter-maritzburg: University of Natal Press, Shuter and Shooter, 1989), 49–82; Guy, "Gender Oppression."

30.   Belinda Bozzoli, "Marxism, Feminism, and South African Studies," *Journal of Southern African Studies* 9, no. 2 (1983): 139–71.

31.   Simon J. Maphalala, *Aspects of Zulu Rural Life during the Nineteenth Century* (KwaDlangezwa: University of Zululand, 1985); Jennifer Weir, "'I Shall Need to Use Her to Rule': The Power of 'Royal' Zulu Women in Pre-colonial Zululand," *South African Historical Journal* 43, no. 1 (2000): 3–23; Weir, "Chiefly Women and Women's Leadership in Pre-colonial Southern Africa," in *Women in South African History*, ed. Nomboniso Gasa (Cape Town: HSRC Press, 2007), 3–20; Sifiso Ndlovu, "A Reassessment of

Women's Power in the Zulu Kingdom," in Carton, Laband, and Sithole, *Zulu Identities*, 111–21.

32. Sean Hanretta, "Women, Marginality and the Zulu State: Women's Institutions and Power in the Early Nineteenth Century," *Journal of African History* 39, no. 3 (1998): 389–415.

33. Shireen Hassim, "Family, Motherhood and Zulu Nationalism: The Politics of the Inkatha Women's Brigade," *Feminist Review* 43 (1993): 1–25.

34. Waetjen, *Workers and Warriors*, 63–68.

35. Eva Jackson, "Exceptions That Prove the Rule? A Discussion of Vundlazi of the Izinkumbi in Natal, and Female Chiefship in Precolonial and Early Colonial Southeast Africa" (paper presented at the South African Historical Conference, Durban, 2011).

36. Susan Geiger, "What's So Feminist about Doing Women's Oral History?," *Journal of Women's History* 2, no. 1 (1990): 169–83.

37. In addition to the interviews I undertook in Mbambangalo and Mkhambathini, this chapter also draws upon the interviews conducted by Sinomlando fieldworkers in rural Nxamalala, to the west of Pietermaritzburg, and housed at the Alan Paton Centre, Pietermaritzburg. These interviews focused on the role of religion and the church during uDlame.

38. Jill E. Kelly, field notes, 30 January 2010.

39. Nwando Achebe discusses a similar experience in her own fieldwork in the introductory chapter of Nwando Achebe, *Farmers, Traders, Warriors, and Kings: Female Power and Authority in Northern Igboland, 1900–1960* (Portsmouth: Heinemann, 2005).

40. Veronica D., interview by the author and Thandeka Majola, 23 May 2011, Maqongqo.

41. On calls to be "mothers of the nation" by both parties, see Debby Gaitskell and Elaine Unterhalter, "Mothers of the Nation: A Comparative Analysis of the Nation, Race, and Motherhood in Afrikaner Nationalism and the African National Congress," in *Women-Nation-State*, ed. Nira Yuval-Davis and Floya Anthias (New York: St. Martin's Press, 1989), 58–78; Hassim, "Family, Motherhood and Zulu Nationalism."

42. Thombi G., interview by the author and Thandeka Majola, 27 January 2011, Maqongqo.

43. Thombi G., interview.

44. Nikiwe M., interview by the author and Thandeka Majola, 4 March 2011, Maqongqo. See also Thombi G., interview; Khethi Z., interview by the author and Thandeka Majola, 2 March 2011, Imbubu; Ntombinazi Z., interview by the author and Thandeka Majola, 25 March 2011, Maqongqo.

45. Ntombi N., interview by the author and Thandeka Majola, 17 January 2011, Imbubu.

46. Ntombinazi Z., interview.

47. Thobekile Maphumulo, interview by the author and Thandeka Majola, 8 February 2011, Camperdown.

48. Veronica D., interview.

49. Doris M., interview by the author and Thandeka Majola, 16 June 2011, Haniville.

50. Philisile N., interview by the author and Thandeka Majola, 25 May 2011, KwaNyavu.

51. Eugenia Lindiwe Zamandelu Sikhosana, "A Critical Study of the Contemporary Practice of Ululation (Ukukikiza) and Its Current Social and Cultural Values among the Zulus" (PhD diss., University of Zululand, 2002), 172–73.

52. This section has benefited from discussions with Sifiso Ndlovu, Lauren Jarvis, and Ndubueze Mbah. Comparisons might be made to the Ohafia practice of *ije akpaka*, where women dressed as male warriors both to authorize men to go to war and to protect them. See Leonard Ndubueze Mbah, "Emergent Masculinities: The Gendered Struggle for Power in Southeastern Nigeria, 1850–1920" (PhD diss., Michigan State University, 2013). There is oral evidence of King Shaka's aunt Mnkabayi, often called the regent queen, dressing as a man. See Ndlovu, "Reassessment."

53. Timothy Smith, testimony to the Truth and Reconciliation Commission, November 1996, Pietermaritzburg, http://www.justice.gov.za/trc/hrvtrans/hrvpmb /pmb7_11.htm (accessed 24 December 2011).

54. Nsuze kaMfelafuti, in *The James Stuart Archive of Recorded Oral Evidence Relating to the History of the Zulu and Neighbouring Peoples*, ed. Colin de B. Webb and John B. Wright, vols. 1–5 (Pietermaritzburg: University of Natal Press, 1976). Stuart also documented this practice, as well as others observed by women during wartime, in his 1913 account of the Zulu Rebellion. James Stuart, *A History of the Zulu Rebellion 1906* (Cambridge: Cambridge University Press, 2013).

55. Eileen Jensen Krige, *The Social System of the Zulus* (Pietermaritzburg: Shuter and Shooter, 1988), 277.

56. A. T. Bryant, *A Zulu-English Dictionary* (Pinetown: Mariannhill Mission Press, 1905), 549–50.

57. Axel-Ivar Berglund, *Zulu Thought-Patterns and Symbolism* (London: C. Hurst, 1976), 363–71.

58. Philisile N., interview.

59. See, for instance, the testimonies of Maziyana kaMahlabeni, Ngidi kaMcikaziswa, and Mtshayankomo kaMagolwana. Other testimonies refer less explicitly to women's fighting. That "unarmed women" were not killed suggests there were armed women. For an example, see Mqaikana kaYenge, in Webb and Wright, *James Stuart Archive*.

60. For a discussion of amabutho, see Weir, "Chiefly Women." For women's conflicts, see Helen Bradford, "'We Are Now the Men': Women's Beer Protests in the Natal Countryside, 1929," in *Class, Community, and Conflict: South African Perspectives*, ed. Belinda Bozzoli (Johannesburg: Ravan Press, 1987); Lauren V. Jarvis, "'The Maidens Were Fighting for Shembe': Women and Violence in the Nazareth Baptist Church, 1910–1939" (paper presented at the South African Historical Society, Durban, 2011).

61. Jo Beall et al., "African Women in the Durban Struggle, 1985–1986: Towards a Transformation of Roles?," in *South African Review*, vol. 4, ed. Glenn Moss and Ingrid Obery (Johannesburg: Ravan Press, 1987), 93–103; Cock, *Colonels and Cadres*; Janet Cherry, "'We Were Not Afraid': The Role of Women in the 1980s' Township Uprising in the Eastern Cape," in Gasa, *Women in South African History*, 281–313; Raymond Suttner,

"Women in the ANC-Led Underground," in Gasa, *Women in South African History*, 233–55.

62. Florence N., interview by the author and Thandeka Majola, 7 March 2011, Maqongqo.

63. Ntombi N., interview.

64. Khethi Z., interview.

65. Theni N., interview by the author and Thandeka Majola, 27 May 2011, Haniville.

66. Khethi Z., interview.

67. Doris M., interview.

68. Iris Berger, "Rebels or Status Seekers? Women as Spirit Mediums in East Africa," in *Women in Africa: Studies in Social and Economic Change*, ed. Nancy Hafkin and Edna Bay (Stanford, CA: Stanford University Press, 1976), 157–81; Deborah Gaitskell, "Devout Domesticity? A Century of African Women's Christianity in South Africa," in *Women and Gender in Southern Africa to 1945*, ed. Cherryl Walker (Cape Town: David Philip, 1990), 251–72; Cynthia Hoehler-Fatton, *Women of Fire and Spirit: History, Faith, and Gender in Roho Religion in Western Kenya* (New York: Oxford University Press, 1996); Dorothy L. Hodgson, *The Church of Women: Gendered Encounters between Maasai and Missionaries* (Bloomington: Indiana University Press, 2005).

69. A vast literature has shown how African men and women made Christianity their own and suggests no need to distinguish between African Christianity and traditional religion. At what point do one's religious beliefs become part of one's culture and moral ethnicity? Do they always remain separate, and did women envision them as separate? For the Zulu Christians of the later nineteenth and early twentieth centuries known as *kholwa* (believers), their Zulu background became an important political tool and part of their identity. This is a large question perhaps best suited for its own study. Here I will follow Denis and refer to them as two separate but complementary tools used by women.

70. Philippe Denis, "Prayers and Rituals to the Ancestors as Vehicles of Resilience: Coping with Political Violence in Nxamalala, Pietermaritzburg (1987–1991)," *Journal of Theology for Southern Africa* 128 (2007): 37–52.

71. Ntombinazi Z., interview.

72. Thombi G., interview.

73. Nikiwe M., interview.

74. Thombi G., interview.

75. Florence N., interview.

76. Nikiwe M., interview.

77. Busisiwe T., interview by the author and Thandeka Majola, 21 March 2011, Maqongqo.

78. Nompumelelo M. and Mirriam T., interviews by Lindiwe Mkasi, HC07C16 English transcript, 16 September 2005, APC.

79. Thuleleni M., Irinah G., and Thokozile T., interview by Lindiwe Mkasi, HC07C03 English and Zulu transcripts, 16 September 2005, APC.

80. Busisiwe T., interview.

81. Krige, *Social System*, 159.

82. Ntombi N., interview.

83. Florence N., interview.

84. Nikiwe M., interview.

85. Generational tensions within and between the movements of the era have been examined by both Belinda Bozzoli and Ari Sitas. Bozzoli highlights the internal division between youth and adults during the Alexandra Rebellion, while Sitas shows the ways in which the comrades movement was more than just unemployed black youth. Belinda Bozzoli, *Theatres of Struggle and the End of Apartheid* (Athens: Ohio University Press, 2004); Ari Sitas, "The Making of the 'Comrades' Movement in Natal, 1985–91," *Journal of Southern African Studies* 18, no. 3 (1992): 629–41.

86. Xaba, "Masculinity," 110.

87. Mchunu, "Culture Change."

88. Bozzoli, *Theatres of Struggle*.

89. Tryphina G., interview by Cosmos Mzizi, HC07C04 Zulu transcript, 13 March 2003, APC.

90. Florence N., interview.

91. Eunice D., interview by the author and Thandeka Majola, 7 March 2011, Maqongqo.

92. Bonangani N., interview.

93. Khethi Z., interview.

94. Alzina H., interview by Cosmos Mzizi, HC07C07-2 English transcript, 2 September 2003, APC.

95. Harriet Ngubane, *Body and Mind in Zulu Medicine: An Ethnography of Health and Disease in Nyuswa-Zulu Thought and Practice* (New York: Academic Press, 1977), 83, 141.

8

~~~~~~

Sorting and Suffering

Social Classification in Postgenocide Rwanda

JENNIE E. BURNET

In Rwanda, the shibboleth of genocide forced a clear yet sometimes arbitrary demarcation between Hutu and Tutsi. This violent delineation had an enduring impact on the lived experience of intersecting systems of social classification (gender and ethnicity) in the aftermath of the 1994 genocide. Many of the chapters in this book describe ethnicity as a social resource that women mobilize to claim their rights or to reject men's narratives of history. This chapter explores the more sinister aspects of ethnicity and the dangerous material consequences of rigidly defined oppositional categories. Drawing on the methods the science historian Geoffrey Bowker and the sociologist Susan Star used to trace the ways that "the lives of individuals are broken, twisted, and torqued by their en-counters" with the racial classification system in South Africa, I examine how gender and ethnic social classifications affected the lives of ordinary women in the aftermath of the genocide.[1] Gender and ethnic social classifications in the aftermath of the genocide marginalized women who did not fit into the social categories deployed in the dominant discourse about the genocide, civil war, and national history.

Between 6 April and 4 July 1994, at least 500,000 Rwandans, primarily Tutsi but also politically moderate Hutu and others defined as "enemies of Rwanda," lost their lives in a state-sponsored genocide.[2] The genocide occurred in the context of a civil war that had begun on 1 October 1990, when the Rwandan Patriotic Front (RPF) rebel group attacked Rwanda with the intention of liber-ating the country from President Juvénal Habyarimana's dictatorship.[3] The civil war continued throughout the early 1990s until Habyarimana, facing dramatic military losses and continued pressure from bilateral aid donors, was forced to the negotiating table. The 1993 Arusha Peace Accords brought an official end to hostilities and outlined a transition plan to move the country to multiparty politics and democratic elections. The transition was brought to an abrupt halt on 6 April 1994, when President Habyarimana's plane was shot down by unknown assailants. Hutu extremists then took control of the government and perpetrated a genocide against Tutsi and others defined as "enemies" of the state.

While many scholars tackled the meanings of ethnic classification in pregenocide Rwanda, few wrote about ethnicity in postgenocide Rwanda. Investigating or writing about ethnicity in Rwanda after the genocide was not only extremely difficult because of the potential psychological and emotional risks to research participants but also dangerous for researchers. Under the RPF's policy of national unity, which emphasized the unity of all Rwandans and forbade discussions about ethnicity, it was impossible to ask research participants direct questions about ethnicity. In the late 1990s and through the 2000s, Rwandan government authorities, local Rwandan associations, and international nongovernmental organizations required questions about ethnicity to be removed from interview guides, questionnaires, and surveys. During the bulk of my ethnographic research in Rwanda between 1997 and 2002, this policy was what the anthropologist Michael Taussig has called a public secret, something that is unstated but universally known.[4] In 2001, a law on discrimination and sectarianism codified this policy into law and defined divisionism as "the act of any speech, written statement, or action that divides people" and a crime punishable by one to five years in prison.[5] The 2003 constitution stated that the Rwandan people should resolve to "fight the ideology of genocide and all its manifestations and to eradicate ethnic, regional and any other form of divisions." Neither the 2001 law nor the 2003 constitution clearly defined divisionism or genocidal ideology. As a result, the government used these laws to silence citizens who publicly criticized the RPF, its leaders, or its policies and to suppress movements or political parties opposed to RPF rule.

In this chapter, I examine the ways that systems of gender and ethnic classification in postgenocide Rwanda made certain Rwandan women socially invisible and excluded them from important aspects of social reproduction. These social classification processes increased their suffering by bringing past violence into their present lives. Through a case study of three categories of women living in the borderlands of social classifications in postgenocide Rwanda—raped maidens, Tutsi wives of prisoners, and Hutu genocide widows—I demonstrate that these categories of women do not fit into the intertwined systems of ethnic and gender classification. Because of this mismatch between the dominant systems of social classification and these women's social status, they suffered the symbolic violence of not existing in the collective social imagination. This symbolic violence held material implications and thus further compounded their poverty and the consequences of physical violence they had experienced. Nonetheless, these women exercised their agency to rebuild their lives despite the structural and symbolic violence that ethnic sorting inflicted on them.

Sorting:
Social Classification in Precolonial and Colonial Rwanda

Virtually any glyph of Rwandan society states that the population is comprised of three "ethnic groups": Tutsi at 15 percent of the population, Hutu at 85 percent, and Twa at less than 1 percent.[6] Yet the origin of these widely cited statistics is unclear. They themselves form part of the mythicohistories, a term I borrow from the anthropologist Liisa Malkki, that structure reality.[7] Although the terms Hutu, Tutsi, and Twa are quite old in Rwandan social discourse and predate the colonial era, their meanings and importance have changed dramatically over time and varied by region.[8] What scholars today call "ethnicity" in Rwanda has not been marked by differences in language, culture, religion, or territory in recorded history. This fact calls into question whether ethnicity is the best label for this classification system. Despite the widely accepted mythico-history of separate origins for the three so-called groups, historical linguistic and archaeological evidence indicate that the people who populated what today is Rwanda have shared similar ways of life, language, and culture since approximately 500 BCE. This shared cultural heritage was what made them Rwandans.

Nonetheless, we should not be seduced by idyllic depictions of a precolonial Rwanda where social harmony and ethnic equality were the predominant features. The politicization of the categories Hutu, Tutsi, and Twa began in the mid to late nineteenth century when Mwami Rwabugiri imposed corvée labor on Hutu peasants throughout the kingdom but exempted Tutsi peasants.[9] These classifications were further politicized in the colonial encounter. Belgian colonizers brought their own nineteenth-century ideas about race and experiences of ethnic difference and mapped them onto the indigenous categories "Hutu," "Tutsi," and "Twa." Colonial administrators and Catholic missionaries believed that Tutsi were descendants of so-called Nilotic peoples from the Horn of Africa or even possibly remnants of a lost tribe of Israel. From their perspective, Tutsi were seen as more Caucasian than the Negroid Hutu. The colonialists praised the beauty of Tutsi women, with their so-called European features: straight, thin noses; long, graceful arms and legs; and light, clear skin.

Table 1. Gender classifications in Rwanda

Male	Female
	uruhinja (newborn)
	umwana (child)
umuhungu (son-boy)	*umukobwa* (daughter-girl)
umusore (bachelor)	*umwari* (maiden)
umugabo (husband-man)	*umugore* (wife-woman)
	umutegarugori (wearer of the *urugori* [wife-mother])
umupfakazi (widower, widow)	
umusaza (old man)	*umukecuru* (old woman)
[no male analogue]	*indushyi* (vulnerable [person], referring to a rejected wife)

Alongside ethnic classification, the system of gender classification in Rwanda was historically quite different from the dichotomous distinction between men and women common in Europe, North America, and the rest of the West. In Rwanda, gender was constructed two-dimensionally not only by sex but also by age or life status. In the precolonial and colonial periods, gender categories in Rwandan society were embedded in one's role in society rather than on a simple distinction between males and females. Age and life status served as structural elements for the ways in which a person is gendered at a given stage of life. Newborns and children under the age of four were generally treated the same by their parents, relatives, and community members regardless of their sex. There were no gender differences in customary dress, hairstyle, or bodily decorations for infants. Around the age of four, distinctions between boys, literally "sons" in Kinyarwanda, and girls, literally "daughters" in Kinyarwanda, began to be made as they took on specific roles in the household. Distinctions in age status were just as important as sex distinctions. Even today in Rwanda, both urban and rural dwellers make clear and strict distinctions between daughters-girls (*abakobwa*) and wives-women (*abagore*), as well as between sons-boys (*abahungu*) and husbands-men (*abagabo*). No boy can become a man until he is a husband and father, fulfilling all the attached responsibilities (providing a house, a livelihood, and social stability). And no girl can become a woman until she is a wife and mother.

Female roles in Rwandan society were largely determined by marital or reproductive status. As a society relying primarily on agriculture or pastoralism, access to land was of vital importance for all Rwandans. According to custom, female Rwandans' access to land was assured through their relationships with male kin.[10] The first category, maidens, refers to unmarried female Rwandans ranging in age from sixteen to twenty-nine. "Maidens" is my translation of the

Kinyarwanda term *abari*, meaning roughly "girls ripe for marriage," which has no exact equivalent in standard American English. The archaic "maidens," with its connotation of virginity, is a close match. The term *abari* has a more positive connotation than abakobwa because it explicitly refers to a young woman's physical readiness to bear children and become a wife and mother. Maidens were integral to the family unit, performing important chores around the home such as cooking, cleaning, and fetching water, and they cultivated food crops alongside their mothers and other siblings. Once a maiden left her father's home and married, she became part of her husband's patrilineage and relied on her husband, brothers-in-law, and sons for access to land. Wives were the economic (as well as spiritual and moral) center of the *inzu* (literally "house," referring to the conjugal household comprised of husband, wife, and children). Motherhood was the best light in which females could be seen in Rwandan society, and a maiden only truly became a wife upon bearing children.[11] In the recent past, a wife was responsible for cultivating all food for the household on land belonging to her husband or his lineage.[12] A husband focused on the production of cash crops, managed the livestock, or migrated in search of paid labor. Upon the death of her husband, a widow (*umupfakazi*) who had produced a son for her husband's lineage retained the right to cultivate her deceased husband's landholdings, managing them for her sons until they were old enough to receive their inheritance and become heads of their own households. In old age, a widow relied on her sons and daughters-in-law to care for her. On the other hand, a widow who had not produced a son for her husband's lineage was labeled *indushyi* (literally "vulnerable") and returned to her father's (or, in his absence, one of her brothers') household.[13] Her deceased husband's landholdings reverted to his patrilineage. The indushyi's patrilineage was expected to provide a portion of land for her to cultivate until she remarried and left to join her new husband's lineage. Rwandan men, on the other hand, acquired land directly either through inheritance or through land-tenure agreements, exchanging labor and a portion of the harvests or milk for access to agricultural fields or pastureland. While these gendered land-tenure practices continued long into the postcolonial period, the meanings and importance of ethnicity changed significantly during colonialism.

The degree to which the colonial encounter changed the implications of gender and ethnic classification systems is illustrated by the transformations in the meaning of a Rwandan proverb: "Abagore ntibafite ubwoko." Today in Rwanda, the standard translation for this proverb is "Wives have no ethnicity." However, the Kinyarwanda word *ubwoko*, translated here as "ethnicity," literally means "sort" or "type" and can be applied to monkeys, trees, or bananas as easily as to people. Prior to the 1950s, ethnicity was not the primary way that Rwandans classified each other. At that time, the term *ubwoko*, when referring to human beings, meant the combination of a person's social attributes relevant to a given context. In the 1960s, when asked, "Ubwoko bwawe n'ubuhe?" (What is your type?) by a foreign scholar, male respondents spontaneously gave their clan and lineage name, for example, "Abasinga Rumanzi."[14] Female respondents responded the same way or might ask for clarification whether the asker wanted to know her birth clan and lineage or her clan and lineage through marriage. In Rwanda today, however, the same question, "Ubwoko bwawe n'ubuhe?" is immediately understood by both men and women to be asking, "What is your ethnicity?" a taboo question under the current government's policy of national unity.

Coming back to the meaning of this proverb, perhaps the best translation would be "Wives have no classification [of their own]." On most occasions when Rwandans used this proverb with me, they were trying to explain a wife's subordination to her husband—it was a statement more about public perceptions of the household and how a wife was obligated to support her husband's and his lineage's interests instead of her own (i.e., her father's or brothers') lineage. Rwanda is a patrilineal society, and traditionally a daughter's or wife's social classification and identity were determined by the men she was related to—as a girl, her father or brothers, and as a wife, her husband, father-in-law, or brothers-in-law. While according to tradition daughters and wives did not have their own ethnic classification, the colonial encounter added European ideas about "blood" and dual inheritance to the strictly patrilineal inheritance of ethnic classification that previously existed in Rwandan society. Before colonialism, aspects of social identity other than ethnicity, such as lineage, clan, hill, and region, were of much greater importance than the social categories Hutu, Tutsi, and Twa.

The late colonial and early postcolonial periods had a profound effect on the implications of ethnic classification for all Rwandans. Colonial policies had politicized ethnicity by formally excluding Hutu from the colonial administration and exempting Tutsi of all social classes from corvée labor. At independence a small cadre of educated Hutu male elite called for a popular democracy and transition of power to the hands of the Hutu ethnic majority. From 1959 until 1961, sporadic communal violence punctuated the transition with Tutsi men targeted for beatings, which sometimes resulted in death, and Tutsi houses burned to the ground.[15] The emergence of Hutu extremism in reaction to the RPF incursion in 1990 and the advent of multiparty politics in the early 1990s started a new era of prominence for these classifications, which had largely receded into the background of daily life for Rwandans in the 1980s. The early 1990s also brought the gradual normalization of political violence, targeting Tutsi and others defined as "enemies of the state." The 1994 genocide rendered these classifications unequivocal questions of life and death.

Beyond its inherent sorting out of ethnic classifications for everyone, the genocide was gendered. Female Tutsi were frequently raped, forcibly taken as "wives," or sexually tortured before being killed.[16] Rape itself was a weapon of the genocide. The genocide targeted the normally privileged role of Rwandan wives as mothers. Female Tutsi were told that they were being impregnated with Hutu fetuses in order to "wipe out" the "Tutsi race." Others were told that bullets should not be wasted on them because they would "die of AIDS," presumably contracted during the rapes.[17] Extremist rhetoric also targeted Tutsi beauty and desirability—militiamen were promised the opportunity for sexual intercourse with Tutsi women. Beauty as a marker of Tutsiness was so strong in the popular imagination that female Hutu who were perceived as beautiful risked being mistaken for Tutsi and raped, sexually tortured, or even killed.[18]

The fate of ethnically mixed families in the genocide illustrates the penetration of European ideas about blood and dual inheritance into the traditional, strictly patrilineal inheritance of ethnic classifications. In the 1970s and 1980s in Rwanda, marriage between Hutu and Tutsi was quite common. Although intermarriage was discouraged among Hutu men at the top of the government and officially forbidden for army officers, even these men sometimes married Tutsi women.[19] Prominent Hutu politicians, army officers, and businessmen who did not take Tutsi wives often had Tutsi mistresses.[20] Like the prototypical trophy wife in the United States, a beautiful (presumably Tutsi) wife or mistress was evidence of a man's stature.

While it may seem logical that intermarriage between Hutu and Tutsi, as well as the attendant offspring of these unions, would inoculate the country against genocide, it was not effective. Although official orders were to kill all Tutsi, wives, maidens, and children were sometimes spared. It was an unofficial policy to spare the Tutsi wives (or mistresses) and children of Hutu men during the first month and a half of killing.[21] The genocide organizers realized that killing the wives and children of Hutu men risked jeopardizing the cooperation of these men in the genocide. It was not until the Hutu extremist government and Rwandan military began losing the war against the RPF rebels that orders to eliminate the Tutsi wives and children of Hutu men, "to cut the tree at its roots" in the parlance of extremist propaganda, were issued nationwide.

National Unity:
Social Classification in Postgenocide Rwanda

The classificatory systems of gender and ethnicity were the product of changing constellations of social, economic, and political power and the violent sorting of ethnic categories throughout the 1990s. The violent demarcation of ethnicity

Table 2. Social classification in postgenocide Rwanda

Tutsi	Hutu
inzirakarengane (victims)	*abicanyi* (perpetrators)
abarokotse (survivors)	*abafunze* (prisoners)
abapfakazi b'itsembabwoko (genocide widows)	*abacengezi* (infiltrators)
abaturutse hanze or *abarutashye* (old returnees)	*abatingitingi, abatahutse,* or *abahungutse* (new returnees)

during the genocide had an enduring impact on lived experiences of social classification. Yet the ethnic classification system underwent further transformation in the years after the genocide. The policy of national unity made open discussions about ethnicity taboo, but Rwandan society was far from unified, and ethnic distinctions remained salient. As I have argued elsewhere, state practices of national memory and the amplified silence regarding Hutu victims of the genocide maintained an ethnic dichotomy (Hutu/Tutsi) by politicizing victimhood and emphasizing the distinction between victim and perpetrator in national ceremonies commemorating the genocide.[22] In national mourning ceremonies and the dominant public discourse, the terms *victim* and *perpetrator* (or *killer*) stood in for the ethnic terms Tutsi and Hutu. The hegemony of public discourse and the state's power to define who was innocent and who was guilty, who was victim and who was perpetrator undermined the RPF's professed ideology of national unity and reinforced ethnic categories of social classification.

Within this context, a new language for discussing ethnicity emerged. Rwandans and foreigners working in Rwanda began to talk about ethnic classification in terms of experiential categories focused on the 1994 genocide and two major refugee flows: the first, mainly Tutsi refugees who left between 1959 and 1973 and returned after the 1994 genocide; and the second, mainly Hutu refugees who left in 1994 and returned in 1996 or 1997. While this new set of categories may have been more accurate in that it focused on individuals' experiences rather than on imagined, innate, ethnic essences, it maintained a polar distinction between Hutu and Tutsi. Terms synonymous with Tutsi included *inzirakarengane* (victims), *abarokotse* (survivors), *abapfakazi b'itsembabwoko* (genocide widows), and *abaturutse hanze* or *abarutashye* (old returnees, referring to Tutsi who returned from long-term exile).[23] Terms synonymous with Hutu included *abicanyi* (perpetrators), *abafunze* (prisoners), *abacengezi* (infiltrators), and *abatingitingi, abatahutse,* or *abahungutse* (new returnees, referring to Hutu who went into exile in 1994 and returned in 1996 and 1997).[24]

While this new constellation of words may have been more accurate in that it focused on individuals' experiences, it polarized discussions of the genocide by leaving no space in public discourse or mourning practices for Hutu genocide victims and by globalizing blame on Hutu, regardless of whether they participated in the genocide or not. For Rwandans in ethnically mixed families, this polarizing discourse excluded their experiences of violence: they could not be victims of violence at the hands of the genocide perpetrators because they were not genocide victims or survivors, and they could not be victims of violence at the hands of the RPF because in the hegemonic national discourses about violence, the RPF only committed violence against genocide perpetrators. Thus, their experiences of violence were erased from the national imagination. Furthermore, this set of categories reinforced the distinction between Hutu and Tutsi among those Rwandans (Hutu, Tutsi, Twa, and those of mixed heritage) who grew up inside the country.

In April 1995, Paul Kagame, then Rwanda's vice president, summarized the double bind of Hutu opponents of the genocide in his response to a journalist's question about rumors of imminent massive reprisals against Hutu that were circulating widely in April 1995: "There are many ways to analyze this phenomenon. First is that this fear [of reprisals against Hutu] could be justified. A lot of people know that they committed or were complicit with some crimes, and they are afraid of being held responsible. The second explanation is a long history of intoxication—they always told the population that Tutsi are dangerous, that they wanted power."[25] In this statement, Vice President Kagame deployed a linguistic device of coded ethnic talk that Rwandans heard clearly but that foreign observers could not detect. In his speeches over the years, Kagame frequently used two terms in opposition with each other: *abantu* (people) and Banyarwanda (Rwandans). In this opposition, the generic abantu is understood to refer to Hutu, while the more specific term, Banyarwanda, literally "Rwandans" but also "the people to whom Rwanda belongs," is understood to mean Tutsi in general but more specifically Tutsi RPF-supporters. Thus, in this particular speech, Kagame only used the term *abantu*, but Rwandan listeners immediately understood that this word meant Hutu because of the history of rhetorical pairing of these words. So, in this speech Vice President Kagame blamed the (Hutu) people either for their participation in or complicity with the genocide or for their willingness to believe propaganda against Tutsi and the RPF. The vice president did not propose a possible third explanation: that the people's fears were justified because RPF soldiers had been killing civilians, both Hutu and Tutsi. Although these killings were well known among Rwandans inside the country, they were rarely reported by human rights organizations.[26] The Rwandan government prevented international human rights monitors and humanitarian aid workers from investigating these killings by preventing their access to the regions where these killings were occurring. The most that the human rights organizations could do was report that the RPF-led government tightly controlled access to local communities throughout 1994 and 1995.[27] Rwandan citizens who opposed the killings—whether Hutu or Tutsi— kept their mouths shut in order to avoid becoming victims as well.[28] Men, male youth, and male adolescents were more likely to be arrested or killed than women, maidens, or children because it was assumed that males were more likely to have participated in the genocide or to mount armed resistance to the new government.

To illustrate the contingency of ethnic classification, which begins to seem cut-and-dried when discussed abstractly, let me relate an ethnographic vignette about two brothers. The first brother, Petero, was in his late twenties and a student at the national university when I met him in 2000. He was also a soldier in the Rwandan Patriotic Front. Before the genocide, Petero had worked in a parastatal company (a company belonging in whole or in part to the state and having political authority) in Kigali. Although Petero had wanted to go to the university and had excellent scores on national exams, he was not awarded a coveted place at the national university. Even though he had managed to change his official ethnic identity (meaning the one marked on his national identity card) from Tutsi to Hutu, his parents did not have the necessary connections to secure him a place at the university. Under President Habyarimana's patrimonial rule, having the "correct" ethnicity was not enough, as the state and its benefits were shared among a limited network of families and friends from the mountains of northwestern Rwanda.

In 1994, Petero escaped the killing squads by fleeing across the battle lines to the RPF side. His national identity card, marked Hutu, did not offer him any protection from the Interahamwe militiamen because his prototypical Tutsi appearance belied the ethnicity marked on his identity card.[29] Like most able-bodied men and adolescent boys who managed to cross the front lines, Petero was conscripted into service with the RPF. In the years after the genocide, Petero tried to demobilize, but the army refused to release him and instead commissioned him as an officer. The army sent him to study at the national university, which afforded him a civilian lifestyle, at least for a few years. After the genocide, the government issued new identity cards without any indication of ethnicity, and open discussions of ethnicity were forbidden, but ethnic distinctions still remained salient for Rwandans in everyday life. Due to his appearance, his membership in the RPF army, and his status as a genocide survivor, he was perceived as Tutsi.

While Petero was classified as Tutsi, his older brother Yohani, who had the same father and mother as Petero, was classified as Hutu. Before the genocide Yohani was a soldier in the Rwandan military, Forces armées rwandaises

(FAR). When the genocide began, Yohani remained with his unit. The fate of most Tutsi soldiers in the FAR was execution by firing squad.[30] However, Yohani, with a less obviously Tutsi physiognomy, had successfully passed for Hutu during his entire military career, and he managed to maintain this disguise during the genocide. Yohani remained with his unit and retreated into exile before the advancing RPF lines. Yohani eventually returned to Rwanda in 1998 after spending two years in refugee camps in eastern Zaire plus over a year in the rain forests following the RPF's attacks on the camps in 1996.

As a recently returned refugee in postgenocide Rwanda and as a former FAR soldier, Yohani was classified as Hutu in the minds of most Rwandans who knew anything about his recent personal history. His siblings, on the other hand, were all perceived as Tutsi. In this ambiguity, Yohani returned to the community where his mother had lived before her death of natural causes in 1993.

Suffering:
The Torque of Social Classification

While in many ways highly ambiguous, this system of ethnic classification played a foundational role in social interactions in the late 1990s and early 2000s. Especially among Rwandans without kin or friendship ties predating the genocide, these categories served as an initial filter of understanding (or lack thereof) among strangers or acquaintances. When combined with other categories of social classification such as gender, they created social capital—or, in most cases, the lack of social capital—that shaped individual agency. In the rest of this chapter, I explore the ways that the lives of certain female Rwandans were "torqued" and their suffering prolonged because they did not fit into the "Aristotelian ideal types of social classification" in postgenocide Rwanda.[31] The gendered social classifications—maidens, wives, and widows—are at the heart of this discussion. Official state policy largely focused on distinguishing between males who had perpetrated genocidal violence (i.e., Hutu) and males who been victims of this violence or liberated the nation through fighting with the RPF (i.e., Tutsi). Because of women's less frequent implication in genocidal violence and greater survival rates, wives, maidens, and widows largely felt the intertwined systems of gender and ethnicity in different ways from men.

Raped Maidens

As discussed above, cultural scripts placed women and girls under the protection of men: before marriage, that of their father, brothers, and uncles; and after marriage, that of their husband, brothers-in-law, and father-in-law. Thus, the major preoccupation for a maiden in Rwanda, as in many other places in the world, is to get married, because it is the only way for her to gain some autonomy, albeit autonomy as the "heart of the household."[32] In the wake of the genocide, maidens faced a difficult terrain fraught with dangers. There were limited opportunities for them to enter into socially recognized marriages because of the demographic realities in the aftermath of the 1994 genocide.

The genocide and war caused a demographic shift in Rwandan society that lasted for several years.[33] The targeting of Tutsi men and boys in the genocide meant that genocide survivors were disproportionately female. Male genocide survivors were mobilized as RPF soldiers to help fight the war. Hutu men and boys were more likely to flee the advancing RPF in 1994 for fear of being killed or imprisoned; wives sometimes remained behind in the hopes of retaining the family's property rights over homes and farmland and to prevent looting. As internally displaced persons and refugees began to return home in 1994 and 1995 and as RPA soldiers shifted from combat to policing duties, the demographic situation began to return to a more normal equilibrium. The mass return of refugees in 1996 and 1997 quickly helped equalize the gender gap; however, the mass arrest of returning refugee men and adolescents on genocide charges meant that a significant proportion of Hutu men were part of the population but not accessible for marriage. Recruitment of Rwandan male youth for the RPA invasion of Zaire and ongoing RPA engagement in the Congo Wars (1997–2003) also siphoned off many men of marrying age. In certain communities, the gender gap remained significant, particularly among people of marriageable age. As a result, the demographic situation limited maidens' marriage opportunities in some communities more than others.

Beyond the demographic issue, the civil war and genocide's economic devastation reduced maidens' marriage opportunities. To enter into a legitimate marriage, meaning one recognized socially and legally, a bachelor needed to prove his ability to support a family. In rural Rwanda, such proof entailed access to farmland and building a house. In urban Rwanda, a stable job or solvent business sufficed. A bachelor also needed the required bridewealth, which in the past had been furnished by his lineage. Since the vast majority of personal property, including bank account balances, and real estate was looted in the genocide or left behind in the flight to safety or into exile, most Rwandans, whether genocide survivors or not, had to begin their lives again from "less than zero," as one genocide widow put it, making a bridewealth out of the reach of many bachelors and their lineage.

Beyond these material obstacles to marriage, maidens faced social obstacles that hinged on the symbolism of marriage in Rwandan culture. Many Tutsi maidens who survived the genocide had been raped or forced into so-called marriages with Hutu militiamen. Virginity, or at least the illusion of virginity, is a fundamental characteristic of a desirable bride in Rwanda. While brides today may rarely be virgins, they must have maintained the public illusion of virginity. For maidens raped during the genocide, entering into a legitimate marriage was virtually impossible unless their rapes were kept secret.

Maidens who were able to keep their rapes secret still had to cope with the psychological consequences of their experiences and, in some cases, the rumors about their rapes that circulated in the community. Maidens lucky enough to be courted faced difficult decisions whether to reveal what had happened to them. Caught in a double bind, these maidens feared being jilted by their boyfriends or fiancés if they remained silent about their rapes because the men might assume they were "loose women" (a vernacular term synonymous with "slut" or "prostitute") when the men discovered the maidens were not virgins. Or the maidens might be jilted if they revealed the truth about what had happened to them in the genocide because they could be perceived as "tainted" by their contact with Hutu militiamen.

Two categories of maidens found it impossible to hide their rapes: those who became pregnant and those who contracted HIV. After the genocide, these maidens were viewed and continue to be viewed today as tainted by the touch of the Interahamwe militias. Some of the single mothers faced rejection by surviving family members who denounced them as "collaborators" of the genocide perpetrators. The children who resulted from these rapes were also stigmatized: they remained as living reminders of their mother's shame. Maidens who became single mothers faced a social dead end: they could not advance to the next stage of life as a wife and mother and were stuck in a figurative no-woman's-land of single motherhood.

I met one such single mother, Placidia, along with her five-year-old son in 2000. Placidia was the sister of Petero and Yohani discussed earlier. I met Placidia when Petero invited me to attend Yohani's wedding celebration. On the morning of the celebration, we stopped to visit Placidia on the way to the event. After visiting with her, we went on to the reception hall, where I helped the wives and maidens prepare food. I noticed that Placidia was conspicuously absent from the preparations. Later during the wedding mass and reception, I again noticed that Placidia did not attend, although the celebration was taking place in her family's home community, where she continued to live with her son. At the time I had no idea that Placidia's son was born of rape. It was only several months later that I had an explanation for her absence. Petero was lamenting the "trouble," as he called it, that Placidia was causing in their brother's marriage. I asked Petero why Placidia would want to cause problems.

PETERO: I guess maybe it's out of jealousy. Placidia is stuck there in our mother's house. She can't get married—no one will have her.

JENNIE BURNET: Why not?

PETERO: Because everyone knows she was raped, even if we never talk about it.

If she were a widow, it might be different. But they [meaning potential suitors] see him [her son]. Most survivors [read "Tutsi"] can't stomach the idea of adopting a Hutu bastard. It would take a really strong man to withstand all that.

When I was trying to marry Jane [a woman with whom Petero had a son], Placidia meddled. She kept telling me that Jane wasn't a good wife for me. Now she's doing the same to Yohani, though he's already married—spreading rumors about his wife.[34]

Petero was sympathetic to his sister's situation even if he was exasperated. He added, "We try to be patient with her. She's suffered a lot. She continues to suffer. . . . It's not easy." While he did not say so explicitly, Petero recognized that a large part of his sister's problem, the root cause of her jealousy, was that she was cut off from traditional means of social reproduction and from legitimate social standing as a wife and mother. She could not be recognized as a legitimate wife and mother because she had never been married, and she probably never would be due to her tainted status as a maiden who had been raped by Interahamwe militiamen. As a result, she sought power when and where she could by influencing her younger brothers' marriage and courting decisions.

Tutsi Wives of Prisoners

In postgenocide Rwanda, thousands upon thousands of Hutu men were imprisoned on accusations of genocide for up to ten years or more. At its peak in 1999, the Rwandan prison population was estimated to be 150,000, according to Human Rights Watch: the vast majority was awaiting trial on charges of genocide. While it is possible that the majority of prisoners participated in the genocide, as the government maintained throughout the late 1990s and early 2000s, several thousand had been imprisoned simply because they were Hutu and male or because someone had fabricated charges against them. Due to masculinity's strong association with aggression and violence, it was often assumed that all Hutu men, youth, and adolescents had participated in the genocide. In the years immediately following the genocide, it was extremely easy to get someone arrested on suspicions of genocide. Although officially accusations from three independent parties were required, in most cases a single accusation was enough to get someone arrested. Once a person was in prison, investigations moved extremely slowly due to the overload of cases and lack of personnel in the justice system. As a result, the falsely accused faced what appeared to be indefinite detention at the time. Thousands died while in prison awaiting trial due to the horrific conditions in the overloaded prisons, jails, and impromptu detention centers.

Regardless of whether they were guilty or innocent, many of these male prisoners had families on the outside. In fact, their lives depended on their kin on the outside who brought them food, drinking water, and clothing. The Rwandan government at best provided minimal food rations for prisoners and at times did not provide any food at all. Prisoners' families, whether they were Hutu (the majority) or Tutsi (a significant minority), faced many difficulties. As the families of prisoners they were presumed to be perpetrators themselves or at least to be genocide sympathizers in the eyes of many Tutsi. When they took supplies to the prison, they were required to stand in long queues for hours outside. The weekly queues further marked them as perpetrators in the eyes of community members who passed by. In many communities, genocide survivors heckled the families waiting outside the prisons and threw rotten food or rocks at them. Prison guards insulted them, mistreated them, and often exacted bribes in the form of cash or sexual favors from the women and girls.

Tutsi wives of imprisoned Hutu men usually found themselves marginalized from every traditional support mechanism, including their husband's patrilineage, their own patrilineage, and the community. In some cases, the husband's patrilineage had opposed the marriage on the basis of ethnic difference in the first place. In other cases, members of the husband's patrilineage had come to oppose the marriage because they blamed the Tutsi wife for their son's imprisonment. They viewed their Tutsi daughters-in-law as RPF accomplices (*ibyitso*) or as cockroaches (*inyenzi*), expressing their dislike in the same terms used by the Hutu extremists to characterize Tutsi during the early 1990s and the genocide.[35] Like raped maidens, these women were in effect removed from the ethnic community and its protection.

In many cases, Tutsi wives of prisoners were completely bereft of kin because their entire patrilineage was wiped out in the genocide. They often found that their few surviving kin blamed them for the genocide because they had married Hutu. Surviving kin viewed their Tutsi sisters as being both literally and figuratively in bed with the enemy. They saw Tutsi wives of Hutu men as collaborators in extremist Hutu politics and the genocide. Some of these Tutsi wives of prisoners knew or at least suspected that their husbands had participated in or even organized massacres during the genocide. They faced difficult decisions about whether to reveal what they knew about their husbands' actions (actions that sometimes had resulted in the wives' own family members—even children— dying terrible deaths) to promote justice for genocide victims and survivors or to remain silent to preserve the sanctity of their marriages and what little kin support remained.

Beyond this marginalization at the hands of kin, Tutsi wives of prisoners were denied the moral, spiritual, and economic assistance some wives and widows found in associational life. Tutsi wives of prisoners were usually excluded from genocide survivor organizations because the members did not perceive Tutsi wives of Hutu men as real genocide survivors. While associational life, particularly among Rwandan women, flourished in the years after the genocide, prisoners' families could not create their own organizations because such efforts were perceived by the government as inherently political and were opposed on the grounds that they promoted "a genocidal ideology."[36]

I met Dolores in 2001 when she worked for an American NGO in Kigali. Over several months I came to learn her story in snippets recounted here or there either by her or by a coworker. Dolores was in her forties and married, and she had several children. Her husband was imprisoned in the Kigali Central Prison on genocide charges. Under the Habyarimana government, he had been a member of the MRND, the political party of President Habyarimana, and a highly placed bureaucrat. Each Saturday Dolores dutifully brought food to her husband, waiting in the long queues outside the prison, except for the last Saturday of each month, when there was *umuganda*, community work projects held nationally. At work Dolores was usually cheerful although matter-of-fact and very direct in social interactions, which was atypical for Rwandans. Occasionally, she would show exasperation as she exited the office of her direct supervisor, an American who was very demanding and, in Dolores's opinion, often unreasonable. Over coffee one morning Dolores's coworker recounted in Dolores's presence how her husband treated her during their marriage.

> Don't you know!?! Her husband was a notorious Interahamwe. He was a racist from the beginning [shortly after their wedding]. He always treated her badly, but things really heated up after the war started. He used to make her undress and stand completely naked beside the bed all night long so that he could look at her *if he wanted to*. If she would lie down in the bed to sleep, he would shove her out onto the floor and yell at her and make her stand there naked.
>
> [In the daytime] when he wanted something, he would order her around and call her inyenzi [cockroach]. All day she worked as a secretary [and gave her salary to him], and then at night she was a slave.
>
> They say he had a lot of people killed in the genocide.

On another occasion, when Dolores mentioned that her entire Saturday had been wasted waiting outside the prison, I asked her why she brought food and water to her husband if he had treated her so badly. She said, "I don't have a choice. You see, my in-laws have already taken one house. They would like to see me and the children put out on the street so that they can have the one we are in. I have to take care of my husband so that he will keep them from taking the house." What she did not say, but what I could guess based on the experiences of other Tutsi wives of prisoners I knew, was that her in-laws demanded money from her, saying that she was rich because she worked for Americans. She had learned to explain away her earnings with stories of the children's tuition, uniforms, and other needs. While Dolores's (Hutu) in-laws continued to make kinship demands of her, they refused to honor their kinship obligations to her because they suspected her of having divided (ethnic) loyalties.

I lost touch with Dolores for several years, but I eventually learned she had immigrated to the United States. She brought her children to join her one by one. Then she died. According to a Rwandan woman who had worked with her, Dolores had been poisoned by her in-laws who were furious that she had left Rwanda. I asked the woman how she knew it was a case of poisoning. She responded, "That's what everyone says. Who else would want to cause her harm?"

Months later I spoke with an American woman who had worked with Dolores at the NGO. I asked her about Dolores, pretending that I did not know Dolores was dead. The woman told me that Dolores had committed suicide. I explained that I had heard a rumor that she had been poisoned by her in-laws. The American woman explained:

> She definitely killed herself. It's terrible. She worked so hard to get here [to the United States]. —— [another American who had worked at the NGO] helped her to get the visa, then she stayed and applied for asylum. She worked really hard and then brought her sons. She escaped from her husband and in-laws.
>
> It seems she started having problems. She became depressed. She started having flashbacks and other signs of [psychological] trauma. I think she must have believed that if she left Rwanda and came to the United States, all her problems would be solved and her life would be easy. When it didn't turn out that way, she ended it.

Committing suicide is an extreme way to exercise agency in difficult circumstances and is not an option that I would characterize as resisting systems of social classification. While Dolores's case had a tragic ending, other Tutsi wives of prisoners have fared better. Some managed to escape their husbands or in-laws by leaving Rwanda or becoming financially independent and getting a divorce. Others who believed their husbands were innocent did what they could to exonerate them. In some cases they failed, but in others they succeeded. These women faced the challenge of reintegrating their husbands into society— a society that scarcely resembled the pregenocide society they had known.

Hutu Genocide Widows

Following the genocide, many widows (whether they were widows due to natural causes, to genocide, or to RPF-perpetrated killings) found themselves in precarious situations because the male kin who protected their rights and guaranteed them access to land were absent.[37] Widows from ethnically mixed marriages faced the worst of it, as they often found themselves caught between the two families, with neither family willing to fulfill traditional kin obligations to the widow or her surviving children.

Intermarriage between Hutu and Tutsi was very common from the 1970s onward, especially in central and southern Rwanda. The genocide did not start in this region until late April 1994, but then the killing was very effective because most Tutsi had gathered at government offices, schools, or churches. Because of the frequency of intermarriage and a greater representation of Tutsi in the population (around 40 percent, according to the 1990 census), the genocide decimated the population. Entire hills in Butare Prefecture (now South Province) remained empty because the few survivors with property on them were too afraid to live far from government offices or roads.

The situation of a women's group in a rural area of southern Rwanda illustrates the impact of the genocide on social reproduction for women in ethnically mixed marriages. The group was comprised of Hutu genocide widows. Ranging in age from approximately twenty-three to sixty-six, the widows met weekly to study the Bible and work together. They shared many of the same problems, having dealt with social, political, and economic marginalization at the hands of kin and local authorities.

At a meeting in 2000 I asked the widows whether they had difficulties with their patrilineal kin. After a very long silence, one widow responded angrily, "All widows in our situation have problems with their family." The group leader interrupted her, saying, "You mustn't lie. There are also those who protected their families." Other group members then offered examples from the group where affinal kin had protected (or tried to protect) their Tutsi brothers-in-law, nephews, and nieces. Members of the group then explained that a Hutu genocide widow's relationship with her patrilineage depended upon how her brothers had behaved during the genocide: "There were Hutu men who protected their sisters' children; in these cases, there is no problem between the widow and her family. On the other hand, there were others who, instead of protecting their nieces and nephews, killed them, most of them indirectly—they went discreetly to call the Interahamwe from another hill [to do the killing]. The widows who lost their children like that—understandably, they have many problems with their families. Some have no relations with them at all." Some of the genocide widows' brothers were in prison accused of genocide. Those widows whose brothers had helped them during the genocide did not hesitate to take food to their brothers in prison.[38] As one widow explained, "I take food to my two brothers in prison each week. [Both brothers were single, so they did not have wives or children to bring them food.] They protected my children [during the genocide], but they went to kill others." Some widows who knew or believed that their brothers were responsible for killing their sisters' husbands or children would not take them food. Yet their resistance to kinship obligations came at a cost; they could not rely on their own patrilineage for assistance, whether economic, social, or emotional.

I asked the widows whether they had encountered difficulties with their affinal (i.e., Tutsi) kin, such as disputes over land or property. The widows remained silent for a few minutes and looked down at the ground, a sign of sadness or shame. One widow finally spoke up. She said, laughing softly instead of crying, "You have to understand, for most of us there is no one left. They are all gone. There is no one left for us to have a conflict with."[39] Another widow responded: "Of course, for the few Hutu genocide widows who still have in-laws there have been problems, especially when the widow's brothers were responsible for killing her husband and children. In these cases, her in-laws will reject her. They refuse to let her cultivate. They take any remaining children and send her away." A third widow added: "I know of one [Hutu widow] whose sisters-in-law survived. They were widows too, but they came home to their own patrilineage's land since all their brothers had been killed. They did not throw their sister-in-law out. They live together now as neighbors without any trouble. They help each other like sisters." Following this group interview, my research assistant and I discussed whether these women were speaking in general or whether they were telling their own stories. In the end we concluded that it was probably a mix of the two, but, regardless, we did not have the detailed community information necessary to contextualize their narratives.

During another visit in 2001, the widows explained how they had been excluded from development assistance set aside for genocide survivors. According to one widow,

> In 1994 and early 1995, AVEGA gave us cooking pots, plates, cups, clothing, shoes, and seed. But when the foreigners [meaning international agencies] came to build houses for genocide survivors, we were not included. They built for other widows [of the genocide] first. Certain individuals [the widows intentionally did not name anyone] did not want us included on the lists. They said, "You have male kin [i.e., fathers and brothers]. They can build for you. You don't need any help." Even male genocide survivors received houses in the new villages, but we were forgotten.

The widows went on to explain that many of them were about to become homeless because the government building in which they had lived for four years was being reclaimed by the local government office to hold community food stores as part of a food security project sponsored by the World Food Program. The women were uncertain what to do and lamented the fact that no one in the community seemed to recognize their difficulties.

The previous burgomaster (the administrative head of the commune), who held the position from 1996 until 1999, was a genocide survivor. It was widely rumored that he had sought revenge against Hutu in the community. In 1999, the Ministry of Local Affairs removed him from office when his abuses of power came to light thanks to an investigative news article published in a Kinyarwanda newspaper. As he still lived in the community and wielded a great deal of influence, few people would state explicitly what he had done. Nonetheless, it was clear to my research assistant and me that the women believed that the burgomaster had excluded them from the original list of genocide survivors in need of housing assistance.

Because of the Hutu widows' ambiguous status as "survivors" within the discourse promoted by the Rwandan government and its attendant, invisible classification system, community members felt justified in their "lack of pity," as the widows described it. Hutu neighbors remained complacent in the belief that the government or international aid organizations would help the Hutu genocide widows because only "survivors benefit from development assistance," as more than one rural Hutu said to me over the course of my research. Tutsi neighbors, on the other hand, believed that members of the widows' own patrilineage should take care of them. So these widows were left largely to their own devices, which were circumscribed by the customary law of land tenure and their extreme poverty.

In a return visit to the same group in 2007, I caught up on their news. Six of the twenty members had died, leaving behind nine orphans, whom the group did their best to help. Thanks to the assistance from Caritas Christi, the social support arm of the Roman Catholic diocese, the widows had received assistance in building houses in late 2001. Unlike most assistance projects coordinated by international NGOs, their houses were built with the free labor of prisoners on their own land on the hill rather than in a new village. During our brief meeting, I asked them about the progress of *gacaca*, the grassroots courts created by the government to prosecute genocide perpetrators in their local communities before judges elected from the local community. The widows told me that two of their members had been elected as judges, one at the cell level and the other at the sector level.

When I asked them about the reintegration of perpetrators into the local community, the widows gave me what sounded like a rehearsed, politically correct answer; they said that everything went well.

> The prisoners had received awareness raising at a reeducation camp [*ingando*, required of all released prisoners] before coming home to the hill. We saw that when they arrived on the hill, they had changed a lot. They prayed a lot. You could see that they were true Christians. They approach the population to ask forgiveness from the people against whom they had committed genocide [meaning those whose family members they had killed]. They go help others. They go to explain to prisoners the benefits of confessing and asking for a pardon.[40]

I doubted the widows' account was complete, since many other people in the same community had explained that the reintegration of released prisoners and confessed genocide perpetrators was sometimes very difficult and tense. I then asked the widows whether they still had difficulty getting along with their husband's kin or their own kin. They said that they had never had a problem with their husband's kin. When I read to them from the interview transcript, they insisted that they had never told me they had problems with their families, and they said that I was mistaken.

Following the interview, I looked again at my records and field notes from the interviews in 2000 and 2001 to check whether I could have mixed up the interviews. My research assistant and I discussed the situation. She also remembered the same women's group, and her recollection matched the information written in the interview transcript. We puzzled over the possible reasons for the widows' change in attitude and recollection. My assistant hypothesized that since the women had solved their most serious economic problems by receiving assistance to rebuild their houses, they no longer remembered the cold shoulder they had received from kin and neighbors in the years immediately after the genocide. Her hypothesis is certainly plausible. Another possibility is that the women did not feel comfortable responding as honestly in 2007. Given the rehearsed response we received to the questions about gacaca, I suspected the women again perceived me as an outsider and closed the veil of secrecy that shrouds rural life in Rwanda and obscures it from outsiders, whether foreign or Rwandan.[41]

Conclusion

Raped maidens, Tutsi wives of prisoners, and Hutu genocide widows inhabited a gray, gendered, ethnic zone in the postgenocide national imagination; they stood at the point of friction, a term I borrow from the anthropologist Anna

Tsing, between lived reality and discourse.[42] The intersection of gender and ethnicity prolonged their suffering by bringing the past violence of genocide into the lived present. Raped maidens were excluded from legitimate forms of social reproduction due to their tainted status, and they were largely bereft of kin, many of whom had been decimated in the genocide. Tutsi wives of prisoners and Hutu widows of the genocide were disenfranchised from both Hutu and Tutsi family networks. These women's marginal status made it acceptable for people to exclude them from the balanced reciprocity of kin relations and communal life. This exclusion further compounded these women's poverty and created additional obstacles to rebuilding their lives.

In postgenocide Rwanda the dominant narrative focused on national unity and reconciliation and promoted a national Rwandan identity that formally eschewed ethnic distinctions. Ethnic categories nevertheless remained salient and were reinforced by the genocide commemoration ceremonies. Because raped maidens, Tutsi wives of prisoners, and Hutu widows of the genocide confounded the social logic of ethnicity, these women had few opportunities to subvert the dominant discourse or to deploy ethnicity as a "livelihood asset," as Heidi Gengenbach describes in chapter 2 of this volume. Nonetheless, in the messiness of quotidian life, ad hoc accommodations were made. Single mothers were called "wives-women" (abagore) by their neighbors, and they wore the urugori, a headband worn above the ears and customarily reserved for married women who had borne a child, to community festivities such as weddings. When the gacaca process brought the release of tens of thousands of prisoners in 2005, Tutsi wives of prisoners welcomed home their husbands and did their best to help them adjust to life outside of prison in a society greatly changed. Hutu genocide widows slowly rebuilt their lives with little assistance from kin or from programs designed to assist the vulnerable, and they focused their energy on raising their surviving children.

With time, these women remade their lives and normalized their statuses in the new social structure. Many women replaced the emotional and financial support of kin with the camaraderie and solidarity they found in women's associations or farming cooperatives. The few who had the financial means to do so returned to school to earn bachelor's and even master's degrees and then went on to successful careers as leaders of women's civil society organizations, representatives of the Rwanda Patriotic Front political party, or members of parliament.

NOTES

1. Geoffrey C. Bowker and Susan Leigh Star, *Sorting Things Out: Classification and Its Consequences*, Inside Technology (Cambridge, MA: MIT Press, 1999), 26. I use the

terms *ethnic* and *ethnicity* to refer to the distinctions between Hutu, Tutsi, and Twa in Rwanda throughout this chapter. Most scholars of Rwanda have preferred to use these terms instead of *tribe* and *race*. However, as discussed later in this chapter, the distinctions between Hutu, Tutsi, and Twa operate like racial categories, meaning that the categories *allegedly* correspond to sets of biological attributes and do not correspond to differences in language or culture.

2. Estimates of how many people died in the 1994 genocide vary widely. While how many died is irrelevant to whether or not the killings in Rwanda in 1994 were genocide, the issue is highly politicized, so it is necessary to indicate the sources. The number I use here comes from Alison Des Forges, *Leave None to Tell the Story: Genocide in Rwanda* (New York: Human Rights Watch, 1999), 15. For more on the numbers of dead, see Scott Straus's analysis in *The Order of Genocide: Race, Power, and War in Rwanda* (Ithaca, NY: Cornell University Press, 2006), 41–64.

3. The Rwandan Patriotic Front (RPF) is the current ruling party in Rwanda. Founded in Uganda in the late 1980s, it mounted an armed resistance to President Habyarimana's rule. The RPF ended the genocide in July 1994 by taking military control of the country. Its armed wing, the Rwandan Patriotic Army, became the new national army, the Rwandan Defence Forces, and its political wing, the Rwandan Patriotic Front, became the ruling political party.

4. Michael T. Taussig, *Defacement: Public Secrecy and the Labor of the Negative* (Stanford, CA: Stanford University Press, 1999), 51.

5. Republic of Rwanda, "Law No 47/2001 of December 2001 Instituting Punishment for Offences of Discrimination and Sectarianism," in *Official Gazette of the Republic of Rwanda*, Special issue, December 2001.

6. See, for example, Gérard Prunier, *The Rwanda Crisis: History of a Genocide*, 2nd ed. (New York: Columbia University Press, 1997), 5. These statistics were also reported in the CIA Factbook up until 2010, "Rwanda," https://www.cia.gov/library/publications/the-world-factbook/geos/rw.htm (accessed 15 January 2010). Ethnicity was removed from the Rwanda entry in the 2011 edition of the CIA Factbook online.

7. Liisa Malkki, *Purity and Exile: Violence, Memory, and National Cosmology among Hutu Refugees in Tanzania* (Chicago: University of Chicago Press, 1995).

8. Catharine Newbury has documented the transformation in the categories "Hutu" and "Tutsi" during the late precolonial and colonial periods in her book *The Cohesion of Oppression* (New York: Columbia University Press, 1988).

9. Jean-Paul Kimonyo, "La relation identitaire hutu/tutsi," in *Ruptures socio-culturelles et conflit au Rwanda*, ed. Centre de gestion des conflits–Université national du Rwanda, Cahiers du Centre de gestion des conflits (Butare: Centre for Conflict Management, National University of Rwanda, 2001), 88.

10. Jennie E. Burnet and Rwanda Initiative for Sustainable Development, "Culture, Practice, and Law: Women's Access to Land in Rwanda," in *Women and Land in Africa: Culture, Religion and Realizing Women's Rights*, ed. Lynne Muthoni Wanyeki (New York: Zed Books, 2003), 176–206.

11. David Lee Schoenbrun, *A Green Place, a Good Place: Agrarian Change, Gender*

and Social Identity in the Great Lakes Region to the 15th Century (Portsmouth, NH: Heinemann, 1998), 151–54.

12. Villia Jefremovas, "Loose Women, Virtuous Wives and Timid Virgins: Gender and Control of Resources in Rwanda," *Canadian Journal of African Studies* 25, no. 3 (1991): 378–95; Villia Jefremovas, *Brickyards to Graveyards: From Production to Genocide in Rwanda* (Albany: State University of New York Press, 2002), 87.

13. The term *indushyi* was also applied to daughters who "divorced" their husbands (i.e., who returned home from failed marriages). In cases of divorce, a wife would leave with children perceived as being too young to be separated from their mother (below the age of eight or nine). Older children remained with their father or his patrilineage.

14. The twelve clans of Rwanda are not ethnically exclusive, and all include Hutu, Tutsi, and Twa—an apparent mystery, since clan affiliation is inherited patrilineally, like ethnic classification. David Newbury, "The Clans of Rwanda: An Historical Hypothesis," *Africa* 50, no. 4 (1980): 389–403.

15. Newbury, *Cohesion of Oppression*, 197; Prunier, *Rwanda Crisis*, 49–53.

16. Human Rights Watch (HRW), *Shattered Lives: Sexual Violence during the Rwandan Genocide and Its Aftermath* (New York: Human Rights Watch, 1996).

17. Interviews by the author, 1997, 1998, 1999, and 2000, Rwanda.

18. On the desirability of Tutsi women and Hutu extremist propaganda, see chapter 4 of Christopher C. Taylor, *Sacrifice as Terror: The Rwandan Genocide of 1994* (London: Berg Publishers, 1999), 151–79.

19. Taylor, *Sacrifice as Terror*, 166–67.

20. Taylor, *Sacrifice as Terror*, 165–66.

21. Des Forges, *Leave None*, 296.

22. Jennie E. Burnet, "Whose Genocide? Whose Truth? Representations of Victim and Perpetrator in Rwanda," in *Genocide: Truth, Memory, and Representation*, ed. Alex Laban Hinton and Kevin O'Neill (Durham, NC: Duke University Press, 2009), 80–110; Jennie E. Burnet, *Genocide Lives in Us: Women, Memory, and Silence in Rwanda* (Madison: University of Wisconsin Press, 2012). Uli Linke's work on public memory and symbolic violence in Germany after 1945 is relevant to the themes I consider in this chapter; see Uli Linke, "Archives of Violence: The Holocaust and the German Politics of Memory," in *Annihilating Difference: The Anthropology of Genocide*, ed. Alexander Laban Hinton (Berkeley: University of California Press, 2002), 229–70; Linke, "The Limits of Empathy: Emotional Anesthesia and the Museum of Corpses in Post-Holocaust Germany," in Hinton and O'Neill, *Genocide*, 147–91.

23. The terms *abaturutse hanze* and *abarutashye* denote the same thing: people who returned from outside. The two phrases have very different connotations. Abaturutse hanze is more commonly used by the Rwandan population and is neutral. Abarutashye is used by old returnees when talking about themselves; the word sounds arrogant because it implies that they returned from outside *victoriously*. In other words, they see themselves as synonymous with members of the RPF, which won the war.

24. The Kinyarwanda term *abicanyi* means "killers," but in postgenocide Rwanda the word has become synonymous with "perpetrators." The Kinyarwanda term

abacengezi means "infiltrators." Ironically, the same term was used by the Habyarimana regime and especially the Hutu Power extremists to label the RPF soldiers believed to be hiding in the civilian population.

25. *Le soir*, 7 April 1995, quoted in Claudine Vidal, "Les commémorations du génocide au Rwanda," *Les temps modernes* 613 (2001): 1–46, quotation on 8, my translation.

26. Interviews by the author, 1998, 1999, 2000, 2001, 2005, Rwanda.

27. Human Rights Watch (HRW), *World Report 1995* (New York: Human Rights Watch, 1995); Human Rights Watch (HRW), *World Report 1996* (New York: Human Rights Watch, 1996).

28. Interviews by the author, 1997, 1998, 2000, 2005, Rwanda.

29. The Interahamwe began as the youth wing of the MRND political party led by President Habyarimana. Interahamwe members underwent paramilitary training in the years leading up to the genocide. During the genocide, the Interahamwe became a civilian militia and the primary force of killers in the genocide.

30. Des Forges, *Leave None*, 266–70.

31. Bowker and Star, *Sorting Things Out*, 223.

32. The phrase "heart of the household" comes from a Kinyarwanda proverb, "Umugore n'umutima w'urugo" (The wife is the heart of the house).

33. Burnet, *Genocide Lives in Us*, 65–66.

34. Yohani's wife was a triple outsider: she was born outside the community, she was Hutu, and she had grown up in Congo.

35. Interviews by the author, 1999, 2000, 2001, 2002, Rwanda.

36. Interviews by the author, 1999, 2000, 2001, 2002, Rwanda.

37. The designation "widow of the genocide" is semiofficial. There are genocide widows' organizations throughout the country associated under a national organization, Association des veuves du génocide d'avril 1994 (AVEGA).

38. At the time this interview was conducted in 2001, over 130,000 Rwandans were imprisoned, accused of genocide. In general, prisoners depended on family members to bring them food and drinking water several times a week.

39. In the course of my interviews with women in Rwanda, I found that frequently they would smile or laugh softly when recounting heart-wrenching stories. I came to understand these actions as culturally appropriate expressions of grief. Rwandan society does not encourage expressions of emotion.

40. Interview by the author, 21 May 2007, South Province.

41. Danielle de Lame has written in great detail on secrecy in rural Rwanda and the difficulty for outsiders (whether foreign anthropologists or Rwandans from the next hill) to gain access to the "'terribly closed' rural world." See Danielle de Lame, *A Hill Among a Thousand: Transformations and Ruptures in Rural Rwanda*, trans. Helen Arnold (Madison: University of Wisconsin Press, 2005), 14, originally published as *Une colline entre mille, ou, Le calme avant la tempête* (Tervuren, Belgium: Muse´e royal de l'Afrique centrale, 1996).

42. Anna Tsing, *Friction: An Ethnography of Global Connection* (Princeton, NJ: Princeton University Press, 2004).

Part IV

Performing Gendered Ethnic Power

9

Matriliny, Masculinity, and Contested Gendered Definitions of Ethnic Identity and Power in Nineteenth-Century Southeastern Nigeria

NDUBUEZE L. MBAH

The Ohafia people of southeastern Nigeria are not the typical "Igbo" one encounters in Chinua Achebe's *Things Fall Apart* or Elechi Amadi's *The Concubine* whose ancestors the Nigerian anthropologist Victor Uchendu described as being "organized in lineages with patrilineal emphasis, as are those on earth."[1] In precolonial southeastern Nigeria, lineages were central to ethnic differentiation; thus, Uchendu noted, "An Igbo without 'umunna' [patrilineage] ... is an Igbo without citizenship."[2] However, in Ohafia frontier Igbo society, comprised of twenty-six villages and bounded in the north, south, and west by various matrilineal and bilateral non-Igbo ethnic communities in the nineteenth century, ancestral and human lineages were organized with matrilineal emphasis, female political institutions were more powerful and effective than their male counterparts, and women were the breadwinners of their families.[3] Ohafia women's privileged sociopolitical positions, which women in patrilineal Igbo societies lacked, owed a lot to Ohafia's geographical proximity to and cultural similarity with non-Igbo neighboring communities. Hence, women's sociopolitical power was ethnically gendered.

This chapter theorizes ethnicity as a gendered practice by arguing that the gendered struggle for power in Ohafia was manifest in the ideological and political contestations between men and women over the definition of Ohafia-Igbo ethnicity. It demonstrates how men and women performed and expressed their ethnicity, individually and collectively, through lineage practices, marriage contracts, age-grade political organizations, warfare, and rituals. Women were invested in Ohafia-Igbo ethnicity but defined what that meant in a very different way from men. Through interethnic alliances, rituals and discourses that re-affirmed the matrilineage, and consistent exhibitions of superior political power, Ohafia women forged different ideas of ethnic citizenship and promoted gendered forms of ethnicity. Ohafia male society, on the other hand, promoted a militant worldview of Ohafia-Igbo ethnicity, one that they accomplished through warfare, memorialization of a heroic age, and militant conceptions of masculinity. Hence, gender was central to lineage ideologies and ethnic affilia-tions in the Cross River region of Nigeria and constituted the framework for the conveyance of lineage and ethnic differences in Ohafia society.

This chapter contends that the social identification of the Ohafia people as ethnically "Igbo" was constituted in the nineteenth century. The ancestral Ohafia (Mben) who migrated to the eastern limits of Igboland from the Niger-Benue confluence in the 1650s had no clearly defined ethnicity. The construc-tion of Ohafia-Igbo ethnicity was shaped by their settlement in a frontier envi-ronment, their preoccupation with militant slave production in the eighteenth and nineteenth centuries, and their borrowing and adaptation of matrilineal practices and age-grade systems of political organization from their non-Igbo neighbors. The designation of Ohafia as ethnically Igbo also resulted from Ohafia's military conflicts with their non-Igbo neighbors, whose lands they overtook, and their diplomatic alliances with their immediate Igbo neighbors. However, Ohafia's non-Igbo neighbors were simultaneously enemies of Ohafia male warrior groups while intermarrying and making alliances through Ohafia women. Hence, Ohafia society's ethnicity constructed vis-à-vis its matrilineal and bilateral non-Igbo neighbors was situationally gendered.

This chapter, therefore, portrays female power and authority and militant masculinity as politically contested forms of identity in male and female per-formances of Ohafia-Igbo ethnicity. Men's performances of *ufiem* (masculinity) through military distinction and women's expressions of political power pro-duced conflicting social imaginations of Ohafia-Igbo ethnicity in the nine-teenth century as either a heroic Igbo society dominated by male warriors who preyed on non-Igbo neighbors for slaves or a matrilineal non-Igbo society dominated by female breadwinners and political rulers who forged filial links with non-Igbo neighbors.

These disparate visions of Ohafia social identity are captured in the juxta-positional titles of the pioneering scholarship on the society, namely, the

Igboland, Nigeria

anthropologist Philip Nsugbe's *Ohaffia: A Matrilineal Ibo People*, and the historian Onwuka Njoku's *Ohafia: A Heroic Igbo Society*.[4] These two different ways of understanding Ohafia-Igbo ethnicity are reinforced in the subjective discourses of Ohafia men and women, the historical memories and stereotypes of Ohafia's multiethnic neighbors, late nineteenth-century reports of European missionaries and colonial officers, and historical and anthropological scholarship.

This chapter begins with an examination of the continued impact of the historical memories of Ohafia men and women on the social definition of Ohafia-Igbo ethnicity in the fieldwork context. It then provides a brief historical background on Ohafia migration and settlement and examines the Ohafia lineage structure as a gendered practice in two respects.

The preoccupation of Ohafia men with slave production and military defense of their society in the nineteenth century strengthened the patrilineages as major units of male political organization and thereby linked the Ohafia people politically and culturally with the rest of patrilineal Igbo society. Ohafia military conflicts with its immediate non-Igbo neighbors over landownership alienated the latter culturally and politically and provided practical reasons for Ohafia people to identify more closely with their Igbo neighbors through ritual kinship contracts known as *ukwuzi*. In contrast, through interethnic marriages that strengthened matrilineal ties across ethnic boundaries, Ohafia women linked Ohafia, culturally and politically, with matrilineal and bilateral non-Igbo ethnic communities, as opposed to the patrilineal Igbo society. Moreover, through public ritual discourses, Ohafia women defined Igbo people as ethnic outsiders to Ohafia while identifying individual non-Igbo matrikin as legitimate Ohafia citizens. The gendered uses of lineages to define ethnic identification and the fact that Ohafia men and women reinforced their ethnic identities in their daily practices suggest that ethnicity was not a static concept in this frontier "Igbo" society but rather an appropriable ideology constantly in flux and reinvented in the lived experiences of Ohafia people.

Lastly, this chapter interrogates the concept of ethnic citizenship through an examination of the gendered uses of Ohafia age-grade political organization and various definitive discourses deployed by Ohafia men and women in ritual situations. This study of subjective gendered conceptions of Ohafia-Igbo citizenship is divided into three sections. The first section discusses women's age-grade political organization and rituals as a window into their specific definitions of what it meant to be Ohafia-Igbo. It shows that in addition to matrilineage ideologies, patrilineage residential arrangements also shaped Ohafia women's vision of ethnic citizenship. Hence, in her study of patrilineal Birom women of Nigeria, the social anthropologist Audrey Smedley cautioned against essentializing patriliny as patriarchy and matriliny as matriarchy, since women played critical roles in reinforcing patrilineal ideologies.[5] The second section examines the emergence of the masculine warrior ethnicity metanarrative. The goal is to demonstrate that men and women embraced the idea of Ohafia-Igbo ethnicity in different ways as a result of their proximity to bellicose and matrilineal/bilateral non-Igbo neighbors and their gendered social roles and positions. The last section analyzes the public space as a domain of gendered status performance and contested definitions of Ohafia-Igbo ethnicity between men and women.

Gendered Memories and Ethnicity Constructs in the Fieldwork Context

I was born and raised in a patrilineal Igbo society of southeastern Nigeria, so my encounter with the Ohafia society was one of strange familiarity. Some of the immediate cultural differences that established my outsider status within the society, however, included the Ohafia dominant matrilineage principles; the relative disregard for kola nut culture and a preference instead for alcohol libation and application of *nzu* (white chalk) to welcome visitors, a practice that historian Ugo Nwokeji has equated with pan-Igbo ethnicity; and the Cross River Igbo dialect of Ohafia, which is unintelligible to the average Igbo-language native speaker.[6] The preeminent autonomy that Ohafia women continue to enjoy in their society, their unparalleled consciousness of past female power and authority, and their eagerness to comment on this historical awareness set them apart from my previous understanding of Igbo sociopolitical life. However, my native fluency in the Igbo language facilitated quicker learning of the Ohafia-Igbo dialect. I also found many Ohafia cultural practices familiar and intelligible compared to my own lived culture.

The one challenge I was conscious of at the onset of my research was the silence of Ohafia female voices in both published literature and archival sources. Smedley has pointed out that "it is an often unacknowledged reality that male scholars have been restricted in their access to women's private lives by the conventions of the societies they studied."[7] I quickly discovered that, as a male, capturing Ohafia women's perspectives was a methodological challenge that required moving from the familiar world of men—a reflection of my existing contacts and acquaintances—to the unfamiliar world of women. After I was introduced to the *ezie-ogo* (male king) of Elu Village (the most senior Ohafia village), his cabinet members presented me with a list of names of knowledgeable local historians from twenty-two Ohafia villages, all of whom were male. When I asked for the names of women, some of the elders joked that women had no knowledge of Ohafia history, but that if I insisted on talking to women, the *ezie-nwami* (female king) and her cabinet could be invited to the male king's palace for me to interact with them. I soon discovered that Ohafia men's and women's historical narratives presented conflicting versions of Ohafia's social identity, and my position as a researcher was often perceived as an opportunity to project a specific gendered vision as authoritative.

I later gained access to women through informal referrals from elderly male collaborators, who confessed their lack of knowledge about women's socialization, political organizations, and worldviews. These women, whose life histories I documented, later referred me to the female king of their village. At the palaces of Ohafia female kings, I learned that it was laughable to think that the male king could summon the female king and her cabinet to his palace to answer my interview questions, since women's political institutions were autonomous and more effective than their male counterparts. Ohafia women embraced the interviews to demonstrate their consciousness of past female power and authority, which they lost upon colonial rule at the turn of the twentieth century.[8] They often transformed the interview sessions into public performances in front of awed audiences of younger women, children, and men. They danced and mocked men, reemphasizing their power to "teach men lessons" when neces-sary. Whereas Ruth Finnegan noted that the performative nature of oral history before participatory audiences impacts the meaning produced, Barbara Cooper shows that the performative nature of oral evidence enables us to explore the social production of memory, self, and subjectivity.[9]

Ohafia women forced the researcher to focus not only on discourse but also on practices, which are also evidence of agency, self-representation, and consciousness.[10] These gendered practices that capture the divergent social visions of Ohafia-Igbo ethnicity embody successive historical experiences in the region. They are sites for the re-creation and contestation of gendered power and constitute the definition and redefinition of social and individual identities, as well as changing conceptions of traditions that shape knowledge production in the society. Ohafia-Igbo women's rituals such as *uzo-iyi* (virginity testing) and *ije akpaka* (ritual declaration of war), political resistance strategies such as *ibo ezi* (strike and boycott) and *ikpo mgbogho* (social ostracism), and material culture practices such as the raising of ancestral pot monuments (*ududu*) constitute what the historian Jan Vansina has described as the practi-cal uses of traditions.[11] In the Ohafia case, the performance and reproduction of tradition in the fieldwork context are ways for women to define the history of their social formation and their place within it. These practices are simulta-neously contemporary performances of female power and authority and gen-dered memorializations of the past. They center women in Ohafia history, in the anthropologist Janice Boddy's words, as "culture producers and social actors."[12] These practices elucidate women's vision of Ohafia social identity as matri-lineal and culturally oriented toward non-Igbo ethnic communities. Thus, whereas Ohafia men define ethnicity through oral traditions, women did so through rituals and performative histories such as political songs and dances.

Personal interviews began with life histories, emphasizing socialization from childhood to adulthood and social mobility. From this subjective reflec-tion about the past, research collaborators then provided what Louise Tilley has described as histories of social relations.[13] The result was that whereas men's historical narratives emphasized Ohafia's military tradition in the con-texts of migration and settlement, head-hunting and slave production, my female respondents emphasized the centrality of the matrilineage to women's sociopolitical power. Women's historical accounts differ from men's because they are more gender inclusive. While women described the superiority of their political institutions and their ability to exercise judicial authority over both women and men, a power that men lacked, they also described women's indispensability to men's warfare and performance of ufiem, showing that masculinities and femininities were mutually constitutive. Women emphasized their superior position within the matrilineage, which reflects their dominance of the agro-based economy, their right to own farmland (in contrast to patrilineal Igbo women), and their position as breadwinners of their families in the nineteenth century. Lastly, they speak of their ability to negotiate marriages and divorces easily, in contrast to the fates of their sisters in patrilineal Igbo society, and attest that this facilitated their historical negotiation of multiple ethnicities in a borderland region.

The worldviews of Ohafia women provide an indispensable critical lens to reexamine the accepted male historical narratives. They enable the researcher to probe the meaning behind the assertions of most Ohafia men. What do men mean when they say, "Our women don't have much role to play in the history of the community; women are to be seen, not to be heard"? And why did most male collaborators take this position despite affirming the eminent historical sociopolitical power and independence of Ohafia women? Most male collaborators agreed that Ohafia women possessed more powerful, more effective, and more coercive sociopolitical institutions before the twentieth century. Yet these men described a history without women—a history of warfare and conquest, head-hunting and bravery, slave production, male-exclusive secret societies, and male socialization from *igba nnunu* (to kill a hummingbird—the first "head" a boy-child "cuts") to *igbu ishi* (to "cut a head" in battle in order to achieve adult masculinity). This history by men about men is preserved in the historical lore of the society, which glorifies Ohafia's heroic past and constitutes the masculinist vision of Ohafia-Igbo ethnicity.

From a methodological standpoint, one cannot historicize the constitution of Ohafia-Igbo ethnicity without accounting for the tensions in men's and women's subjective narratives. The oppositional social image of Ohafia society evident in the gendered discourses shows that the definition of Ohafia-Igbo ethnicity was ideologically contested between men and women. The very historical processes through which Ohafia society became ethnically Igbo were gendered domains of historical experience, including migration and settlement, head-hunting and slave production, and the gendered adaptation of age-grade political systems and lineage practices.

Migration, Settlement, and Slave Production: The Masculinist View of Ohafia-Igbo Ethnicity

How did Ohafia become ethnically Igbo? Did a previous matrilineal society adopt patriliny and identify as Igbo, or did an Igbo society adopt matrilineal

traits and set itself apart? In the view of most Ohafia male collaborators, becoming Igbo was a military affair. Ohafia ancestors, known as Mben, had
migrated from the Niger-Benue confluence to Umunede and Owan near Benin
before the sixteenth century, but the military expansion of the Benin Kingdom
between 1480 and 1517 forced the Mben to migrate first to the western and
eastern banks of the Niger River at Aniocha and Ndoni and eventually to Ibeku,
in the heartland of Igboland, by the end of the sixteenth century.[14] Following a
military confrontation between the Mben and their Ibeku hosts, the former left
Ibeku to found the following communities on the western bank of the Cross
River by the 1650s: Abam, Ohafia, and Ada.[15] Ohafia arrival in the Cross River
region triggered extensive demographic transformations among the various
ethnic groups in the area.[16] Ohafia migrants displaced most of the aboriginal
Ekoi and Ibibio peoples from their territories west of the Cross River, pushing
the latter east of the river. Ohafia military displacement of Ekoi and Ibibio
communities resulted in the emergence of mixed Igbo-Ibibio-Ekoi towns in
the region in the seventeenth century, including Ihe, Ukwa-Igbo, Isu-Igbo,
Ikwere, and Arochukwu.[17]

The displaced non-Igbo peoples viewed the Ohafia as land-grabbers, and,
according to Chukwuma Azuonye, "the young were reminded of their duty
to retake all the stolen land or at least render them unsafe for human habitation."[18] Until the 1890s, Ohafia people engaged in intergroup warfare with
these eastern neighbors for territorial defense.[19] Prior to Ohafia arrival, Ibibio,
Ekoi, Biase, and Ogoja peoples engaged in head-hunting expeditions as a psychological means of defense and embarked on raids occasioned by drought,
seasonal hunger (unwu), and crop failure.[20] In a bid to regain their lost land
between 1700 and the 1890s, they employed these defense mechanisms against
the Ohafia.[21] In turn, the Ohafia imitated the war tactics of their hostile neighbors, often taking the battle to the doorsteps of their enemies, beating them at
their own game, and successfully taking their heads to deter them from venturing
into Ohafia domains.[22] Hence, various scholars have noted that head-hunting
developed as a defensive warfare tactic of the Cross River ethnic communities,
including Ekoi, Efik, Biase, Ibibio, Ogoja, and Igbo peoples during this period.[23] This head-hunting tradition, still celebrated in Ohafia today through the
war dance in memorialization of a "heroic age" and militant masculinity, has
shaped the masculinist vision of Ohafia-Igbo ethnicity.[24] In this view, Ohafia
people are "Igbo" because they defended Igboland from military and cultural
encroachment by non-Igbo hostiles while maintaining ancestral and ritual kinship with their immediate Igbo neighbors.[25]

However, in order to defend themselves, Ohafia people adopted the better-
organized paramilitary institutions of their matrilineal and bilateral Ibibio and

Ekoi eastern neighbors. These borrowed practices include a well-integrated age-grade system with elaborate rites of passage, which ensured a substantial reserve of on-call, battle-ready, able-bodied men; exclusively male secret societies that reinforced the unity of the patrilineages; and a village residential layout akin to a military garrison, which inscribed militant notions of masculinity within the Ohafia physical landscape (what I have elsewhere theorized as a "geography of masculinity").[26] The borrowing of institutions from non-Igbo ethnic groups and their gendered adaptation within Ohafia imbued the society with a sociopolitical system more akin to those of its non-Igbo neighbors (particularly the Biakpan, Ikun, Biase, Yako, and Mbembe).[27] Thus, in contrast to most Igbo communities, which possessed a lineage-based political system and where age grades were mostly convivial, the Ohafia political system was based on pyramidal age-grade organizations between 1800 and 1900.[28] The masculinist image of Ohafia-Igbo ethnicity does not account for the cultural similitude between Ohafia and its non-Igbo neighbors.

Between the 1660s and 1840s, Ohafia also maintained a diplomatic alliance (*ukwuzi*) with the commercial town of Arochukwu. Ohafia male warriors raided Ibibio and Ekoi territories for slaves, which they supplied to Aro merchants, who traded the slaves at the coastal towns of Itu and Bonny in exchange for European commodities.[29] In this system, Ohafia was guaranteed access to a widespread network of Aro-controlled markets in southeastern Nigeria for the disposal of its slaves and could acquire choice European goods, especially guns, textiles, metal wares, and beads.[30] Ohafia warriors contributed about 35 percent of the slaves taken from the Bight of Biafra for the Atlantic market, and the political economy of slave production reshaped lineage practices within Ohafia.[31] The transfer of personal property, particularly land, guns, and brass rod currency, from father to son and beyond the control of matrilineages increased in the nineteenth century as part of *ogaranya* (wealth) status performance among Ohafia men.[32] This emergent inheritance practice placed a new emphasis on the social importance of fathers and the patrilineage over matrilineage rights of inheritance.[33] It also increasingly oriented Ohafia toward a social identification as ethnically Igbo.

The military tradition of Ohafia male society became essential to definitions of individual social status in the nineteenth century and sheds more light on the emergence of a militant view of Ohafia-Igbo ethnicity. The hostile environment in which the Ohafia settled was fundamental to the evolution of what Njoku and Azuonye describe as a "heroic age" (the eighteenth and nineteenth centuries) that placed emphasis on militant conceptions of manhood and honor.[34] In the late eighteenth and early nineteenth centuries, most Ohafia warriors who raided Ibibio, Ekoi, and Biase territories often captured female slaves and cut male heads as proof of their bravery and claim to the social status of ufiem in the society. Warriors who failed to bring back human heads were ridiculed as *ujo* (cowards), such that Ohafia male society was divided between ufiem and ujo.[35] Men who attained ufiem enjoyed many privileges in Ohafia society. They married the choicest women and were exempted from minor public works. They often disinherited the ujo of their property. In public, they wore distinct regalia to mark their social status, especially the red *jooji* wrapper cloth (a nineteenth-century, Manchester-made textile used as a status symbol in the Cross River region) and a red-and-white-striped cap.

This gendered ideology of Ohafia warfare was a major factor in the production of more female slaves and children than male slaves from southeastern Nigeria during the eighteenth and nineteenth centuries, in contrast to the demography (male-female ratio) of slave supplies from other parts of West Africa.[36] Following the 1807 abolition of the Atlantic slave trade, the domestic slave trade expanded in southeastern Nigeria.[37] Whereas many Ibibio and Ekoi female slaves captured by Ohafia warriors became Ohafia wives, others were sold in the domestic markets at Itu, Asan, Bende, and Uzuakoli, where they fetched more money than male slaves.[38] By preferring to marry ufiem over ujo and taunting ujo in public, Ohafia women bought into the warrior model of Ohafia-Igbo ethnicity, but the large-scale incorporation of non-Ohafia female slaves as Ohafia wives and citizens through membership in the matrilineages generated critical and discriminatory discourses from indigenous Ohafia women and constituted gendered contestations over the definition of legitimate Ohafia-Igbo citizenship.[39]

As the anthropologist John McCall noted, the goal of attaining ufiem placed an emphasis on "going out into the realm beyond the limits of the familiar Ohafia world, . . . confronting the unknown, prevailing against alien forces and conquering them on their own ground. Returning with the head completed the act of incorporation."[40] By converting their non-Igbo neighbors into slave sources, Ohafia warriors cultivated an ideological distance from these societies and earned a (dis)reputation as "Aro mercenaries," headhunters, and cannibals in the views of European missionaries and colonial officials, who sought justification for opening the southeastern Nigerian hinterland to Christianity, trade, and effective colonial occupation in the late nineteenth century.[41] The "heads" that Ohafia warriors had cut militarized changing notions of masculinity in the society. In the course of the Atlantic slave trade, live captives would be substituted for heads brought home by warriors to ensure their attainment of ufiem. By the same logic, after the 1900s, the academic degree and the Mercedes-Benz became "heads" that, when brought home, established the passage to full adulthood and status as a local hero.[42] In effect, by 1900, there was a social equation of Ohafia-Igbo ethnicity with warrior masculinity.

The major outcomes of Ohafia male intergroup relations were mutual hostilities with non-Igbo neighbors and diplomatic relations with Igbo neighbors. In both cases, ethnicity was defined through a militant metanarrative of Ohafia-Igbo identity in relation to both Igbo and non-Igbo peoples in the region. This was in contrast to women's performance of their ethnicity.

Matriliny as a Lens into the Matrifocal Configuration of Ohafia-Igbo Ethnicity

British colonial anthropologists such as G. T. Basden, Daryll Forde, G. I. Jones, and C. J. Mayne noted the unusual predominance of matrilineal elements among a number of Cross River communities that had been classified as Igbo following British colonial rule in 1901. These scholars were uncomfortable describing these societies, including Ohafia, Abam, Afikpo, and Ada, as Igbo, since they were not patrilineal, so they called them the "Cross-River Igbo."[43] This designation, which distinguished these societies from the rest of Igboland, acknowledged the existence of Igbo and predominantly Ekoi and Ibibio cultural practices within these societies. Ohafia women's narratives of how their society became Igbo shed light on this phenomenon.

Matrilineality became coterminous with Ohafia-Igbo ethnicity soon after their settlement in the region immediately west of the Cross River around the seventeenth century.[44] As latecomers to their present environment, Ohafia people absorbed the matrilineal inheritance practices of their alienated eastern neighbors.[45] While descent came to be traced through both the matriline and patriline among Ohafia people, the patrilineage existed in gross inferiority vis-à-vis the matrilineage.[46] It is apt to examine Ohafia's dominant matrilineage principles for two reasons. First, in contrast to the rest of patrilineal Igboland, membership in an Ohafia matrilineage was the major parameter of legal citizenship (rights and duties based on social definitions of descent, belongingness, inheritance, succession, and burial) in the nineteenth century.[47] Second, the gendered uses of lineages defined the historical processes of Ohafia's ethnic identification. Matrilineages reflect practices and institutions that dramatize female power and authority, capture alternate female conceptions of Ohafia-Igbo ethnicity, and shed light on how Ohafia women defined themselves as outliers vis-à-vis the larger Igbo community. Patrilineages, on the other hand, became the major basis for the organization of male warriors, military defense, and slave production, which shaped the masculinist discourse of how Ohafia became ethnically Igbo.

Matrifocal narratives of Ohafia-Igbo ethnicity emphasize the Ohafia's cultural exchanges with their non-Igbo neighbors upon settlement. Ibeku, the heartland Igbo society where the ancestral Ohafia (Mben) lived for some time before migrating to their present location, was patrilineal.[48] Upon settlement in the Cross River region, however, Ohafia people found themselves on the fringe of Igboland, where until the nineteenth century they were cut off from most of Igboland by dense forests and narrow, steep-sided valleys and therefore almost entirely isolated.[49] Ohafia's geographical isolation from the rest of Igboland meant that it remained much more accessible from and in more constant inter-action with the territories of its alien and hostile non-Igbo neighbors.[50] Through intermarriages with aboriginal Ibibio, Yako, Mbembe, and Biase matrilineal and Yako peoples, Ohafia immigrants gained access to farmlands and in the process developed matrilineal practices.[51] As Ohafia men were preoccupied with the defense of their new territory, the bulk of farmwork was transferred to women, and after so many generations of controlling farmland, women became the sole transmitters of the right of its ownership.[52]

Some Ohafia oral traditions link the origins of matriliny to the active role women played in the foundation of new villages by assisting their community in times of crisis or rescuing male individuals from difficult situations.[53] Others ascribe the origin of matriliny to ancestresses who individually founded a village.[54] As Nsugbe rightly pointed out, it is not the historical truth of these traditions that makes them important as much as their role in validating the structural principles upon which crucial social relations were built before colo-nial rule.[55] Several Ohafia oral traditions show that women's control of farm-land through the matrilineage, their dominance in agricultural production, their emergence as breadwinners, their right (as opposed to their husband's) to inherit their children upon divorce, their leadership of the matrilineage units, and their ritual practices assured them a central place in the maintenance of the matrilineage as the dominant lineage ideology in the society.[56] Lineage ideologies became central to women's conception of their relationship with Ohafia's multi-ethnic neighbors and, consequently, their definition of Ohafia-Igbo ethnicity.

As a set of principles subject to appropriation by different historically situated individuals, lineage ideologies reflect Michel Foucault's notion of power as situ-ational, in flux, and manifest in effective practices.[57] The historically situated po-sitions of men and women within the matrilineage enabled Ohafia women, not men, to determine the dominant kinship affiliation across ethnic boundaries. Through intermarriage with nonpatrilineal and non-Igbo ethnic communities, Ohafia-Igbo women transformed the multiethnic Cross River region into a network of matrilineal kin relationships, such that various Ibibio and Ekoi ethnic communities have had chiefs of Ohafia maternal descent.[58] Since all children belonged to their mother's matrilineage, Ohafia women who married outside Ohafia produced children who had property and citizenship rights both within Ohafia and in their father's ethnic homelands. Thus, in the second half of the nineteenth century, individuals were occasionally invited from outside Ohafia to succeed to matrilineally inherited political offices within Ohafia.[59] Interethnic marriages thus enabled the fluidity of ethnic identities. This was not possible in the rest of patrilineal Igbo society and demonstrates a different conception of ethnicity in Ohafia. Moreover, by alluding to matriliny as central to female power and authority and a threat to male power, authority, and autonomy inherent in the militant concept of Ohafia-Igbo ethnicity, Ohafia men and women recognize the ideological and cultural differences that exist between their society and other patrilineal Igbo societies, as well as the similarities they share with nonpatrilineal and non-Igbo ethnic communities in the Cross River region.

Lineages are best viewed as practices that are adaptable and change over time. It was people's practices that constituted lineages, continued to give lineage its meaning, and ushered in significant changes in lineage ideologies over time.[60] It is in this sense that Ohafia-Igbo people describe their society as matrilineal until the mid-nineteenth century, when they increasingly became bilateral and increasingly claimed Igbo ethnicity. Recounting the changes in lineage ideology, Ohafia men and women cite the increase in individual property ownership (as opposed to ownership by the matrilineage), the transmission of estates from father to son (as opposed to inheritance by uterine siblings), and a father's (as opposed to maternal uncles') assumption of responsibility for the welfare of his children.[61] In fact, the conception of lineages as practices enables the understanding of gendered agency in the definition of Ohafia-Igbo ethnicity. As gendered practices, matrilineage and patrilineage express two separate visions of Ohafia-Igbo ethnicity, captured in Ohafia idioms: "Anyi eri ala a nne" (We eat through the mother) and "Ohafia wu mba ji ishi, acho ishi" (Ohafia is a community in search of military glory). Whereas the first expression epitomizes the matrilineage and the centrality of female economic (breadwinners and controllers of landed estates) and political power as foundational to Ohafia-Igbo identity, the latter invokes the warrior image of Ohafia society and the significance of patrilineage units as the basis of Ohafia paramilitary organizations.

Even though most Ohafia men attest that the matrilineage was a dominant feature of their society that distinguished them from the rest of patrilineal Igbo society, they tend to equate Ohafia-Igbo ethnicity with certain masculine attributes such as head-hunting and warfare and have fostered the patrilineage as the major organizational unit for male society. While Ohafia women did not necessarily oppose warfare and indigenous conceptions of ufiem, they sought to define a different Ohafia-Igbo identity that conflicted with the masculinist vision. Women were involved in the organization of warfare and in the celebration of warrior ufiem, and some Ohafia women performed masculinity.[62] So, in a sense, they bought into the masculinist vision. However, through collective political actions, women championed a social vision of Ohafia society as matrilineal, dominated by powerful female political institutions, female breadwinners, and a ritual-sacral matriarchy whose legacies are preserved through the raising of female ancestor shrines (ududu—pot monuments). Moreover, Ohafia women exploited the matrilineage to maintain an ideological and cultural distance from the patrilineal Igbo and an intercultural and diplomatic network with the various non-Igbo matrilineal and bilateral ethnic groups in the Cross River region. Women created these long-lasting kinship networks across cultural and linguistic boundaries primarily through marriage practices.

Ohafia Gendered Political Organization and the Performance of Ethnic Citizenship

Politics was an arena of gendered struggle for power and the definition of Ohafia-Igbo ethnicity in the nineteenth century. The age-grade system of Ohafia political organization, which they adopted from their non-Igbo neighbors, set them apart from the rest of Igboland, which had a lineage-based system of political organization and was thus an ethnic configuration that was neither wholly Igbo, Ibibio, nor Ekoi.[63] Whereas the age grade served a primary military purpose among the Ibibio and Ekoi and was merely a loosely integrated and largely social and convivial association in patrilineal Igbo societies, in Ohafia it became central to contested definitions of ethnicity between men and women. Here, the age grade served as a major institution for male socialization, the organization of warfare, and the performance of ufiem, while for women it became a major framework for female socialization and the exercise of political power and authority over both men and women. Thus, the sociopolitical uses of age grades in pre-twentieth-century southeastern Nigeria were ethnic in nature, and the gendered adaptation of the age-grade system within Ohafia transformed it into an institution for contested definitions of Ohafia-Igbo ethnicity between men and women because warrior masculinity and dominant female political power were antithetical social images of Ohafia-Igbo ethnicity.

Gendered socialization within the Ohafia age-grade system began in childhood. Boys and girls born within a three-year age bracket were grouped into the same age grade, and this grouping was repeated every three years for each new set of three-year-olds.[64] The gendered distinction of girls from boys began informally through play, whereas the anthropologist Robert Rattray noted in the case of the Asante in Ghana that young children were daily "undergoing unconscious instruction, mostly perhaps by a process of imitation of their elders."[65] In Ohafia, this gender distinction culminated in the boy's performance of igba nnunu (to shoot and kill a hummingbird using a bow and arrow) and the girl's performance of *ino nhiha* (menstruation seclusion).[66] The former introduced a boy into the world of men, and the latter enabled a girl to attain womanhood. From informal associations (up to eighteen years), the age grade gained formal recognition (eighteen to thirty-six years) and later (thirty-six to forty-five years) organized itself into two gendered political organizations.[67] The female members formed a political association known as *ikpirikpe ndi inyom*, while the male members constituted an equivalent organ called *akpan*. In practice, the akpan worked under the leadership of the male king to form a men's court in charge of male affairs, while the ikpirikpe, under the leadership of the female king, constituted the women's court in charge of female affairs.[68]

The following examination of Ohafia women's political organization in the nineteenth century demonstrates that women made use of both matrilineages and patrilineages in defining Ohafia social identity vis-à-vis its Igbo and non-Igbo neighbors. It also shows that Ohafia women practiced cross-ethnic political organizations while at the same time distancing themselves from Igbo and non-Igbo neighbors through matrifocal conceptions of Ohafia-Igbo ethnic citizenship. In effect, Ohafia women did not simply seek to define themselves as Igbo or Ibibio or Ekoi; they strove to construct themselves in a way that reinforced the sociopolitical privileges they enjoyed in their society. Thus, if lineage practices and political systems evidence ethnic identification in southeastern Nigeria, it becomes difficult to define Ohafia as Igbo or Ibibio or Ekoi. Hence, this chapter posits ethnicity as gendered and dynamic social practices that distinguish a community from the dominant stereotypes of its immediate neighbors.

The makeup of the Ohafia female court distinguished it from women's political organizations in patrilineal Igbo societies. The Ohafia female court comprised an assembly of wives and an assembly of daughters, similar to those that existed in other Igbo societies.[69] However, unlike in the rest of Igboland, these female assemblies did not exist independently of each other in Ohafia, because endogamous marriage practices within Ohafia patrilineages, which were considered an abomination in other Igbo societies, ensured the existence of women who were simultaneously wives and daughters in each Ohafia village.[70] This duo social status of Ohafia women shaped their conceptions of legitimate Ohafia-Igbo ethnic citizenship. Through critical discourses and rituals of exclusion and inclusion examined below, Ohafia women defined women who did not meet the criteria of wife-cum-daughter as ethnic outsiders to Ohafia.

In fact, the female king earned the right to govern the female court by being both daughter and wife of a royal patrilineage. As argued elsewhere, the concept of female king (a woman who is king over women) as distinct from male king (a man who is king over men) in pre-twentieth-century Ohafia emphasized the autonomy of the female sphere in defining politically acceptable notions of ethnic citizenship in the society.[71] Through their offices, Ohafia female kings forged cross-ethnic sisterhood alliances across village groups in other Igbo areas, which enabled women to effectively implement boycotts against men (ibo ezi) in order to coerce compliance with their political decisions, control the setting of the annual farming calendar, and prohibit male participation in certain economic activities.[72] Ibo ezi involved the entire female folk of one village deserting their homes in protest and seeking refuge in other villages or in neighboring ethnic communities. Njoku has described it as women "voting with their feet" and concurs that the effectiveness of this strategy rested primarily with the fact that Ohafia women exercised control over food production, preparation, and distribution.[73] Ibo ezi was a realization of cross-ethnic female group solidarity but did not necessarily orient Ohafia toward being Igbo.[74]

The degree of political power that Ohafia women possessed before twentieth-century British colonial rule facilitated the emergence of men in dominant positions of power set them apart from the rest of Igboland. Ohafia women made use of both physical force and rituals to enforce their rule. In fact, rituals were mechanisms for the exercise of female power and authority. They were, as the French sociologist Georges Balandier noted, "instruments of political action just as much as rulers and bureaucracy."[75] Through rituals of excommunication and reincorporation, Ohafia women established themselves as guardians of public morality and definers of Ohafia-Igbo citizenship and ethnicity. This chapter therefore posits political power as the exercise of "coercive influence" based on the threat or use of sanctions, control over public morality and communal values, and control over the distribution of material resources.[76]

In an interview with the female court of Akanu Village, Ohafia, Nnenna Emeri stated:

> If men violated the laws upheld by women, they were held to severe obligations and punishments. . . . If a man abused his wife physically or verbally in relation to her sexuality, or accused her of sleeping with other men, once women learned of it, and are invited by the women of that patrilineage to come and deal with such a man, the ikpirikpe [the women's court] went and showed him that there was a power above him. . . . And once they came in, if the man was not cooperating, they may put him down and urinate upon him![77]

Urinating upon men was Ohafia women's manifestation of what the historian Judith Van Allen has described as "sitting on a man" and what Shirley Ardener has described as African women's "sexual insult" upon men, employed to enforce women's political decisions.[78] The ability of women to punish men as individuals and as a group distinguished ikpirikpe as more than a protest organization (like the Igbo women's assembly); it was a formal political entity that constantly governed societal mores. It is plausible that the matrifocal principles of citizenship, inheritance, and political succession in nineteenth-century Ohafia encouraged an intense preservation of women's civil rights.[79] Thus, southeastern Nigeria women's political power was ethnically gendered.

Urinating upon men was part of a larger mechanism known in Ohafia as *ikpo mgbogho* (to desecrate, ostracize, and pronounce an individual socially dead) and typified women's show of power and authority.[80] Ohafia women applied ikpo mgbogho in all cases of domesticity that threatened the moral integrity of women, including abortion and divorce.[81] This punishment was followed by a cleansing ritual (*iyi ose*) of the repentant accursed individual by the womenfolk, which involved yet another level of social degradation and re-birth, after which the individual could be readmitted as a legitimate member of society.[82] The cleansing ritual involved a dramatic reconfiguration of Ohafia society's "moral imagination," for by focusing on the human body as the locus of personhood and the material manifestation of self, the ritual positioned women as the definers of the metanarrative of right and wrong and the conditions under which an ostracized individual was reintroduced as a legitimate member of society.[83] Through rituals of excommunication and reincorporation, Ohafia women controlled the social perception of individuals and reinforced women's power to define Ohafia-Igbo citizenship.

The intersection of political power and definitions of ethnic citizenship in Ohafia women's rituals is further manifest in two biannual rites: *idighi omara* (the land purification rite) and uzo-iyi (virginity testing). Both were distinguished by significant age-role inversions, where virgin girls assumed the role of a public supreme court of critical opinion, primarily against the male elders of the society. Here, ritual ceremonies were transformed into political platforms for registering dissent and bringing to public ridicule male elders who had committed social ills in secret, even in the privacy of their homes, in order to restore moral purity in the society.[84] However, during these rituals, Ohafia women sang songs that discriminated against Igbo and Ibibio wives as foreigners and equated these nonindigenous Ohafia women and their daughters with slaves and the expensive property of Ohafia matrilineages.[85]

This discourse referred to the fact that since Igbo and Ibibio wives did not have a matrilineage within Ohafia, they became citizens by becoming a member of their husband's matrilineage. It was more expensive to marry wives from neighboring Igbo societies, and most Ibibio wives were slave captives. In both cases, such foreign wives assured the continuity of Ohafia matrilineages, especially where a descendant daughter was lacking.[86] The inability to have a female child was a calamitous challenge to Ohafia women's negotiation of ancestral

honor. It meant that the individual woman would have no ududu ancestral pot
raised in her name upon her death, a ritual that would enshrine her as an ancestral matriarch of her matrilineage.[87] In order to overcome this challenge, many
Ohafia women married expensive wives from patrilineal Igbo societies, thereby
becoming female husbands. Through these wives, Ohafia female husbands
begot daughters who memorialized them as matriarchs of their matrilineages.[88]
The female definition of legitimate citizenship was thus directly linked to dominant matrilineage principles and women's performance of respectable social
status.

However, by qualifying the "Igbo" and "Ibibio" as property, slaves, foreign,
and strangers, Ohafia women defined them as two dominant ethnic groups between which their society struggled to define itself. This speaks to how Ohafia
women positioned themselves as different from Igbo and different from other
matrilineal and bilateral groups in the region. Indeed, Ohafia women's rituals
were avenues for the configuration of Ohafia-Igbo ethnicity and the definition
of legitimate individual citizenship, since women reinforced the matrilineage
as the major corporate group within which property was inherited and through
which individual identity was defined. They also located the female body as a
site of great moral anxiety and for the negotiation of various forms of identity,
including the lineage seniority of settlement, slave or freeborn status, Ohafia
citizenship or foreign origin, aboriginal or visitor status, childhood or womanhood, sexual purity or sexual defilement, and a just social system or a corrupt
moral order. The ritual songs emphasize the role of women as breadwinners
and equate motherhood and womanhood with community survival.[89] Ohafia
men define warrior masculinity as central to communal welfare and Ohafia-
Igbo ethnicity in the same way.[90]

Masculinity, Ritual, and the Male Performance
of Ethnic Citizenship

Whereas Ohafia women's discourses, rituals, and practices created and sustained indigenous notions of inclusivity and exclusivity that came to define the
processes of ethnic identification within the society, Ohafia men's masculinity
practices militarized the social image of Ohafia-Igbo ethnicity. In contrast to
women's emphasis on the matrilineage and motherhood, the dominant expressions of ethnic citizenship and autochthony of settlement by Ohafia men reified
the patrilineage. In this sense, as Jean Davison shows, it was the cultural meaning
that individuals and groups attached to lineages that gave them meaning.[91]
These ethnicity expressions include (1) traditions of origin based on symbolic
ufiem characters such as the *dibia* (medicine men) and the wrestler-warrior;[92]

(2) ritual reaffirmations of patrilineage seniority in the course of various masculinity performances and rituals;[93] and (3) the organization of warriors according to patrilineage units and the equation of Ohafia-Igbo ethnicity with igbu ishi (head taking). For instance, until the late nineteenth century, the establishment of new nuclear family homesteads and patrilineage compounds and their incorporation as legitimate parts of the village group required ritual acts involving the sacrifice of human heads obtained by male warriors who performed ufiem. Through this process, patrilineage shrines and communal deities were also instituted.[94] The parameter of legitimate citizenship as far as Ohafia male society was concerned was the possession of these ufiem institutions and symbols.[95]

Moreover, a legitimate Ohafia male ancestor was one who received the deification ceremony of *idoru-nna* (laying a father to rest), which established him as a powerful patrilineage ancestor.[96] The deceased's eldest son hired the services of a great warrior to perform the ritual war dance of *okerenkwa*. As Ohafia elder Ndukwe Otta stated, this warrior was considered a "man" not "because he has a penis [but] because he had accomplished the requirements of manhood in Ohafia."[97] Legitimate Ohafia-Igbo male ancestors were those who received the honor of okerenkwa. Individuals who did not receive the honor of okerenkwa were believed to belong neither in the world of the living nor in the world of the dead.[98] Thus, juxtaposed to its female counterpart, the male definition of ethnic citizenship was directly linked to patrilineage ideologies and men's performance of respectable social status.

There were two institutional practices that imbued Ohafia-Igbo ethnicity with militant notions and patrilineage ideologies: secret societies and the Ohafia war dance. The anthropologist Simon Ottenberg noted in the case of the Afikpo-Igbo, who are the immediate northern neighbors of Ohafia, that secret societies united the various patrilineages in the village in a structural opposition to the diversity of the matrilineages.[99] Ohafia men adopted four secret societies (*obon*, *akang*, *ekpe*, and *okonko*) from their non-Igbo neighbors in the eighteenth and nineteenth centuries.[100] Whereas the first three served military training purposes, okonko was used to facilitate cross-ethnic trading voyages throughout the Cross River region, since it guaranteed security and immunity to multiethnic members.[101] Okonko spread quickly from the Ibibio ethnic community of Calabar to Igboland in the nineteenth century, so much so that the social anthropologist Patrick Nwosu asserted that okonko came to represent Igbo ethnic identity and that without it a community was without a name.[102] However, whereas okonko was open to both men and women among the Ibibio and in other Igbo communities such as Amuzo-Ihe, in Ohafia, it excluded women and became an ufiem institution through which wealthy Ohafia men performed ogaranya (wealth) masculinity.[103] Through these societies, Ohafia male society constructed its power of control over "sons" and reinforced the patrilineage as a prominent domain for the definition of Ohafia male citizenship.[104] This is perhaps why Ottenberg stated that in nineteenth-century Ohafia, "politics seems patrilineal rather than matrilineal."[105]

The Ohafia war dance has perhaps played the most dramatic role in popularizing a militant image of Ohafia-Igbo ethnicity. The war dance was a masculine genre of music and dance in which the lead dancer carried a headdress bearing human skulls. Since the colonial period, the human skulls have been replaced with wooden sculptures. Before the twentieth century, the war dance was performed within Ohafia to acknowledge individual accomplishments of ufiem. It was performed at funerals of ufiem to honor their memory and at the coronation of male kings to legitimate their assumption of office. In the course of the Nigerian-Biafran civil war (1967–70), the war dance served to drum up confidence and raise hopes in the region.[106] It was performed at Nigerian universities to launch history journals (such as *Ikenga*) that celebrated pan-Igbo ethnicity and at intercultural and interstate art competitions in Nigeria to showcase Igbo ethnic heritage.[107] When the corpse of the erstwhile Biafran leader Odumegwu Ojukwu was flown to Lagos in 2012, the war dance was headlined to celebrate Ojukwu as a national hero. The dance is today showcased on national television in Nigeria and in the United Kingdom.

As a memorialization ritual, the war dance propagates the militant image of Ohafia-Igbo ethnicity.[108] Its performance entrenched the view of Ohafia as a land of noble warriors and has encouraged the misrepresentation of Ohafia women as subservient in mainstream literature, thereby clouding the earlier preeminence of female power in precolonial Ohafia society. The dance performance structured the social perception of the society's gender system as one comprising visible male warriors and invisible female farmers and has been a major internal factor in the equation of Ohafia ethnicity with head-hunting since the turn of the twentieth century.

Njoku writes that nothing dramatizes Ohafia's military propensity in the past as much as the people's war dance.[109] McCall adds that the war dance reflected Ohafia internalization of warfare and was an expression of manhood and Ohafia-Igbo ethnic identity.[110] In the war dance, the past and present become interpermeable, experience is structured, and history is reconstituted.[111] Through dancing, men linked their sense of personhood and masculinity and their somatic knowledge of themselves with a continuum of experience that extends beyond individuals to encompass a corpus of ancestral knowledge.[112] Azuonye described the war songs as the principal channel through which Ohafia cultural traditions and ideals of personal success and veneration of heroic ancestors were transmitted to younger generations, inspiring them to emulate the example of their forebears. Through constant performance, the war dance and songs became philosophical traditions and the expression of a community's identity and history.[113]

As a performance of military heroism and a record of the heroic deeds of the ancestors, the war dance was central to the social production of warriors as the dominant ufiem in nineteenth-century Ohafia society, as well as the dominant social vision of Ohafia as a warrior Igbo society.[114] The vision of the war dancers bearing human skulls obtained from head-hunting became the dominant social characterization of Ohafia society by successive historical actors in the region, including missionaries, colonial officials, academic researchers, Igbo and non-Igbo neighbors, and some Ohafia people themselves.

Ufiem Confronts Female Power and Authority: Performing Ethnicity in the Public Space

The social performances of ufiem and of female power and authority in nineteenth-century Ohafia transformed the public space into an arena of gendered struggle for power and the definition of ethnic identity. Ufiem performance in Ohafia society gendered the landscape itself—it created a "geography of masculinity" characterized by the establishment of male cultural symbols in public spaces.[115] These include the patrilineage *obu* (meeting house), which marked the inception of the public sphere within the Ohafia architectural village structure; the wooden *ikoro* (war drum) occupying the village square, where successful warriors presented the heads they had taken for social recognition; and shrines that sought to delineate a public sector of male domination and simultaneously the spatial-cultural limits that women and ujo (cowards) could never trespass. Until today, Ohafia women were forbidden to pass through the patrilineage shrines unless the women were virgins.[116]

The lack of female access to a patrilineage shrine—a mound of stones hedged in by two trees—may at first appear to have no apparent gendered power implications; however, its continued existence highlights the persistent inscription of gender ideologies within the landscape itself—ideologies that came to shape the notion of female political invisibility and inferiority vis-à-vis men. These physical constructs played a significant role in the construction of the dominant ufiem by providing the public platforms for the performance of warrior masculinity, but they also constituted historical and cultural evidence that Ohafia men rely upon to legitimate a masculinist ethnic vision.[117]

The masculinization of the patrilineage obu in the nineteenth century was in direct structural opposition to the absence of matrilineal residential compound units, and its location in the center of the village defined a public sector of male visibility.[118] The preservation of male cultural artifacts (ancestor shrines) in the patrilineage obu as a result of colonial government intervention (which transformed the obu into museums) at the turn of the twentieth century and the destruction of women's matrilineage ududu as a result of successive missionary and indigenous converts' evangelization efforts and religious zeal have shaped historical memories of gendered power and gendered visions of Ohafia-Igbo ethnicity.[119] The postcolonial visibility of male cultural relics informs men's insistence that women were peripheral to Ohafia society and inspires women's reenactments of historic female power and authority through time-tested punitive and boycott strategies and rituals to recenter themselves in Ohafia history.

Men's appropriation of public spaces for ufiem performance and women's transformation of public spaces into the most effective platforms for registering political dissent and asserting political authority over both men and women indicate that the public space was an arena of gendered contestation and thus an apposite context for studying the gendered struggle for power and definition of ethnic identity. It was through their performances of overwhelming authority that the female court came to be socially perceived as a supreme public court that simultaneously becomes a litigant who never loses, an arbiter who often votes in its own favor with its own feet (boycott), and an enforcer of its own ruling. The female courts marched more often than their male counterparts. They were the ones who constantly transformed private and secret disagreements into public spectacles, subject to the entire society's moral debate through cross-ethnic mobilization. Indeed, the public space was the most important and effective platform for Ohafia women's assertion and performance of political power in the nineteenth century.

Conclusion

Ethnicity was a gendered practice in nineteenth-century Ohafia society. Conflicts over gendered forms of ethnicity were evident in oppositional lineage ideologies, contested definitions of legitimate citizenship, and performances of gender identity and political authority. The historical contexts of Ohafia ethnicity formation included the migration and settlement of the Ohafia people in a borderland region in the seventeenth century, their preeminent role in militant slave production for the Atlantic and domestic markets in the eighteenth and nineteenth centuries, their commercial relations with their non-Igbo neighbors, and, to a lesser degree, the late nineteenth-century incursion of European missionaries and colonial officials. However, Ohafia women and men daily performed their ethnic identities, and when one puts one's ear to the ground, one hears the drumbeats of the ants, male and female, each playing a different tune.

Women exploited the matrilineage to maintain a cultural distance from the patrilineal Igbo and a kinship network with the various non-Igbo matrilineal and bilateral ethnicities in the Cross River region. However, women's cross-ethnic political strategies linked them with neighboring Igbo communities. Moreover, Ohafia women exploited both the patrilineage residential system of their society and the incorporative matrilineage ideology to define legitimate female citizens as individuals who were simultaneously wives and daughters while discriminating against Igbo and Ibibio people as ethnic outsiders to Ohafia. In the same vein, Ohafia men propagated a militant image of Ohafia-Igbo ethnicity through warfare and slave production that alienated their non-Igbo neighbors, ufiem performances that celebrated warriors above other categories of masculinity, and war dances that memorialized the "heroic age" of the nineteenth century. Yet Ohafia male society borrowed secret societies from their non-Igbo neighbors. While these societies promoted patrilineages as major units of male political organization and identified Ohafia with the rest of patrilineal Igbo society, they also made Ohafia's political systems simulative of those of their non-Igbo neighbors.

Thus, nineteenth-century Ohafia may not wholly be characterized as Igbo or Ibibio or Ekoi, since both Ohafia men and women possessed specific historical ideologies about what being Ohafia-Igbo meant. Without the lens of gender, it is impossible to understand the meanings and historical processes of Ohafia's emergence as an Igbo ethnic society in the nineteenth century because men and women brought different historical motivations and interpretations to bear on the social definition of Ohafia-Igbo ethnicity. The case study of Ohafia reinforces the overarching arguments of this book that ethnicity was not a gender-neutral identity, since it was defined through a gender-differentiated individual quest for social mobility, collective political mobilization, and the adaptation of cultural practices from neighboring communities. Both ethnicity and gender were constituted in everyday practices and livelihoods. Moreover, the active role that women played in the historical processes of Ohafia-Igbo ethnic identification challenges the male-centered metanarratives of ethnicity in Africanist scholarship.

NOTES

This chapter is a result of my dissertation research from July 2011 to July 2012, facilitated by a Wenner-Gren Foundation Dissertation Fieldwork Grant, as well as predissertation research conducted in 2009 and 2010, funded by the Michigan State University Department of History. My sources include field observations, photographs, video recordings, and 170 oral interviews conducted over a period of eleven months in Ohafia, southeastern Nigeria, as well as archival research at the British National Archives, Kew; the National Library of Scotland, Edinburgh; and the Nigerian National Archives in Enugu, Ibadan, and Lagos.

1. Victor C. Uchendu, *The Igbo of Southeastern Nigeria* (New York: Holt, Rinehart and Winston, 1965), 12.

2. Uchendu, *Igbo*, 13.

3. See Leonard Ndubueze Mbah, "Emergent Masculinities: The Gendered Struggle for Power in Southeastern Nigeria, 1850–1920" (PhD diss., Michigan State University, 2013).

4. Philip O. Nsugbe, *Ohaffia: A Matrilineal Ibo People* (Oxford: Oxford University Press, 1974); Onwuka Njoku, *Ohafia: A Heroic Igbo Society* (Ohafia, Nigeria: Whytam Press, 2000). See also Chukwuma Azuonye, "The Heroic Age of the Ohafia Igbo," *Genève-Afrique* 28, no. 1 (1990): 7–35.

5. Audrey Smedley, *Women Creating Patrilyny: Gender and Environment in West Africa* (Walnut Creek, CA: AltaMira Press, 2004), 1–3.

6. Ugo G. Nwokeji, *The Slave Trade and Culture in the Bight of Biafra: An African Society in the Atlantic World* (New York: Cambridge University Press, 2010). See also Elizabeth Isichei, *A History of the Igbo People* (London: Macmillan, 1976), 86.

7. Smedley, *Women Creating Patrilyny*, 1.

8. This subject has been explored elsewhere. See Mbah, "Emergent Masculinities," chap. 5.

9. Ruth Finnegan, *Oral Literature in Africa* (Oxford: Oxford University Press, 1970), 2–3; Barbara Cooper, "Oral Sources and the Challenge of African History," in *Writing African History*, ed. John Edward Philips (New York: University of Rochester Press, 2005), 202–7.

10. Anthony Giddens, *New Rules of Sociological Method: A Positive Critique of Interpretative Sociologies* (London: Hutchinson, 1976); Pierre Bourdieu, *Outline of a Theory of Practice* (Cambridge: Cambridge University Press, 1977); Pierre Bourdieu, *The Logic of Practice* (Cambridge: Polity, 1990); Pierre Bourdieu and John B. Thompson, *Language and Symbolic Power* (Cambridge, MA: Harvard University Press, 1991); Henrietta Moore and Meghan Vaughan, *Cutting Down Trees: Gender, Nutrition and Agricultural Change in the Northern Province of Zambia, 1890–1990* (Portsmouth, NH: Heinemann, 1994).

11. For detailed discussions of women's rituals, see Mbah, "Emergent Masculinities," chap. 2. *Uzo-iyi* is women's ritual purification of the land and holding of a supreme court of public opinion, in which young virgin girls served as oracles and judges. *Ije akpaka* is women's ritual declaration of warfare, which authorized men to go to war. *Ibo ezi* is women's mass desertion of their homes in protest, and *ikpo mgbogho* is women's punitive death sentence. Jan Vansina, *Oral Tradition as History* (Madison: University of Wisconsin Press, 1985), 40.

12. Janice Boddy, *Wombs and Alien Spirits: Women, Men, and the Zar Cult in Northern Sudan* (Madison: University of Wisconsin Press, 1989), 4–5.

13. Stephan Miescher, "The Life Histories of Boakye Yiadom: Exploring the Subjectivity and Voices of a Teacher-Catechist in Colonial Ghana," in *African Words, African Voices: Critical Practices in Oral History*, ed. Luise White, Stephan Miescher, and David William Cohen (Madison: University of Wisconsin Press, 1985), 163; Louise A. Tilley, "People's History and Social Science History," *Social Science History* 7, no. 4 (1983): 457–74.

14. C. J. Mayne, "Intelligence Report on the Ohafia Clan, 1934," 11–12, Chief Secretary's Office (CSO) 26/3, file 29196, Nigerian National Archives Ibadan (NAI); Njoku, *Ohafia*, 2–3; Nsugbe, *Ohaffia*, 12–18; Isichei, *History*, 51–52; Daryll Forde and G. I. Jones, *The Ibo and Ibibio-Speaking Peoples of South-Eastern Nigeria* (London: International African Institute, 1950), 54; Kenneth O. Dike, *Trade and Politics in the Niger Delta, 1830–1885: An Introduction to the Economic and Political History of Nigeria* (Oxford: Clarendon Press, 1966), 24; John N. Oriji, *Traditions of Igbo Origin: A Study of Pre-colonial Population Movements in Africa* (New York: Peter Lang, 1994), 149–50; Nkparom C. Ejituwu, *A History of Obolo (Andoni) in the Niger Delta* (Oron: Mason Publishing Company, 1991), 28; G. I. Jones, *Annual Reports of Bende Division, South Eastern Nigeria, 1905–1912* (Cambridge: University of Cambridge, 1986), 1, 63–64; Oji K. Oji, "A Study of Migrations and Warfare in Ohafia" (BA thesis, University of Nigeria, Nsukka, 1974), 6–15.

15. Forde and Jones, *Ibo and Ibibio*, 53–56, 85; Oriji, *Traditions*, 151; Nnenna E. Obuba, *The History and Culture of Ohafia, Covering from about 1432 to 2008: Collated Oral Tradition* (Ebem, Ohafia: Lintdsons Publications, 2008), 2–5; Nsugbe, *Ohaffia*, 11–18; Njoku, *Ohafia*, 9.

16. Jones, *Annual Reports*, 1; Nsugbe, *Ohaffia*, 35, 116–18; Kenneth O. Dike and Felicia Ekejiuba, "The Aro State: A Case-Study of State-Formation in Southeastern Nigeria," *Journal of African Studies* 5, no. 1 (1978): 273; R. Harris, "The Influence of Ecological Factors and External Relations on the Mbembe Tribes of South-East Nigeria," *Africa* 32 (1962): 43–47; Obuba, *History and Culture*, 8; Nsugbe, *Ohaffia*, 35.

17. Forde and Jones, *Ibo and Ibibio*, 52; A. E. Afigbo, *Ropes of Sand: Studies in Igbo Culture and History* (Ibadan: Oxford University Press, 1981), 229–30; G. I. Jones, *The Trading States of the Oil Rivers* (Oxford: Oxford University Press, 1963), 134; Felicia Ekejiuba, "The Aro System of Trade in the Nineteenth Century," *Ikenga: Journal of African Studies* 1, no. 1 (January 1972): 13–34; David Northrup, *Trade without Rulers* (Oxford: Oxford University Press, 1978), 35.

18. Azuonye, "Heroic Age," 13.

19. Nsugbe, *Ohaffia*, 27–28; Azuonye, "Heroic Age," 21–23; Monday Abasiattai, *Akwa Ibom and Cross River States: The Land, the People and Their Culture* (Calabar: Wusen Press, 1987), 55.

20. For descriptions of the psychological means of defense, see "Africa, West Coast, 1890," 348–59, Foreign Office (FO) 84/2020, British National Archives (hereafter cited as BNA); Azuonye, "Heroic Age," 14.

21.   "Southern Nigeria Original Correspondence, 1903," 18–20, 44–54, 173–87, 263–65, Colonial Office (CO) 520/20, BNA; Azuonye, "Heroic Age," 13; Njoku, *Ohafia*, 68.

22.   Nna Agbai Ndukwe, interview by the author, 10 August 2010, Elu Village, Ohafia; Mr. Arunsi Kalu, interview by the author, 15 August 2011, Amangwu Ohafia; Harris, "Influence," 46–47.

23.   Njoku, *Ohafia*, 87; Azuonye, "Heroic Age," 14; Nsugbe, *Ohaffia*, 27, 56.

24.   Azuonye, "Heroic Age," 9–14; Njoku, *Ohafia*, 68–72; Chukwuma Azuonye, "The Narrative War Songs of the Ohafia Igbo: A Critical Analysis of their Characteristic Features in Relation to their Social Functions" (PhD diss., University of London, 1979), 32.

25.   Njoku, *Ohafia*, 84; Arthur Glyn Leonard, "Notes of a Journey to Bende," *Journal of the Manchester Geographical Society* 14 (1898): 196–97; Nsugbe, *Ohaffia*, 13–15.

26.   Mbah, "Emergent Masculinities," chaps. 3–4. See also Njoku, *Ohafia*, 68; Nsugbe, *Ohaffia*, 51; Chieka Ifemesia, *Traditional Humane Living among the Igbo: An Historical Perspective* (Enugu: Fourth Dimension Publishers, 1979), 76–80.

27.   For gendered adaptations, see Mbah, "Emergent Masculinities," chaps. 2–4. These adaptations are discussed again later in this chapter.

28.   Nsugbe, *Ohaffia*, 58, 69; Forde and Jones, *Ibo and Ibibio*, 52; Njoku, *Ohafia*, 26, 59; M. M. Green, *Ibo Village Affairs* (London: Frank Cass, 1947), 25; Afigbo, *Ropes of Sand*, 22; U. O. Eleazu, "Traditional Institutions and Modernization," *Ohafia Review* 1 (April 1981): 9; Uchendu, *Igbo*, 84; C. K. Meek, *Law and Authority in a Nigerian Tribe: A Study in Indirect Rule* (London: Oxford University Press, 1937), 198.

29.   "Southern Nigeria Protectorate Original Correspondence, May–August, 1901," 510–14, CO 520/8, BNA; Northrup, *Trade without Rulers*, 119; Nsugbe, *Ohaffia*, 31.

30.   For details of Ohafia-Aro alliance, see Mbah, "Emergent Masculinities," chap. 3.

31.   Ugo U. Nwokeji, "African Conceptions of Gender and the Slave Traffic," *William and Mary Quarterly* 58, no. 1 (January 2001): 53, 61–65; Ugo U. Nwokeji, "The Atlantic Slave Trade and Population Density: A Historical Demography of the Biafran Hinterland," *Canadian Journal of African Studies* 34, no. 3 (2000): 617–26.

32.   See Mbah, "Emergent Masculinities," chap. 2, for detailed discussion.

33.   Mayne, "Intelligence Report," 47; A. K. Uche, *Customs and Practices in Ohaffia* (Aba, Nigeria: A. K. Uche, 1960), 39–40; Obuba, *History and Culture*, 54; Nsugbe, *Ohaffia*, 122–23; Mbah, "Emergent Masculinities," chap. 2; Simon Ottenberg, *Double Descent in an African Society: The Afikpo Village-Group* (Seattle: University of Washington Press, 1968), 199–202.

34.   Azuonye, "Heroic Age," 9, 13–14; Njoku, *Ohafia*, 68–72.

35.   Azuonye, "Narrative War Songs," 32; Njoku, *Ohafia*, 62–63, 72–80; Uka, "A Note on the 'Abam' Warriors of Igbo Land," *Ikenga: Journal of African Studies* 1, no. 2 (1972): 78; John C. McCall, *Dancing Histories: Heuristic Ethnography with the Ohafia Igbo* (Ann Arbor: University of Michigan Press, 2000), 68; Ndukwe Otta and Elder Uduma Uka, interview by the author, 14 August 2010, Ebem Village, Ohafia.

36.   The unusually high percentage of females in the number of slaves exported from the Bight of Biafra shaped what is meant by "creole" in the Americas. D. B. Chambers, "Tracing Igbo into the African Diaspora," in *Identity in the Shadow of*

Slavery, ed. Paul E. Lovejoy (New York: Continuum, 2000), 55–71; M. D. Philip and S. Hawkins, *Black Experience and the Empire* (London: Oxford University Press, 2004); D. B. Chambers, *Murder at Montpelier: Igbo Africans in Virginia* (Jackson: University Press of Mississippi, 2005); M. A. Gomez, "A Quality of Anguish: The Igbo Response to Enslavement in the Americas," in *Trans-Atlantic Dimension of Ethnicity in the African Diaspora*, ed. Paul E. Lovejoy and David V. Trotman (New York: Continuum, 2003), 82–95.

37.   Afigbo, *Ropes of Sand*, 241–42; Mbah, "Emergent Masculinities," chaps. 4–5.

38.   Jones, *Annual Reports*, 70; Mayne, "Intelligence Report," 50; CO520/8, "Southern Nigeria Protectorate Original Correspondence, May–Aug., 1901," 574; Chief Idika Aso, interview by the author, 12 August 2010, Asaga Village, Ohafia; Chief Udensi Ekea, interview by the author, 4 August 2010; Vasco U. Iro, ezie-ogo of Nkwebi Village, interview by the author.

39.   For Ohafia women's marriage preferences, see Azuonye, "Narrative War Songs," 15; Uka, "A Note," 78; McCall, *Dancing Histories*, 80; Mr. Arunsi Kalu, interview by the author; Ndukwe, interview; Chief Emeh Okonkwo, interview by the author; Chief Kalu Awa Kalu, interview by the author; Chief K. K. Owen, interview by the author; Chief Olua Iro Kalu, interview by the author.

40.   McCall, *Dancing Histories*, 74.

41.   Isichei, *History*, 81–87; Frank Ashcroft, "Report on Calabar Mission: Tour of the Calabar Mission Districts," 19–31, MS 7796, *West Africa*, Church of Scotland Mission Archives (hereafter cited as CSM), National Library of Scotland (hereafter cited as NLS), Edinburgh; United Free Church of Scotland, "The Recent Expedition against the Aros," *Missionary Record of the United Free Church of Scotland*, nos. 1–164 (1902): 453, CSM, NLS; Charles Patridge, *Cross River Natives* (London: Krauss Reprint, 1905), 70; Leonard, "Notes," 190–201; A. G. Leonard, *The Lower Niger and Its Tribes* (London: Macmillan, 1906); P. A. Talbot, *The Peoples of Southern Nigeria: A Sketch of Their History, Ethnology, and Languages with an Account of the 1921 Census*, vol. 3 (London: Oxford University Press, 1926), 18; G. T. Basden, *Among the Ibos of Nigeria* (London: Frank Cass, 1921 [1966]), 37, 208–9; G. T. Basden, *Niger Ibos* (London: Frank Cass, 1938 [1966]), 377–88; K. O. Dike, *Trade and Politics in the Niger Delta, 1830–1885* (Oxford: Clarendon Press, 1956); K. O. Dike and F. I. Ekejiuba, *The Aro of South-Eastern Nigeria, 1650–1980: A Study of Socio-economic Formation and Transformation in Nigeria* (Ibadan: University Press, 1990); Northrup, *Trade without Rulers*; J. N. Oriji, "Slave Trade, Warfare and Aro Expansion in the Igbo Hinterland," *Genève-Afrique* 24, no. 2 (1986): 107–14; Azuonye, "Heroic Age," 8–35; John McCall, "Dancing the Past: Experiencing Historical Knowledge in Ohafia, Nigeria," *Passages* (Evanston, IL: Northwestern University Program of African Studies, 1993), 6.

42.   McCall, *Dancing Histories*, 73.

43.   Forde and Jones, *Ibo and Ibibio*, 9–10, 52; Basden, *Niger Ibos*, 268; Mayne, "Intelligence Report," 39.

44.   Njoku, *Ohafia*, 15; Azuonye, "Narrative War Songs," 22; Abasiattai, *Akwa Ibom*, 50.

45. Nsugbe, *Ohaffia*, 116–18. The Afikpo-Igbo society, which shares a boundary with the Biase ethnic group, also had a stronger matrilineage system than other Igbo societies. Simon Ottenberg described the Afikpo as a double-descent Igbo society as opposed to a patrilineal society. See Ottenberg, *Double Descent*; David Uru Iyam, *The Broken Hoe: Cultural Reconfiguration in Biase Southeast Nigeria* (Chicago: University of Chicago Press, 1995), 29–32.

46. Nsugbe, *Ohaffia*, 90–115.

47. Mbah, "Emergent Masculinities," 123–32.

48. Mayne, "Intelligence Report," 47; Nsugbe, *Ohaffia*, 16–18.

49. Njoku, *Ohafia*, 67; Azuonye, "Heroic Age," 9; Nsugbe, *Ohaffia*; Stella Attoe, *A Federation of the Biase People: Origin and Development of Biase Ethnicity, 1750–1950* (Enugu: Harris Publishers, 1990); S. O. Jaja, E. O. Erim, and Bassey W. Andah, eds., *History and Culture of the Upper Cross River* (Enugu: Harris Publishers, 1990); Iyam, *Broken Hoe*, 4, 29–32; Abasiattai, *Akwa Ibom*, 8–11, 27–40, 48; Sandy O. Onor, *The Ejagham Nation in the Cross River Region of Nigeria* (Ibadan: Kraft Books, 1994), 13–31; Kannan K. Nair, *Politics and Society in South Eastern Nigeria, 1841–1906* (London: Frank Cass, 1972), 3–4.

50. Azuonye, "Heroic Age," 9.

51. Nsugbe, *Ohaffia*, 18.

52. Nsugbe, *Ohaffia*, 21; Azuonye, "Heroic Age," 18.

53. Obuba, *History and Culture*, 4; Ndukwe, interview; Mr. Arunsi Kalu, interview by the author; Chief Eke Emetu, interview by the author; Chief Emeh Okonkwo, interview by the author; Chief Kalu Awa Kalu, interview by the author; Chief K. K. Owen, interview by the author; Chief Olua Iro Kalu, interview by the author.

54. See Mbah, "Emergent Masculinities," chap. 2; Mayne, "Intelligence Report," 18–21.

55. Nsugbe, *Ohaffia*, 112.

56. These oral traditions are documented in Mbah, "Emergent Masculinities," chap. 2.

57. Michel Foucault, *Discipline and Punish: The Birth of the Prison* (New York: Vintage Books, 1995).

58. Njoku, *Ohafia*, 68.

59. Chief Kalu Awa Kalu, interview by the author; Otta and Uka, joint interview; Ndukwe, interview; Mr. Arunsi Kalu, interview by the author; Chief Eke Emetu Kalu, interview by the author; Chief Emeh Okonkwo, interview by the author; Chief Olua Iro Kalu, interview by the author; Ezie-Nwami Ucha Oji Iwe of Elu Village and her cabinet, group interview by the author; Ikpirikpe Ndi Inyom of Akanu Village, group interview by the author, 3 November 2011; Mecha Ukpai Akanu, Ezie-Ogo of Amangwu Village, and members of the men's court, group interview by the author.

60. Frederick Cooper, "Conflict and Connection: Rethinking Colonial African History," *American Historical Review* 99 (1994): 1535, 1544, has observed that individuals were remaking the meanings of institutions even as they used them. This is what Franz Boas called the "genius of the people." See L. L. Langness, *The Study of Culture* (Novato,

CA: Chandler and Sharp, 2005), 22; Claude Lévi-Strauss, *Structural Anthropology*, vol. 2 (New York: Basic Books, 1976), 4; Adam Kuper, *Anthropology and Anthropologists: The Modern British School* (London: Routledge and Kegan Paul, 1996), 47–48; A. R. Radcliffe-Brown, *A Natural Science of Society* (Chicago: University of Chicago Press, 1957), 45, 55.

61. Nsugbe, *Ohaffia*, 122–23; Otta and Uka, joint interview; Chief Kevin Ukiro, interview by the author; Mr. Arunsi Kalu, interview by the author.

62. Mbah, "Emergent Masculinities," chaps. 2, 3, and 4.

63. Nsugbe, Njoku, and Azuonye concur that the Ohafia-Igbo adapted the better-organized age-grade system of their non-Igbo Cross River neighbors during the "heroic age" (1650–1850). Afigbo, *Ropes of Sand*, 22; Njoku, *Ohafia*, 59; M. M. Green, *Ibo Village Affairs: Chiefly with Reference to the Village of Umueke Agbaja* (London: Frank Cass, 1947), 25. For a detailed study of the Ohafia age-grade political system, see Mbah, "Emergent Masculinities," chap. 2.

64. Njoku, *Ohafia*, 26; Nsugbe, *Ohaffia*, 58; Ndukwe, interview; Mr. Arunsi Kalu, interview by the author, 15 August 2011, Amangwu Village, Ohafia.

65. Uduma O. Uduma, *The People of Ohafia Ezema* (Aba, Nigeria: Arinson Publishers, 2007), 54; Uka, "A Note," 77; Robert S. Rattray, *Ashanti Law and Constitution* (Oxford: Clarendon Press, 1929), 11–13.

66. Mama Docas Kalu and Mama Mary Ezera, joint interview by the author, 10 August 2010, Elu Village; Nmia Nnaya Agbai, interview by the author, 18 August 2011, Elu Village; Ikpirikpe Ndi Inyom of Akanu Village, group interview by the author, 3 November 2011, Akanu Village; Mr. Arunsi Kalu, interview by the author; Mama Orie Emeh and Chief Mrs. Grace Ojieke, interview by the author, 18 August 2011, Elu Village.

67. Njoku, *Ohafia*, 28.

68. Onwuka E. Oti, *The Age Grade System and Otomu Ceremony in Ohafia* (Aba: EMS Corporate, 2007), 11; Mbah, "Emergent Masculinities," chap. 2.

69. Kamene Okonjo, "The Dual Sex Political System in Operation: Igbo Women and Community Politics in Midwestern Nigeria," in *Women in Africa*, ed. Nancy Hafkin and Edna Bay (Stanford, CA: Stanford University Press, 1976); Ifi Amadiume, *Male Daughters, Female Husbands: Gender and Sex in an African Society* (London: Zed Books, 1989); Njoku, *Ohafia*, 24; Nwando Achebe, *Farmers, Traders, Warriors and Kings: Female Power and Authority in Northern Igboland, 1900–1960* (Portsmouth, NH: Heinemann, 2005), 164–71.

70. For endogamous marriage practices in the Ohafia patrilineages, see Nsugbe, *Ohaffia*, 72–79. In Ohafia, only the matrilineage is exogamous.

71. Mbah, "Emergent Masculinities," chap. 2.

72. Nsugbe, *Ohaffia*, 68; Njoku, *Ohafia*, 24; Ikpirikpe Ndi Inyom of Akanu, group interview.

73. Njoku, *Ohafia*, 24.

74. Ikpirikpe Ndi Inyom of Akanu, group interview.

75. Georges Balandier, *Political Anthropology*, trans. A. M. Sheridan Smith (London: Penguin, 1970), 36.

76. The term "coercive influence" is from Nina Mba, *Nigerian Women Mobilized:*

Women's Political Activity in Southern Nigeria, 1900–1965 (Berkeley, CA: Institute of International Studies, University of California, 1982), vii–viii.

77.   Nnenna Emeri, group interview with Ikpirikpe Ndi Inyom of Akanu Village; Ezie-nwami Ogbonne Kalu, interview by the author, 17 November 2011, Uduma Ukwu Village; and Ezie-nwami Mmia Abali of Eziafor Village, interview by the author, 17 December 2011.

78.   Judith Van Allen, "'Sitting on a Man': Colonialism and the Lost Political Institutions of Igbo Women," *Canadian Journal of African Studies* 6 (1972): 165–81; Shirley Ardener, "Sexual Insult and Female Militancy," in *Perceiving Women*, ed. Shirley Ardener (New York: John Wiley, 1975), 29–53.

79.   Mayne, "Intelligence Report," 23–24.

80.   Njoku, *Ohafia*, 25.

81.   Nmia Nnaya Agbai, interview by the author.

82.   Ikpirikpe Ndi Inyom of Akanu Village, group interview.

83.   Julie Livingston, *Debility and the Moral Imagination in Botswana* (Bloomington: Indiana University Press, 2005), 1, 2, 6. For a comparable case, see Victor Turner, *Schism and Continuity in an African Society: A Study of Ndembu Village Life* (London: Manchester University Press, 1957), 161–69.

84.   For detailed discussion of these rituals, see Mbah, "Emergent Masculinities," chap. 3.

85.   See Mbah, "Emergent Masculinities," chaps. 1–2.

86.   Ikpirikpe Ndi Inyom of Akanu Village, interview; Otta and Uka, joint interview; Chief Kevin Ukiro, interview by the author, 10 August 2010, Asaga Village, Ohafia; Njoku, *Ohafia*, 26.

87.   See Mbah, "Emergent Masculinities," 89–149, for discussion of *ikwu* and *ududu*.

88.   Mbah, "Emergent Masculinities," chap. 5.

89.   Mr. Arunsi Kalu, interview by the author; Nmia Nnaya Agbai, interview by the author; Obuba, *History and Culture*, 19–20. See also Karen E. Flint, *Healing Traditions: African Medicine, Cultural Exchange, and Competition in South Africa, 1820–1948* (Athens: Ohio University Press, 2008), 37–89; Livingston, *Debility*, 64–106.

90.   Mr. Davidson Kalu Oki, interview by the author; Dibia Kalu Uko, interview by the author; Ndukwe Otta and Uduma Uka, joint interview by author, 16 September 2011, Asaga Village, Ohafia; Chief Dr. (Dibia) Azueke Kalu, interview by author, 22 September 2011, Okon; elders of Nde Nbila compound, interview by the author, 15 September 2011, Okon; elders of Nde Oka compound, interview by the author, 14 and 15 September 2011, Okon.

91.   Jean Davison, *Gender, Lineage, and Ethnicity in Southern Africa* (Boulder, CO: Westview, 1997), 50.

92.   See Mbah, "Emergent Masculinities," chap. 3, for these traditions, which served to (1) make sense of a situation whereby the first settlers lost their political authority to a second group of later migrants into the region, (2) justify a history in which a group of people who were originally not Igbo and not of the *mben* (the core of Ohafia original migrants and settlers in the region) stock became legitimate Ohafia citizens, and (3) to

emphasize the indispensable significance of the *dibia* institution to the society's welfare. Dibia Agwu Arua, interview by the author, 4 August 2010, Okon Village, Ohafia; Mr. Davidson Kalu Oki, interview by the author, 5 August 2010, Okon Village, Ohafia; Dibia Kalu Uko, interview by the author; Dibia Uche Dimgba, interview by the author, 22 September 2011, Okon Village, Ohafia.

93. The social performance of ufiem among hunters required that after a hunter had killed a wild animal he presented parts of the kill to the various patrilineage compounds in his village in order of lineage seniority, thereby validating his social belongingness and the historical order of lineage seniority. Nna Kalu Awa, interview by the author, 26 November 2011, Amuma Village; Chief Torti Kalu, interview by the author, 26 November 2011, Amuma; Mr. Nsi Kalu, interview by the author, 26 November 2011, Amuma; Obuba, *History and Culture*, 22.

94. Obuba, *History and Culture*, 26; Chief K. K. Owen, interview by the author; Nna Agbai Ndukwe, interview by the author; Chief Eke Emetu Kalu, interview by the author; Chief Emeh Okonkwo, interview by the author.

95. Dibia Kalu Uko, interview by the author; elders of Nde Odo compound, Akanu Village, group interview with the author, 2 November 2011, Akanu Village, Ohafia.

96. Chief Eke Emetu Kalu, interview by the author; Ottenberg, *Double Descent*, 193, 197–98.

97. Otta and Uka, joint interview.

98. Otta and Uka, joint interview.

99. Ottenberg, *Double Descent*, 147ff.

100. Chief Oluka Mba, interview by the author, 3 November 2011, Nde-Ibe Village, Ohafia; Mr. E. I. Udensi of Eziukwu compound, 5 September 2011, interview by the author, Okagwe Village, Ohafia, Local Government Council Office, Ebem; Chief Kalu Awa Kalu, interview by the author; elders of Nde Odo compound, group interview with the author; Njoku, *Ohafia*, 29.

101. Mbah, "Emergent Masculinities," chap. 4; Ifemesia, *Traditional Humane Living*, 93; "Okonko Club: Activity of," File No. 8/8/433, RIV PROF. (Cross Rivers Province), Nigerian National Archives Enugu (NAE).

102. Patrick U. Nwosu, "The Age of Cultural Hybridisation: A Case Study of Okonko Society vis-à-vis Christianity in Igboland," *Anthropologist* 12, no. 3 (2010): 162.

103. "Okonko Club: Activity of." For a detailed discussion of ogaranya, see Mbah, "Emergent Masculinities," chaps. 4 and 5.

104. Njoku, *Ohafia*, 30; Obuba Igu, *The Advent of Catholicism in Umuahia Diocese: The Ohafia Experience* (Umuahia, Nigeria: Felly, 2005), 50. For a detailed discussion of structural lineage oppositions, see Mbah, "Emergent Masculinities," chap. 2; Ottenberg, *Double Descent*, 147–48, 192–202. For similar discussion of the patriarchal role of patrilineage male elders in sons' initiations, see Basden, *Among the Ibos*, 240–42, on analysis of iba na maw and ikpu ani.

105. Simon Ottenberg, "Ohafiia: A Matrilineal Ibo People by Philip O. Nsugbe," *Africa: Journal of the International African Institute* 46, no. 3 (1976): 296.

106. Ndukwe, interview.

107. Onwuka Njoku, interview by the author, 12 July 2010, History Department, University of Nigeria Nsukka.

108. Otta and Uka, joint interview; Nna Agbai Ndukwe, interview by the author; Godwin Nwankwo Uko, Ezie-Ogo of Amankwu Village and his cabinet members, group interview by the author; Anaso Awalekwa, Ezie-Ogo of Ndea-Nku Village and members of the men's court, group interview by the author.

109. Njoku, *Ohafia*, 54.

110. John McCall, "The Atlantic Slave Trade and the Ohafia Warrior Tradition: Global Forces and Local Histories," in *Repercussions of the Atlantic Slave Trade: The Interior of the Bight of Biafra and the African Diaspora*, ed. Carolyn Brown and Paul Lovejoy (Trenton, NJ: African World Press, 2010), 75–76.

111. McCall, *Dancing Histories*, 65.

112. McCall, *Dancing Histories*, 63.

113. Azuonye, "Narrative War Songs," 50–52; Nsugbe, *Ohaffia*, 34.

114. Azuonye, "Heroic Age," 23.

115. Mbah, "Emergent Masculinities," chap. 5.

116. Elders of Nde Odo compound, Akanu Village, group interview by the author.

117. Nsugbe, *Ohaffia*, 49–51.

118. Ottenberg, *Double Descent*, 25–93, 192–93; Mbah, "Emergent Masculinities," 214–19.

119. Mama Orie Emeh and Chief Mrs. Grace Ojieke, interview by the author; Mama Docas Kalu and Mama Mary Ezera, group interview by the author; Chief Kevin Ukiro, interview by the author; Ndukwe, interview; Mr. Arunsi Kalu, interview by the author; Chief Eke Emetu Kalu, interview by the author; Chief Kalu Awa Kalu, interview by the author; Chief K. K. Owen, interview by the author; Chief Olua Iro Kalu, interview by the author.

10

//

Shaming Men, Performing Power

Female Authority in Zimbabwe and Tanzania on the Eve of Colonial Rule

HEIKE I. SCHMIDT

In October 1992, I arranged for a meeting with *muzvare* Muparutsa, senior female member of the Mutasa royal lineage and guardian of the Mahemasimike granite formation and the surrounding area, a spiritual landscape in the Honde Valley, eastern Zimbabwe.[1] Together with Rosemary Muparutsa, a close relative of the muzvare (here meaning daughter of a chief; also chieftainess) whom I had asked to be the go-between, and Mona Lisa Sakarombe, a young woman also of the royal totem and a descendant of a female chief who facilitated my introduction and translations, we ascended Mahemasimike.[2] The elderly *sabhuku* (subchief; pl. *wasabhuku*) Tegwe joined us, showing the way and explaining the sacredness of the site. As we climbed, sabhuku Tegwe emphasized the spiritual prohibitions and mapped a landscape of ancestral graves, mnemotopes of war from the 1970s, and shifting land-use practices due to the ongoing drought. Upon arrival at the muzvare's homestead, I found, to my surprise, that what I had hoped would be a rather intimate first meeting turned out to be an event that took place at her chiefly *dare*, the assembly place under a shade tree, where a small crowd of men and women was already seated, including the subchiefs from the area, who all were male. The male elders decided that the meeting could not commence without soft drinks and sent teenage boys to dash down the hill to the next store at the valley bottom to fetch crates. After their return, panting from exhaustion after their long run, and once the bottles were distributed to everybody's satisfaction, the muzvare appeared from her hut—a tiny, frail elder assisted by two younger women.

The seating arrangement was typical for such an occasion: men on one side, women on the other, women on mats on the ground, the subchiefs on stools, other male elders also somewhat elevated on tree trunks, young men on the margins on the ground.[3] The muzvare sat with us women on the mats. Each question I asked was translated by Mona Lisa Sakarombe, answered by sabhuku Tegwe or discussed by him and the other wasabhuku, and then passed on by Rosemary Muparutsa to the muzvare to be answered or commented upon. Then, Rosemary Muparutsa repeated the muzvare's words, and so on. After a while I attempted to challenge these filters of articulated meaning and was unexpectedly successful. I asked what age the muzvare was, which caused the men to laugh and shake their heads at such an obviously useless question. But the muzvare, ignoring the chain of communication, piped up and said proudly, "My mother was four months pregnant with me the last time the *madzviti* raided this area!"[4] This reference to invading warriors from the Gaza state in today's Mozambique dates muzvare Muparutsa's birth to 1888 or 1889.[5] She continued to talk of her life as a muzvare. She explained that she had never been married. She used to have a big herd of livestock, and in the evening when the boys returned from grazing her animals, she would watch the boys and choose the finest looking to spend the night with her. At that explanation the men lowered their heads and shook them in horror. The old woman chuckled and pointed a rather long, bony finger at an elder, explaining that he was wearing a red kerchief that indicated he suffered from age-related impotence. She continued: "And that one too! Aaaaaand that one!" The women and young men struggled to keep their composure, while the older men snickered at those identified but also looked deeply worried, because they feared she might go on.

The gendered shaming performed by muzvare Muparutsa on the occasion of the interview significantly shifted the discursive framework and firmly asserted her role as the senior political and spiritual authority.[6] The palpable tension between the muzvare's position of authority and prevailing heteronormativity manifested itself in the ambiguity of the performance of gendered power. In terms of social differentiation, the muzvare's followers were of commoner lineages, while she belonged to the royal family. On the occasion of the meeting, however, the chain of communication, with male elders vetting questions and answers, provided a setup that left control with the men. This was further embodied by the spatial articulation of status hierarchies in the seating arrangement. According to the vernacular understanding of showing respect toward another person, this may be expressed through keeping one's head lower; hence, children, youths, and women sit on the ground, while men sit elevated, and women are expected to serve food, their heads lowered, and enter a room on their knees. The muzvare, however, while sitting on the ground with the other women, would not entirely put up with such an arrangement. She chose to communicate directly with me, breaking the protocol of rearticulated meaning, and with a tremendous sense of humor, she mocked the men through asserting her control over the sexuality of her male subjects, going as far as directly shaming some of the elders.[7] Red, understood to be a spiritual color, is to be worn by male elders to signify old age impotence, but it is not to be talked about. Significantly, the wasabhuku used the occasion of the meeting to initiate a court case in which they challenged her recent decisions regarding land allocation. Muzvare Muparutsa presided. During the interview she had taken control and shamed the elders, who now addressed her as *changamire*, an honorary title typically reserved for royal men. The muzvare in turn clapped her hands in greeting and affirmation like a man, still sitting on the ground, yet also embodying manliness. After much deliberation she closed the case with a simple, "I have decided," confirming her earlier directives. At least at that meeting she was not further challenged.

The significance of this at first sight seemingly trivial episode for the discussion of gender, power, and ethnicity lies in two aspects. First, hierarchies of difference and entitlement to resources and prestige were determined by one's totem, inherited patrilineally, drawing the line between royals (with the totem *shumba*, lion) and commoners (with a range of totems). The ethnic identity of being Manyika, in contrast, tribalized during the colonial period, spanned articulations of differentiation in the rural areas, provided a sense of belonging, and has tended to remain inclusive to this day, both for women and men.[8] Second, what stands out is the performativity of gendered power and the embodiment of gender relations through public shaming, both of which in this case are enshrined in kinship and not ethnic terms.

This chapter takes a comparative approach to the study of eastern Zimbabwe and southwestern Tanzania during the late nineteenth and early twentieth centuries. It focuses on royal women who significantly challenged gender normativity through performing power vis-à-vis their subject populations and through their roles within the polity. In Zimbabwe, power relations between ruler and subject population were articulated in terms of kinship; in contrast, in Tanzania, power relations were articulated in terms of ethnicity.

Any study of elite women by definition cannot be representative for their society. However, a strong voice, asserted by female elders, is not uncommon either in Zimbabwe or in Tanzania.[9] It can be argued that as much as conflict and dispute, especially in the arenas of court hearings and petitions, may have been the exception rather than the rule, they still have served as crucial pathways for historians to gain an understanding of everyday negotiations of identity, power, and status.[10] Similarly, elite women's lives provide unusual insight into the connections between the moral and political debate over gender, ethnicity, and power in more general terms.[11] The findings presented here challenge the current understanding of the creation of tradition and tribes, which tends to privilege political identities and agency over social cohesion, civic virtue, and belonging, in other words, "political tribalism" over "moral ethnicity," to use the historian John Lonsdale's terminology.[12] There has been a tendency in the existing historiography to reproduce the colonial gaze, which focused on tribalism and expressed an understanding of "primitive societies" determined by tribal identities rooted in traditions based on primordialism and claims of shared descent, societies that were naturally ruled by men with women marginalized. One consequence has been the pronounced silence in the historiography of East and southern Africa on female political authorities and instead a focus on women as (re)producers.[13] What this chapter shows is that in some cases ethnicity, gender, and kinship may be so closely interwoven that, in terms of expressing power differential within a society, they may become coterminous and perhaps even congruent. More specifically, in the two African societies examined, the Mutasa area in Zimbabwe and Ungoni in Tanzania, centralized political power was legitimated through a gendered ideology of kinship and of ethnicity.

This chapter argues that practices of female political authorities publicly shaming men were an effective way of reminding commoners of a chieftainess's royal prerogative and hence of central royal power. The very embodiment of power through women questioned subject masculinity by putting subjects' perception of the male role in society to shame. Shaming hence was a political tool that effectively reproduced royal hegemony in terms of either kinship in eastern Zimbabwe or ethnicity in southern Tanzania.[14] Either way, these women who were born or married into the ruling lineages successfully employed what social anthropologist David Parkin has labeled "semantic creativity," reasoning that "power rests not simply on the acquisition of land and material objects but rather derives from unequal access to semantic creativity, including the capacity to nominate others as equal or unequal."[15] If one follows anthropological debate further, with W. Arens and Ivan Karp's argument that power may be "recognized as a pervasive social resource, which provides the ideological bases for various domestic and public relationships," then at least some of these royal women were indeed linchpins in the political makeup of their societies, as their embodied performance legitimized centralized political power where it mattered most: at the margins, sites of political contestation, and places invested with deep spiritual meaning.[16] The contrasting case studies examined in this chapter demonstrate that it is a fallacy to assume that ethnicity necessarily plays a predominant role in negotiating social differentiation within a given society. In what follows, both case studies will be introduced in turn before some comparative conclusions are drawn.

Chieftainess Muredzwa:
Power and Kinship in Mutasa (Zimbabwe)

In the early 1990s *mambo* (king, paramount ruler) Abishai Mutasa (1982–94) revived the office of female chief in the Mutasa paramountcy in eastern Zimbabwe, and he did so without the knowledge of local government authorities.[17] He emphasized that he had inherited the structures of authority, such as the forty-two chieftaincies and the institution of female political offices, from his "great-grandfather" Tendai and that he thus appointed women to the vacant female chieftaincies in areas where Tendai had prescribed that only women could rule—even when this met with local resistance, as in the case of chieftainess Muredzwa II.[18] Her predecessor Muredzwa was probably born before 1870, and she died in 1949.[19] She was the second of four of mambo Tendai Mutasa's children with his first wife.[20] Her older sister was Chikanga, who was a chieftainess herself, and Chimbadzwa and Kadzima were her younger brothers, both of whom were to rule as mambo.[21] From the late nineteenth century to the height of her struggle against colonial land appropriation, chieftainess Muredzwa carried significant authority among her followers and was the most senior woman in the entire polity. She was the most prominent *ishe* (male or female chief) within the mamboship, she was a *mhondoro* (chiefly spirit medium), and she was to become the most senior woman in the royal lineage (*samukadzi*), which gave her a singularly important role in succession decisions. Muredzwa's life and political standing were unique and yet serve well to illustrate the intersection between gender, chiefly power, and a sense of belonging to the polity that in this case was at best marginally informed by a shared sense of ethnicity. Political and cultural identities were shaped and reworked on a much more local level than the paramountcy, which carries the dynastic name Mutasa and not the ethnic label Manyika. Manyika denotes the local Shona dialect and is the name that became tribalized during the colonial period.

The Mutasa polity had gained geopolitical importance in the late nineteenth century as Portugal and the Moçambique Company, on the one hand, and Cecil John Rhodes's British South Africa Company (BSAC) and British interests, on the other, competed over the area and eventually delineated the colonial border between Southern Rhodesia and Portuguese East Africa, which severed a smaller part of the Mutasa area when it became Portuguese territory. With the loss of its political independence, the mambo became a colonial chief who was denied special status within the colony as "king" or even "paramount chief," a practice that continued with political independence in 1980. Against the backdrop of the European scramble over Africa and competition by other African polities, mambo Tendai attempted to stabilize hegemony by drastically raising the number of his chieftaincies to forty-two, including at least ten chieftaincies, or almost one-quarter of all offices, reserved for women only to rule.[22] Tendai apparently believed that a gubernatorial system of trusted followers would both guarantee political stability in the polity and be an effective defense mechanism against intruders.[23] He either appointed female royals to rule in their own right in chieftaincies he created or assigned the women to the areas of warrior chiefs where the woman's relationship with the chief was more ambiguous. In the latter case, deserving young men of commoner lineages provided military protection of the frontier, and the role of female royals was apparently to balance the men's power by representing the mambo through the women's kinship status and spiritual authority.[24] By the late nineteenth century, most, and possibly all, mediums of mhondoro were women. Cosmologically, the role of medium is to be the spirit's mere vessel when the spirit manifests himself or herself, but mediums and their attendants are in fact regarded as ritual experts and may be of great importance to the social well-being of rural communities. Muzvare Muparutsa, for example, provided spiritual protection to fighters in Zimbabwe's liberation war of the 1970s.[25]

In the Mutasa polity, the office of female chief contrasted with that of male chief in significant aspects. While male chieftaincies are hereditary offices, there is no line of descent for female chiefs, as each individual is selected by the mambo from among the royal lineage, while it is understood that the specific *dunhu* (area of a chieftaincy) can only be ruled by a woman. Tendai chose to appoint prepubescent girls, who were prohibited from marrying but expected to have children. The biological father of the female chief's children, who was usually from the subject population where she was posted, was not to be known, and chieftainesses were the sole exception where the totem was passed from mother to child instead of father to child. Both sons and daughters were then of the royal totem, as was their mother, and they were nominally understood to be the mambo's children.[26] Evidence suggests that Tendai chose females for office who were spiritual authorities or showed signs of becoming so, as was certainly the case with three chieftainesses: his daughters, Muredzwa and Chikanga, and also Muparutsa.[27] During the colonial period, some female chiefs married, but the arrangement was matrilocal, as an elder explained: "Because she is a chief, she cannot be taken to another land."[28] Moreover, no bridewealth was to be paid by the groom's family, according to another elder: "If you want to marry her, you do not pay *chuma—roora* [bride-price]—but you are made a servant to that woman. She cannot be married and have a wedding. If she takes over the chieftainship, whoever wants to marry her has to become her *muranda*."[29] Muranda translates as "servant or subject of a chief who is not of the royal lineage."[30] Marrying a chieftainess is said to be unpopular with men: "A woman who is chosen to be mambo [here: ruler] is not easy to marry!"[31] During restoration in the early 1990s, mambo Abishai Mutasa adapted the qualifications for office to current times by choosing postmenopausal women, arguing that one could no longer appoint young girls or expect a woman to refrain from marrying.[32]

Looking back to the eve of colonial rule, an argument in favor of female officeholders was that females were less likely to rebel against or break away from centralized authority because they could not fulfill the role of military leader or succeed to the throne.[33] Occurrences in the late nineteenth century undermine this contention. The female chiefs Muredzwa and Chikanga left the mamboship temporarily with their brother Chimbadzwa in protest against their father, Tendai. They had fallen out with the mambo after the death of their mother, Tendai's chief wife, in 1896. They accused one of the junior wives of being responsible for their mother's death. When Tendai did not agree to punish the accused, the three siblings and five hundred of their followers sought refuge in the neighboring Makombe paramountcy, their father's archrival at the time. They returned the following year.[34] This was a great affront against the mambo for several reasons, most directly because it was an act of disobedience but also because Makombe, whose paramountcy was located in the east and northeast, had been enemy territory for some time. As it has been argued elsewhere, the fallout between Tendai and his chiefly children together with a drought may have culminated in preventing the mambo from participating in the First Chimurenga (1896–97), the anticolonial uprising in the then company-ruled Southern Rhodesia.[35] The incident is significant because it illustrates the importance of the senior royal children in Mutasa, where women's political descent could at times be voiced just as powerfully as that of men. While Chimbadzwa, as the eldest son, was king-designate, his sisters, Chikanga and Muredzwa, were chieftainesses. Both women had been directly appointed by Tendai as part of his attempt to stabilize his realm and were posted almost to create a buffer zone around the polity's heartland. Expecting political loyalty from one's daughters and other female kin may have been an important reason for appointing female authorities, yet other factors must have at least contributed, because such loyalty was not necessarily forthcoming, as the 1896 episode demonstrates.

It is of significance that, after being chosen for office as young girls, female chiefs underwent aspects of the bridal experience in this patrilocal society, where the bride leaves her immediate kin to prove herself with her husband

and in-laws, away from home and without intimates or relatives close by. Growing up and becoming a woman through marriage was a process most women underwent, and it was concomitant to a female chief becoming a figure of authority, depending initially and heavily for advice from her subject population on local matters and guardianship until she could live a full life as a royal ruler over commoner lineages.[36] This ambiguity in the process of gaining authority while already in the position of power is reflected in the usage of the terms *muzvare* and *nehanda*. Muzvare translates not only as "daughter of a chief" and "chieftainess" but also as "unmarried woman," a status that every woman passes through during her lifetime. Carried as a title for political office, muzvare may denote the unique reproductive status of these select women who retained control over their sexuality by choosing their sexual partners and over their offspring because the biological father is unknown. Nehanda may refer to a female chief's subject population and translates as "son-in-law lineage" without an equivalent for male chiefs. The appellation emphasizes at the same time the gendered kinship character of political power and community through the marriage-generated category and also signifies the power differential between royal and commoner.[37]

Mambo Abishai Mutasa as a young boy grew up listening to chieftainess Muredzwa's stories. He emphasized that Muredzwa was not to be toyed with at the apex of her political power: "You know, even the Native Affairs [Department; Native Commissioner's Office], if she came there during those days, they would be very, very scared of her. She was a wild woman! If they *dare* to [say] things that she didn't like, she would even spit on them! Oh, this woman was a rough rider—so to speak."[38] The description "rough rider" was well earned, because early on Muredzwa affronted representatives of the Native Department when the BSAC made the first attempt to collect hut tax in the northern Nyanga portion of the mamboship in 1900 and when land rent was introduced in 1904. With the mamboship split between two districts and in anticipation of resistance against the payments, the native commissioners (NCs) Inyanga and Umtali, together with a small patrol of the British South Africa Police, assembled the political authorities for a two-day meeting in March 1904. With the exception of two officeholders, all 350 chiefs, subchiefs, and their subordinate "kraalheads" attended, albeit with an attitude that was apparently "far from respectful." Spokesperson for the chiefs was Muredzwa, who stated clearly that they had no intention of working for or paying tax to settlers, while taxation by the government was a different matter. With large-scale land alienation already manifest, the chieftainess added that resettlement was only acceptable if that meant staying close to the home area.[39] What ensued was a protracted battle in which she fought to retain control of her dunhu. Amidst Muredzwa's struggle for her land, she proved herself to be a worthy patron of her subjects in other aspects also. She used to kill game with a gun given to her by her father and distribute the meat among her people.[40] In times of famine, she used cattle from her large herd as drought relief. But she was also feared. Many people worked in her fields, a prerogative of male and female chiefs, and had to pay fines of food and cattle when they broke the rules of her land.[41]

The struggle over Muredzwa's land culminated in the mid-1930s after the Rhodesia Wattle Company bought about 10,500 acres to establish a forestry plantation, most of which was part of the chieftainess's dunhu.[42] When the colonial authorities instructed her to move because her area had been designated commercial land, Muredzwa was the only chief in the area who absolutely refused to abandon her land. Initially, the wattle estate manager conducted meetings with the elders and offered a labor agreement. Such arrangements, common at the time, allowed households to remain on the plantation and to cultivate limited areas of land if, in turn, the adult male members of the household worked at least 150 days per year for the company.[43] After several unsuccessful mediation attempts with the local population, sometime in 1936 the NC finally called a meeting, which was attended by the manager of the Wattle Company and the assistant chief NC, who addressed the chiefs and headmen, insisting on the labor agreement if they wanted to avoid resettlement. An elder recalled: "So assistant chief [native] commissioner told the gathering: 'Now you people, this area was bought by Wattle Company.' And then, 'You people will be moved sometime. You agree?' And then the chiefs said, 'Yes, we agree.' But ishe Muredzwa refused, she said, she stood up and said, 'I don't agree—to say my place has been bought!'"[44]

Muredzwa is remembered to have addressed the estate manager directly: "'What are you saying? You want me to move? I'm not moving! You are moving!' So the white man said, 'Oh, you're talking nothing! What power has she?'"[45] Soon the settlers learned to appreciate this woman's power. What followed was Muredzwa's forced removal and that of her followers, which, however, did not end her resistance. She is remembered to have manifested her spiritual authority. When the Wattle Company cleared the land, built housing for the management, and began planting, Muredzwa, medium of an ancestral lion spirit, mhondoro, called upon the ancestors, who appeared as lions. Two varying accounts speak of her spiritual prowess. Mambo Abishai Mutasa recalled: "In the night he [the estate manager] was there with his wife and his servants. The same night . . . the house was surrounded by lions. They didn't sleep that day, thinking the lion may probably break in. . . . In the morning he just disappeared."[46] The second account of Muredzwa's spiritual power is less dramatic. A man from the affected area emphasizes her success in restricting the land alienation:

There were lions who passed by. They [estate workers] got three lions. They [the workers] passed there at night, just about seven or half past seven. And when they stopped, the lions stopped also, looking at each other. Then they said, "You know, the problem is that woman, that woman ishe Muredzwa, she is causing all that." Then this man [the manager] said, "I want to shoot them!" "Oh, please, don't. Don't do that, because if you shoot, there will be a lot of problems. Don't do anything, leave it!" Well, they left. He [the manager] said, "But what's the problem? How can the chief bring lions and all that?" They said, "That's what we African people believe in, that she was responsible to bring the lions."

Then the next morning, they talked about it. The interpreter told the Wattle Company manager, "Isn't the area you've got enough? Because it's nonsense to have all this. We won't work well, because the lions will hunt us." So this man agreed, he said, "OK, let's make a new plan. The road is the boundary." They agreed.[47]

Even though the plantation area was apparently somewhat reduced in size, when planting at the wattle plantation went ahead, the trees withered, a development believed by those in the area to have been caused by Muredzwa.

Muredzwa's spiritual authority informed mambo Abishai Mutasa's choice of her successor, Muredzwa II, at least in part because the chieftainess's spirit was in the process of manifesting itself at the time of her successor's installation. Meanwhile, some of her subject people claimed that the severe 1991–92 drought was due to Muredzwa II's improper installation over the male chieftaincy Nyamaende, whose officeholders had been responsible for the rainmaking rituals.[48] The original Muredzwa was not a spirit medium who could call the rains to come, a *mhondoro remvura*, but she was spiritual guardian of her dunhu, and her spiritual powers were associated with rain, as reported by the Methodist missionaries: "Whenever she left for Bingaguru [the mamboship headquarters] rain would follow behind to rub off her footprints so that enemies would not follow."[49] She has been described as "rain queen," likely linked with some concept of fertility.[50] Muredzwa was perceived at the time and is remembered as particularly powerful today because she combined a striking personality with political and spiritual authority, all of which set her apart from the male rulers in the Mutasa paramountcy. Her father's initial trust in anointing her as chieftainess, the spiritual authority she acquired during the course of her life, and eventually her status as senior woman of the royal lineage were all specific to female authorities only. In the end, Muredzwa's political role was eventually as much challenged by her experiences as a mother as by the imposition of colonial rule.

Muredzwa gave birth to thirteen children, of whom only four survived: her firstborn was Mukonyerwa, a daughter; then she bore twins three times and triplets once, all of whom were killed, as was the custom with multiple births, which are common in her line of the royal lineage. Her second surviving child was Chirema (Josuah); then she had a daughter called Murenjekwa (Theresa) and finally another daughter, Nenhu (Dorcas). It is not known what impact it had upon her that nine of her children were killed.[51] Muredzwa's youngest child, her daughter Nenhu (ca. 1902–72), was born with a deformed body, remained small, and could not walk. The chieftainess consulted healers throughout the area, but to no avail. Then, in 1918 the Great Revival of the American Methodist Episcopal Church occurred. It spread from its headquarters at Old Mutare Mission in the Mutasa area: small groups of believers went to the villages to convert people and demonstrate the experience of possession by the Holy Spirit. Apparently, John Cheke and David Mandisodza, two of the revivalists, convened a meeting at the chieftainess's homestead, while healing occurred nightly among believers who prayed in the hills. One man sat on each side of Muredzwa's daughter, and John Cheke shouted in his prayer: "Dorcas, in Jesus's name, you rise and walk!" Nenhu rose and walked upright for the first time in her life, albeit with difficulty and leaning on a stick. Nenhu was then baptized Dorcas and became a dedicated churchgoer for the rest of her life.[52] At least three of Muredzwa's four children converted to Christianity. According to church accounts, Muredzwa immediately dropped her ancestral beliefs on that occasion, even though she had resisted conversion to Christianity before. This is probably an exaggeration, because Muredzwa had already allowed her children to attend mission schools before 1918. Her firstborn daughter, Mukonyerwa, was one of the brides in the spectacular "Quintet Wedding" of four Christian couples at Old Mutare Mission in 1906, which served to demonstrate the early influence of the mission church at a time of still low conversion rates.[53] What followed Nenhu's healing was Muredzwa's slow rapprochement to Christianity, which culminated in her losing her spiritual powers.[54] Later, between 1949 and 1951, the colonial government enforced the eviction of Muredzwa's followers from their land, but she had already left a few years earlier, after she had resigned from her office.[55]

In the last decade of her life, Muredzwa was neither a chieftainess nor a spirit medium any longer. But she was still the senior female of the royal lineage, the samukadzi. As such, she commanded great authority in family matters, which in particular referred to gender relations within the royal lineage. Hence, mambo Mutasa explained, the samukadzi is the only person the ruler has to listen to. Muredzwa now lived with the Chimbadzwa family, headed by her younger brother's son, in the heartland of the polity. Throughout the century the Chimbadzwa house had put forth a claim to rule. But they kept being turned down on the grounds that Chimbadzwa, Tendai's firstborn son, did not constitute a line of chiefly descent because he had not ruled himself. Chimbadzwa had been acting mambo when his father was old but had pre-deceased him. The claim of this house relied to a great extent on Muredzwa's support.[56] The last succession dispute in her lifetime occurred in 1948. At that point she was simply ignored by the elders and the representatives of the district administration.[57] Muredzwa was now an old woman who no longer held spiri-tual or political authority, a shadow of the powerful spokesperson she used to be. Muredzwa died in 1949. At the peak of her power, chieftainess Muredzwa was an imposing figure for her family, her followers, the settlers, and the colonial administration. It might well be due to her "rough rider" appearance and her direct and at times confrontational approach that more subtle nuances of every-day practices of power and authority are not transmitted in written sources or personal and social memory.

In the same way that Muparutsa shamed her male followers and performed power in a gendered manner in the 1990s, a hundred years earlier Muredzwa and other chieftainesses had also controlled their own sexuality and that of their young male subject population. In addition, being nehanda (a member of the commoner lineage) entailed a variety of responsibilities for young men, including herding the chieftainess's livestock and serving as warriors and body-guards. Muredzwa, Chikanga, and their aunt Nyakuwanikwa, mambo Bvumbi's daughter,[58] are reported to have moved with fifty to sixty young men when they traveled. According to oral tradition, Nyakuwanikwa even led her warriors into a battle for the mamboship.[59] A Victorian description from the early 1890s by British nurses of their encounters with Nyakuwanikwa and Chikanga empha-sizes further their bending of gender normativity and command over their sub-ject male population. The nurses describe Nyakuwanikwa's visit: "She accepted tea, passing her mug, after drinking, to the two men who sat behind her. These were two of her husbands. We were told that she had several, whom she divorced or knocked on the head as seemed most convenient."[60] On another occasion, Muredzwa's older sister, Chikanga, returned a visit to the nurses accompanied by sixty to seventy men, albeit of all ages, one carrying her baby. The nurses report that she sat elevated while the men sat on the ground and that she had one of them taste the offered coffee, which she then declined. As had her half-sister Nyakuwanikwa before, she asked for alcohol, and, according to the nurses, "we told her that 'firewater' was the drink of men, not women, but we could not make her see the force of the argument."[61] Occasionally, Chikanga, who proceeded to drink "mugsfull" of port wine, which the nurses removed to instead appease the chieftainess with sugar, would interrupt the goings-on when her child cried and briefly leave for breastfeeding outside, where the child had remained with her male bodyguards.[62]

Clearly, the chieftainesses perturbed the British nurses with their power over young men and gender-ambiguous practices, such as demanding alcohol to drink, something that was unthinkable against the backdrop of both Victorian and indigenous gender normativity. Judging from her grandson's memories of just how formidable Muredzwa was when she visited the polity's headquarters, it is difficult to assume anything but that the chieftainesses left a deep impression wherever they set foot. It was their entourage of men who enacted submission through gendered body politics, from controlling young men's sexuality, to carrying a woman's child and handing it to the royal woman for breastfeeding, to inverting the gendered seating arrangement, with the chieftainess elevated over her followers. Such gendered performances resulted in public shaming of male commoners, which in turn daily delineated status hierarchies along the dividing line of lineage membership and hence asserted centralized power. This practice of rule proved stable not only because an ethnic or status label that marks marginality could be disputed but also because kin relations, once established, are difficult for an entire population to challenge, especially when royal privilege is claimed by blood descent.[63] The next section examines southwestern Tanzania, which provides a contrasting example to the Mutasa paramountcy.

Chieftainess Namabengo: Power and Ethnicity in Ungoni (Tanzania)

The two Ngoni polities in southwestern Tanzania, Njelu and Mshope, which date to the mid-nineteenth century, came about concomitantly and coexisted peacefully. Sharing the same ethnicity and historical roots, the two states, each headed by a *nkosi* (king), articulated power very similarly, establishing the rule of an ethnically defined Ngoni political and military elite, which was composed of royal and nonroyal lineages, over the local non-Ngoni populations. Most oral and some written sources from Njelu claim that women in positions of political power were a phenomenon specific to Mshope. Njelu elders tend to mock Mshope for this to this day, and one man rather derisively compared Mshope governance to colonial rule, which permitted women to rule.[64] However, written evidence contradicts this view. The earliest German source on political organization in Ungoni is a report by Tom von Prince, officer in the colonial forces, based on conversations with chief Fussi, a brother of nkosi Mharule (1874–89), and conversations with Rashid, the most prominent locally based coastal slave trader. Prince found that the nkosi attempted to stabilize his rule by settling his seventy "wives" (probably wives and female members of the royal lineage) into four strategically located villages, each presided over by one of his senior wives. The settlements in turn were overseen by four major *manduna* (generals). These female authorities were responsible for brokering communication between the nkosi and his military leaders.[65] The sources on the area reveal a broader picture of the early twentieth century, which saw a range of roles for royal women, who held positions of power and authority, including that of female chief. In a society where ethnic identity was defined male, as will be shown below, nevertheless, at least some royal women had the opportunity to enact centralized power in their own right. One of these women was Namabengo, a member of the royal lineage who became a powerful chieftainess, successfully negotiating the transition period from the intensification of the slave trade in the second half of the nineteenth century to colonial conquest and the establishment of a colonial administration in the area.

In the mid-nineteenth century, initially three Ngoni groups, each under military leadership, settled in southwestern Tanzania after their migration, part of the so-called *mfecane*, the early nineteenth-century period of upheaval in northeastern South Africa.[66] During the early transition from migration to settlement, Zulu Gama and Mbonani Tawete assassinated the third leader, Mputa Maseko, in the early 1860s and established two coterminous kingdoms: the southern Njelu and the northern Mshope polity in an area that became known as Ungoni.[67] In a process that evolved between the mid and late nineteenth century, the strict military and centralized political organization of the migrant kingdoms under the leadership of their nkosi and manduna changed, as both kingdoms adapted to a sedentary lifestyle. What emerged was a patchwork of power relations between "true Ngoni," the "Ngoni," and their subject people, the *sutu*, that was negotiated along the axes of gender and age.

Both Ngoni polities rested their livelihood on establishing tribute-paying relationships with local and neighboring societies and on raiding activities, mostly for slaves, as these were slave-owning, slave-raiding, and slave-trading societies. The collective term for all subject people, *sutu*, reflects a Ngoni perspective and is problematic because it does not distinguish between degrees of submission or integration into one or the other of the two multiethnic kingdoms or differentiate between individuals or even societies. The term *sutu* hence encompasses a range of subjects, from followers paying tribute in foodstuffs to slaves living in Ngoni settlements. In contrast, "true Ngoni" and "Ngoni" are identity categories that denote membership in the ruling ethnicity. True Ngoni, an ascribed status, are understood to be survivors of the initial migration from South Africa or their direct descendants through the male line. Ngoni, in contrast, is an acquired status. Any man, including a slave warrior, could become Ngoni if he proved himself to be a valuable member of the community by submitting war booty to the nkosi. Hence, any true Ngoni or Ngoni who distinguished himself in battle could then advance to become a military or political leader.[68] Ngoni civic virtue, the core issue of debate in moral ethnicity, was over questions of masculinity and military prowess, because the exertion of predominantly military power over subject people defined the political character of the Ngoni polities.[69] It is this very essence of Ngoni ethnic identity that made it a male prerogative.

In contrast to men, it appears that women who were integrated into the kingdoms did not have the option of becoming Ngoni in their own right. Instead, sutu women could associate with Ngoni status through seeking male patronage, while their sons and daughters would be Ngoni as defined by their father's ethnicity. Conversely, even women born to a Ngoni father appear to have affirmed their status by marrying a Ngoni man, not least because otherwise their children would have been considered sutu, with a significant impact on their mother's standing. In fact, one elder translated the kiNgoni word for wife, *mfazi*, as "follower of men."[70] The exception regarding the masculine Ngoni ethnic identity were royal women, whose role, status, and practices parallel those of the Mutasa chieftainesses in important ways, although significant differences can be observed. Similar to their counterparts in eastern Zimbabwe, some of these royal women also shamed men and performed power, although in Ungoni the power differential was articulated through ethnicity and gender.

On the eve of colonial rule, royal women in Ungoni occupied a range of politically important roles in the two polities. As in Mutasa, it appears that they qualified for these roles because of their structural position vis-à-vis the king, and some earned the nkosi's trust through strength of character, as was the case with chieftainess Namabengo. Two differences also become apparent in comparison with eastern Zimbabwe. In Ungoni the royal women comprised not only members of the royal lineage but also, significantly, royal wives. Moreover, these women gained power when they were of marriageable age, hence taking on their responsibilities at a stage of their life cycle that commanded some respect, compared to the prepubescent girls in Mutasa.

Among the Ngoni wives whose responsibilities have been recorded is Nyasele, the senior wife of the ruler of Njelu, *mke mkubwa wa nkosi* (Kiswahili, literally, the king's big or important wife). She was the keeper of his ancestral shrine, which appears to have had some significance. The Benedictine father Franziskus Leuthner was responsible for the destruction of the shrine shortly before the outbreak of the Maji Maji War in the area in 1905, and this was most likely the main reason why he was killed and why the mission stations were attacked with such ferocity. The senior wife was also the gatekeeper to the nkosi, as she was to be approached first in order to be granted an audience with him.[71] In Mshope, a particularly formidable woman was apparently the nkosi's mother, the only Ngoni ruler who offered her hospitality to the Benedictine brother Alfons Adams on his travels. Adams found her living in her own settlement,

Gumbiro, and observed that "she exercised considerable influence on the subjects of the king."[72]

In the early twentieth century, between the two polities at least six royal women occupied a range of important political offices.[73] Some presided over their own house, a settlement consisting mostly of slaves, and generated a wider following by collecting food as tribute and redistributing it.[74] These women effectively managed human, environmental, and economic resources crucial to the well-being of the polity—settled slaves who served as agricultural labor and warriors—and they oversaw central production areas. Apparently, there were four of these houses in Njelu and two in Mshope.[75] The evidence is not sufficient to conclude whether there was a range of formal offices available to royal women or whether such articulations of political and spiritual power were more fluid. The latter would, however, be congruent with the overall power structure of the polities. Still, some royal women, such as Namabengo, rose to directly exert political power as chieftainesses.

In short, comparable with the Mutasa area, geopolitical changes (in the case of Ungoni, the transformation from migrant to settled polities) brought forth opportunities of empowerment for some true Ngoni women. One prominent royal woman in Mshope was chieftainess Namabengo. Nkosi Chabruma chose his sister for her strong-willed character, for her leadership qualities, and for cutting an imposing figure.[76] He positioned her in one of the tribute-paying areas, ethnically Ndendeule, one of the strategically most important locations in the entire polity. Her territory was located on the intersection of one of East Africa's major caravan routes, which connected important Indian Ocean coastal trading towns such as Lindi and Mikindani with the far interior and with the border between the two polities. Namabengo's territory was adjacent to *nduna* (military leader or chief) Songea's headquarters, which in the 1890s became the German district capital named after him.[77] Songea formally served Njelu's nkosi but had gained a semiautonomous warlord status by the end of the nineteenth century, commanding five hundred warriors and playing an important role in the raiding and trading activities in the region.[78] Intentionally or not, Namabengo was an important counterpoint to Songea and represented the Mshope kingdom's political, military, and economic interests in the area, facilitated by her oversight of the caravan route, which provided her with detailed knowledge of economic activities in both Mshope and Njelu. In addition, Namabengo enforced the nkosi's rule by collecting tribute from the local Ndendeule population, having them farm on her behalf, and, possibly already before the imposition of colonial rule, recruiting labor for the maintenance of the caravan route.[79] The nkosi also bestowed upon her the right to hold court and to pass sentence against offenders without recourse to him.[80]

Namabengo demonstrated her political cunning during the Maji Maji War of the early colonial period. The insurgency was primarily directed against the unwelcome presence of outsiders, including the colonial state and its representatives, missionaries, and coastal traders. In Ungoni, it was moreover a conflict that young men joined for the opportunity to reinforce their Ngoni identity and advance their status or they could become Ngoni if they could prove their military prowess in combat.[81] When the German counterinsurgency efforts took full effect starting in November 1905, the strategy was one of total war, which meant that every single captured Ngoni leader who was implicated in the insurgency was executed. In the district capital, Songea, about one hundred male elders were hanged on two occasions in the spring of 1906. Major Johannes, in charge of the counterinsurgency campaign, also imposed the death penalty on royal women. Chieftainess Kommandire joined the war when she seized a trader's goods that he had deposited with her. Johannes had her hanged as an active Maji Maji rebel.[82] He did the same with another royal woman, Mkomanile. The *maji* (war medicine) and the call to join the uprising, which started in the eastern section of the colony, were carried by Omari Kinjala to Ungoni in August 1905. Kinjala was a young Ngindo man from an area east of Songea, and he initially approached Nkosi Chabruma through Mkomanile, a female chief and possibly the nkosi's wife. For a short time, Mkomanile played a crucial part in introducing Kinjala and the war medicine to Ungoni.[83] In contrast, Namabengo was the only Ngoni leader who did not take up arms or flee, nor was she executed. Days before the rising, which began in September 1905, she went to the district headquarters with three male chiefs, assuring the colonial officials of their allegiance. Nevertheless, the men joined the war, as most likely did she, considering that the largest battle of the entire war occurred close to her headquarters. Namabengo must have been aware that her brother, nkosi Chabruma, together with Njelu's nkosi, five thousand warriors, and spiritual authorities, assembled at Old Namabengo to gather forces and confront the colonial troops. In fact, it has been suggested that she "offered both moral and material support during the war" to the warriors.[84] This makes it ever more surprising that Namabengo succeeded in convincing the German authorities that she had remained loyal.

Namabengo appears to have been an imposing figure to anybody who encountered her, and shame is a central theme in the personal and social memory of Namabengo's rule among her former subject population. To this day, male Ndendeule elders remember the humiliation of having been subjected by the Wangoni (the plural of Ngoni) and, worse still, by a woman. One elder related that he had been chosen by her with nine other boys and ten girls as her attendants. They were prepubescent and, so he recalled, her bodyguards. They stayed close to her and slept in her hut to protect her from sexual assault. He described her as a harsh woman and remembered how at her homestead she was constantly accompanied by female servants who even had to clean her, using maize cobs, after she defecated. Namabengo did not marry but "ordered *jumbe* [subchiefs]" to bring chosen men to her to have intercourse. He recalled that she had three children, a son and two daughters. As she drank much, she had two servants whose task it was to assist her with breastfeeding when she was in no condition to do so herself. He responded bitterly to the question of whether her servants were slaves: "They called all of us Wandendeule their *watumwa* [Kiswahili, slaves]" and added that Namabengo herself never did anything— no farming, weeding, or cooking.[85] Finally, in 1921, under British rule, she was deposed when the administration became exasperated with her lack of cooperation and her court convictions, which culminated in her guilty verdict for having pimped women to a nearby military camp.[86]

The parallels between Namabengo and the Mutasa chieftainesses are striking. These were women who had control over their own sexuality and they commanded that of their subject (young) male population; they submitted only to their close relative, who was the head of the polity; they did not act according to expected gender norms in terms of gender division of labor and aspects of behavior that marked status, such as the consumption of alcohol. Most importantly, these women embodied centralized power, shaming subject men into submission in daily interactions through their very position and through public performance. One significant difference between Mutasa and Ungoni, however, was that in the Ngoni polities the power differential between these chosen elite women and their subjugate people was expressed in terms of ethnic difference and not in terms of kinship. The specificity of an ethnically and male-defined slave-raiding, slave-trading, and slaveholding Ngoni elite made for a political environment in which female Ngoni chiefs through their performance of power appear to have emasculated the male members of the subject population to such a degree that up to the present day a person like Namabengo is still remembered with loathing by male elders. In Ungoni sutu women were excluded from becoming Ngoni, and even Ngoni women could not pass their ethnic status on to their children, while at the same time, their ascribed status as true Ngoni or as the nkosi's wives privileged some to exercise tremendous political power and in some cases to have control over their own sexuality.

Conclusion

This comparative study of two areas in Zimbabwe and Tanzania has argued that any understanding of political identity in rural societies south of the Sahara at the turn of the nineteenth century profits from considering ethnicity in relation to gender—understood as gender relations, roles, norms, and symbols. At the same time, ethnicity may be seen as part of a set of identities that are interwoven and complex and embedded in the daily making and unmaking of community. In the Mutasa paramountcy, ethnicity was at best secondary; instead, loyalty to the central power was imagined and practiced in kinship terms and through the reliance on the social, political, and spiritual relevance of an individual's membership in the royal lineage. Loyalty and power were practiced, performed, and spoken through manifestations of gender identity by some elite women. In contrast, in Ungoni, political power rested firmly with the ethnic identities of being true Ngoni or Ngoni, set apart from the multiethnic sutu subject population. The very masculinity of power and ethnicity was paradoxically further enshrined through female power holders, who strengthened the centralized power of the Ngoni polities, even though individual women held at times significant control over their areas of authority. Female authorities were selected because their embodied and performative challenges to heteronormativity among the subject populations served to further stabilize central power. In both cases, gender normativity provided an arena in which royal women performed shaming, which might have served personal gratification and certainly enforced hegemony. Either way, female officeholders, much as they might have been the exception among the overall female population, still played important political roles vis-à-vis both the power centers and their own areas of rule in both regions on the eve of colonial rule. The effect on young men and women who witnessed gender bending can only be guessed at beyond the lingering anger of male descendants of the subject populations.

NOTES

I would like to thank Jan-Georg Deutsch for critical comments and Marcia Wright for encouragement to work on this topic in the earlier stages of research.

1. Muzvare Muparutsa, group interview, 27 October 1992, Mahemasimike, Zimbabwe. All interviews were conducted by the author unless indicated otherwise. With the exception of prominent members of the community who agreed to be referenced by name, in Zimbabwe all interviewees were guaranteed anonymity. For a detailed discussion of the valley and the Mutasa case study, see Heike I. Schmidt, *Colonialism and Violence in Zimbabwe: A History of Suffering* (Oxford: James Currey, 2013).

2. Please note that all vernacular terms used in relation to the Mutasa area in Zimbabwe are ChiManyika, a dialect of Shona, and those used in the discussion of Ungoni in Tanzania are KiNgoni, unless otherwise indicated. While the use of vernacular terms may be distracting to the reader, and a balance needs to be found to retain comprehension, it is significant in providing a specificity of insight and argument that translations into English do not allow.

3. "Elder" denotes the social, not the chronological, age.

4.   Muzvare Muparutsa, group interview.

5.   Reverend E. L. Sells, "The History of Manicaland Rhodesia 1832–1897," 4, boxfile 44, north wall, Old Mutare Mission Archive (hereafter OMMA), Zimbabwe.

6.   Cases of public shaming on the part of male chiefs could not be found for either case study.

7.   Surprisingly little attention has been paid to the topic of shame and shaming in Africa south of the Sahara. For a discussion of shame through the lens of honor, see John Iliffe, *Honour in African History* (Cambridge: Cambridge University Press, 2004).

8.   Schmidt, *Colonialism and Violence*.

9.   Ruramisai Charumbira, "Nehanda and Gender Victimhood in the Central Mashonaland 1896–97 Rebellions: Revisiting the Evidence," *History in Africa* 35 (2008): 103–31.

10.   Derek Peterson, "Morality Plays: Marriage, Church Courts, and Colonial Agency in Central Tanganyika, ca. 1876–1928," *American Historical Review* 111, no. 4 (2006): 983–1010; Richard Roberts, *Litigants and Households: African Disputes and Colonial Courts in the French Soudan, 1895–1912* (Portsmouth, NH: Heinemann, 2005); Elizabeth Schmidt, *Peasants, Traders, and Wives: Shona Women in the History of Zimbabwe, 1870–1939* (Portsmouth, NH: Heinemann, 1992); Martin Chanock, *Law, Custom, and Social Order: The Colonial Experience in Malawi and Zambia* (Cambridge: Cambridge University Press, 1985).

11.   A pathbreaking volume, albeit almost exclusively on West Africa, was Flora Kaplan's *Queens, Queen Mothers, Priestesses, and Power: Case Studies in African Gender* (New York: New York Academy of Sciences, 1997).

12.   For the shift from the invention to the creation of tradition, see Terence Ranger, "The Invention of Tradition Revisited: The Case of Colonial Africa," in *Inventions and Boundaries: Historical and Anthropological Approaches to the Study of Ethnicity and Nationalism*, ed. Preben Kaarsholm and Jan Hultin (Roskilde: Roskilde University Press, 1994), 5–50. For the debate, see Thomas Spear, "Neo-traditionalism and the Limits of Invention in British Colonial Africa," *Journal of African History* 44, no. 1 (2003): 3–27. See also John Lonsdale, chap. 11, "The Moral Economy of Mau Mau: The Problem," and chap. 12, "The Moral Economy of Mau Mau: Wealth, Poverty, and Civic Virtue in Kikuyu Political Thought," in *Unhappy Valley: Conflict in Kenya and Africa*, vol. 2, ed. Bruce Berman and John Lonsdale (Oxford: James Currey, 1992), 265–504.

13.   An early and important exception for East Africa is Marcia Wright's work on Ufipa female authorities. See her recent publication, "Mama Adolphina Unda (c. 1880–1931): The Salvation of a Dynastic Family and the Foundation of Fipa Catholicism, 1898–1914," in *The Human Tradition in Modern Africa*, ed. Dennis Cordell (Lanham, MD: Rowman and Littlefield, 2012), 123–38.

14.   Please note that the term *patriarchy* is avoided entirely. Its implications of a stable category of maleness and a male system of domination are not useful for historical analysis.

15.   David Parkin, introduction to *Semantic Anthropology*, ed. David Parkin (London: Academic Press, 1982), xlvi, cited in W. Arens and Ivan Karp, introduction to *Creativity*

of Power: Cosmology and Action in African Societies, ed. W. Arens and Ivan Karp (Washington, DC: Smithsonian Institution Press, 1989), xiv.

16. Arens and Karp, introduction, xxi.

17. Schmidt, *Colonialism and Violence*, chap. 2.

18. Mambo Mutasa, interview, 7 March 1992, Watsomba, Zimbabwe.

19. NC Umtali to PNC Manicaland, 21 November 1958, PER5 (file name) Chief Mutasa, Provincial Administrator's Office (hereafter cited as PAO), Mutare, Zimbabwe.

20. The written sources identify Muredzwa as Tendai's daughter. For the view that she was his aunt, see Zeki Mutasa, interview, 5 January 2014, Harare, Zimbabwe.

21. Mambo Mutasa, interview, 7 March 1992; Shepherd Machuma, "Mtasa," boxfile 248, shelf d, north wall, OMMA. Chimbadzwa served as acting *mambo*.

22. Jason Machiwenyika, lesson 112, "The History and Customs of the Manyika People and Manyika," MA/14/1/2, National Archives of Zimbabwe, Harare, Zimbabwe; PER5 Chief Mutasa, PAO; PER5 Chief Mutasa, District Administrator's Office, Mutasa, Zimbabwe; Appointment of Chief Mutasa of the Manyika Tribe, NC Umtali, box number 57577, National Record Center, Harare, Zimbabwe; Shepherd Machuma, "Treatment of Women and Their Role in the Society," ca. 1970, boxfile 275, shelf d, north wall, OMMA; Selwyn Bazeley, "Manyika Headwomen," *NADA* 7 (1940): 3–5; Rose Blennerhassett and Lucy Sleeman, *Adventures in Mashonaland* (London: Macmillan, 1893), 131–34.

23. Mambo Mutasa, interview, 7 March 1992.

24. BVM, interview, 13 August 1992, Honde Valley, Zimbabwe; H. H. K. Bhila, *Trade and Politics in a Shona Kingdom: The Manyika and Their Portuguese and African Neighbours 1575–1902* (Burnt Mill: Harlow, 1982), 23; J. G. Storry, "The Settlement and Territorial Expansion of the Mutasa Dynasty," *Rhodesian History* 7 (1976): 26–27.

25. DMF (a female Muparutsa elder), interview, 27 October 1992, Honde Valley, Zimbabwe.

26. Muzvare Muparutsa, group interview; Muredzwa II, group interview, 24 October 1992, New Reserve, Zimbabwe; AUM (one of Muredzwa's grandsons), interview, 28 February 1992, Mutare, Zimbabwe; Mambo Mutasa, interview, 7 March 1992. See also Shepherd Machuma, "Persons: Life History of Joshua Muredzwa," boxfile 262, shelf d, north wall, OMMA.

27. Bhila, *Trade and Politics*, 16.

28. BDM, interview, 13 August 1992, Honde Valley, Zimbabwe.

29. BXM, interview, 13 August 1992, Honde Valley, Zimbabwe.

30. See M. Hannan, *Standard Shona Dictionary*, repr. ed. (Harare: College Press, 1987).

31. BVM, interview. Another man recalled that his father was warned not to marry the daughter of chieftainess Muredzwa. AUM, interview, 2 October 1992, Mutare, Zimbabwe.

32. Mambo Mutasa, interview, 7 March 1992.

33. Bhila, *Trade and Politics*, 23.

34. Bhila, *Trade and Politics*, 223–27, 244–46.

35. Bhila, *Trade and Politics*, 239–42. This argument is not entirely convincing, because Tendai had collaborated with the BSAC against his son Chimbadza's urging in the early 1890s.

36. In her treatment of gender and ethnicity, Jean Davison discusses ethnicity as an enlargement of lineage and hence kinship relations, an argument that does not apply in the discussed case studies. See Davison, *Gender, Lineage, and Ethnicity in Southern Africa* (Boulder, CO: Westview, 1996).

37. A particularly intriguing comparative case study is Dahomey, where the status of subjugation was expressed in gendered terms. Any dependent of the king, especially when living in the royal capital, Abomey, could be referred to as royal wife, regardless of his or her sex. Edna Bay, *Wives of the Leopard: Gender, Politics, and Culture in the Kingdom of Dahomey* (Charlottesville: University of Virginia Press, 1998), 20. The historical sociologist Oyèrónké Oyěwùmí cautions that approaching African identities with the assumption that categories of historical analysis such as gender are universal can lead to major misconceptions. Oyèrónké Oyěwùmí, *The Invention of Women: Making an African Sense of Western Gender Discourses* (Minneapolis: University of Minnesota Press, 1997).

38. Mambo Mutasa, interview, 5 November 1992, Watsomba, Zimbabwe.

39. Umtali District, Quarterly Reports, December 1900, N9/3/3; Inyanga District, Monthly Reports, March 1904, N9/4/18; and CNC Mashonaland, Annual Reports 1908, N9/1/11, all in National Archives of Zimbabwe.

40. Mambo Mutasa, interview, 8 August 1992; Machuma, "Mtasa."

41. For the prerogatives of male and female chiefs, see Machuma, "Mtasa"; AUM, interview, 3 October 1992. For fines, see AUM, interview, 28 February and 3 October 1992.

42. AUM, interview, 3 October 1992; "Nyamkwarara Valley Tribe to Be Moved to New Home," *Rhodesia Herald*, 1 May 1973. Wattle is the wood used to make houses with mud.

43. "Report on the Tenant Area; Stapleford Forest Reserve, by K. W. Groves, October 1956," 15, Private Papers A, Zimbabwe.

44. AUM (who was present at the meeting), interview, 3 October 1992.

45. Mambo Mutasa, interview, 5 November 1992.

46. Mambo Mutasa, interview, 5 November 1992.

47. AUM, interview, 3 October 1992.

48. Mambo Mutasa, interview, 7 March, 8 August, and 5 November 1992, Watsomba, Zimbabwe; AUM, interview, 3 October 1992; DFM, interview, 24 October 1992, New Reserve, Zimbabwe; Muredzwa II, group interview.

49. Machuma, "Mtasa."

50. Shepherd Machuma, "Dorcas Muredzwa," boxfile 212, shelf d, north wall, OMMA.

51. Machiwenyika, lesson 41.

52. Shepherd Machuma, files "Revival," boxfile 264, and "Mabvumi," boxfile 271, shelf d, north wall, OMMA; AUM, interview, 3, 17, and 28 October 1992, Mutare, Zimbabwe, Machiwenyika, lesson 62.

53.   Machuma, "Revival."

54.   Much of the existing literature on women and missions has emphasized the spaces of negotiation and change mission education and missionaries as patrons opened for African women, while the loss of spiritual authority for women that accompanied this religious transformation has largely been neglected. See, for example, Elizabeth Schmidt's otherwise excellent and still-pathbreaking work *Peasants, Traders, and Wives*.

55.   AUM, interview, 3 October 1992.

56.   NC Umtali to PNC Manicaland, 21 November 1958 and 28 January 1959; and Bvumbi Mutasa to the DC Umtali, 22 November 1965, both in District Administrator's Office, Mutasa.

57.   Mambo Mutasa, interview, 21 August 1992, Watsomba, Zimbabwe.

58.   Zeki Mutasa, interview, 11 January 2014, Harare, Zimbabwe.

59.   Machiwenyika, lesson 21.

60.   Blennerhassett and Sleeman, *Adventures in Mashonaland*, 153ff. The account continues: "Curiously enough, in the kraals governed by a chieftainess the other women are in a state of, if possible, more abject subjection than when under the rule of a chief. The men seem to revenge on their wives the respect they are forced to show to their queen."

61.   Blennerhassett and Sleeman, *Adventures in Mashonaland*, 254.

62.   Blennerhassett and Sleeman, *Adventures in Mashonaland*, 254.

63.   In Zimbabwe during the liberation war of the 1970s, one struggle that manifested itself in rural areas was that between commoner and royal lineages. See Norma Kriger, *Zimbabwe's Guerrilla War: Peasant Voices* (Cambridge: Cambridge University Press, 1992), chap. 2; Norma Kriger, "The Zimbabwean War of Liberation: Struggles within the Struggle," *Journal of Southern African Studies* 14, no. 2 (1988): 304–22.

64.   Lazarus Ulangani Tawete, interview, 21 March 2001, Namatuhi, Tanzania. For the view that there had been only one female chief, Mkomanile, between both polities and that she had been merely appointed regent for her still underage son, see Bertram Mapunda, "Reexamining the Maji Maji War in Ungoni, with a Blend of Archaeology and Oral History," in *Maji Maji: Lifting the Fog of War*, ed. James Giblin and Jamie Monson (Leiden: Brill, 2010), 224, 227.

65.   Tom von Prince, "Aus dem deutsch-ostafrikanischen Schutzgebiete," *Mitteilungen aus den Schutzgebieten* 7 (1894): 219. See also Peramiho Chronik, vol. 2/I, 5 June and 30 October 1909, Peramiho Abbey Archives, Tanzania.

66.   Thomas Spear, "Zwangendaba's Ngoni 1821–1890: A Political and Social History of a Migration," *Occasional Paper* 4 (Madison: African Studies Program, University of Wisconsin, 1972). For the *mfecane* debate, see Carolyn Hamilton, *The Mfecane Aftermath: Reconstructive Debates in Southern African History* (Johannesburg: Witwaters University Press, 1995).

67.   For the early history of the Songea Ngoni, see Patrick Redmond, *The Politics of Power in Songea Ngoni Society, 1860–1962* (Chicago: Adams Press, 1985), chap. 1; and Elzear Ebner, *The History of the Wangoni and Their Origin in the South African Bantu Tribes* (Ndanda-Peramiho, Tanzania: Benedictine Publications, 1987).

68. Edmund Simba, interview, 21 March 2001, Mpitimbi, Tanzania; nkosi Xaver Usangira Gama, interview, 3 March 2001, Ndirima, Tanzania. The office of chief was officially abolished in Tanzania after independence in 1963. In Njelu, the nkosi is still regarded as paramount ruler, though without direct political and certainly no military power.

69. For the most useful discussion of Ngoni political and social organization from ca. 1860 to 1905, see Redmond, *Politics of Power*, chaps. 2 and 3. For another example that illustrates the connection between ethnicity and masculinity, see Alan Isaacman and Barbara Isaacman, *Slavery and Beyond: The Making of Men and Chikunda Ethnic Identities in the Unstable World of South-Central Africa, 1750–1920* (Portsmouth, NH: Heinemann, 2004).

70. Tawete, interview. For ritual power, see Maji Maji Memorial Committee, interview, 28 March 2001, Songea, Tanzania. For political change and enlargement of women's roles in the Zulu Kingdom in the early nineteenth century, see Sean Hanretta, "Women, Marginality and the Zulu State: Women's Institutions and Power in the Early Nineteenth Century," *Journal of African History* 39, no. 4 (1998): 389–415.

71. Maji Maji Memorial Committee, interview; Ebner, *History of the Wangoni*, 136ff.

72. Alfons Adams, *Im Dienste des Kreuzes: Erinnerungen aus meinem Missionsleben in Deutsch-Ostafrika* (St. Ottilien: St. Benediktus Missionsgenossenschaft, 1899), 137. An unpublished English translation is located at the Peramiho Mission.

73. Nkosi Xaver Usangira Gama, interview; Simba, interview; Tawete, interview; and Sister Asumpta Ngonyani (a Benedictine nun), interview, 2 April 2001, Songea, Tanzania.

74. Adams, *Im Dienste des Kreuzes*, 137; "'The Story of the Likuyu Area' related to me by Jumbes Mabukusera and Hangahanga," 25 April 1938, 19, ACC/24/1/1, Tanzania National Archives (hereafter cited as TNA), Dar es Salaam, Tanzania.

75. Philip Gulliver, "An Administrative Survey of the Ngoni and Ndendeuli of Songea District" (1954), 24, manuscript located at the Peramiho Mission.

76. Kanisius Ngonyani Mshenge Daraja, interview, 27 March 2001, Namabengo, Tanzania; Motoulaya Ngonyani, interview by G. P. Mpangara, 4 April 1968, Ungoni, Maji Maji Records 6/68/4/3/2, 3; Issa Ngula Fusi and Hussein Ndunya, interview by G. P. Mpangara, 26 April 1968, Ungoni, Maji Maji Records 6/68/4/3/10, 2, Dar es Salaam, Tanzania. See also Maji Maji Memorial Committee, interview. One member of the committee stated that women were chosen for their leadership qualities.

77. The fact that chieftainess Mkomanile's headquarters were located at Kitanda at the northern caravan route further confirms the strategic posting of these women.

78. Redmond, *Politics of Power*, 69.

79. Donatus Ngonyani Makisio, interview, and Kanisius Ngonyani Mshenge Daraja, interview, 27 March 2001, Namabengo, Tanzania.

80. Daraja, interview.

81. For the causes of the Maji Maji War in Ungoni, see Heike Schmidt, "The Maji Maji War and Its Aftermath: Gender, Age, and Power in South-Western Tanzania, c. 1905–1916," *International Journal of African Historical Studies* 43, no. 1 (2010): 27–62.

82. Testimony by Askari Ibrahim Ali Habshi, Ssongea, 16 December 1907, Finanzielle Folgen des Maji-Maji-Aufstandes, G3/77, TNA. Jim Giblin and Jamie Monson have suggested that the correct name is Nkomanile, not Mkomanile, and that Nkomanile is identical to Kommandire. The few written sources available, however, use the spelling Mkomanile, and while not conclusive, the evidence suggests that these are in fact two different women. Giblin and Monson, "Section Three: At the Apex of Violence. Maji Maji in Songea," in Giblin and Monson, *Maji Maji*, 182n1.

83. R. M. Bell, "The Maji-Maji Rebellion in Liwale District," Songea, 23 March 1941, 29–31, ACC 16/37/29, TNA; testimony by Habshi; Ebner, *History of the Wangoni*, 139; Susana Mbeya, interview by G. P. Mpangala, 4 April 1958, Ungoni, Maji Maji Records 6/68/4/3/1, 1; Andreas Haule, interview by G. P. Mpangala, 17 April 1968, Ungoni, Maji Maji Records 6/68/4/3/3, 2. For a more detailed account of Mkomanile and an account of the war in Ungoni, see Heike Schmidt, "'Deadly Silence Predominates in the District': The Maji Maji War and Its Aftermath in Ungoni," in Giblin and Monson, *Maji Maji*, 183–219. For a different interpretation of Mkomanile, see Mapunda, "Reexamining the Maji Maji War," 223–28.

84. Bertram Mapunda and G. P. Mpangara, *The Maji Maji War in Ungoni* (Dar es Salaam: East African Publishing House, 1969), 21. Redmond, on the other hand, suggests that as a woman Namabengo would hardly have been asked to participate in the war, an interpretation that is contradicted by her elevated position (*Politics of Power*, 122). See also Anonymous, "Die Ereignisse im Bezirk Ssongea von Beginn der Unruhen bis Mitte November 1905," *Deutsch-Ostafrikanische Zeitung*, 7 January 1906.

85. Daraja, interview.

86. Songea District Office, Songea District Book, vol. C, ACC 155, TNA.

11

Muslim Women Legislators in Postcolonial Kenya

Between Gender, Ethnicity, and Religion

OUSSEINA D. ALIDOU

The politics of Kenya have been widely perceived by many Kenyan and non-Kenyan observers as prone to ethnic concerns and conflicts.[1] The state is seen to be ethnocratic, with the president and the elite from his ethnic group wielding disproportionate power.[2] Many regard the politics of elections and representation as riddled with ethnic considerations, and voting is said to take place primarily along ethnic lines.[3] As a result, frustrations with and disputes about election results have sometimes resulted in major episodes of interethnic violence, as happened in 1992 and 2007, for example. In 1992, Kalenjin men viciously attacked members of the Gikuyu ethnic group residing in the Rift Valley Province in an attempt to alter the demographics of the region in favor of a then Kalenjin president, Daniel arap Moi, and his political party, the Kenya African National Union, just weeks before the 1992 general elections. Similarly, a dispute over the results of the presidential elections of 2007 led to weeks of bloody interethnic violence that left over one thousand Kenyans dead.

As one would expect, all these conflicts have had a strong material basis tied to inequalities in resource distribution.[4] These political struggles may themselves take the form of ethnicity. But even in this case, there is often the hand of the political elite seeking to exploit ethnic difference for politico-economic ends. Whatever the case, it is partly due to this interplay between politics and ethnicity that Kenya decided to move away from a unitary state in which the central government was supreme to a devolved system of government in which power is shared with subnational authorities, which came into effect with the March 2013 elections.

But do women parliamentarians respond to the question of ethnicity differently in their political calculations than men do, especially if Islam is an attendant attribute of the identity of those women? Muslim women in Kenya come from a wide range of ethnic and regional constituencies. In some of these, such as the Swahili, Somali, and Digo, Muslims are in the majority. In others, such as the Kikuyu and Luo, they constitute a minority. Depending on which statistics one looks at, the proportion of Muslims in Kenya ranges from 15 to 20 percent in a population of over 40 million people. Focusing on the experiences of two Muslim women legislators, or members of Parliament (MPs), as they are known in Kenya, this chapter shows that the majority or minority status of Muslims in any ethnic constituency affects how Muslim women politicians from those communities relate to their work both inside and outside the legislative bodies.

Islam places primary emphasis on the notion of the *ummah*, the multiracial, multiethnic community of believers. The bonds holding members of this quasi-religious political entity are expected to be stronger than those of any other group defined by any other parameter. And because Islam is often described as a total way of life, the ummah can be seen as a macroethnic affiliation of transnational scope. Though the two women MPs discussed here are from different Kenyan ethnicities, it was to be expected perhaps that they would develop a special relationship on account of their macroethnic identity as Muslims at the national stage of political competition. In other local contexts, however, the challenge to them is always that of striking the right balance in expressing multiple identities—macroethnicity (Islamic), local ethnicity, gender, marital identity, and so forth. Yet their consciousness of belonging to the ummah never deters them from continuously seeking to build transreligious bridges at the national level for the common good of women and children.

As citizens of a country in which the political moment demands greater representation of minorities like Muslim women, the projection of an ethnoreligious self gives the Muslim women MPs a certain advantage nationally. Supporting Muslim women politicians has now become an important signifier of how politically representative political parties aspire to be. This same politics of representation, however, makes it imperative that the Muslim women continue to affirm their ethnoreligious identity locally but within a secular understanding of politics. For it is in this secular political disposition that they are able to forge lines of political action beyond ethnicity and religion, fully aware that women in general suffer many similar experiences from the impact of male-framed articulations of one kind or another.

It is true, of course, that even Muslim male politicians within Muslim-minority constituencies have to be mindful of winning the support of their non-Muslim constituents. However, there is much less pressure on Muslim male politicians to explain their efforts to appear religiously inclusive than there is on Muslim women politicians. Because both the local ethnic community and the wider Muslim community regard the woman as the custodian of culture, the Muslim woman MP has to appear secular and inclusive and be a model of the best values of her ethnocultural and Islamic traditions. If she appears to have abandoned the belief in woman's custodial role of her culture, she stands the risk of losing the support of both her Muslim and non-Muslim constituents among whom male-defined conceptions of the role of women in society holds immense sway. From the Muslim point of view, then, a Muslim male politician who donates money to help his Christian constituents construct a church, for example, is often judged less harshly by his ethnic compatriots than a Muslim woman MP who makes the same interfaith gesture.

One of these women MPs is Dr. Ummi Naomi Shaban, a dentist by training who has been serving in Kenya's legislature as an elected member of Parliament since 2002. Shaban is a divorced mother of three, and her ethnic affiliation is Taita, one of the largest ethnic groups in the Coast Province. In her constituency—officially called Taita/Taveta constituency—which elected her to Parliament, the Taita are the majority, but Taita of Muslim faith, as Shaban is, constitute a tiny minority. In a sense, then, as in the case of her competitors, Shaban's ethnic identity was an asset in her bid for a parliamentary position to the extent that she shares the cultural and linguistic identity of the dominant section of her electorate. On the other hand, her Muslim identity might have been a liability in an ethnic group in which the majority is not Muslim. Shaban therefore had to play down—but not deny—her Islamic identity to a greater extent than a Muslim male politician would have been expected to and project an orientation of religious inclusiveness to win the support of her non-Muslim constituents, who happen to be the majority. This portrayal of a religiously neutral disposition has become even more paramount since the recent upsurge of evangelical Christianity in Kenya.[5]

The other MP presented in this chapter, and who started as a young un-married politician and has served as a nominated MP since 2002, is Amina Abdallah. A small number of Kenyans are nominated to the Parliament either to increase representation from marginalized groups and/or to bring on board relatively well-known citizens with skills, experience, and training that are deemed valuable to the business of the legislative body. From the 1990s onward, the winds of change have called for a pluralism that is more representational and have put pressure on all political parties to use their slots for nominated

MPs to gain the support of underrepresented groups, including women, from across the country. Under the country's current constitution, nominated MPs are chosen by their respective political parties rather than elected by a constituency. Until the elections of 2013, there were only twelve nominated MPs, making up less than 5 percent of the legislative body.

Abdallah is a Kenyan of mixed descent: her father is of Yemeni origin, and her mother is from the northeastern region of the country and is of Borana descent, an ethnic group that is considered predominantly nomadic in lifestyle. She grew up in the town of Moyale, near Kenya's northern border with Ethiopia, which she describes as "a very marginalized post of the country" that is hardly accessible due to very poor infrastructure. It is impoverished and has very low literacy rates. Here the majority of the constituents are of Muslim faith. By 2002, her party, the Kenya African National Union (KANU), had introduced an affirmative action seat that, in Abdallah's words, was intended to "give minority groups and special interest groups a chance to come to Parliament so that they can use it as a stepping stone to get to Parliament as elected members or use this opportunity to raise issues about minorities here." And it was through the affirmative action plan that Abdallah was nominated to Parliament. Her selection as a nominated MP helped her political party gain a foothold among the nomadic communities of the Eastern Province and Northeastern Province, as well as among Muslims and women.

Even though these two women legislators self-identify as Muslim, they take a wholly secular approach to politics in order to broaden their potential electoral constituency. That is why they sought (and continue to seek) political leadership through a secular political party like KANU rather than through a faith-based political party like the Islamic Party of Kenya (IPK). Although all the political parties discriminate against women, the Muslim women MPs argue that they stand a better chance of achieving their leadership goals through secular parties than through faith-based parties. The continued patriarchal interpretation of Islam, even within the context of political pluralism at the national level, has constrained leadership opportunities for Muslim women in Kenya. On the other hand, the women's own political party was keen on highlighting their minority ethnic status and their religious identity as a way of promoting an image of a national—that is, multiethnic, multiracial, and multireligious—party.

To reiterate, then, Muslim women MPs have consistently taken the position that forging transethnic and transreligious alliances with other women politicians in Parliament is essential in their mission to promote the legislative welfare of women and children, both nationally and within their communities of faith and ethnicity. In doing so, however, they have been equally conscious of the need to reaffirm their ethnoreligious identities in a context in which the question of minority representation is now lodged deep in the heart of national politics. At the same time, women have to continue performing a balancing act because of their expected role as custodians of their ethnoreligious culture, working for ethnic and religious unity of women while embodying ethnoreligious culture in their personal lives.

Gendered Expectations and Discrimination in Politics

In order to overcome discrimination in politics, women had to conform to some of the gendered expectations in their ethnoreligious communities. Like most women politicians in Kenya, these two Muslim women politicians had to contend with the forces of patriarchy, both within and across ethnic lines from the very beginning, when they publicly declared their intentions to serve as politicians in the legislative assembly. Even as the momentum for pluralistic representation continued to grow, many Muslim men and the predominant conservative Muslim organizations in Kenya continued to believe that political leadership in the public sphere was the exclusive preserve of men. Shaban recounts how her ethnic culture and Islamic arguments were invoked in order to prevent her from vying for a parliamentary seat in the Coast Province and describes the types of violence unleashed against her as a result of her resistance:

> The first time I tried, I tried to compete in a by-election in my constituency, was when my former MP had resigned. That was in 2001. But culturally it has taken a long time for people to realize that even women should try to compete for such a position. First of all, the first resistance I felt was from the males, the male elders who sent a delegation to come and tell me [as a woman] to stop doing politics. So you can see where we started. But of course, if you are focused and you want to be there, it is difficult; it is not easy. You will be insulted. I was insulted. But, fortunately, I had the support of the women and the youth.
>
> [In the process of campaigning,] my car was broken into pieces. I had another car, and the second car was burnt. A friend's car, he had lent me his car for campaign, it was burnt. My home was almost burnt, for they poured the petrol all around it. But they did not burn it. That was in 2001. But again, that did not deter me. So the following year again, I was there on the spot again to try. This time around, I made it, I made the points. And of course, the insults were fewer because they thought, this one will not stop. The insults got less, they were less interesting.[6]

New to the game and with cultural forces against her, Shaban lost in her first bid. But, refusing to be intimidated and having learned some important strategic lessons from her first experience, she went on to compete again for the same seat in the 2002 general election, and this time she succeeded.

Even after her election, however, Shaban continued to experience the hostility of men and women; people of both genders believed that on religious and/or ethnocultural grounds she should not be serving her society at that level of legislative leadership:

> But for the Muslim women, of course, you realize that because people want to keep off the women, they also misquote the Qur'an, saying that women are not meant to lead. They misquoted it, because I have not seen it anywhere, retained anywhere. They misquoted it. But again, this is just to lock out the women. Again, like I am saying, [in] African culture, not only in East Africa but in West Africa as well, the women have always been looked at as children. They are supposed to be children and looked at as minors. But as time is getting on, we are trying to get our rights in the society, and we are going to stay, we are here to stay. We hope we will be able to carry onboard other women, the youth also, to include them onboard.

Women's marital status was one of the most important ways that women were expected to conform to ethnoreligious assumptions if they wanted to serve. While senior or married women have been more acceptable in a male-dominated public politics, the fact that Abdallah was a young unmarried woman in Parliament was a major source of pressure for her. She quickly realized that expectations of her performance are gendered. Her Borana Muslim commu-nity in particular put pressure on her because the community sees itself as re-sponsible for monitoring the moral and sexual conduct of a never-married Muslim woman. A young Muslim woman must uphold family honor through the preservation of her virginity until her first marriage. Failure to obey this code of honor has been the source of family psychological and/or physical vio-lence against young women among the conservative Muslim families to which Abdallah belongs. This patriarchal cultural concern regarding family honor is at the root of long-standing cultural practices such as female genital cutting among Muslim Boranas and Somalis in Kenya and Somalia, demonstrating once again how particular readings of Islam become wedded to ethnic traditions.

Furthermore, given her unmarried status, Abdallah constantly feels under pressure to demonstrate that her nomination to Parliament was based on the merits of her candidacy and not on some undeserving favoritism arising from some association of personal intimacy with a powerful politician within the nominating political party:

> One of the biggest challenges that I got the first week that my name was announced was "Who is she? Whose girlfriend is she? Why is she here?" For me, I already had

plans to do whatever I was going to do. But I thought that now that I have issues, I have to reduce my problems because I was coming in to an avenue, a career that people think is reserved for men. And then, not only was I coming to the career reserved for men, I was coming to a career that stereotypes the community that I come from, not only the religion but the region and tribe I am supposed to have come from.

As indicated earlier, Abdallah's father is of Yemeni origin, and her mother is of Borana descent and is from the northeastern region of the country, an area that is considered poor and "backward." In the stereotypical imagination of many non-Muslim Kenyans, all these factors—questionable citizenship, poverty, and illiteracy—are in turn a reflection of Abdallah's Muslim upbringing. Compounding all these negative factors at the time she was first seeking office was the fact that she was young and single: "The only thing I had was a good education. But everything else from me was wrong. I was single, I was from a marginalized community, I was a Muslim, and I was a woman. So I was combining too many negatives, and I needed to neutralize some issues. So although I was single, I had to very quickly make the decision to change that. And I think that helped a lot." So soon after her initiation into parliamentary politics, Abdallah proceeded to marry the man to whom she was already engaged. She decided to get married earlier than she had planned in order to gain some cultural capital and legitimacy to better pursue her chosen career in politics.

In sum, then, Muslim women politicians in Kenya have had to confront challenges that are deeply rooted in the culture of the legislative assembly itself and in the society at large. Some of these are directly linked to the fact of male dominance in the respective ethnic groups of the politicians. Others are tied to specific interpretive preferences of Islamic doctrine and practices as articulated by local *ulema* or Muslim scholars. And in the Kenya Muslim context, the ethnic and the religious often come together to reinforce each other in ways that sometimes act to the detriment of Muslim women politicians.

Uniting against Stereotypes

What is remarkable about both Abdallah and Shaban is the sisterhood that binds them in their struggle as Muslim women in public politics as they confront all sorts of adversities. Being senior in age, profession, and public politics and having gone through the violent experience of fighting for a legislative political seat as a divorced woman, Shaban offered herself as a mentor to Abdallah. She helped Abdallah to develop strategies for winning the confidence of the electoral constituency in the upper Eastern Province where she was running. One of these strategies included getting married in order to neutralize political opponents who might use her unmarried status for negative attacks. Aspiring to a parliamentary seat made Shaban a target of disparaging patriarchal attacks because she was a divorcée and single mother. She did not want her mentee to undergo similar experiences:

> As the community kept talking about [Amina], even the members of Parliament who were Muslims were not amused about the fact that she is basically the one who is being nominated. She is on the top of the list of the nominees. But for my part, that time I had to talk very forcibly [in support of] Amina because I had looked at her CV. I knew what she has done for the party, and I thought this girl is meant to be here, she is meant to be with us. . . . But of course, I was one of the people who were telling her, "Get married and very fast. Since you are engaged, can you do that?" [*laughs*] . . . "Can you do that? By the time you are going for election, I do not want you to face what I faced. It is not a good thing."

This combination of ethnocultural factors worked to the disadvantage of women seeking to be MPs. Both Shaban's status as a divorced woman running a woman-headed household with three children and Abdallah's status as a single woman became ethnoreligious liabilities for the two women politicians. Shaban notes that, as a result,

> as much as one would like to do certain things, all female members of Parliament do not have a social life. Socially, you don't have a social life, whether married or single. You don't have that social life. You can't afford to have it, because everybody is like in a telescope. Actually, they put you under a microscope, and they have to look at each atom in your body and think, "Have you done the right thing today?" So there you are, you are put on the spot. You have to know how to carry yourself morally [to know] what kind of respect you command from the people. It is like you are put on that lens by your constituency and also nationally.

These ethnoreligious considerations that frame the lives of Muslim women MPs are some of the conditions that have led them to take a gendered approach to ethnicity and religion in pursuit of their parliamentary objectives.

Abdallah finds that Muslim men and women across ethnic groups, in fact, are the worst offenders against their fellow Muslim sisters who are presented with leadership opportunities that could advance their collective cause:

> Yes, whether or not it matters, [Shaban] is right: You are put under the microscope. For example, as she was telling you, the Muslim members of Parliament were bigger opponents of my nomination than non-Muslims. Then, when you come to the women's movement, Muslim women were the first to say, "We don't want her. She does not represent us." Even if they are not in the same party as you. So that in itself you have to be ready for. You have to be ready for criticism

on things you have done and things you have not done. Even if you are married, even if you try to remove the loopholes as much as you can, politics is such that we operate on rumors, rumors to finish your opponent or potential opponent. Every day you wake up, you say, "Oh, God, I am keeping this marriage, so that nobody says anything about me." They would still say something about you. You cannot be too happy. If you laugh too loudly with a guy, you are having some- thing with that man! [*laughs*] So for a woman, in this profession, you have to do a hundred and fifty percent better than a man, and you have to do things that would divert people's attention from you, the social being. And even when you do well, they would still find something bad to say about you.

Abdallah found it hard to cope with the problem of stories made up to dis- parage women politicians in societies that are primarily oral. This is especially true of nomadic communities of the Northeastern Province, where oral art forms are alive and well. Orality itself becomes a fertile condition for reimagining reality in the image of one's value system.[7] As Abdallah observes: "For a Muslim woman, it is even worse, because you are from a community that is very oral, especially like the Somalis. Most people who have not gone to school are very oral. So they have so much to talk [about] and to come up with . . . any time you don't overfocus on making sure they don't have other issues to talk about you [*laughs*]." Orality, then, provides infinite space for multiple repetitions and improvisations, allowing "rumormongers" to take hold of a tiny bit of information, factual or otherwise, and embellish it with multiple layers of imaginative narrations that could seriously disparage or even destroy a politi- cian. These two women politicians cope with these challenges from within and outside of their own culture by uniting together.

Women MPs and Media Misrepresentation

Women MPs have also had to work together across ethnic and religious divides in order to counter negative media representation. Both Abdallah and Shaban denounce how the male-dominated media reinforce patriarchal discrimina- tion of women in political executive positions either by refusing to grant them fair coverage of their political achievements or by portraying them through negative stereotypes. This is why the two Muslim women MPs celebrated the appointment of Martha Karua, a woman, as Kenya's minister of constitutional affairs, even though Karua comes from an ethnic group, the Gikuyu, that is perceived to be potentially hegemonic.[8] In her position, Karua received fre- quent coverage in both print and electronic media, putting women's executive abilities and achievement in high politics in the limelight. As Shaban explains:

The women of Kenya, because of the marginalization of women in the country and voting trend in this country, when a woman comes to Parliament, she really works very hard to retain her seat because she is perceived as . . . [*pause*] they look at her as the weaker sex and also a person who cannot make decisions. So we are all, by society at the same level, at par. In our Parliament, the standards of performance where women are concerned have been very high. They have been very good. Except that because of the general misconception that women are non-performers, you find that even the media are not concerned about what women [parliamentarians] talk about or what they say and their contributions. So you find that their only interest is . . . I will put it this way: even the lousiest of the male [Parliament] members, when he says something, it will be reported all over. Yet when a woman gives a contribution it is not reported. . . . But we are lucky this time because the deputy leader of government business happens to be a woman [Martha Karua], who is a minister of constitutional affairs. It is a plus. It has never [before] happened, and to us it is a plus. And at least every day we get to hear her talk. We believe that as time goes on, people will appreciate women more, and more women will be elected in the next general election, because, without blowing trumpets, I believe our women have really worked, including the nominated women. The elected and the nominated women, we both worked in our own areas of interests.

In Shaban's view, then, the media have been complicit in erasing the contributions of women in Parliament and in making them "invisible" irrespective of their ethnic affiliation. Consequently, women MPs have to work twice as hard, support each other, and perform immensely better than their male counterparts just to be visible.

Both Muslim women MPs take on the mainstream media bias, supporting Joyce N. Omwoha's insightful analysis in "'The Woman's Place . . .': Media and (Mis)representation of Women in Political Leadership Positions in Kenya" of how the media use humiliation and ridicule to negatively depict women political leaders and/or deliberately fail to report their accomplishments to the public.[9] Omwoha provides concrete examples of negative media coverage of prominent women political leaders such as Martha Karua, former minister of justice and constitutional affairs, and Margaret Wanjiru, a member of Parliament for the Starehe constituency of Nairobi. Such media (mis)representations suggest that Kenyan women are simply unfit for public political leadership. As Omwoha comments regarding Kenya's first litigation case involving a political satirical cartoon, "Ms. Martha Karua, former Minister of Justice and Constitutional Affairs and arguably the most high profile female politician in Kenya, sued the *East African Standard* over a caricature of her that appeared in April 25, 2010, issue of *Penknife* [magazine]."[10] Elsewhere in the article she adds:

In a robbery incident in 2003, Kenyans really got excited and amused when the Minister (Ms. Martha Karua) was carjacked at around midnight and the only person she was with at the time was one Catholic priest father Wamugunda. Caroline Mutoko, a presenter in a popular radio station in Kenya, had a field day asking her eager listeners all sorts of hypothetical and hilarious rhetorical questions addressing the mystery as to what the minister may have been up to with the father before they were carjacked. A newspaper article published by the *Daily Nation*, on December 12, 2003, headline was "Martha: I owe no one an explanation."[11]

Such awareness of media misrepresentations of women in public office has led some Muslim women political leaders such as Shaban to invest energy in persuading reporters who are sensitive to gender mainstreaming to publicize women's achievements in legislation and their success in securing resources for the development of their electoral constituencies. In addition, as I have demonstrated elsewhere, the political liberalization processes of the 1990s resulted in the intensification of Muslim minority efforts to gain greater political representation as equal citizens within the Kenyan nation through effective use of Muslim-owned print and electronic media such as Radio Rahma, Iqra, Radio Salaam, FM Pwani, and others.[12] These Muslim-owned media outlets have increasingly become venues in which Muslim women political leaders and community activists can present their agenda for women, the Muslim communities, and the nation at large to the public.

The two Muslim women MPs always understood, furthermore, that there are issues that concern women across religious and ethnic lines and that to be nationally effective they cannot be isolationist. As a result, they have always sought to cross their boundaries of identity to work with other women MPs. Abdallah, for example, worked closely with Njoki Ndungu, another woman MP of Gikuyu, Christian background, to campaign for the enactment of the Sexual Offences Bill, which eventually became law. In fact, as I have demonstrated elsewhere, it is one of the remarkable qualities of Muslim women leaders that they have always sought to forge links across boundaries of ethnicity and religion in their efforts to promote the interests of their specific communities and of women in the nation at large.[13]

Performing Diversity through the Politics of Dress

Partly because of the attitudes they encounter in Parliament and the pressure from their own constituents, the women have to maintain a delicate balance between their ethnoreligious identities and political identities as members of Parliament. Performing this balancing act is most visible in the politics of dress.

Muslim women MPs often use dress politics in order to fight the stereotypes and discrimination they face by virtue of their faith-based minority status and to mark their participation in national politics. They employ dress politics to resist assimilation to the dominant non-Muslim majority's adoption of a Western-inspired dress code, on the one hand, and to raise national consciousness about the diversity of Muslim communities within Kenya, on the other hand. Their mode of dress is partly a response to societal expectations for women to embody and represent their ethnic culture and partly a way of signaling an ethnoreligious presence in the space of national politics. As stated earlier, Muslims are found in virtually every ethnic group in Kenya, sometimes constituting the majority (as in the case of the Digo, Somali, and Swahili) and sometimes a minority (as among the Taita, Kikuyu, and Luo). Some call themselves Muslims by birth, and others refer to themselves as "reverts," meaning returning to their original religion. The general belief here is that all people in the world are, in fact, born Muslim—that is, submitting to the will of one God—and those who grow up as members of other faiths but later adopt Islam are simply reverting to the religion of their birth. Being a Muslim in a predominantly Muslim area has implications for Muslim women and men different from those of being a Muslim in a predominantly non-Muslim area.

Coming from a minority position (as women) within a Muslim-majority and a Muslim-minority community, respectively, both Abdallah and Shaban challenge the homogenizing tendency of the politics of representation in Kenya. In the case of Shaban, dress politics has an additional meaning partly because of her popular middle name, Naomi. This is a name she was given by a female neighbor and friend of her mother, and it stuck. Though born of Muslim parents, then, Shaban is widely referred to by a name, Naomi, that is not Islamic and that is not common among Kenyans of Christian faith either. Among non-Muslims who know little or nothing about her background, her name often raises questions about her faith. Instead of adopting the *buibui* style of dress of the Swahili (a traditional long black outer dress with an attached head and facial cover) or the more modern *abaya* type (a more recent, often imported loose robe-like overgarment with a separate head piece), however, Shaban gets her dress inspiration from West Africa, which, in her opinion, expresses the union of African and Islamic culture, on the one hand, and neutralizes a too overt expression of religious identity, on the other. Her public attire is African in style and origin but meets the Islamic requirements of dress for women. In her words:

> Again, the way Amina and I myself dress has made a bit of a difference in Parliament. A bit [of a] difference because we see people dress more like us. [*laughs*]

Yeah! [*laughs*] Before, people were used to suits and what have you; we are seeing a difference in leadership. Now you have a function, you go there. You can't tell who is a Muslim, who is a Christian. You can't tell, because morally the culture is all the same. I think our African culture and Muslim [culture] are interrelated. They are interrelated. For instance, if you go to West Africa, you can't really tell who is Muslim and who is a Christian by the way people dress. Among the women, you can't tell, and even among the men, you can't tell.

In a sense, then, the two women have adopted different strategies of identity politics in their style of dress. Shaban has adopted a mode of dress that makes her comfortable with both her Muslim and African identity and that at the same time does not mark any sectarian distance from Kenyans of non-Muslim faith. Shaban comes from a constituency where Muslims are a minority, and her religiously neutral dress allows her constituents of non-Muslim faith to be comfortable with her and to trust her ability to represent their interests without religious bias. Yet she still dresses in a style that conforms to the ethnic and religious expectations of her community with regard to women's public attire. Abdallah, on the other hand, has adopted a modern dress style for her public appearance that is clearly associated with Muslim faith and identity. It strongly affirms the continued need for greater representation of the Muslim minority in Parliament. Because she comes from a predominantly Muslim constituency, her dress satisfies the moral standards of her Borana constituents. Just as important, it is seen as an act of courage for her to mark her Muslim identity in an institution of power controlled almost entirely by Kenyans of non-Muslim faith. To the extent that her attire signals her ethnoreligious identity, Abdallah has to rely exclusively on her interpersonal skills to reach across boundaries of religion and ethnicity in her role as a member of Parliament.

The decision to mark Muslim identity by wearing modern Muslim attire is particularly significant in light of the derision that Islamic dress has elicited from some non-Muslim citizens, including national leaders in Kenya. For example, Minou Fuglesang points out the public attempt of Christian-centric Kenya president Daniel arap Moi to humiliate Muslims by demeaning coastal Swahili Muslim women's wearing of the buibui in a 1985 speech delivered in Mombasa. According to the *Message*, a local newspaper, "President Moi in his recent tour of Mombasa asked Muslim women not to wear the *bui-bui* as it did not reveal their beauty. The president said, 'Women in Mombasa should not wear the *bui-bui* because if you cover your faces with the *bui-bui*, nobody will know if you are beautiful. You will also miss the chance of someone to marry you.'"[14]

In light of such pronouncements and the attitudes that underlie them, one can appreciate why Muslim women politicians take it on themselves to signify their Muslimness through dress discourse in Parliament, a site whose defining principle of composition is representativeness. The semiotics of this dress act becomes significant not only for political relations within the Kenya Parliament but also for how the constituents see themselves (re)presented. Mary Porter also elaborates on how the public school uniform worn in Mombasa, which meets Islamic dress requirements for women, is politicized to mark the Muslim distinctiveness of Swahili adolescent girls.[15] In sum, this discourse suggests the tension between belonging to an ethnoreligious community, with its internal histories of hierarchies and normative gender ideology, and belonging to a country as members of a religious minority that Muslim women continue to experience. And Muslim women MPs respond to these ideologies differently in their modes of dress, sometimes depending on whether they come from Muslim-majority or Muslim-minority ethnic constituencies.

The Strategy of Secular Politics

In spite of their overt display of Muslim women's identity through their mode of dress, however, the Muslim women MPs adopt a secular politics as parliamentarians, associating themselves with political parties that claim neither a religious nor an ethnic base. Neither of the two women politicians, for example, chose to work with the IPK, which was formed in the early 1990s and which assumes an Islamic-centered approach to national politics. Both MPs stress their commitment to serving Muslim and non-Muslim constituents through the adoption of secular politics, for secular politics is strategically necessary for broadening their electoral constituency, which is multiethnic and multireligious. This is crucial especially because very few Muslims participate as candidates in electoral politics, even in communities where they are the majority. Both MPs have well-thought-out strategies for winning or retaining parliamentary seats.

Secular politics that is anchored neither in religious nor in ethnic competition is deemed important even in constituencies where Muslims are the majority. According to Abdallah, there is a general tendency among Muslims in many parts of the country not to register as voters because of what she calls "a slum upbringing." As an underprivileged minority, many Muslims in her constituency live in slums where bread-and-butter issues like jobs, housing, sanitation, and medical care take precedence over all else. In such a situation, and in the context of a generalized Muslim belief that women should not assume a public leadership role, Muslim women MPs cannot rely exclusively on the ethno-Muslim vote and have to adopt a politics that appeals to Muslims and to constituencies of other faiths and ethnic affiliations. For Shaban and Abdallah, the strategy of secular politics is as effective as it is necessary for their work. On the other hand, a Muslim male politician in a Muslim-majority constituency, even if it is multiethnic, can rely primarily on the religious card for his election campaign: it is almost seen as the right and responsibility of Muslim men, but not of Muslim women, to be in positions of public leadership advocating for the rights and resources of their Muslim constituents.

For Shaban, who represents a Christian-majority constituency, the imperative of secular politics applies not only to her work in Parliament but also to her regular engagement with her constituents. Though a Muslim, she may on occasion even be required to support the construction of a Christian church. Such action on her part may upset some of her Muslim constituents, and she finds that she has to rationalize it to them as much as to herself:

> If I can add, the other problem we face because of our secular nature of the country generally, even if you start at home, most of the constituencies even where I come from [Taita in the Coast Province] are Christian. There is no way I will be told, "Look, [Christians in your area] they are building a church," and I look the other way. You understand. So I must give them some of my contribution, because I think that basically we are praying to the same God, although they use a different route. I should also encourage them in their own way.

Shaban sees hope in the young as well. Increasingly, the young of virtually every ethnic group are crossing religious boundaries in their relationships. Inter-religious marriages are rising. And even though one of the spouses ends up converting in order to bring up the children within one faith, the growing incidence of Christian-Muslim marriage is defusing religious tensions and making it easier for Shaban to support the religious aspirations of her constituents who belong to a different community of faith.

Even more than Abdallah, Shaban, who comes from a Muslim-minority coastal constituency, is always walking a tightrope between her Muslim community of faith and her non-Muslim constituents, without whose support she could never have gotten voted into Parliament. It is partly for this reason that a culturally neutral attire worn widely by Muslim women in West Africa plays out well in her area. A dress that places emphasis on her Africanness essentially reinforces her embrace of secular politics in the public arena. Shaban would also be careful not to ally herself with the religious efforts of one community of faith at the neglect of others. She would always maintain an even hand in her support of the institutional religious needs of her constituents, be they of Muslim Christian or Hindu affiliation or members of indigenous ethnic religions.

Conclusion

The narrative analysis of the interviews with the two Muslim women MPs in Kenya reveals that the 1990s democratization process opened up doors of opportunity for women in general and for Muslim women in particular, giving them the chance to participate as political actors in public politics in the nation. However, that process has not been able to transform the patriarchal ideology rooted in both ethnic cultures and religious interpretations, which seek to prevent women from participating in electoral politics and from seeking executive political seats, such as the Parliament, on equal terms with men.[16] Despite the constraints of ethnoreligious patriarchy, Muslim women who experience multiple, gendered marginalization as members of a religious minority and as ethnic minorities contend that the democratization process offers them a terrain on which to contest these negative forces within their communities and within the nation at large.

This analysis also highlights the ways in which Muslim women MPs subvert ethnic-based and religious-patriarchal representations of women in order to achieve some practical gains on behalf of women and themselves as political leaders. We begin to understand why they opt more for a secular rather than a faith-based politics as they seek to reach out to and win the support of their multiethnic and multireligious constituencies in spite of the fact that one religion or one ethnic group may be the predominant one. The constitution itself defines Kenya as a "secular state," but one within which all communities of faith are to be treated equally and protected. This is a provision that provides ample room for advocating for the rights of ethnic and religious minorities in Kenya without resorting to a faith-based politics of the kind that inspired the Islamic Party of Kenya and that could potentially threaten religious coexistence in this multireligious nation. And in this orientation toward a transethnic and transsectarian politics, Muslim women leaders have often been pioneers in the forefront of creating a new national sensibility.

As pointed out at the beginning of this chapter, scholars such as Stephen Ndegwa have argued that elite male politics in Kenya is predominantly ethnocentric and hierarchically gendered, with men dominating especially for reasons of competition over resources.[17] In support of this argument, Aquiline Tarimo further elaborates on the ethnocentric alignment of religious clergy in Kenya to the detriment of the national collective common good.[18] Given this patriarchal hegemonic deployment of ethnicity in national politics, when women politicians have formed associations in postcolonial Kenya, they have tended to be more issue based than ethnicity or religion based.[19] For the women, it is the promotion of transethnic and interfaith alliances and understanding that will guarantee more equitable distribution of resources in the nation and promote social justice for all, as revealed in the coalitions that Naomi Shaban and Amina Abdallah have engaged in with non-Muslim women. Competing in a male terrain of parliamentary politics, the women perform gendered ethnic and religious symbols that draw on the strength of their ethnic base for purposes of national politics. These women are less concerned with ethnoreligious identity as they seek other, more substantive goals in finding connections across boundaries.

On the other hand, women politicians also have to perform their expected role as embodying ethnoreligious culture in their personal lives, in their mode of dress, and on the issues where they choose to focus their energies. The women politicians do not see this accommodation of male-defined roles as surrendering to the male-dominated culture but as an opportunity to play with those symbols in a way that allows the women to both affirm their culture and transcend it in their political practice. In the process, they get the legitimacy they seek from their local communities, which they are then able to galvanize very effectively in pushing for a women-centered agenda nationally.

NOTES

1.   Stephen Ndegwa, "Citizenship and Ethnicity: An Examination of Two Transition Moments in Kenyan Politics," *American Political Science Review* 91, no. 3 (1997): 599–616; Aquiline Tarimo, "Politicization of Ethnic Identities and the Common Good in Kenya" (Santa Clara University, Markkula Center for Applied Ethics, April 2008, http://www.scu.edu/ethics/practicing/focusareas/global_ethics/kenya.htm); Godfrey Mwakikagile, *Ethnic Politics in Kenya and Nigeria* (Huntington, NY: Nova Publishers, 2001).

2.   Wanjiru Nyaguthii Kamau-Rutenberg, "Feuding in the Family: Ethnic Politics and the Struggle for Women's Rights Legislation" (PhD diss., University of Minnesota, 2008); Felicia A. Yieke, "The Discursive Construction of Ethnicity: The 2007 Kenya General Election" (paper presented at the Council for the Development of Social Science Research in Africa, Egerton University, Kenya, 7–11 December 2008).

3.   Grace Nyatugah Wamue, "Revisiting Our Indigenous Shrines through *Mungiki*," *African Affairs* 100, no. 400 (2001): 460; Felicia A. Yieka, "Ethnicity and Development in Kenya: Lessons from the 2007 General Elections," *Kenya Studies Review* 3, no. 3 (2011): 8–19; Federico Battera, "Ethnicity and Degree of Partisan Attachment in Kenyan Politics," *Journal of Asian and African Studies* 48, no. 1 (February 2013): 114–25.

4.   Andrea Rigon, "Fragmentation and Democratic Transformations in Kenya: Ethnicity as an Outcome rather than a Cause (1992–2013)," ISPI Analysis no. 170, May 2013, http://www.ispionline.it/sites/default/files/pubblicazioni/analysis_170def_2013 .pdf.

5.   Julie Hearn, "The 'Invisible' NGO: US Evangelical Mission in Kenya," *Journal of Religion in Africa* 32, no. 1 (February 2002): 32–60.

6.   All interviews quoted here with MP Dr. Ummi Naomi Shaban and MP Amina Abdallah were conducted at the Kenya Parliament Buildings with the author in 2006. See also Ousseina D. Alidou, *Muslim Women in Postcolonial Kenya: Leadership, Representation, and Social Change* (Madison: University of Wisconsin Press, 2013), 84–114.

7.   Zainab Mohamed Jama, "Fighting to Be Heard: Somali Women's Poetry," *African Languages and Cultures* 4, no. 1 (1991): 43–53; Lidwien Kapteijns, "Gender Relations and the Transformation of the Northern Somali Pastoral Tradition," *International Journal of African Historical Studies* 28, no. 2 (1995): 241–59; Said Samatar, *In the Shadow of Conquest: Islam in Colonial Northeast Africa* (Trenton, NJ: Red Sea, 1992); Richard J. Hayward and I. M. Lewis, eds., *Voice and Power: The Culture of Language in Northeast Africa: Essays in Honor of B. W. Andrzjewski* (London: School of Oriental and African Studies, 1996).

8.   Karua resigned from her ministerial post in President Kibaki's regime on 6 April 2009, citing frustrations in exercising her duties. "Statement on Martha Karua's Resignation," *Pambazuka News*, 9 April 2009, http://www.pambazuka.org/en/category/comment /55471.

9.   Joyce N. Omwoha, "'The Woman's Place . . .': Media and (Mis)representation of Women in Political Leadership Positions in Kenya," in *Beyond Tradition: African Women and Cultural Spaces*, ed. Toyin Falola and S. U. Fwatshak (Trenton, NJ: Africa World Press, 2011), 133–49.

10.   Omwoha, "'The Woman's Place,'" 143.

11.   Omwoha, "'The Woman's Place,'" 143.

12.   Ousseina Alidou, "Muslim Women, Rights Discourse, and the Media in Kenya," in *Gender at the Limit of Rights*, ed. Dorothy L. Hodgson (Philadelphia: University of Pennsylvania Press, 2013), 180–200; Esha Fakhi Mwinyihaji, "Muslim Women in Media and Politics: Fighting for Legitimacy," *Global Journal of Human Social Science, Sociology, Economics and Political Science* 12, no. 9 (June 2012): 39–42.

13.   Alidou, *Muslim Women in Postcolonial Kenya*.

14.   Minou Fuglesang, *Veils and Videos: Female Youth Culture in the Kenya Coast* (Stockholm: Stockholm University, 1994), 205.

15.   Mary A. Porter, "Resisting Uniformity at Mwana Kupona Girls School: Cultural Production in an Educational Setting," *Signs* 23, no. 3 (1998): 619–43.

16.   For ethnic cultures, see Kamau-Rutenberg, *Feuding*; for religious interpretations, see Tarimo, "Politicization."

17.   Ndegwa, "Citizenship and Ethnicity."

18.   Tarimo, "Politicization."

19.   Kamau-Rutenberg, *Feuding*, 86–87.

Afterword

Reflections on Gender, Ethnicity, and Power

DOROTHY L. HODGSON

One day in the early 1990s as I sat with Koko, an elderly Maasai grandmother, enjoying the sunshine outside her hut in rural Tanzania, I asked her to tell me about her many children, grandchildren, and great-grandchildren—where they lived, whom they had married, what they did. Her murky, cataract-filled eyes and wizened face masked a sharp, witty mind. One by one she listed her children, male and female, and named their husbands or wives . . . with notable exceptions. Occasionally she would just say "Mayiello" (I don't know) about a wife, then quickly name the next person. I was initially mystified by these muttered ramblings as compared to her clear, lucid recollections of the names and clans of most of the spouses—even for those sons and grandsons who had married six or seven times. I pressed, and she responded: "They are not Maasai; I can't know them; they don't count."

Koko's strategically uneven memory and pointed remarks speak to the continued salience of ethnicity for many Africans, however problematic the concept may be for scholars, politicians, and others. Her response also confirms the theme of this volume about the value of taking gender seriously when analyzing ethnic memories, performances, practices, and silences. Like the women in the Mara Region of Tanzania who talked to Jan Bender Shetler in detail about their social networks, Koko was an oral archive of social relationships in her community—but an archive that, like most archives, had notable silences and absences. For her, only "real Maasai" (*Maasai piwa*) "counted," and the Arusha, Meru, and other women whom some of her sons and grandsons had married were condemned to obscurity, withered branches of the family tree with no name, no clan, no memory.

In an early book, I argued for the importance of analyzing what I called the "interconstruction of gender and ethnicity": "These axes of difference interact over time to produce, reproduce, and transform one another. Gender and ethnicity are both dynamic, historical categories that mutually constitute one another, along with other social differences such as age, class, and citizenship."[1] For Maa speakers in East Africa, the contours and content of "becoming Maasai" and "being Maasai" have shifted in marked but overlapping ways over time—from colonists' division of Maa speakers into "tribes" based on their primary livelihoods during the early colonial period (thus "Maasai" pastoralists, "Arusha" agropastoralists, "Dorobo" gatherer-hunters); to the emergence of male-dominated images of "Maasai" pastoralists that obscured the roles and responsibilities of female Maasai; to more recent efforts by primarily male activists to try to at once transcend and strengthen Maasai identity by becoming "indigenous."[2] None of these phases can be understood without close attention to the shifting gender dynamics that shaped the changes, consequences, and outcomes of ethnicity, as well as its very experience and expression.

The contributions in this volume build on this insight, and on the important work of other scholars like Sandra Greene and Elizabeth Schmidt, to explore the gendering of ethnicity through richly detailed historical and ethnographic studies from across sub-Saharan Africa.[3] The gendering of ethnicity is revealed in the mundane details of everyday life (Urban-Mead, Healy-Clancy, Gengenbach), struggles over political authority and power (Schmidt, Sanders, Mbah), and moments of ethnic conflict and strife (Kelly, Burnet). The challenge, of course, is to "see" gendered ethnicity in the historical record (Shetler, Fry), a challenge that all of the chapters overcome with effort and ingenuity.

So what are some of the insights provided by these chapters into the gendering of ethnicity? How does paying attention to the role of gender in the formation of ethnic identities and, simultaneously, the role of ethnicity in the formation and contestation of gendered identities shape our understandings of not just gender and ethnicity but also the lives and livelihoods of people past and present? Since Jan Bender Shetler has framed the book with a thoughtful introduction and organized the chapters into useful sections, I have the freedom to ponder, probe, and peruse. Thus the following thoughts are not a systematic review of the authors' contributions but musings about intriguing connections and contrasts.

First, many of the chapters demonstrate the centrality of women's work—especially their language and labor—to the production, reproduction, and, at times, transcendence of ethnic meanings, practices, and boundaries. Women shared their understandings of ethnicity with their children, grandchildren, and each other through stories, prayers, and oral histories (Shetler, Kelly, Mbah). They established and maintained interethnic relationships through joking relationships, nicknames, and other linguistic strategies (Gengenbach, Shetler). But their labor and livelihoods also informed their ethnic claims, connections, and concealments (Gengenbach, Fry). Heidi Gengenbach's comparative study of the salience of ethnicity for women in two different districts at two different times in Mozambique suggests the pragmatics of ethnic identifications. In the 1990s, women in Magude District in postconflict Mozambique drew on their ethnic affiliations to form female-centered webs of economic and social support to help each other recover and rebuild. For them, ethnicity was an asset, a form of social capital that provided access to land and other resources. In contrast, the women she met in Cheringoma in 2007 and 2008 were completely uninterested in, if not actively dismissive of, their Sena ethnicity. Their livelihoods now depended on casual part-time work located within or near their homesteads, making localized relationships far more central to their economic security and well-being than broader ethnic claims. Of course, the reproduction of ethnicity was not always the work of women. Shetler describes how in the Mara Region of Tanzania, it was men, through their stories, who emphasized their ethnic identity, while Ndubueze L. Mbah explores how men and women performed and practiced distinct versions of Ohafia-Igbo ethnicity over time in Nigeria.

Women's stories, work, and networks were also central to the forging of interethnic bonds. Most rural women who worked as traders were necessarily multilingual, dependent on their communication skills for the success of their commerce. In patrilocal societies, women who married in as "outsiders" (whether from the same or a different ethnic group) formed webs of female support, and their extended kin relations often provided access to key resources in times of insecurity, whether land, water, or entrance into elite schools (Shetler, Gengenbach, Urban-Mead). Urban women and men from different ethnic backgrounds had other opportunities to meet, connect, and possibly even marry. Schools, religious institutions, and political associations provided key sites for interethnic interactions, including the East African Revival (Shetler), the African Association of East Africa (Sanders), and prayer unions and women's clubs (Healy-Clancy). According to Ethan R. Sanders, for example, female members of the African Association of East Africa in the 1930s and 1940s came from a wide range of occupations and ethnicities, and most were living outside of their "indigenous" areas. The organization provided them an opportunity to achieve new kinds of leadership positions, as well as to forward their own supra-ethnic political agendas, such as changing the regulations regarding the brewing of alcoholic beverages. Similarly, Meghan Healy-Clancy shows how the urban, elite, educated men and women in South Africa who called themselves "New Africans" worked to transcend what they perceived as the outdated, splintering effects of ethnicity through the formation of a transethnic identity forged, in part, by the promotion of interethnic companionate marriages "between equals."

The historical moment mattered as well, of course. Although struggles between men and women over the meanings and practices of ethnicity long preceded colonial rule (Mbah, Schmidt), colonial efforts to produce "tribes" were profoundly gendered, as were the lenses through which colonial officers saw ethnicity, with profound effects on social relations.[4] But anticolonial and nationalist efforts in Tanzania, South Africa, and elsewhere to diminish the salience of ethnicity so as to encourage identification with the nation also had important consequences. Jennie E. Burnet's chapter on postconflict Rwanda is perhaps the most disturbing in terms of showing the gendered effects of state-led antiethnicity campaigns. She examines how systems of gender and ethnic/racial classifications made certain Rwandan women invisible, including raped "maidens," the Tutsi wives of prisoners, and Hutu genocide widows. The euphemisms that replaced ethnicity, such as "survivors" and "victims" for Tutsi and "perpetrators" and "prisoners" for Hutu, reflected a stark moral ethnic landscape of good and evil that belied the complicated ethnic interconnections, politics, and positionings of the two groups before, during, and after the genocide.

Dominant norms of masculinity and femininity were conveyed in ethnic terms, and dominant ethnic norms of behavior were often expressed in gendered terms, whether the prestigious *ufiem* masculinity among Ohafia-Igbo (Mbah) or women's efforts to create a separate Fingo ethnic identity that was distinct from the more patriarchal Xhosa in the Cape Colony in 1835 (Fry). Jill E. Kelly, for example, shows how Zulu women provided an alternative meaning and practice of ethnicity as a counterpoint to male representations and practices during the uDlame, a time of intense violence in the 1990s. While Zulu men displayed their Zuluness by carrying weapons and fighting, Zulu women wielded their own "cultural weapons," consisting of their spiritual beliefs and practices.

Together, these chapters provide vivid, compelling examples of the interconstruction of gender and ethnicity and thus the need to make gender a central analytic in any study of ethnic boundary makings and boundary crossings. At a minimum, they certainly challenge earlier claims that "women have no tribe." But they do much more. The historical depth and geographic range of the contributions demonstrate that the meanings and practices of both ethnicity and gender were dynamic and contested, shaping and shaped by institutions, processes, and forces both new and old, including lineage practices, resource struggles, education, Christianity, Islam, migration, colonialism, nationalism, and emerging class distinctions. Sometimes men and women shared common understandings of ethnic identity; at other times the signification and perform- ance of ethnicity was deeply divided by gender. Differences among women and men—especially of generation and class—shaped their approaches to and in- vocations of ethnicity. Sometimes ethnicity was stressed and even politicized; at other times it was underplayed, ignored, or actively disavowed. Ethnicity was often blurred and complicated by other forms of belonging such as class, citizen- ship, and religion. Ethnicity was evident in times of crisis and conflict but also in mundane, everyday relations, networks, and practices. Its salience could fade during certain historical moments and resurge during others. The idiom of ethnicity was used to express ideas of power, authority, prestige, and more. Whatever the dynamics, however, all of these chapters show the centrality of gender, especially the often-overlooked ideas and practices of women, to the practice, politics, power, and passion of ethnicity.

As the anthropologist Wim van Binsbergen, known for his belief that ethnicity was merely a colonial creation, famously lamented in 1981 about his research in Zambia, "How did the Nkoya, against so many odds, manage to convince me that they were a 'tribe'?"[5] The continued salience and power of ethnicity as a mode of belonging, an idiom of power, and a source of pride in the contemporary African world despite modernist dreams, nationalist fantasies, and cosmopolitan connections has bewildered and beleaguered scholars and policy makers alike. Part of the answer, I would argue, lies in the limited under- standing to date of the roles, practices, and ideas of African women, past and present, in the formation, contestation, and continuity of ethnic identifica- tions. With the publication of this volume, such oversights are no longer plau- sible or possible. Future scholars must take seriously the centrality of gender to ethnicity and ethnicity to gender in order to understand the complicated histo- ries and dynamics of the lives and livelihoods of African men and women.

NOTES

1.   Dorothy L. Hodgson, *Once Intrepid Warriors: Gender, Ethnicity, and the Cultural Politics of Maasai Development* (Bloomington: Indiana University Press, 2001), 14.

2.   Hodgson, *Once Intrepid Warriors*; Dorothy L. Hodgson, *The Church of Women: Gendered Encounters between Maasai and Missionaries* (Bloomington: Indiana Univer- sity Press, 2005); Dorothy L. Hodgson, *Being Maasai, Becoming Indigenous: Postcolonial Politics in a Neoliberal World* (Bloomington: Indiana University Press, 2011).

3.   Sandra Greene, *Gender, Ethnicity, and Social Change on the Upper Slave Coast: A History of the Anlo-Ewe* (Portsmouth, NH: Heinemann, 1996); Elizabeth Schmidt, *Mobilizing the Masses: Gender, Ethnicity, and Class in the Nationalist Movement in Guinea, 1939–1958* (Portsmouth, NH: Heinemann, 2005).

4.   See, for example, Hodgson, *Once Intrepid Warriors.*

5.   Wim van Binsbergen, "The Unit of Study and the Interpretation of Ethnicity," *Journal of Southern African Studies* 8, no. 1 (1981): 67.

Suggestions for Further Reading

Achebe, Nwando. *Farmers, Traders, Warriors, and Kings: Female Power and Authority in Northern Igboland, 1900–1960*. Portsmouth, NH: Heinemann, 2005.

Allman, Jean, Susan Geiger, and Nakanyike Musisi. "Women in Colonial Africa: An Introduction." In *Women in African Colonial History*, edited by Jean Allman, Susan Geiger, and Nakanyike Musisi, 1–15. Bloomington: Indiana University Press, 2002.

Amadiume, Ifi. *Male Daughters, Female Husbands: Gender and Sex in an African Society*. London: Zed Books, 1987.

Askew, Kelly. *Performing the Nation: Swahili Music and Cultural Politics in Tanzania*. Chicago: University of Chicago Press, 2002.

Barth, Frederick. *Ethnic Groups and Boundaries: The Social Organization of Culture Difference*. Oslo: Universitetsforlaget, 1969.

Berger, Iris. "'Beasts of Burden' Revisited: Interpretations of Women and Gender in Southern African Societies." In *Paths towards the Past: African Historical Essays in Honor of Jan Vansina*, edited by Robert W. Harms, Joseph C. Miller, David S. Newbury, and Michele D. Wagner, 123–41. Atlanta, GA: African Studies Association Press, 1994.

———. "Fertility as Power: Spirit Mediums, Priestesses and the Pre-colonial State in Interlacustrine East Africa." In *Revealing Prophets*, edited by David Anderson and Douglas H. Johnson, 65–82. Athens: Ohio University Press, 1995.

Bivins, Mary Wren. *Telling Stories, Making Histories: Women, Words, and Islam in Nineteenth-Century Hausaland and the Sokoto Caliphate*. Portsmouth, NH: Heinemann, 2007.

Bowker, Geoffrey C., and Susan Leigh Star. *Sorting Things Out: Classification and Its Consequences*. Inside Technology. Cambridge, MA: MIT Press, 1999.

Boydston, Jeanne. "Gender as a Question of Historical Analysis." *Gender and History* 20, no. 3 (November 2008): 558–83.

Bozzoli, Belinda. "Marxism, Feminism, and South African Studies." *Journal of Southern African Studies* 9, no. 2 (1983): 139–71.

Bozzoli, Belinda, and Mmantho Nkotsoe. *Women of Phokeng: Consciousness, Life Strategy, and Migrancy in South Africa, 1900–1983*. Portsmouth, NH: Heinemann, 1991.

Bradford, Helen. "Women, Gender and Colonialism: Rethinking the History of the British Cape Colony and Its Frontier Zones, c. 1806–70." *Journal of African History* 37, no. 3 (November 1996): 351–70.

Brooks, George E., Jr. "The Signares of Saint-Louis and Goree: Women Entrepreneurs in Eighteenth-Century Senegal." In *Women in Africa: Studies in Social and Economic Change*, edited by Nancy Hafkin and Edna Bay, 19–44. Stanford, CA: Stanford University Press, 1976.

Brubaker, Rogers, and Frederick Cooper. "Beyond 'Identity.'" *Theory and Society* 29 (2000): 1–47.

Butler, Judith. *Gender Trouble: Feminism and the Subversion of Identity*. New York: Routledge, 1990.

Carton, Benedict, John Laband, and Jabulani Sithole, eds. *Zulu Identities: Being Zulu, Past and Present*. Pietermaritzburg: University of KwaZulu-Natal Press, 2008.

Channock, Martin. *Law, Custom, and Social Order: The Colonial Experience in Malawi and Zambia*. Cambridge: Cambridge University Press, 1985.

Charles, Nickie, and Helen M. Hintjens, eds. *Gender, Ethnicity, and Political Ideologies*. New York: Routledge, 1998.

Cohen, David William, and E. S. Atieno Odhiambo. *Burying SM: The Politics of Knowledge and the Sociology of Power in Africa*. Portsmouth: Heinemann, 1992.

Cooper, Barbara MacGowan. *Marriage in Maradi: Gender and Culture in a Hausa Society in Niger, 1900–1989*. Portsmouth, NH: Heinemann, 1997.

Cooper, Frederick. *Colonialism in Question: Theory, Knowledge, History*. Berkeley: University of California Press, 2005.

Couzens, Tim. *The New African: A Study of the Life and Work of H. I. E. Dhlomo*. Johannesburg: Ravan, 1985.

Davison, Jean. *Gender, Lineage, and Ethnicity in Southern Africa*. Boulder, CO: Westview, 1997.

Dubow, Saul. "Ethnic Euphemisms and Racial Echoes." *Journal of Southern African Studies* 20, no. 3 (September 1994): 355–70.

Edmondson, Laura. *Performance and Politics in Tanzania: The Nation on Stage*. Bloomington: Indiana University Press, 2007.

Erlank, Natasha. "Gender and Masculinity in South African Nationalist Discourse, 1912–1950." *Feminist Studies* 29, no. 3 (Fall 2003): 653–71.

Gaitskell, Debbie. "Devout Domesticity? A Century of African Women's Christianity in South Africa." In *Women and Gender in Southern Africa to 1945*, edited by Cherryl Walker, 251–72. London: James Currey, 1990.

Gasa, Nomboniso, ed. *Women in South African History: They Remove Boulders and Cross Rivers = Basus'iimbokodo, Bawel'imilambo*. Cape Town: HSRC Press, 2007.

Geiger, Susan. "Engendering and Gendering African Nationalism." In *In Search of a Nation: Histories of Authority and Dissidence in Tanzania*, edited by Gregory Maddox and James L. Giblin, 278–89. Athens: Ohio University Press, 2005.

———. *TANU Women: Gender and Culture in the Making of Tanganyikan Nationalism, 1955–1965*. Portsmouth, NH: Heinemann, 1997.

Gengenbach, Heidi. *Binding Memories: Women as Makers and Tellers of History in Magude, Mozambique.* New York: Columbia University Press, 2005. Gutenberg-e electronic book.

Greene, Sandra E. *Gender, Ethnicity, and Social Change on the Upper Slave Coast: A History of the Anlo-Ewe.* Portsmouth, NH: Heinemann, 1996.

Guy, Jeff. "Gender Oppression in Precapitalist Societies." In *Women and Gender in Southern Africa to 1945*, edited by Cherryl Walker, 33–47. Cape Town: David Philip, 1990.

Hamilton, Carolyn. *Terrific Majesty: The Power of Shaka Zulu and the Limits of Historical Invention.* Cambridge: Cambridge University Press, 1998.

Handrahan, Lori. *Gendering Ethnicity: Implications for Democracy Assistance.* London: Routledge, 2002.

Hanretta, Sean. "Women, Marginality and the Zulu State: Women's Institutions and Power in the Early Nineteenth Century." *Journal of African History* 39, no. 3 (1998): 389–415.

Harms, Robert. *Games against Nature: An Eco-cultural History of the Nunu of Equatorial Africa.* Cambridge: Cambridge University Press, 1987.

Hassim, Shireen. "Family, Motherhood and Zulu Nationalism: The Politics of the Inkatha Women's Brigade." *Feminist Review* 43 (1993): 1–25.

Hawthorne, Walter. *Planting Rice and Harvesting Slaves: Transformations along the Guinea-Bissau Coast, 1400–1900.* Portsmouth, NH: Heinemann, 2003.

Hay, Margaret Jean. "Local Trade and Ethnicity in Western Kenya." *Economic History Review* 2, no. 1 (1975): 7–12.

Healy-Clancy, Meghan. "Women and the Problem of Family in Early African Nationalist History and Historiography." *South African Historical Journal* 64, no. 3 (September 2012): 450–71.

———. *A World of Their Own: A History of South African Women's Education.* Pietermaritzburg: University of KwaZulu-Natal Press, 2013.

Higgs, Catherine. "African Women's Self-Help Organizations in South Africa, 1927–1998." *African Studies Review* 47, no. 3 (December 2004): 119–41.

Hinton, Alexander Laban, and Kevin Lewis O'Neill. *Genocide: Truth, Memory, and Representation.* Durham, NC: Duke University Press, 2009.

Hobsbawm, Eric, and Terence Ranger. *The Invention of Tradition.* Cambridge: Cambridge University Press, 1983.

Hodgson, Dorothy L. *Being Maasai, Becoming Indigenous: Postcolonial Politics in a Neoliberal World.* Bloomington: Indiana University Press, 2011.

———. *The Church of Women: Gendered Encounters between Maasai and Missionaries.* Bloomington: Indiana University Press, 2005.

———. *Once Intrepid Warriors: Gender, Ethnicity, and the Cultural Politics of Maasai Development.* Bloomington: Indiana University Press, 2004.

———, ed. *"Wicked" Women and the Reconfiguration of Gender in Africa.* Portsmouth, NH: Heinemann, 2001.

Hofmeyr, Isabel. *"We Spend Our Years as a Tale That Is Told": Oral Historical Narrative in a South African Chiefdom.* Portsmouth, NH: Heinemann, 1993.

Hughes, Heather. "Lives and Wives: Understanding African Nationalism in South Africa through a Biographical Approach." *History Compass* 10, no. 8 (August 2012): 562–73.

Iliffe, John. *Honour in African History*. Cambridge: Cambridge University Press, 2005.

Isaacman, Allen, and Barbara S. Isaacman. *Slavery and Beyond: The Making of Men and Chikunda Ethnic Identities in the Unstable World of South-Central Africa, 1750–1920.* Portsmouth, NH: Heinemann, 2004.

James, Deborah. *Songs of the Women Migrants: Performance and Identity in South Africa.* Edinburgh: Edinburgh University Press for the International African Institute, 1999.

Jeater, Diana. *Marriage, Perversion, and Power: The Construction of Moral Discourse in Southern Rhodesia, 1894–1930.* Oxford: Clarendon Press, 1993.

Johnson, E. Patrick. "Race, Ethnicity, and Performance." *Text and Performance Quarterly* 23, no. 2 (April 2003): 105–6.

Kanogo, Tabitha. *African Womanhood in Colonial Kenya, 1900–50.* Athens: Ohio University Press, 2005.

Klumpp, Donna, and Corinne Kratz. "Aesthetics, Expertise, and Ethnicity: Okiek and Maasai Perspectives on Personal Ornament." In *Being Maasai: Ethnicity and Identity in East Africa,* edited by Thomas Spear and Richard Waller, 195–222. Athens: Ohio University Press, 1993.

Kurien, Prema. "Gendered Ethnicity: Creating a Hindu Indian Identity in the United States." *American Behavioral Scientist* 42, no. 4 (January 1999): 648–67.

La Hausse, Paul. *Restless Identities: Signatures of Nationalism, Zulu Ethnicity and History in the Lives of Petros Lamula and Lymon Maling.* Pietermaritzburg: University of Natal Press, 2000.

Landau, Paul S. *Popular Politics in the History of South Africa, 1400–1948.* Cambridge: Cambridge University Press, 2010.

Lee, Christopher J. "Do Colonial People Exist? Rethinking Ethno-Genesis and Peoplehood through the Longue Durée in South-East Central Africa." *Social History* 36, no. 2 (2011): 169–91.

Lonsdale, John. "African Pasts in Africa's Future." *Canadian Journal of African Studies/ Revue canadienne des études africaines* 23, no. 1 (1989): 126–46.

———. "Authority, Gender and Violence: The War within Mau Mau's Fight for Land and Freedom." In *Mau Mau and Nationhood: Arms, Authority and Narration,* edited by E. S. Atieno Odhiambo and John Lonsdale, 46–75. Oxford: James Currey, 2003.

———. "Kikuyu Christianities." *Journal of Religion in Africa* 29, no. 2 (1999): 206–29.

———. "Moral Ethnicity and Political Tribalism." In *Inventions and Boundaries: Historical and Anthropological Approaches to the Study of Ethnicity and Nationalism,* edited by Preben Kaarsholm and Jan Hultin, 131–50. Roskilde: International Development Studies, Roskilde University, 1994.

Mann, Kristin. *Marrying Well: Marriage, Status, and Social Change among the Educated Elite in Colonial Lagos.* New York: Cambridge University Press, 1985.

Marks, Shula. *Not Either an Experimental Doll: The Separate Worlds of Three South African Women: Correspondence of Lily Moya, Mabel Palmer, and Sibusisiwe Makhanya.* London: Women's Press, 1987.

———. "Patriotism, Patriarchy and Purity: Natal and the Politics of Zulu Ethnic Consciousness." In *The Creation of Tribalism in Southern Africa*, edited by Leroy Vail, 215–40. Berkeley: University of California Press, 1989.

Martin, Phyllis M. *Catholic Women of Congo-Brazzaville: Mothers and Sisters in Troubled Times*. Bloomington: Indiana University Press, 2009.

McClintock, Anne. *Imperial Leather: Race, Gender, and Sexuality in the Colonial Contest*. New York: Routledge, 1995.

Miescher, Stephan, and Lisa Lindsay, eds. *Men and Masculinities in Modern Africa*. Portsmouth, NH: Heinemann, 2001.

Mutongi, Kenda. *Worries of the Heart: Widows, Family, and Community in Kenya*. Chicago: University of Chicago Press, 2007.

Odhiambo, E. S. Atieno, and John Lonsdale. *Mau Mau and Nationhood: Arms, Authority and Narration*. Athens: Ohio University Press, 2003.

Okonjo, Kamene. "The Dual Sex Political System in Operation: Igbo Women and Community Politics in Midwestern Nigeria." In *Women in Africa: Studies in Social and Economic Change*, edited by Nancy Hafkin and Edna Bay, 46–56. Stanford, CA: Stanford University Press, 1976.

Oyěwùmí, Oyèrónkẹ́. *The Invention of Women: Making an African Sense of Western Gender Discourse*. Minneapolis: University of Minnesota Press, 1997.

Parkin, David, and David Nyamwaya, eds. *Transformations of African Marriage*. Manchester: Manchester University Press, 1987.

Peterson, Derek R. *Ethnic Patriotism and the East African Revival: A History of Dissent, c. 1935–1972*. Cambridge: Cambridge University Press, 2012.

Posner, Daniel. *Institutions and Ethnic Politics in Africa*. Cambridge: Cambridge University Press, 2005.

Presley, Cora Ann. "The Mau Mau Rebellion, Kikuyu Women and Social Change." *Canadian Journal of African Studies* 22, no. 3 (1988): 502–27.

Ranger, Terence. *The Invention of Tribalism in Zimbabwe*. Gweru, Zimbabwe: Mambo Press, 1985.

———. *Voices from the Rocks: Nature, Culture and History in the Matopos Hills of Zimbabwe*. London: James Currey, 1999.

Schlee, Gunther. *Identities on the Move: Clanship and Pastoralism in Northern Kenya*. New York: Manchester University Press, 1989.

Schmidt, Elizabeth. *Mobilizing the Masses: Gender, Ethnicity, and Class in the Nationalist Movement in Guinea, 1939–1958*. Portsmouth, NH: Heinemann, 2005.

Scott, James. *Domination and the Arts of Resistance: Hidden Transcripts*. New Haven, CT: Yale University Press, 1990.

Scott, Joan Wallach. "Gender: A Useful Category of Historical Analysis." In *Gender and the Politics of History*, 28–52. New York: Columbia University Press, 1999.

Scully, Pamela. *Race and Ethnicity in Women's and Gender History in Global Perspective*. Washington, DC: American Historical Association, 2006.

Shadle, Brett L. *"Girl Cases": Marriage and Colonialism in Gusiiland, Kenya, 1890–1970*. Portsmouth, NH: Heinemann, 2006.

Smedley, Audrey. *Women Creating Patrilyny: Gender and Environment in West Africa.* Walnut Creek, CA: AltaMira Press, 2004.

Sofos, S. A. "Inter-ethnic Violence and Gendered Constructions of Ethnicity in Former Yugoslavia." *Social Identities* 2, no. 1 (1996): 73–91.

Spear, Thomas, and Richard Waller. *Being Maasai: Ethnicity and Identity in East Africa.* Athens: Ohio University Press, 1993.

Stern, Steve J. *The Secret History of Gender: Women, Men, and Power in Late Colonial Mexico.* Chapel Hill: University of North Carolina Press, 1995.

Taussig, Michael T. *Defacement: Public Secrecy and the Labor of the Negative.* Stanford, CA: Stanford University Press, 1999.

Thomas, Lynn M. "Love, Sex, and the Modern Girl in 1930s South Africa." In *Love in Africa*, edited by Lynn M. Thomas and Jennifer Cole, 31–57. Chicago: University of Chicago Press, 2009.

———. "The Modern Girl and Racial Respectability in 1930s South Africa." In *The Modern Girl around the World: Consumption, Modernity, and Globalization*, edited by Alice Weinbaum et al., 96–119. Durham, NC: Duke University Press, 2008.

Tripp, Aili Mari, Isabel Casimiro, Joy Kwesiga, and Alice Mungwa, eds. *African Women's Movements: Transforming Political Landscapes.* Cambridge: Cambridge University Press, 2009.

Tsing, Anna. *Friction: An Ethnography of Global Connection.* Princeton, NJ: Princeton University Press, 2004.

Vail, Leroy, ed. *The Creation of Tribalism in Southern Africa.* Berkeley: University of California Press, 1991.

Van Allen, Judith. "'Aba Riots' or 'Igbo Women's War'? Ideology, Stratification, and the Invisibility of Women." In *Women in Africa: Studies in Social and Economic Change*, edited by Nancy J. Hafkin and Edna G. Bay, 59–85. Stanford, CA: Stanford University Press, 1976.

van Binsbergen, Wim. "The Unit of Study and the Interpretation of Ethnicity." *Journal of Southern African Studies* 8, no. 1 (1981): 51–81.

Waetjen, Thembisa. *Workers and Warriors: Masculinity and the Struggle for Nation in South Africa.* Urbana: University of Illinois Press, 2004.

Walker, Cherryl, ed. *Women and Gender in Southern Africa to 1945.* Cape Town: David Philip, 1990.

———. *Women and Resistance in South Africa.* London: Onyx Press, 1982; Cape Town: David Philip, 1982, 1991.

Webster, David. "Abafazi Bathonga Bafihlakala: Ethnicity and Gender in a KwaZulu Border Community." In *Tradition and Transition in Southern Africa*, edited by Andrew D. Spiegel and Patrick A. McAllister, 243–49. New Brunswick, NJ: Transaction, 1991.

Wells, Julia. "Eva's Men: Gender and Power in the Establishment of the Cape of Good Hope, 1652–1674." *Journal of African History* 39, no. 3 (1998): 417–37.

White, Luise. *The Comforts of Home: Prostitution in Colonial Nairobi.* Chicago: University of Chicago Press, 1990.

Young, Crawford. *The Politics of Cultural Pluralism*. Madison: University of Wisconsin Press, 1976.

Yuval-Davis, Nira. *Gender and Nation*. London: Sage, 1997.

Contributors

OUSSEINA D. ALIDOU (PhD, Indiana University, linguistics) is an associate professor in the Department of African, Middle Eastern and South Asian Languages and Literatures, affiliate graduate faculty of the Department of Anthropology and Women's and Gender Studies, and the director of the Center for African Studies at Rutgers University–New Brunswick. Her research focuses mainly on the study of Muslim women as agents of social and political change in postcolonial African societies such as the Republic of Niger and Kenya, Muslim women's discourses and literacy practices in African Muslim societies, comparative African women's literature, gendered discourses of citizenship and belonging, and the politics of cultural production in Muslim African countries. She is most recently the author of *Muslim Women in Postcolonial Kenya: Leadership, Representation, and Social Change* (2013). Her book *Engaging Modernity: Muslim Women and the Politics of Agency in Postcolonial Niger* (2005), a runner-up for the Aidoo-Schneider Book Prize of the Women's Caucus of the Association of African Studies, explores women's agency through their contributions in religious and secular education, public politics, and the performing arts. Her other publications include *Post-conflict Reconstruction in Africa*, coedited with Ahmed Sikainga (2006), and *A Thousand Flowers: Social Struggles against Structural Adjustment in African Universities*, coedited with Silvia Federici and George Caffentzis (2000).

JENNIE E. BURNET (PhD, University of North Carolina, Chapel Hill, anthropology) is an associate professor of anthropology at the University of Louisville. Her research interests include gender, ethnicity, race, war, genocide, and reconciliation in postconflict societies in the African Great Lakes region. Her book *Genocide Lives in Us: Women, Memory, and Silence in Rwanda*, published in the University of Wisconsin Press series Women in Africa and the Diaspora, won the 2013 Elliot P. Skinner Award from the Association for Africanist Anthropology. She has published articles in *Politics and Gender*, *African Studies Review*, *African Affairs*, and *Journal of Genocide Studies and Prevention*. Her current research examines the roles of rescuers during the 1994 genocide of Tutsis in Rwanda.

POPPY FRY (PhD, Harvard University, history) is an assistant professor of history at the University of Puget Sound. She has published on early nineteenth-century ethnic conflict and on politics in the Cape Colony. She is currently completing a book on Fingo ethnicity in the nineteenth century.

HEIDI GENGENBACH (PhD, University of Minnesota, history; MA, Tufts University, humanitarian assistance) is an assistant professor of history at the University of Massachusetts–Boston. Her doctoral research on women's oral and material forms of historical memory in southern Mozambique has been published in the *Journal of Women's History* and the *Journal of Southern African Studies* and in the electronic book *Binding Memories: Women as Tellers and Makers of History in Magude, Mozambique* (2005). Her current research focuses on gendered histories of food system interventions in conflict settings, particularly central Mozambique, northern Uganda, and northern Ethiopia.

MEGHAN HEALY-CLANCY (PhD, Harvard University, African studies) teaches in the programs in social studies and in women, gender, and sexuality studies at Harvard University. She is a social and cultural historian of modern southern Africa who is centrally interested in how social institutions and politics in the region have been gendered, and how this history intersects with other African and global histories of gender. She is the author of *A World of Their Own: A History of South African Women's Education* (2013). Her current research examines how ideas and practices of family have shaped political projects in twentieth-century South Africa. Toward this end, she has coedited *Ekhaya: The Politics of Home in KwaZulu-Natal, South Africa* (2014); she also served as guest editor for a special issue of the *African Studies Review*, "The Politics of Marriage in South Africa," in which this essay first appeared.

DOROTHY L. HODGSON (PhD, University of Michigan, anthropology) is a professor of anthropology at Rutgers University, the former director of the Rutgers Institute for Research on Women, president-elect of the African Studies Association, and a past president of the Association for Feminist Anthropology. As a historical anthropologist, she has worked in Tanzania, East Africa, for over twenty-five years on topics such as gender, ethnicity, cultural politics, colonialism, nationalism, modernity, the missionary encounter, transnational organizing, and the indigenous rights movement. She is the author of *Being Maasai, Becoming Indigenous* (2011), *The Church of Women* (2005), and *Once Intrepid Warriors: Gender, Ethnicity, and the Cultural Politics of Maasai Development* (2001), among other publications. Her work has been supported by awards from the Rockefeller Foundation's Bellagio Center, National Endowment for the Humanities, John Simon Guggenheim Memorial Foundation, Fulbright-Hays, American Council for Learned Societies, National Science Foundation, American Philosophical Society, Wenner-Gren Foundation, Social Science Research Council, and Center for Advanced Study in the Behavioral Sciences.

JILL E. KELLY (PhD, Michigan State University, history) is an assistant professor of history at Southern Methodist University. Her current manuscript project examines the historical roots of South Africa's transition-era civil war and competition over land and chiefly authority in twentieth-century KwaZulu-Natal. Her work has appeared in the *African Historical Review*, and her interests include Zulu, gender, and contemporary history.

NDUBUEZE L. MBAH (PhD, Michigan State University, African history) is an assistant professor of history at the State University of New York, Buffalo (UB). Mbah utilizes oral history, emic interpretations of material culture, and gendered rituals to study masculinities, female power, ethnicity, slavery, religion, and colonialism in southeastern Nigeria. His research has focused on the relationship between changes in women's sociopolitical power and the shifting constructions and performances of masculinity in nineteenth- and twentieth-century West Africa as a lens into the transition from the precolonial period, characterized by more powerful and effective women's political institutions, to the colonial period of male political dominance. His current project, "'Missionary Redemption,' Slavery and the Emergence of 'Atlantic Citizens' in the Bight of Biafra in the 19th Century," focuses on new forms of slavery and dependencies that developed in West Africa as a result of European and African missionaries' manumission of slaves in the ports of Calabar and Bonny and loaning these "freed slaves" out as indentured servants in German Cameroon, Spanish Fernando Po, and the British-controlled "free territory" of Sierra Leone.

ETHAN R. SANDERS (PhD, University of Cambridge, history) is an assistant professor of history at Regis University in Denver, Colorado. He has previously published on several aspects of the political and religious history of East and Central Africa, and his present work focuses on the intellectual history of a number of early twentieth-century pan-African activists in East Africa and a project on the global dynamics of the Zanzibar Revolution. He is currently working on a book titled "Building the African Nation: The African Association and Pan-African Politics in Colonial East Africa."

HEIKE I. SCHMIDT (DPhil, University of Oxford, modern history) is a lecturer in modern history at the University of Reading. She is the author of *Colonialism and Violence in Zimbabwe: A History of Suffering* (2013) and the coeditor of *African Modernities: Entangled Meanings in Current Debate* (2002). She has published articles in the *International Journal of African Historical Studies*, *Journal of the History of Sexuality*, *History in Africa*, *Journal of Southern African Studies*, *L'homme*, *Environment and History*, and *Sociologus*. Schmidt's research interests comprise Zimbabwe and Tanzania during the nineteenth and twentieth centuries and topics such as violence, gender, memory, landscape, and colonialism.

JAN BENDER SHETLER (PhD, University of Florida, history) is a professor of history at Goshen College. She conducted most of her field research in the Mara Region of

Tanzania collecting oral tradition and in the archives. Her work has explored the history of social memory, identity, environmental relations, and place from precolonial times to the present. Other research includes work in Harar, Ethiopia. She has edited a number of collections of locally written histories from the Mara Region, including *Telling Our Own Stories: Local Histories from South Mara, Tanzania* (2003), which was a finalist for the 2005 Paul Hair Prize (African Studies Association) and a Choice Outstanding Academic Title for 2003. She is currently working on a book manuscript, "A Gendered History of Social Network Memory in the Mara Region, Tanzania, 1880–Present." Recent publications include a book, *Imagining Serengeti: A History of Landscape Memory in Tanzania from Earliest Times to the Present* (2007); articles for diverse interdisciplinary journals, including *Journal of Peace Research, Journal of Religion, Conflict and Peace, Studies in World Christianity, Journal of African History*, and *International Journal of African Historical Studies*; and a chapter in the edited volume *The Spatial Factor in African History*.

WENDY URBAN-MEAD (PhD, Columbia University, history) is an associate professor of history in the Master of Arts in Teaching Program at Bard College. Her book *The Gender of Piety: Intersections of Faith and Family in Matabeleland Zimbabwe since 1900* is forthcoming. Her work on Zimbabwe is based on extensive oral history research conducted continuously since 1997. She has published articles on gender and Christianity in southern Africa in *Women's History Review* and *Journal of Religion in Africa* and chapters in *Women in African Colonial Histories* (ed. Jean Allman, Susan Geiger, and Nakanyike Musisi) and *Competing Kingdoms: Women, Mission, Nation, and the American Protestant Empire, 1812–1960* (ed. Kathryn Kish Sklar, Barbara Reeves-Ellington, and Connie Shemo). She is coeditor of *Social Sciences and Missions*.

Index

WOMEN IN AFRICA AND
THE DIASPORA

Surviving the Slaughter: The Ordeal of a Rwandan Refugee in Zaire
Marie Béatrice Umutesi; translated by Julia Emerson